Power, Production and Social Reproduction

Also by Isabella Bakker

Rethinking Restructuring: Gender and Change in Canada

The Strategic Silence: Gender and Economic Policy

Also by Stephen Gill

American Hegemony and the Trilateral Commission

Atlantic Relations: Beyond the Reagan Era

Chiku Seiji no Saikochiku: Reisengo no Nichibeiou Kankei to Sekai Chitsujo
(Restructuring Global Politics, in Japanese translated and edited by Seiji Endo)

Globalization, Democratization and Multilateralism

Gramsci, Historical Materialism and International Relations

Innovation and Transformation in International Studies (edited with James Mittelman)

International Political Economy: Understanding Global Disorder (with Robert Cox, Björn Hettne, James Rosenau, Yoshikazu Sakamoto and Kees van der Pijl)

Power and Resistance in the New World Order

The Global Political Economy: Perspectives, Problems and Policies (with David Law)

Power, Production and Social Reproduction

Human In/security in the Global Political Economy

Edited by

Isabella Bakker and Stephen Gill
York University
Toronto
Canada

Editorial Matter and Selection and chapters 1 and 2 © Isabella Bakker and Stephen Gill 2003
Chapter 4 © Isabella Bakker 2003
Chapters 10 and 11 © Stephen Gill 2003
Remaining chapters © Palgrave Macmillan 2003

All rights reserved. No reproduction, copy or transmission of this publication may be made without written permission.

No paragraph of this publication may be reproduced, copied or transmitted save with written permission or in accordance with the provisions of the Copyright, Designs and Patents Act 1988, or under the terms of any licence permitting limited copying issued by the Copyright Licensing Agency, 90 Tottenham Court Road, London W1T 4LP.

Any person who does any unauthorised act in relation to this publication may be liable to criminal prosecution and civil claims for damages.

The authors have asserted their right to be identified as the authors of this work in accordance with the Copyright, Designs and Patents Act 1988.

First published 2003 by
PALGRAVE MACMILLAN
Houndmills, Basingstoke, Hampshire RG21 6XS and
175 Fifth Avenue, New York, N.Y. 10010
Companies and representatives throughout the world

PALGRAVE MACMILLAN is the global academic imprint of the Palgrave Macmillan division of St Martin's Press LLC and of Palgrave Macmillan Ltd. Macmillan® is a registered trademark in the United States, United Kingdom and other countries. Palgrave is a registered trademark in the European Union and other countries.

ISBN 1–4039–1320–X hardback
ISBN 1–4039–1793–0 paperback

This book is printed on paper suitable for recycling and made from fully managed and sustained forest sources.

A catalogue record for this book is available from the British Library.

Library of Congress Cataloging-in-Publication Data
Power, production, and social reproduction : human in/security in the global political economy / edited by Isabella Bakker and Stephen Gill.
   p. cm.
  Studies inspired by a series of meetings, beginning with the conference "Feminist Perspectives on the Paradoxes of Globalization," sponsored by the Heinrich Böll Stiftung in Berlin on November 3–5, 1999, and followed up finally by "Gender, Economy and Human Security," a conference held in Toronto at York University in October 2001.
  Includes bibliographical references and index.
  ISBN 1–4039–1320–X —— ISBN 1–4039–1793–0 (pbk.)
   1. Globalization—Social aspects. 2. Power (Social sciences) 3. Sexual division of labor. 4. Equality. 5. Basic needs. 6. Feminist economics. I. Bakker, Isabella, 1956– II. Gill, Stephen, 1950–

HF1359.P69 2003
303.48'2—dc21

2003053607

10 9 8 7 6 5 4 3 2 1
12 11 10 09 08 07 06 05 04 03

Printed and bound in Great Britain by
Antony Rowe Ltd, Chippenham and Eastbourne

For
Gerda, Karl and Milly

Contents

Acknowledgments — x
Contributors — xi
Preface: Hybridizing a New Intellectual Space — xiii

Part I: Perspective and Framework

1. **Global Political Economy and Social Reproduction** — 3
   Isabella Bakker and Stephen Gill
   Governance, Reproduction and World Order — 5
   Crises and Contradictions: Labor and Social Reproduction — 6
   Human In/Security and Global Political Economy — 8
   Changing Global Conditions of Existence and Three Concepts of Security — 9
   The Dialectic of the Old and the New — 12

2. **Ontology, Method, and Hypotheses** — 17
   Isabella Bakker and Stephen Gill
   Towards a Feminist Historical Materialist Ontology — 19
   A Methodological Sketch — 23
   Key Hypotheses — 27
   Transformations in Political-Juridical and Political Economy Frameworks — 29
   Transformations in Social Reproduction and Structures of Exploitation — 32

Part II: Governance and World Order

Governance and World Order: Introduction to Part II — 43
Tim Di Muzio and Alejandra Roncallo

3. **Globalization, In/Security, and the Paradoxes of the Social** — 47
   Janine Brodie
   Globalism and Human In/Security — 49
   (Re-)Forming the Social — 52
   Globalization and Social Welfare — 55
   The Paradox of Scale — 58
   The Paradox of Necessity — 60
   The Paradox of Sustainability — 61
   Conclusion — 64

4. **Neo-liberal Governance and the Reprivatization of Social Reproduction: Social Provisioning and Shifting Gender Orders** 66
   Isabella Bakker
   Neo-liberal Governance and Conceptual Silences 69
   The Shifting Gender Order 74
   Social Reproduction and Neo-liberal Restructuring 76
   Conclusion: Neo-liberal Governance and Human Security 80

5. **Constitutionalism in a Modern Patriarchal State: Japan, the Sex Sector and Social Reproduction** 83
   Seiko Hanochi
   Japan's Constitutional Development 84
   Meiji Constitutionalism as a Reaction to International Colonialism 86
   From the Anti-Prostitution Law to the Global Sex Trade 90
   Globalizing New Constitutionalism and the Sex Industries 92
   The Racist Nature of the Global Sex Industries 95

Part III: Crises, Tensions and Contradictions

Crises, Tensions and Contradictions: Introduction to Part III 99
Tim Di Muzio

6. **Financial Crises and Social Reproduction: Asia, Argentina and Brazil** 103
   Brigitte Young
   Intensified Globalization, Financial Crises and Social Reproduction 104
   Changing Governance Frameworks 107
   East Asian Financial Crises and their Impact on Social Reproduction 111
   Financial Crises and Paid Reproductive Work 115
   Argentina and Brazil: The Shift to a Neo-liberal Governance Framework 118
   What is to be Done? 121

7. **Power, Production and Racialization in Global Labor Recruitment and Supply** 124
   Randolph B. Persaud
   Migration Theory 127
   Racial and Cultural Aspects of Disposability 133
   Labor Supply and Labor Control: Colonies and Elsewhere 134
   Globalization and Labor Supply 137
   Conclusion 144

8. **Social Reproduction of Exclusion: Exploitative Migration and Human Insecurity**   146
Kinhide Mushakoji
Socioeconomic Insecurity: Filipina "Entertainers" in Japan   147
Informalization, Occultation and Reproduction of the Sex Industry Workforce   150
Insecurity, Biological Reproduction and Provisioning of Care   152
Formal, Informal and the "Quotidian"   153
Encounters: Forces of Informalization and Counter-Informalization   155
Concluding Reflections: Insecurity and Global Political Economy   158

Part IV: Human In/Security on a Universal Scale

Human In/Security on a Universal Scale: Introduction to Part IV   163
Isabella Bakker, Stephen Gill and Tim Di Muzio

9. **Food Security and Social Reproduction: Issues and Contradictions**   169
Philip McMichael
Food Security in the Development Project   170
Reframing "Food Security" as a Market Good   171
"Food from Nowhere"   177
The Corporate Relation   180
Biotechnology and Food Security   182
Food Sovereignty and Food from Somewhere   185
Conclusion   188

10. **Social Reproduction of Affluence and Human In/Security**   190
Stephen Gill
The Global Hierarchy of Socio-economic In/Security   191
The Social Reproduction of Affluence: The US Case   196
Conclusion   203

11. **National In/Security on a Universal Scale**   208
Stephen Gill
Securing the World Market   209
Full Spectrum Dominance and Globalization: US National Security Strategy   214
Prospects for World War III?   217

Bibliography   224
Index   238

Acknowledgments

We are very grateful for financial and other support from the following institutions: the Social Science and Humanities Research Council of Canada, the United Nations Development Fund for Women (UNIFEM), Robert Drummond, Dean of the Faculty of Arts, York University, the Office of the Vice President, Research and Innovation, York University, the Heinrich Böll Stiftung, Berlin and the International Studies Association.

All the work in this book is original except for Chapter 7, by Randolph Persaud, which is a rewritten and revised version of his article, Racial Assumptions in Global Labor Recruitment and Supply, *Alternatives: Global, Local, Political*, Volume 26 (4) 2001: 377–99, Copyright © 2001 by Lynne Rienner Publishers. We thank the publisher for permission to reprint this revised work.

The making of this book involved a significant number of people and we would like to say a big thank you to the following people. We thank our outstanding editor Amanda Watkins and her colleagues at Palgrave Macmillan, notably Guy Edwards, Tracey Day, Ray Addicott, Oliver Howard and Tony Hooper for their exemplary work. We also thank our friends the Scarth Family: Peter, Vanessa, Greg and Luke Scarth for their collective efforts in facilitating the design concept for the book cover, and Peter in particular who painted the original. We are also particularly grateful to three York graduate students who helped us as excellent research assistants: Sonam Dolma, Alejandra Roncallo and Tim Di Muzio. Special thanks go to Tim Di Muzio for doing much of the painstaking work on the index and Tyler Attwood for proofreading.

We would also like to acknowledge the intellectual and personal debts that we owe to a number of colleagues, students, friends and family. These include: Aijaz Ahmad, Greg Albo, Rob Albritton, Beate Andrees, Sedef Arat-Koc, Harry Arthurs, Anke Bakker, Rawidda Baksh-Soodeen, Drue Barker, Tony Beck, Lourdes Beneria, Sarah Bernstein, Kate Bezanson, Janine Brodie, Ray Broomhill, Debbie Budlender, Nilufer Cagatay, Barbara Cameron, Marjorie Cohen, Judy Cornish, Robert and Jessie Cox, Matt Davies, Ann Denholm Crosby, Diane Elson, Sakiko Fakkuda-Parr, Judy Fudge, Christina Gabriel, Millicent Gill, Caren Grown, Carolyn Hannan, Adam Harmes, Andrea Harrington, Jeffrey Harrod, Richard Higgott, Sue Himmelweit, Emma Hooper, Laurie Ivsich, Hande Keklik, Jamie Kennedy, Rob Langham, Lorren Leveille, Silke Lock, Meg Luxton, Martha MacDonald, Birgit Mahnkopf, Kim Meimaroglou, Mary Mellor, Craig Murphy, Nigmendra Narain, Janice Newton, Jonathan Nitzan, Sule Ozler, Leo Panitch, V. Spike Peterson, Lisa Philipps, Sol Picciotto, Ann Porter, Rhonda Sharp, Scott Sinclair, Malinda Smith, Kathie Steinhoff, Angie Swartz, Bruce Tate, Dagmar Vinz, Leah Vosko, Sylvia Waterman-Anderson, Brigitte Young, and, last but not least, five anonymous reviewers who each made useful and constructive suggestions for this book.

We of course apologize for anyone wrongly omitted from this list.

Contributors

Isabella Bakker is Chair, Department of Political Science, York University, Toronto. She has held visiting positions at the European University Institute, Free University Berlin, and Rutgers University. Her published work includes *The Strategic Silence: Gender and Economic Policy* (1994), *Rethinking Restructuring: Gender and Change in Canada* (1996), and numerous other works on Gender and Restructuring, Fiscal Policy, Political Economy of State Finance, Governance and Globalization. Bakker has been a Principal Consultant to the UNDP for the 1999 and 2000 *Human Development Reports* and Senior Consultant to the UN/UNIFEM report, *The Progress of the World's Women* (2000).

Janine Brodie is Chair, Department of Political Science, University of Alberta, Edmonton. Her work focuses on Canadian Politics and Political Economy, Gender and Politics, and Governance and Globalization. Her most recent publications include *Reinventing Canada: Politics of the 21st Century* (2003, co-editor) and *Critical Concepts: An Introduction to Politics* (1999 editor, 2nd edition, 2001). Brodie has been an active participant in the policy process, and she has written research reports for Status of Women Canada, North-South Institute, the Royal Commission on Electoral Reform and Party Financing, and the Attorney General of Ontario. In 2002 she was elected Fellow, Royal Society of Canada.

Tim Di Muzio is a PhD candidate in Political Science at York University, Toronto.

Stephen Gill is Professor of Political Science at York University, Toronto, specializing in Political Economy and International Studies. Gill has been a visitor at the following universities: Warwick, UCLA, Tokyo, Manchester, La Trobe (Melbourne) and he is Senior Associate Member, St. Antony's College, Oxford. In 2003 he was elected Fellow, Royal Society of Canada. His publications include *The Global Political Economy* (1988 with David Law), *American Hegemony and the Trilateral Commission* (1990), *Gramsci, Historical Materialism and International Relations* (1993), *Globalization, Democratization and Multilateralism* (1997) and *Power and Resistance in the New World Order* (2002).

Seiko Hanochi is a PhD candidate in Political Science at York University, Toronto. An activist as well as a scholar, she was recently the co-organizer of the Beijing Plus Five Global Feminist Symposium in New York in 2000.

Philip McMichael is Chair, Department of Development Sociology, Cornell University, Ithaca, New York. He specializes in Development Studies, Political Economy, Politics of Agrarian and Food Systems. He edited *Food and Agrarian*

Orders in the World-Economy (1995), *The Global Restructuring of Agro-Food Systems* (1994) and authored the award-winning *Settlers and the Agrarian Question* (1984). His most recent book is *Development and Social Change: A Global Perspective* (2nd edition, 2000). McMichael is the former President of the Research Committee on the Sociology of Agriculture and Food of the International Sociological Association. He is a member of the FAO's Scientific Advisory Council on Food and Nutrition.

Professor Kinhide Mushakoji is one of the world's leading authorities on Global Affairs and Peace Research and author of many works in these fields. A former President of the International Political Science Association, between 1976 and 1989 he was Vice-Rector of the United Nations University in Tokyo and Professor of Peace Research at Meiji Gakuin University (1989–99). He has been a visitor at numerous institutions, including: the East-West Center, Hawaii and Princeton and Northwestern Universities. Mushakoji remains active in numerous peace-oriented and Political Science associations, editorial boards and political movements; for example, as Director, International Movement Against All Forms of Racism and Discrimination.

Randolph B. Persaud is Associate Professor in the School of International Service, American University, Washington, D.C., specializing in Political Economy and International Studies. He has served as the Director of the Interdisciplinary Council on the Americas, and is Co-Director of Comparative and International Race Relations at American University. Persaud's most recent work includes *Counter-Hegemony and Foreign Policy: The Dialectics of Marginalized and Global Forces in Jamaica* (2001). He was co-editor (With R. B. J. Walker) of a Special Issue of *Alternatives* (2001) 26 (4): *Race in International Relations*.

Alejandra Roncallo is a PhD candidate in Political Science at York University, Toronto.

Brigitte Young is Professor of Political Science at the University of Münster, Germany. She is Germany's leading Feminist scholar in International and Comparative Political Economy. In 1999 she was appointed Expert Adviser to the high-level Commission of Inquiry of the German Parliament on Globalization of the World Economy. Her English-language publications include *Triumph of the Fatherland: German Unification and the Masculinization of Women* (1999).

Preface:
Hybridizing a New Intellectual Space

This book seeks to open an intellectual space to allow for movement towards a more realistic, critical, and interdisciplinary perspective on Global Political Economy. It reflects our shared sense of both the promise and the limitations of our respective intellectual frameworks – Political Economy (Feminist and Critical) and International Studies – in the context of analyses of intensified globalization. We each have worked within and sought to contribute to the development of our respective traditions over the years as a part of an open, reflexive dialogue. In this work we try not only to build upon, but also go beyond aspects of these traditions and to make a practical contribution to debates over state power and public policy.

Thus our book seeks to initiate the development of a hybrid perspective and intellectual framework. It outlines a number of research hypotheses that allow us to focus on the interconnections between questions of power, production and social reproduction in the contradictory totality of the emerging world order. We – and the other contributors – apply this framework to interpret and explain a number of concrete links between local, national, regional and global dimensions of the restructuring of capital. In this context the various authors explore a global dialectic of dominant and subordinate power connected to questions of human in/security and social reproduction. This dialectic is shaped by the social relations of gender, race and class, as well as by patterns of ideology, interest and identity. Here we are particularly interested in the interactions between transformations in power and production and the redefinition of the governance of social provisioning. In this context, the book seeks to begin to analyze how structures of power/production/social reproduction relate to world orders, and how different identities are formed and articulated; in particular, gender orders.

What we hope this book will achieve is to highlight some of the contributions that can come from our respective and mutual fields of interest. We also hope it can provide an outline for a new synthesis to help make for theoretical development, the aim of which is to develop a more comprehensive, critical and radical perspective on the transformations in world order. We hope that our readers will take our arguments as being suggestive rather than definitive, since we are fully aware that this is the beginning of a research program that requires much more empirical investigation in and across the different regions of the world. We also fully expect that empirical work associated with this research program will bring to light many new complexities as well as challenges for theoretical development, attendant upon the scope and the depth of the historical changes associated with an era of intensified globalization. Thus we will seek to move forward and ascertain how far and in what ways our hypotheses begin to correspond to the complexity of changing global conditions of existence.

Next we would like to say a word about the longer process involved in the production of this book. The catalyst for this project was a conference organized by Brigitte Young and sponsored by the Heinrich Böll Stiftung in Berlin, Feminist Perspectives on the Paradoxes of Globalization held on November 3–5, 1999. This conference brought together scholars and activists from Britain, Germany, Canada, Japan and the United States with the specific goal of building a dialogue and research agenda for Feminists interested in a Political Economy approach and Critical scholars of International Studies. Both sets of scholars were interested in alternative approaches to structure and agency, transnational politics and conceptions of the economic and political. Out of that very exciting and productive public event, a group of scholars came together in meetings in Berlin, Toronto and New Orleans. Elmar Altvater generously hosted a working group meeting in Berlin in November 2000. Several scholars in this volume organized panels at meetings of the International Studies Association in Chicago in February 2001 and in New Orleans in March 2002. Finally, a follow-up conference to Berlin was held in Toronto at York University in October 2001 on Gender, Political Economy and Human Security, organized by the editors. Since the first Berlin conference, contingencies of history have influenced our thinking on issues of power and security, as well as production and social reproduction. Major events such as 9/11 and the war on Iraq in 2003 brought into sharp relief the pressing questions of human in/security, national security and security of capital dealt with throughout this book. We sincerely hope that we can make a contribution to the way in which these questions are considered, debated and applied.

Finally, the reader will see that this book is organized into four parts, and with the exception of Part I (which constitutes the introduction and perspective of the book as a whole), each has a short introductory piece that frames the issues and gives a summary of the arguments to be made.

Isabella Bakker and Stephen Gill
Toronto
April 14, 2003

Part I:
Perspective and Framework

1
Global Political Economy and Social Reproduction

Isabella Bakker and Stephen Gill

Chapter 1 serves as the general introduction to this book, and it should be read in conjunction with Chapter 2, which outlines ontological and methodological issues, and sketches our main hypotheses.

The aim of this book is to bring together theories and concepts from Feminist and Radical Political Economy and Critical International Studies, and to harness them to a more encompassing methodological and theoretical perspective with which to study some of the new conditions of existence in the global political economy. It seeks to provide a new approach based on an effort to synthesise the moments of power, production and social reproduction in patterns of intensified globalization. We see this as both theoretical and practical, in so far as our theorization of the world is connected to the way in which we perceive the potential and limits for action and transformation within that world.

Of course it not self-evident how to do this. In this context, even the most critical approaches to understanding the global political economy have sought to explain its crises and transformations mainly in terms of power and production or as primarily involving the interplay between states and markets (Cox 1987; Strange 1994). What the critical International Political Economy literature has so far largely failed to fully integrate into explanations of the restructuring of world society is the analysis of transformations in fundamental social processes, and the mechanisms and institutions upon which societies and communities as well as power and production, are built.

Such processes, mechanisms and institutions correspond to what Feminist theory calls social reproduction, which we elaborate in Chapter 2 along with other key concepts. Indeed, public and private forms of power regulate the three main aspects of social reproduction usually identified in the Feminist literature: biological reproduction, reproduction of labor power, and social practices connected to caring, socialization and the fulfillment of human needs (Bakker 1999). This involves public policy and provisioning associated with health, education, welfare and socialization of risk, institutions and relations that shape how the social, political and moral order are understood and evaluated (UNDP 1999).

Thus our book interrogates key aspects of intensified globalization, many of which are overlooked or downplayed by other approaches, particularly those premised on the narrow ontology of states and markets. Therefore in this work, following an ontological and theoretical reflection in Chapter 2, we shall explore three sets of interrelated questions and themes, principally related to the governance of production/social reproduction and the conditions for human security. These issues are related to a world order context where the power of capital has been extended globally, and where certain powers of the state are being reinforced and re-focused to promote both greater national security, and greater security for capital in more liberalized frameworks of global accumulation.

Our three themes tend to overlap across individual contributions, since they relate to a central hypothesis of this work, namely the emergence of a global contradiction between the extended power of capital (and its protection by the state) and not only sustainable but also progressive forms of social reproduction for the majority of the world's population. Here we use the term "contradiction" to help explain how opposing elements in a historical conjuncture or moment have emerged/are emerging to constitute struggles between different social forces – struggles that may result in structural transformation. When such issues are put in the context of a discussion of the simplified model of the contradiction between capital and social reproduction, such contradictions are not simply logical, and indeed are not "overdetermined" by historical laws. The contradiction between the extended power of capital and capacities for social reproduction is conditioned by social struggles. Indeed, key aspects of such struggles may connect to very longstanding forms of historical conflict, such as the conflict over primitive accumulation (for example, the alienation of public/common land, and more recently privatization of state assets) that date at least from the enclosure movement of the sixteenth century. Some are more recent, such as those associated with the struggles to establish and institutionalize more democratic forms of political representation and also to create social protection and welfare provisions in capitalist social formations. The key point that is reflected in the chapters that follow is that such struggles are ongoing, and for many people concern questions of life and death. This is because primitive accumulation is in effect expropriation/dispossession of the means of subsistence for local communities and primary producers (for example, see Chapter 9 by Philip McMichael).

Governance, reproduction and world order

The *first* set of themes to be explored involves the (global) *governance* of social and economic reproduction. This encompasses legal and constitutional mechanisms and associated forms of global regulation associated with new patterns of accumulation and their cultural manifestation in an emergent "market civilization" and world order (Gill 1995a).

By governance we do not mean "governance without government," since there is often both a public and a private face to governance processes and mechanisms, and it is governments that ultimately pass laws and implement them. Governance involves ideas that justify or legitimate political power and influence, institutions through which influence is stabilized and reproduced, and patterns of incentives and sanctions to ensure compliance with rules, regulations, standards and procedures. Governance thus entails both public and private forms of power, institutions of state and civil society, and it operates either within particular localities, or across national boundaries in regional or global frameworks.

The dominant framework of global economic and social governance is associated with creating a global political economy hospitable to the neo-liberal frameworks of accumulation favored by transnational corporations and large investors that dominate world trade, investment and finance. These agents are drawn principally from the OECD. In this context the liberal reforms associated with the international financial institutions in the former Eastern Bloc and developing countries are linked to concepts of "good governance" premised on reshaping state forms to allow for facilitation and extension of markets as well as, to a limited extent, invigoration of civil society as an agent of development (World Bank 2002). By definition therefore, if such governance involves the extension of markets that facilitate private investment and accumulation, then understanding how new constitutional frameworks have reshaped or channelled the actions or functions of governments also implies the analysis of how private, non-state actors, both within and across nation-states, wield influence and thus shape the use of political power (nationally and transnationally), an issue we return to briefly at the end of this chapter.

In this context, the chapters co-written by the editors (1 and 2) by Janine Brodie (Chapter 3) and Isabella Bakker (Chapter 4) explore how the ontology of the "social" is constituted and more specifically how key institutions and mechanisms of governance associated with social reproduction are being redefined – and more precisely how these are shaped by the discourses of disciplinary neo-liberalism and new constitutionalism (Gill 1998a). Their contributions explore these issues relative to health, welfare and education, and to how extended market disciplines involve new frameworks of law, constitutionalism and regulation, for example, in macroeconomic policy (Bakker 2000). This is also true for regulation of trade and investment such as the new General Agreement on Trade in Services (GATS) at the World Trade Organization to liberalize public and private provision of financial, social, educational and agricultural services. More broadly, therefore, the new governance frameworks are related to transformations in world order and the global political economy: to what Marx called the expanded reproduction of capital and the creation of the world market (Marx 1971, 1976). Indeed, Seiko Hanochi's contribution in Chapter 5 illustrates how patriarchal aspects of the modern Japanese constitutional state, its political economy and system of social reproduction, are reflected in the regulation of sex industries and the trafficking of labor for the sex industries in a wider process of world market formation.

Crises and contradictions: labor and social reproduction

A *second* set of issues addressed relates to *crises, tensions and contradictions* in social and economic reproduction. Here, most of the contributions specifically explore changes in social relations and how they are articulated with strategies to intensify and extend the exploitation of labor in the present era of neo-liberal globalization. Such transnational forms of production and exploitation of labor are related to class-based, racialized, gendered and sexualized aspects of labor supply and control. We emphasize how an expanded notion of labor is required to understand the nexus between production and social reproduction. We link Feminist insights on waged and not-directly-waged labor, to a nuanced, differentiated, and class-based perspective on the global hierarchy of labor. This enables us to identify the very different and unequal conditions of work and labor supply and control, that is, relations of power that apply to different workers.

One distinction that is important is that between so-called "protected" and "unprotected" workers and more generally the differing patterns of power relations of production that apply in different regimes or social modes of production such as those that apply to unprotected (and often undocumented) workers.[1]

For example, the number of workers in the primitive labor market mode seems to be expanding. At the same time, Chapter 7 by Randolph Persaud elaborates some of the complexities of this primitive mode within the lower rungs of a hierarchy of racialized unprotected labor. Persaud documents how casual workers are made "disposable," treated as if they were disposable commodities. Evidence elsewhere in this collection also suggests that the primitive labor market mode is not only increasingly prevalent in the Third World, but also within the leading capitalist societies, and it is often articulated in transnational circuits of labor supply and control. In the urban centers, workers such as these are also often located in the so-called informal sector that provides cheap and disposable services (for example, as maids to professional women, or as manual day-laborers), although the term "informal" conceals as much as it reveals with respect to the social relations of production. Many of these workers are undocumented, or, in official terminology, "illegal." Their precarious and subordinate conditions are frequently worsened by the actions of police forces, which criminalize the victims who are seen to be illegal workers, rather than the perpetrators of this form of extreme exploitation, who may be viewed as legal employers. As Chapter 8 by Kinhide Mushakoji indicates, under these conditions it is often the bosses, including organized criminals, that offer "protection" and "community" after the traditional bonds of the subsistence and peasant-based societies have been destroyed. Harrod indicates that such groups have a propensity to develop a perspective on the world characterized by millenarianism, most recently taking the form of religious fundamentalism, implicitly linking the commodification and atomization of these workers to the emergence of new forms of terrorism (Harrod 2001).

Thus in many parts of the world, labor is divided through practices of discrimination and inequality of treatment, partly because of differences in the constitutional/legal status of different workers and partly by a dramatic contrast in working conditions: the bulk of the world's workers are vulnerable and unprotected. In many respects, from the viewpoint of their employers and local state authorities they are "disposable." Whilst transnationalization of labor flows has a long historical legacy in ancient and more modern forms of slavery, imperialism, colonialism and migrant labor dependencies, the authors in this book highlight the newer aspects in making the current moment of intensified globalization. Indeed, this is reflected, first, in the size and nature of the migrant labor force. The numbers of migrants, according to UN statistics, have more than doubled since 1975. There are now an estimated 175 million migrant workers globally and an increasing number of undocumented workers due to tighter immigration controls. In the United States, for example, the numbers of (documented) migrant workers have increased from 1 to 7 million in the period 1996–2001. Second, the new trend is reflected in the feminization of international migration: women are now believed to constitute 50% of migrants globally. Third, many of these women international migrants are fulfilling the social reproduction needs of receiving societies (Arat-Koc 2003 provides these statistics).

In this context some of the contributions weave together issues and problems that relate to more than one of our themes. Chapter 6, by Brigitte Young, links the global governance theme to crises in Latin America and Asia. She explores how regional economic crises create dislocations with unequal, gendered, racialized and class-based effects and deleterious repercussions for social reproduction, care and provisioning in selected countries in Latin America and Southeast Asia. Bakker in Chapter 4 links this to an analysis that straddles the governance and labor themes. She shows how post-Fordist restructuring of production ("flexible accumulation") involves feminization of labor markets and remaking of gender orders. This has the effect of making established and heretofore protected workers generally less secure, more "flexible" but also, like their unprotected counterparts, more precarious and to a certain extent more "disposable" from the viewpoint of capital. Chapter 7 analyses how labor markets in the Americas are racialized and involve discriminatory strategies of labor control and exploitation, a process that has its lineage in the era of colonial slavery and other institutions such as indentured labor. Chapter 8 analyzes how structures of exploitative migration regulate the supply of hyper-exploited, particularly female labor within Asia.

Human in/security and Global Political Economy

The *third* theme in this collection concerns contemporary aspects of social reproduction and *human in/security* in a global context. This is a theme that is dealt with throughout the collection but in this part of the work we interrogate aspects of the reshaping of the frameworks for human security through an analysis that is both from the "bottom up" and from the "top down." A bottom-up analysis by Philip McMichael, looks at the most fundamental issues of human security for subsistence-based communities as they struggle to secure the means of livelihood in the face of increasing control of food security by market forces and the power of capital – the growing control by agribusiness over global food production and distribution. This analysis takes the perspective of "globalization from below" and links environmental and ecological questions to basic issues of social reproduction and human security, the material basis for the security, survival and sustainability of communities. Chapter 9 is the counterpart to Chapter 10, by Stephen Gill, which deals with "globalization from above." Gill situates his analysis in the context of intensified inequality in global social formation and then links this to prevailing lifestyles and consumption patterns in the USA. Such lifestyles are related to frameworks of disciplinary neo-liberal globalization. The American form of the "social reproduction of affluence" involving the welfare of a relatively small minority of the world's population, however, seems to go with intensified human insecurity for a majority of the world's population, including a substantial portion of the US population, indeed even for large proportions of the populations of the wealthy countries themselves. Efforts to secure this contradictory form of world order are reflected in US state strategies premised on securing the USA as the epicenter of globalization. Globally, this strategy has two main components: (a) US efforts – along with those of other leading capitalist states – to mobilize and to lock in new constitutional governance frameworks to protect the power of capital, and (b) the threatened/actual use of US military power to police, discipline and extend a globalizing world order. This strategy is linked to the UK/US war with Iraq in 2003. Gill's contribution in Chapter 11 therefore shows how, especially after the collapse of the USSR, and particularly following the mega-terrorist attacks on the USA of September 11, 2001 (now referred to in North America as "9/11", the telephone number that is used in emergencies) internal and international frameworks of state security are being redefined in ways that may not only adversely affect social reproduction and human security of the majority of people on the planet, but may also trigger generalized social conflict and war, particularly if no countervailing social and political forces prevent the currently dominant conservative forces in the USA from mobilizing their strategic vision.

In this context many of the contributions here point to the need for political and social mechanisms that might ensure greater human security and progressive forms of human development of the majority of people, taking into account changing global conditions of existence, including those of peace and war.

Changing global conditions of existence and three concepts of security

In the final section of this chapter we indicate some of the general conditions in an era of intensified globalization, since these help us to understand sets of political and social constraints and possibilities for different groups in the hierarchies of world order.

We live in an era of the so-called new inequality (understood not only in terms of the widening disparity in distribution of income and life-chances within societies, but also the widening chasm between rich and poor countries in North and South) (Murphy and Pasha 2002). In this context, the dominant framework for global social and economic development during the past 20 years, which we call disciplinary neo-liberalism, has involved changing conditions of existence for members of world society (UNDP 1994, 1997; UNRISD 1995).

We suggest that this has been linked to a project to extend the power of capital on a world scale. Indeed in important respects, capital's power has become akin to the alien force theorized by Marx. This force now operates in a fluid, transnational framework that involves both old and new forms of power, production and social reproduction. Nevertheless, as the globalization of power intensifies in this neo-liberal framework, this is provoking resistance and a counter-mobilization of new political forces, of both right and left, in a new global politics.

In this context it has become a commonplace of the early twenty-first century to note that we live in an era of intensified globalization characterized by changing frameworks of security/insecurity. But the issue is globalization of what, for whose benefit and with what consequences? And with respect to the question of security: security of what, and for whose benefit?

The contemporary process of globalization involves not only the integration of world market, but also the disintegration of aspects of previous structures of community and political economy, and a transformation of production systems and labor markets where capitalist market forces have become dominant. Globalization is also political, reflected in the spread of liberalism and to a certain extent of liberal democracy; for example, in the proliferation of new constitutional frameworks in the former Eastern Bloc following the collapse of communist rule. Globalization has also been associated with more rapid technological change, particularly in production and communication systems, many linked to new flexible forms of network power and structures of surveillance within and between countries. And globalization has been accompanied by the spread of what could be called an emergent market civilization as transnational corporations and new networks of communication are linked to the spread of consumerism and values of possessive individualism. Such developments of course are not inevitable, as some have claimed, that is they are not "the end of history." Rather as we have already indicated, they involve highly contested processes. Indeed, as Chapter 6 by Young illustrates, the spread of global capitalism seems increasingly to be punctuated by frequent and profound economic and social crises. Many of the growing political conflicts – including the terrorism of the weak – seem to be linked to a generalized and intensifying sense of human insecurity, even for the most powerful.

In sum, this situation of transformation, crisis and insecurity involves the remaking of state authority and challenges to the political legitimacy of elites and ruling classes throughout the world. And in this context human security is a contested concept particularly following the struggles to redefine the security of states (national security) after the mega-terrorist attacks on the USA on 9/11. We believe that it is crucial that civilian populations should be protected from the use of organized violence. We also believe it is crucial that post-9/11 concerns with the security of the state should not obscure the need for governments to provide for basic conditions and indeed improving conditions of human security and human development, as well as respecting and enlarging human rights.

Indeed, our conception of human security follows recent United Nations-inspired work that associates the provision of conditions for human security with those for human rights and human development. As the UNDP put it in 1994, most of the concerns of people today relate to the insecurities that feature in their everyday lives: "threats of disease, hunger, unemployment, crime, social conflict, political repression and environmental hazards. With the dark shadows of the Cold War receding, one can see how many conflicts are within nations, rather than between them" (UNDP 1994: 22). The UNDP notes that such a concept of human security is of universal concern, and not particular to the security of one state, that its components are interdependent, and that it should be centered on the needs of people. It has many components, including economic, food, health, environmental, personal, community and political security (UNDP 1994: 24–40).

Like the concept of national security, human security involves positive and negative dimensions. Its positive elements relate to how human security presupposes a certain level of human (economic and social) development and a set of political freedoms or human rights – for example, freedom of expression and of association under conditions of toleration and absence of repression or violence. Its negative aspect involves freedom from preventable social risks or dangers, freedom from anxieties or fears of arbitrary punishment or exclusion from the rights and freedoms of citizenship, refugee status, or political asylum. It would also involve efforts to lower collective vulnerability to economic and environmental crises coupled to specific compensatory measures to protect the poor who tend to be most vulnerable in situations of economic slump or when environmental factors endanger livelihoods.

Thus in both a positive and a negative sense, the human security of a population involves a collective sense of confidence about the future, premised on a condition where unnecessary dangers associated with everyday life and situations of crisis are minimized or eliminated.[2]

In the context of such questions we are interested in the articulation of world order processes and potentials. We seek to address these issues from the bottom up of world society, for example, the multiple subjectivities and agencies of women and men in specific local contexts, and from the top down, such as the vantage point of the most powerful elements of state and capital with their global reach. Transformations from above and from below constitute intensified globalization. We are interested in how such changes are reflected in and refracted through basic social institutions and provisions of social reproduction and in structures of survival. As we shall see in the contributions of this book, such structures are simultaneously place-bound yet hybridized through the penetration of transnational or global forces.

So what exactly do we mean by global forces and how do they link to basic provisioning of social reproduction? First, for many developing governments a situation of fiscal crisis, compounded by the need to service growing debts, has resulted in savage cutbacks in public provisions for welfare, health and education – essential aspects of social reproduction that underpin a general sense of human security of the majority. Second, as governments have willingly or unwillingly evacuated the state's responsibility for social reproduction, partly due to restructuring from above (often enforced by the external discipline of the IMF, the World Bank and private financial capital) we see new struggles for survival among the very poorest.

One example is the emergence of a grass-roots phenomenon that has been called "the feminization of survival" (Sassen 2000). This concept refers to systematic links between debt servicing and new survival strategies in the developing world. Over the past two decades, at least according to some estimates cited by Sassen, indebted developing countries have repaid four times their original debts whilst at the same time their debt stocks have increased four-fold. Many developing countries use over 50% of their government revenues for debt service (equivalent to 20–25% of their total export earnings). Fear of excommunication from global capital markets skews the composition of state expenditures towards debt servicing, squeezing outlays on primary education and health care by ratios of as much as 10 to 1. As Sassen points out, there is no conspiracy involved here since the context is structural and linked to the power of the capital markets and the associated governing frameworks of economic globalization. Feminization of survival is connected to new frameworks of exploitative migration and oppression, referred to earlier (see also Chapter 2).

So in this book we advance a third concept of security in addition to those of national security and human security: the *security of capital*. It helps to indicate why some state strategies have been reconfigured in the era of intensified globalization and disciplinary neo-liberalism in ways that may have gone with much greater inequality and erosion of material conditions for greater human security, and provisioning for social reproduction. In many respects, because of the pressures of indebtedness and fiscal crisis, much public policy seems to be subordinated to providing maximum security for the owners of capital, including guaranteed repayment of debts, in some cases several times over.

This is why, in today's world, the security of capital generally means reinforced legal and political security for the holdings and power positions of large corporations and wealthy individuals, and creditors more generally.[3] There is, in principle, no reason why legal security for capital could not coexist with national security and better conditions for human security, particularly if the latter were defined in ways that allowed for reasonable provisioning for social reproduction. However, in practice capital wants and has got much more than this. What is in effect being constructed in an American-led world order is a political and juridical framework for global capitalism – a new constitutionalism – that seeks increasingly to "lock in" the rights of capital, whilst simultaneously locking out democratic control over key aspects of the political economy. One result is that the goal of public policy is increasingly premised on increasing the security of ruling classes and the largest property owners, and in some senses minimizing the uncertainty of investors, partly through placing populations and governments under intensified and constant surveillance (Gill 1995b).

The dialectic of the old and the new

The emerging world order and global political economy are being reconstituted by struggles between old and new social forces. For example, there are conflicts over the nature, use and limits of state sovereignty in world politics, particularly as non-territorial frameworks of transnational power/ production/social reproduction are extended, including the transnationalization and spread of primitive labor markets and efforts to institutionalize new forms of discipline over both protected and unprotected workers. Indeed, the question of transnationalization of frameworks of (network) power also includes those forces associated with the unprecedented non-state mega-terrorism of Al-Qaeda and with the growth of transnational crime syndicates – that have a growing role in human trafficking, the transnational sex industry, money-laundering and the illegal arms and drug trade.

At issue with respect to questions of both national and popular sovereignty and frameworks of social reproduction are the largely unregulated offshore world and its tax havens, also crucial here in partially deterritorializing frameworks of power and eroding the traditional tax base of governments. However, it is important to note that the offshore world is itself a creation of states that use their sovereignty within the system to create differential zones of production and exchange (Palan 1998). Offshore facilities – the largest ones being in Switzerland and the City of London, alongside smaller and more literally offshore havens such as the Bahamas and the Cayman Islands – are used not only by transnational crime and terror networks but also by states and wealthy private individuals. However, they are used much more frequently by omnipresent transnational corporations and owners and managers of mobile capital as they seek to maximize profits, and minimize taxes and the effects of environmental and labor regulations in specific jurisdictions. Thus "offshore" facilitates avoidance of local taxes and thus indirectly allows its beneficiaries to escape contributions to the costs of social reproduction that such companies and individuals might otherwise make locally. This hybrid space in the global political economy thus depends on both the territorial power of the state for its creation and maintenance, whilst it facilitates the extension of the power resources and potentials of non-state actors, and private forms of network power and the power and mobility of capital.

Such changes in the global political economy seem to have been accompanied by new frameworks of social reproduction. The emerging framework seems to be linked to the growing atomization of the social relations of production (for example, the growth of both flexible accumulation and primitive labor markets) associated with the dominant global regime of accumulation that we call disciplinary neo-liberalism. It is in effect a globalization of the idea of self-help and possessive individualism, despite some "social safety nets" for those who drop out of the new economic war of all against all. Thus in recent years, the social reproduction of our societies seems to be increasingly marketized, commodified, and, as we have noted, linked to remote, unresponsive and increasingly illegitimate and unaccountable, often distant, alien structures, over which the mass of the world's population seems to have little or no control.

At the same time, however, this situation of transformation, crisis and insecurity involves challenges to the political legitimacy of elites and ruling classes throughout the world, a fact that explains why many of the world's leaders have united under the banner of the "war against terrorism," identifying terror with those that challenge the existing political order, whether such resistance is legitimate or not. Nevertheless, despite efforts to consolidate state powers and the capacities to repress challenges from below, as the globalization of power intensifies, so do the globalization of resistance and a counter-mobilization of new political forces, of right and left.

Indeed, as we have argued in other works, we believe that the making of global society in the twenty-first century will involve the dialectical movement of political forces both locally and globally. It is evident that in many respects, forms of "globalization from below" associated with the lower reaches of the global social hierarchy are not only conditions of existence for "globalization from above" but also form a new moment in global politics, or a "clash of globalizations" (Gill 2002a, 2003a).

In light of such global transformations, this book seeks to point towards the need for radical research agendas for rethinking ontologies of the global political economy. For example, we think that many of the developments outlined in this work may mandate a rethinking of the commodity form of global capitalism. This should also be related to issues of power, production and social reproduction. We think that the key to this rethinking can be found by drawing upon insights from both Radical and Feminist Political Economy. Any such reconsideration would mandate a new conceptual framework and ontology of political economy, connected to the ways in which aspects of human life are increasingly reduced into objects (commodities) for sale and purchase within economistic systems of market exchange. This new ontology might include the multiple forms of commodification, exploitation, and control of labor; the greater commodification of social institutions; accelerating commodification of the human body and the alienation of life-forms and systems of material provisioning more generally. Indeed, these elements normally associated with the exchange form, production and consumption all correspond to the three main components of social reproduction as we have defined them above (see Chapter 2 for elaboration).

Thus rethinking the global political economy would take into account both old and new forms of power, such as the reassertion of certain types of state power in response to traditional interstate security interests (and use of new forms of state-organized violence), as well as new forms of power embodied in non-state actors. Indeed, world order is at a juncture constituted by not only traditional modernist frameworks of power, but also a postmodern, mobile, indeed deterritorialized structure of power that has structural affinities to medieval Europe, one that has been viewed as an emergent postmodern framework (Falk 2003).

In conclusion, the purpose and objectives of this work are two-fold:

- First, this work seeks to initiate a reconceptualization of global political economy by introducing a new perspective on power, production and social reproduction.
- Second, it endeavors to provide an innovative theoretical and empirical framework to permit concrete explanation of the dialectic between national, regional and global restructuring of capital, on the one hand, and the redefinition and reform of social provisioning on the other, in the context of their implications for human in/security.

Thus we hope that the contribution of this book will be both theoretical and practical. It will seek to point towards ways in which a breakthrough in theories of the global political economy might be made. We hope that an innovative theoretical perspective such as the one we seek to foster will help to explain some of the conditions of existence for the members of world society in the early years of the new millennium – and thus key aspects of the political movement of globalization. At the same time we hope that this work will offer some practical insights for understanding the new challenges to public policy connected to globalization; for example, questions of migration, social cohesion, macroeconomics and economic regulation, as well as the humanitarian and ethical questions that form the leitmotif of the chapters of the work.

Notes

1. Harrod and Cox identified at least 12 patterns of power–production relations, or "social modes of production" that coexisted and overlapped in a complex matrix in the global division of labor during the 1980s. These were: subsistence, peasant–lord relations, the primitive labor market, household relations, self-employment, the enterprise labor market, bipartism (co-determination by capital and labor with the state providing the legal framework), enterprise corporatism, tripartism (where the state intervenes more directly in the labor–capital relation and the regulation and rationalization of production relations), state corporatism (as in fascism), communal (for example, the Israeli kibbutzim) and central planning (as in the former Soviet Union). These social modes of production can coexist, although in a given society (or world order) one may be dominant in the sense that it tends to determine the main direction of capital accumulation and the terms under which subordinate modes are articulated in the global division of labor, although in the context of a dialectic of power and resistance. Harrod inverted the priority Cox gave to production by focusing on unprotected workers, and saw the household form as central for social reproduction. See Cox (1987) and Harrod (1987).
2. Of course, the UNDP's 1994 *Human Development Report* that advocated the adoption of a new concept of human security was making a normative claim on behalf of the most vulnerable. Nevertheless, in so far as this might become a covenant of the UN system it would reinforce a sense of universal justice and ethics with the categorical imperative to protect the welfare and everyday security of the most vulnerable as its starting point. The UNDP was also making the implicit historical argument that the post-Cold War order would not be sustainable either in economic,

social, or environmental terms without redistribution to compensate for the effects of crises and growing inequality on world society.
3. Policy-makers also seek to provide security for the world's consumers, defined in terms of their significance and salience for policy by their income, which defines their ability to purchase goods and services. The security of the consumer is seen as a crucial aspect of consumer confidence and as such the propensity to consume.

2
Ontology, Method, and Hypotheses[1]

Isabella Bakker and Stephen Gill

Chapter 2 is concerned to advance some of the theoretical and practical agenda outlined at the end of Chapter 1 by introducing issues of ontology and epistemology so as to outline a methodological sketch to frame a number of our main hypotheses.

Thus a starting point for this work is the construction of an appropriate ontology of the global political economy and the emerging world order. In constructing this ontology we in effect address the need for a more comprehensive approach to the explanation of changing global conditions of existence, or of a totality that consists of a certain contradictory unity, albeit a unity in diversity. We think that this ontology needs to encompass the wider dimension of social life so often referred to in the early Marx (1964) but relatively neglected in his later work. We also think that a radical means to do this was introduced by Gramsci (1971). Namely, we start from the idea that human beings (women and men) make history but – as Marx added – not necessarily under conditions of their own choosing (Marx 1973: 146–7). In other words, social knowledge, human consciousness and patterns of collective action all form part of the making of history.

Of course, Feminist Political Economy has sought to highlight the way in which the making of history is the work of *both men and women*. To recognize this simple fact requires that we pay attention not just to narrowly drawn productivist frameworks of power and production and their power relations. In this regard, we offer an ontology that can incorporate the basic social conditions that make such power and production possible in the first place – including what Feminist Political Economy has called social reproduction, and indeed to recognize that power relations not only serve to define production but also the institutions, processes and practices of social reproduction.

Social reproduction – discussed at greater length below – refers to both biological reproduction of the species (and indeed its ecological framework) and ongoing reproduction of the commodity labor power. In addition social reproduction involves institutions, processes and social relations associated with the *creation and maintenance* of communities – and upon which, ultimately, all production and exchange rests (Bakker 1999). In today's world social reproduction involves institutions that provide for socialization of risk, health care, education and other services – indeed many of the key elements of what the early Marx called "species-being," social institutions that distinguish the life of human beings from that of animals (Marx 1964).[2]

With this stance in mind, at a more historically concrete level of analysis our ontology for analyzing the changing global political economy includes a number of specific historical or constitutive structures associated with the reconfiguration of governance and its relation to the social questions. Thus in the final two parts of the chapter we outline concepts that correspond to the dominant historical structures (understood as the patterned or institutionalized forms of human agency) that we think have served to constitute some of the transformations in the juridical-political, political economy and social dimensions of the world order of the early twenty-first century. These structures include the new constitutionalism, disciplinary neo-liberalism, social reproduction, shifting gender orders, the erosion of the family wage and the feminization of survival.

Our ontology includes not only multiple forms of commodification, but also new patterns of exploitation, and control of labor in the production–reproduction relationship. The ontology should be understood as a transformative *process* that not only entails the constitution and reconstitution of gender, race and class and ideas about gender, race and class as expressed through this greater commodification of social, political and economic institutions. It also entails how a sense of identity and of resistance can be actualized in this new context of intensified globalization. In this context, for example, how women's struggles can confront the connected yet "scattered hegemonies" of global economic institutions, states, patriarchal households and other exploitative structures in ways that both challenge these sites and connections among them, is a key aspect of the politics of a transnational community of women (Nesiah 1993) and of a politics of "transformative resistance" (Gill 2003a) implicit in several Feminist International/Global Political Economy writings.[3] Thus in this work, questions of social reproduction are related not only to the making of history but also to the remaking of theory.

Our concepts are then used to help generate a number of secondary hypotheses that connect to the central hypothesis outlined in Chapter 1: an emerging global contradiction between the extended power of capital (and its protection by the state) and progressive forms of social reproduction or, more broadly, the human security of a majority of the world's population. Our secondary hypotheses concern the reprivatization of the governance of social reproduction and how this is a counterpart to a general increase in the range, depth and scope of socioeconomic exploitation in global capitalism amid wider conditions of primitive or original accumulation. Primitive accumulation is not only reflected in privatization of state assets, a trend that increased massively throughout the 1990s, but also in privatization of parts of the state form itself. There are at least two dimensions to this shift: (a) the privatization of previously socialized institutions associated with provisioning for social reproduction, (b) the alienation or enclosure of common social property which we see as part of a new global enclosure movement. Both of these changes tend to grant more power to capital, while simultaneously undermining socialized forms of collective provisioning and human security.

In addition a growing rate of exploitation (more intensive work and longer hours in order to meet the same social needs) is associated with the restructuring of the family wage, the emergence of what has been termed the feminization of survival, and racialized and gendered patterns of exploitative migration. We see some of these developments as direct or indirect consequences of efforts to extend and institutionalize the power and security of capital – albeit at the expense of greater insecurity for most workers, particularly those women workers at the bottom of the global class and racial hierarchies.

Towards a Feminist Historical Materialist ontology

Ontology in a philosophical sense involves the study of the nature of existence or being, since being is the primary constituent of reality. A social ontology is a conceptualization of the primary constituents of social being and therefore involves a specification of the relation between its primary constituent units, elements or constitutive forces. However, it is important to stress that a social ontology is an historical and human *process*, a process that involves human agency in the creation of the institutions and structures of social life in a given period. A social ontology is therefore a process associated with the reproduction and transformation of dominant and subordinate structures of thought and practice in a given historical period. Thus its specification must necessarily be conditional and open-ended.

Our understanding of the social ontology of the global political economy incorporates the dialectic of structure and agency and power/knowledge as a means to identify the moments not only of power and production, but also of social reproduction in the emerging world order. In relation to production the general point here is that work broadly mediates relations between social and natural orders and combines the theoretical and practical activity of human beings in an understanding of movement and change. This is a process that takes account of past, present and future. By contrast, labor is a particular aspect of work which in a capitalist social formation is that part which is appropriated and controlled by capital in the labor–capital relation.

Gramsci pointed to this distinction with respect to the role of primary education where he argued the central educational principle was the idea of *work*. In primary schools children were taught the basics of natural science as well as civic rights and duties. "Scientific ideas were intended to insert the child into the *societas rerum*, the world of things, while lessons in rights and duties were intended to insert him into the State and into civil society," in ways intended to overcome superstition, folklore and "localistic barbarism." The aim of the primary school was to foster a more modern outlook based on awareness of "the simple and fundamental fact that there exist objective, intractable natural laws to which man must adapt himself if he is to master them" as well as the fact that "social and state laws" exist as "products of human activity, which are established by men [sic] and can be altered by men in the interests of their collective development." The purpose of these state and social laws was to create a human order that best allowed people to "dominate the laws of nature, that is to say [an order] which most facilitates their *work*. For work is a specific mode by which man actively participates in natural life in order to transform and socialize it more and more deeply and extensively" (Gramsci 1971: 34, emphasis in original). This is why Gramsci argued that:

> The idea and the fact of work (of theoretical and practical activity) was the educational principle latent in the primary school, since it is by means of work that the social and State order (rights and duties) is introduced and identified within the natural order. (Gramsci 1971: 34)

Thus for Gramsci work is not primarily a category of Political Economy, it is part of an ontological conception of the world, a world that is grounded in education, culture, and in other institutions of social development. This is also why Gramsci recognized, by contrast, that work in a capitalist society is not only inside a social relation defined by capital (and juxtaposed against capital) in the form of labor, but also a *creative* process that could exist outside of that social relation. As we shall see, this distinction is crucial because it helps to explain how some of the crises and transformations in social reproduction described subsequently in this chapter and throughout this book are connected to how capitalist market forces penetrate into the spheres of society previously shielded from commodification. When capital penetrates into basic social and human institutions it produces destabilizing consequences for social reproduction.

One Socialist Feminist writer has argued that the modern origins of important aspects of this process with respect to social reproduction go back to when goods produced to meet the needs of subsistence "began to be separated out from the consumption of those goods and the generational production of individuals" (Ferguson 1998: 3). Development of markets for commodities (labor and goods) separated social reproduction (including the "production of individuals") from the reproduction of capital. This is because capitalist markets are institutions organized not primarily to meet human needs but to function as mechanisms for the accumulation of capital. Over time, under conditions of the commodification of labor, workers become:

> Dependent on the market for the items they once produced at home (or obtained through the informal economy of bartering, lending and giving)... [Since] without a wage they cannot obtain crucial subsistence goods. It is because of this cycle of dependence that the market actually comes to dominate social reproduction in general. Quite simply, people's ability to sustain themselves and others – to materially reproduce themselves – comes to depend upon their ability to earn a wage to feed, clothe and shelter themselves and their family. (Ferguson 1998: 4)

In other words the social and power relations of capital reduced the creative capacities and potentials of workers to an instrumentality, with the effect that it transformed the advantages of human freedom and its objectification into means to accumulate profit. Thus a contradictory social ontology emerged in the nineteenth century with the creation of market society and wage labor, which became a commodity under the rule of capital. This type of labor is estranged labor, and society – and therefore processes of social reproduction within society – becomes subordinated to an alien power. As nature, people and the means of exchange are reduced to means, social relations are radically redefined.[4]

In this sense commodification of social life and nature is itself an expression of and a means to extend a specific form of social power, and as such it encounters resistance, either in the form of movements for protection or in the context of what can be called socialization. It is in this historical sense that the pure commodification of society is a contradiction in terms (Polanyi 1957; van der Pijl 1998). At the same time, as the chapters by Persaud, Mushakoji and Hanochi all show, the commodity form is not only structured hierarchically in terms of the nature and intensity of exploitation of workers, it is also highly racialized and sexualized. In this sense, and of particular relevance for social reproduction, the commodity form is not generic but gendered.[5]

Thus, whilst our understanding of social ontology (and indeed key aspects of the contemporary historical dialectic) involves the analysis of social relations of production (for example, including the power relations between men and women, lord and peasant, employer and workers, government and governed, dominant and subordinate states) and the mediation and transformation of these relations (and the natural world) through purposive activity, it also includes what Gramsci called the role of human subjectivity and the ways in which this constituted and constrained by different moments of class formation, racialization, sexuality and gender.

Indeed, for Gramsci, the possibility of creativity and liberation for workers is developed through education, culture and politics, since he believed that the creativity of people forged society, culture and history. As such, political struggle could not be narrowly defined. More broadly, Gramsci saw this as forming part of the struggle for hegemony, one that is not confined to the factory, or indeed to the economy, as it is conventionally defined. It also involves the cultural sphere and those elements of social organization and social institutions that we have linked to social reproduction. It had to address not only the separation of mental and manual labor but also that between the "poetic" and "practical" aspects of human activity. However, this is not enough: the question of inequality between men and women must also be posed, which itself is a question of democracy:

> The labourer can become a skilled worker... the peasant a surveyor or petty agronomist. But democracy, by definition, cannot mean merely that an unskilled worker can become skilled. It must mean that every "citizen" can "govern" and that society places him, even if only abstractly, in a general condition to achieve this. (Gramsci 1971: 40)

In conclusion to this section, our ontology assumes that social relations are transitory and are transformed through the activity of human beings, largely connected to and constituted by production/social reproduction – in a specified historical context. In this context, "agency" and "structure" are understood as methodological postulates that help us to identify aspects of the patterning and transformation of social consciousness, social action and social relations in different historical situations. In other words, agency and structure are abstractions from a single set of historical processes, although agency is connected to the formation of historical subjects and the exercise of political will, and as such it is methodologically distinct. We believe that this process cannot be fully understood, indeed is likely to be misunderstood, if it is conceptualized through pure idealism or abstract structuralism, and indeed through the lens of Cartesian dualism that is associated with positivist social science. We also think that such a misunderstanding is likely if the process of historical transformation is theorized in a reductionist way, as is often found in orthodox materialism and mechanical Marxism (for example, what Gramsci called "historical economism") or the methodological individualism of Weberian sociology. Indeed, each of these perspectives can be considered as different forms of reductionism that postulate the determination of historical change by means of reified notions of structure or of agency.

This is why in this book we do not simply equate social reproduction with the care economy, important though this is. We see social reproduction as both a productive potential and a condition of existence for the expanded reproduction of capital and social formation. Put simply, we believe that a more comprehensive and dialectical framework or ontology of global political economy will be one that links different social forces and moments of transformation in power, production and social reproduction.

A methodological sketch

Different instances of power, production/destruction and social reproduction (and of power, resistance, freedom and emancipation) thus constitute the social ontology of the emerging world order. In this sense, our ontology should be understood as an ongoing *process*, a process that involves transformations from above and from below in the hierarchy of global social formation. This world order is, in its present incarnation, gendered and racialized as well as being configured by a complex hierarchy of class relations. In this emerging world order we are seeking to highlight, amongst other things, how transformations related to intensified globalization are in turn reconfiguring gender-based identities and conditions. Indeed, gender inequalities – as the authors in the following chapters illustrate – are constitutive of the very processes at the heart of intensified globalization.

In this context an entry point for the construction of a critical research method can be based on our responses to a number of Feminist insights on redefining what is political and economic activity, and concerning the public–private divide.

For example, some Feminist writers argue that activities associated with social reproduction should be included as "economic activities" (Waring 1999). We see this somewhat differently since we consider the practices associated with social reproduction as part of the *human* constitution (the making) of species-being. Thus we do not separate the economic from the political or the social in this sense since we consider both to be moments in the process of the making of history. The issue therefore is not what is to be included within the sphere of the "economic" but rather how social/material practices are constituted. Thus diverse activities, including labor in the marketplace and work in the home, each form a part of the general reproduction of social/material life.

Also, with respect to the method for locating and explaining the "political" or power relations, a Historical Materialist analysis would always seek to analyze such relations in a concrete historical context. Under given conditions, public forms of authority and rule may be the primary means through which social coordination and social reproduction are articulated. Such a pattern is normally assumed to have existed under communist command systems. By contrast, in modern capitalism, power tends to be hybridized in public/private combinations with respect to capitalist state formations (business has privileged representation within the state) and it is concretized in private property. Here it is worth remembering that, according to a Marxist reading, private property is both the cause and the consequence of alienated labor and with it the expropriation of social, collective or "human property" more generally, in a process sanctioned and enforced by the state (see Marx 1964: 117ff.).[6] Thus a public/private hybrid characterizes the ostensibly private powers that inhere to institutions and agents of civil society (government regulates and authorizes political parties, media organizations, churches and civic groups, and so on) – in ways analogous to how private rights of property are publicly constituted. The same is also true of the family and households.[7]

Further, Historical Materialists influenced by Gramsci have hypothesized not only that capitalist state forms and practices of rule are the result of combinations of public and private power, but also that effective methods, techniques and routines of influence and authority are formed in historical blocs. Such historical blocs are not simply political nor are they exclusively economic or cultural; they must be all three at the same time to effectively reproduce a sustainable form of rule and political order over time. Indeed, any political order is constituted by a range of social practices and cultural institutions connected to the reproduction of the dominant frameworks of understanding and "common sense" as well as those of rule and accumulation. Of course, dominant or supremacist forces associated with the prevailing historical blocs seek to stabilize their cultural and material dominance. However, resistance confronts dominant forces – since resistance is immanent in the contradictory unity of globalization, that is to say resistances are formed in each situation of power relations that involves dominant and subaltern social forces.

Such dialectics of power may be constituted by rival epistemologies as well as political organizations and practical knowledge. Thus the making of history involves the dialectic of political agency and the formation of new potentials of power. Some forms of agency may be confined to a local, immediate perspective, whereas other forms of power and perspective may have potentially universal and hegemonic appeal, and take a long-term, strategic viewpoint.[8]

This is yet another way of repeating our original point that a Feminist Historical Materialist ontological framework concerns how history is created and transformed by people. In this way our methodological framework is grounded in Historical Materialist ontology and it builds on and extends work in critical International Studies, Political Economy and radical Feminism. Writers in the latter tradition have analyzed women's positioning at the crossroads of production and reproduction, and as subordinated in particular ways by the commodity form (Beneria and Sen 1997). Feminists have also stressed how discursive disciplining of thought and action includes how boundaries are constituted in theories of (political) economy – for example, between production and what we refer to as social reproduction of people and communities. Here we extend and apply such work to the analysis of governance processes operating locally and globally in the constitution of world order, political economy and social reproduction. In this regard, governance frameworks are amalgams of discourses and mechanisms of institutionalization and enforcement that combine patterns of consent and coercion, domination and legitimacy.

When Cox originally developed his approach to world order, he saw ideas, institutions and material capabilities as social forces operating in the historical structures of power and production at three basic levels of world order, forms of state and production (Cox 1981). We see these not as levels as such, but as different moments in the constitution of a contradictory totality of world order. Moreover, each moment in the constitution and governance of social forces involves and connects to human capabilities and potentials relative not only to frameworks of power and production but also to social reproduction.[9] For example, with respect to the social forces associated with social reproduction, we want to take into account:

1. *Ideas*, including ideologies, theories and shared perspectives on the world (intersubjectivities) that may include what Gramsci called "the common sense of an epoch" which would include ethics, folklore and "good sense" as well as rationalities and identities of political groups and social subjects.
2. Key *social institutions* through which power, production and social reproduction normally operate: for example, the state, markets, and the family.
3. *Power potentials*, involving mobilization of resources, capabilities and enforcement mechanisms or power potentials of political and social actors.

These moments can be separated methodologically for purposes of exposition but they are linked together in a contradictory totality of world order. With respect to *frameworks of world order*, issues of war and peace, conflict and cooperation, allocation of power and distribution of resources in so-called international organizations or interstate systems and patterns of rivalry connect to power structures and power relations (public and private) that concern the constitution and governance of the world market. As such, they immediately pose the basic contradiction between capital and social reproduction as outlined at the start of this book. That very same contradiction is found in and across forms of governance and political association linked to the regulation and reproduction of capital within particular territories and regions.

Thus any comprehensive analysis of *frameworks of political and civil society* in nation-states or macro-regional associations (such as the European Union) would take into account relationships between social reproduction and the more formal frameworks of the political, partly expressed in state forms, and specifically the historical blocs that give political direction and identity to social and political projects. Thus some forms of state may be governed by historical blocs that are less predisposed than others to allow foreign capital to penetrate within territories for reasons of social protection and self-sufficiency. Indeed, this was a traditional axis of North–South interstate struggle until the early 1980s. Since then the debt crisis and other pressures have led to a specific internationalization of Third World states, allowing for the increasingly free mobility of capital and a loss of self-sufficiency – for example, in food – in ways that seem to have worsened human insecurity and intensified the contradiction between capital and social reproduction. In a similar manner, different forms of *power/production* are connected to issues of *power over* production as well as the *power to* produce. Indeed, any analysis of the power–production nexus must include reference not only to forms of state but also to the specificities of governance, such as those linked to structures of ownership and control (constituted by laws, treaties). It would need to pay attention to varied power relations: for example, between (land)lord and peasant, labor and capital, corporation and union, and between the employer and day-laborers. Such power relations of production may or may not be legally regulated. Moreover such relations have traditionally been mediated by inequalities stemming from racialization, sexuality and gender. Such inequalities in power/production are connected with and influence frameworks of *social reproduction*, involving biological, daily and generational reproduction of labor power and communities, and identities. Indeed these forms of *power/production/social reproduction* are governed by similar processes of commodification, ultimately linked to transforming important aspects of life and nature into commodities, those posing the basic contradiction between capital (which is a form of social power that includes power in and over production) and social reproduction. Thus depletion and destruction of *ecological and biological* structures and systems that sustain life is also linked to intensified commodification and exploitation of life forms and nature. Thus world order issues (for example, the world market for agriculture) connect not only to species-being, but also to the reproduction of the species.[10]

Notwithstanding these elements within the Historical Materialist traditions, Feminist theorists continue to argue, however, that conventional accounts – including many critical ones – are often silent, or at least do not go far enough when it comes to recognizing the gendered (indeed, racialized) character of these material/power potentials, ideas and structures. For example, Feminist writers from the South have consistently demonstrated that the economic subject of restructuring in, for example, the Structural Adjustment Programs of the World Bank is not a gender-neutral, generic subject. Indeed, Feminists have stressed how international financial institutions charged with managing globalization so as to promote a liberal model of development reaffirm a world of self-reliant Davos Men – in an intellectual and political framework that obscures and erases the real-life experiences of most people (Beneria 1999). In particular, the subjective conditions of most women, who are intrinsically tied to social reproduction, are at best assumed or included only to the extent that they mirror the experiences of men. Other Feminists have shown that women have had a fundamentally different relation than men to national and international spaces of production, politics, identity and culture

(Kabeer 1991). This sense of difference and complexity is also true of analyses that highlight practices of racialization and supremacist assumptions connected to the language and cultural representations of frameworks of domination such as colonialism and imperialism, as well as resistance to such practices over many centuries of history.[11]

Thus Critical (Feminist) analyses of the global political economy begin by denaturalizing globalizing capitalism and making explicit its social construction for individuals, groups, nations and civilizations. Indeed, those influenced by heterodox traditions of Historical Materialism approach these questions in a non-reductionist way as did Gramsci's writings on hegemony, power and culture as transformative processes. Thus writers in this tradition have emphasized how social formations and systems of political economy are subject to mutability, transience and transcendence, both within and across particular historical conjunctures (Gill 1997). They have also sought to highlight the crises and contradictions associated with the growth of capital as a social and political force, and the changing structures of world order associated with the rise and fall of empires, hegemonies and other forms of global dominance.[12]

Key hypotheses

We have developed two main hypotheses to guide our research. In the rest of this section we elaborate some of the thinking behind these hypotheses and how we might begin to develop a research program to evaluate them. Our hypotheses are:

1. *There is an emerging contradiction between the global accumulation of capital and the provisioning of stable conditions for social reproduction.* Here we see accumulation and social reproduction as different, albeit contradictory moments in the same system or totality.
2. *This situation is being locked in by neo-liberal new constitutional governance mechanisms*, with damaging effects for the social reproduction of the majority of the world's population.

The dominant framework of global governance is associated with the G7 countries and the international financial institutions. It is linked to a neo-liberal project of reform that seeks to reshape state forms to allow for greater freedom of enterprise, extension of markets for commodities and the mobilization of some parts of civil society to promote growth and development (World Bank 2002). Therefore, and by definition, if governance involves the extension of markets that facilitate private investment and accumulation it also involves new frameworks of power. Thus understanding how such frameworks have reshaped or channelled the actions or functions of governments also implies the analysis of how private, non-state actors, both within and across nation-states, wield influence and thus shape the use of political power (local, national and transnational) and the distribution of global resources for social reproduction.

This type of private, transnational power can be illustrated relative to the new General Agreement on Trade in Services (GATS) mobilized over the past few years, and is currently being extended in the World Trade Organization. The GATS covers virtually all services, and not just tourism. GATS is linked to the framework of "progressive liberalization" that lies at the heart of the new juridical frameworks for the regulation of trade and investment in the global political economy. Since many services are currently publicly provided, many believe that the GATS begins to open up the door to the wider privatization of the state and with it the reprivatization of important institutions of social reproduction, particularly in education, health care and social services. In so far as this is true, a new framework of public and private power is now restructuring frameworks of social reproduction on a world scale.

Thus, for example, new constitutional mechanisms associated with unrestricted free capital mobility coupled to the offshore world of tax avoidance may not only be destabilizing for (national) economic policy as a result of volatile flows of capital, but they may also enable large holders of capital and wealthy private investors (and to an extent highly mobile, professional, elite labor) to be free of the need to contribute substantially to the collective costs of social reproduction (for example, through taxation, training of workers, or other provision of social goods). Partly as a consequence, UN agencies point towards a growing crisis of social reproduction, most acute in poor developing countries (UNDP 2002; UNRISD 1995). This crisis is associated with the fiscal crisis of the state – a crisis also experienced in many more affluent societies. The effects of fiscal crisis and cutbacks in government expenditures for social, educational and health costs affects people in unequal ways, and the poorest tend to be the hardest hit when such provisions are removed or reduced.

This is why questions are being raised worldwide about the political legitimacy, stability and sustainability of new constitutionalism with its ethos of limited government and fiscal discipline, particularly where it is accompanied by regressive regimes of taxation.

Whilst quite a lot of theoretical and empirical work has been done on interrelations between governance frameworks and world order, forms of state and production (for example, how the liberalization of governance may imply an expansion of private forms of power relative to public), very little has been done on connections between these three frameworks of governance and those for social reproduction. Indeed, much more work is needed to interrogate the problems and contradictions associated with the new frameworks of governance. Thus we are interested in the governance of agricultural policies, social welfare, education, as well as the so-called "care economy" which often operates at the level of the household. We are interested in how such provisioning is connected to human security, which we understand in turn as a basic right as well as a condition for social reproduction (UNDP 1994).

Social reproduction and its associated governance frameworks can also be analyzed in terms not only of how they can enhance human rights but also of how they can become productive mechanisms of human development. With respect to the latter, we wish to interrogate how the restructuring of the global political economy and its prevailing governance frameworks may reveal the salience of new sets of *ideas* and broader *discourses* concerning the appropriate role of government and the rights of its citizens. At the *institutional* level, social citizenship, secured and supported by governments, seems to be giving way to market citizenship, where citizens become responsible for helping themselves in a more privatized social order. Indeed, this new notion of citizenship – stripped of post-World War II welfare notions of social justice and an active state – is reflected in the new governance frameworks of the WTO. It signals a new division of responsibility as well as new frameworks for the *allocation of resources* for individual and social welfare between the state, the family, the market, and for the voluntary and informal sectors.

What is needed is analysis that can bring together the changes in ideas, institutions and material resources to assess changes in the public/private distinction over time and across space.[13] This analysis needs to be political and should address the distributional issues associated with the new governance frameworks, for different groups of women and men, depending on race, class and legal status.

In the rest of this chapter we provide conceptual elaboration of new constitutionalism, social reproduction and gender orders and their links to our main hypotheses.

Transformations in political-juridical and Political Economy frameworks

Here we outline two concepts that help us to clarify important aspects of contemporary historical structures in global restructuring. These concepts are *new constitutionalism* and *disciplinary neo-liberalism*. They relate to what the World Bank calls the "worldwide market" revolution, a revolution that involves nothing less than the reconfiguration of forms of state and power/production/social reproduction along largely liberal lines in ways designed to empower private property associated with capital, relative to what Marx called social or "human" property, associated with species-being.

This revolution can be interpreted as part of the historical shift away from Third World post-colonial constitutional frameworks more linked to the New International Economic Order and several UN declarations of the 1970s: covenants that sought to establish different social and economic purposes of the regulation of trade and investment. Liberal frameworks have supplanted these. The introduction of these frameworks has proliferated since the fall of the Soviet Union. As a recent UNDP *Human Development Report* noted: "Indeed, in many respects, the shift has been as revolutionary as that in the formerly communist countries" (1997: 88).

New constitutionalism relates not only to rights and freedoms as usually defined by traditional forms of constitutionalism, but also to microeconomic issues of trade and investment policies and to macroeconomics and the making of monetary and fiscal policy. Thus we can illustrate some of the changes entailed with respect to the liberalization and integration of trade and investment. For example, the GATT system created after World War II regulated trade and investment flows between capitalist, socialist and post-colonial economies. It was a period of *shallow integration* of very differently organized economic systems, articulated in what could be called the *international* political economy. Particularly after the collapse of the USSR, we have now moved into a period of *deepening integration* in an increasingly *global* political economy (Gill and Law 1988; Ostry 1998). The new, more liberal, much more integrated forms of law and regulation, for example, in the World Trade Organization, act as quasi-constitutional devices that intensify pressures (external disciplines) for adjustment of domestic systems and structures in accord with the categorical imperatives of economic globalization. A similar set of pressures and disciplines is reflected in G7/G8 pronouncements, in Structural Adjustment Programs and in the conditionality frameworks of the international financial institutions. They are also reflected in regional trade and investment treaties such as the NAFTA and in the mass proliferation of bilateral trade agreements. Indeed, since the early 1990s, such deeper integration is associated with widening jurisdiction and competence of many international economic organizations, as well as new ones such as the WTO. These plus the many thousands of bilateral trade and investment agreements form part of the new webs of deeper integration.

At the same time, deeper integration has gone with new mechanisms of liberal governance – what we call new constitutionalism. The new networks of laws, rules, standards, as well as regional and national agreements and both new and modified political constitutions that are generally intended in the words of a recent *World Development Report* (World Bank 1997), to "lock in" commitments to liberal governmental and market reforms. The Bank has referred to this process as the creation of an "enabling state," that is a state that is pro-market and is in turn disciplined by market forces and international regulatory and legal frameworks such as those associated with the WTO and the international financial institutions (World Bank 1997: 51). Thus new constitutionalism involves *pre-commitment mechanisms* to lock in not only present governments and citizens to the reforms, but more fundamentally to prevent *future* governments from undoing the reforms. In this way its central purpose is to reconstruct the political and legal terms through which governance and accountability operate not only in the near term, but also in the longer run.

The changes involved include not only the institutionalization of constitutional separation of powers and judicial review and protection for extended private property rights but also institutional and policy changes. For example, in macroeconomic policy, locking-in is associated with independent central banks with low inflation targets, with fixed exchange rates or currency boards as was used in Argentina, as well as with laws that mandate fiscal restraint such as balanced budget laws. In different ways all of these measures can be viewed as quintessential liberal pre-commitment mechanisms (Schneiderman 2000).

Thus new constitutionalism has emerged as one of the means to consolidate or to lock-in the market-based revolution and its disciplines over the past 20 years: the shift in political economy towards disciplinary neo-liberalism. This moment also signals a shift in the organization of social reproduction.

Disciplinary neo-liberalism involves the way that social discipline is increasingly exercised through market-based structures, for example in capital and labor markets. In addition, the state is also subjected to market disciplines: governments now seek to prove their *credibility*, and the *consistency* of their policies according to the degree to which they inspire the *confidence* of investors and, of course, consumers (the "three Cs"). Credibility is defined by the World Bank as the "reliability of the institutional framework" and "the predictability of its rules and policies and the consistency with which they are applied" (Gill 1998b, citing the World Bank 1997: 5). Thus a key issue for contemporary public policy is the need to minimize uncertainty (and maximize the sense of security of property) in the minds of investors/corporate decision-makers. The World Bank stresses the need to strengthen and sustain law and order, to maximize protection of private property, and to apply macroeconomic policies predictably – otherwise, investors do not consider such states credible (World Bank 1997: 4–5).[14]

As such, policy rules and mechanisms to guarantee the rights and security of capital are seen as political counterparts to the discipline of market forces (for example, international capital mobility). Missing from this policy framework are measures to guarantee and secure the rights of workers, and in consequence greater rights and freedom for capital may result in greater exploitation and economic insecurity for workers.

With respect to domestic politics, nearly every new constitution or constitutional revision adopted now contains a bill of rights and commitments to formal electoral democracy. On the one hand, this expands individual freedoms (rights of expression, freedom of conscience, rights of association) yet it also limits the scope of many state actions in both market and civil society by reinforcing the rights of private property. Thus disciplinary neo-liberalism involves a shift towards more limited government in ways that tend to empower large property/capital. Limited government is of course not necessarily weaker government since a free-enterprise-based society still needs regulation to allow market forces to operate; it also requires policing and efforts to sustain the security of the state. Hence the formula "a free economy under a strong state." At the level of world order, of course, the supremacy of American leadership of disciplinary neo-liberalism is armored by the coercive apparatus of the US military, with its capacity for long-distance intervention and war. This capacity is no longer countervailed by that of the Soviet Union, or indeed any single power or group of rivals (US military expenditures dwarf those of the next ten biggest military powers). The Bush Administration announced in 2002 its new doctrine of American military predominance, and its prerogative to engage in preventive and pre-emptive intervention and war to remove potential adversaries. This new doctrine, unleashed in Iraq in 2003, is coupled to its goal of "regime change" to foster electoral democracy, free markets and neo-liberal globalization throughout the world.

Of course, it has become clear that in many situations a commitment to formal electoral democracy and other liberal freedoms may do little to foster improved conditions of social reproduction. One reason for this is connected to the real structures of intensified globalization noted earlier: pressure from fiscal crises and indebtedness has tended to force governments (willingly or unwillingly) either to cutback or to privatize their nationalized and strategic industries and also aspects of health, education and welfare systems. All of these developments may be placing pressure on the resources available for provisioning for social reproduction.

Finally, whilst enabling legal frameworks for realizing human rights and human security exist within multilateral and national frameworks (for example the UN Charter), and indeed theoretically supervene over the economic agreements and mechanisms noted above, they lack the requisite sanctions, dispute settlement mechanisms and enforceability of the legal economic agreements.

Transformations in social reproduction and structures of exploitation

Feminist and other writers have defined social reproduction in varying and contested ways.[15] However, most definitions relate to three aspects or components of social reproduction:

1. *Biological reproduction of the species*, and specifically the conditions and social constructions of motherhood in different societies (as noted, the most common cause of death for women globally remains childbirth).
2. *The reproduction of the labor force*, which involves not only subsistence but also education and training.
3. *The reproduction of provisioning and caring needs* that may be wholly privatized within families, or socialized or, indeed, provided through a combination of the two.

Each of these dimensions of social reproduction relates to what has been called a *gender order* (Connell 1987). Thus Feminist writers have pointed out that all world orders involve specific gender divisions of labor and structures of power that shape symbolic and material representations of gender relations, that is, *gender orders coexist with, serve to shape and are shaped by world orders*.[16] We would also add that a gender order also has racialized and class related dimensions, and its patterns may vary across forms of state, patterns of production and regional or world orders.

For example, *shifts in the governance of social reproduction* can also be analyzed in terms of three dimensions of analysis: micro (individual), meso (institutional) and macro (forms of state and world order). The meso level involves a redefinition of key social institutions, for example in government, the market and the family.

At the *micro level*, the emergence of disciplinary neo-liberalism has entailed a shift in political discourse and social practice involving a reconstitution of the self and the political and social subject. From the vantage point of today's prevailing global governance mechanisms there is a particular definition of the political and social subject that is abstract, generic and ahistorical, that is, in the same way that the commodity labor power is treated in a generic way. This political subject is however, akin to Locke's possessive individual: a generic person that is increasingly reflected in constitutional practice and economic policy. This subject or person is his/her own proprietor (of his/her person/body and capacities) and does not owe society, and vice versa. By implication a possessive individualist program of reform for society would involve a minimum or no socialization of risk at the level of the individual or the community in so far as it entails the private self-regulation of both production and civil society and the limited competence of the state. At the same time, the liberal state that is entailed provides security of property. It protects individuals from expropriation by the state since this is prohibited by constitutional and juridical locking-in mechanisms. Thus limited government is increasingly equated with the protection of civil society and its individual liberties and property rights from the intrusion of the state.

At the *meso level*, therefore, limited government and the juridical separation between state and civil society is emphasized. In recent years in the OECD and more dramatically in the former Eastern Bloc and the developing world there has been a shift to more self-regulating market structures, and thus liberalization of both markets for capital and labor (and land). Levels of unionization throughout the world have fallen and labor markets have become more flexible. One consequence of this has been more precarious employment conditions for both men and women, in both the formal and informal sectors. Feminists refer to this as involving the feminization of labor.[17] What they mean here is that both men and women have seen their working conditions become increasingly insecure and precarious – in ways similar to the conditions of employment for unskilled and semi-skilled female labor that has tended to characterize production in many parts of the world.

These changes seem to be producing some paradoxical cultural and material aspects of globalization. In the North, micro and meso changes are associated with a shift away from the traditional post-war ideology of the nuclear family towards new frameworks of social reproduction increasingly mediated by other discourses of self-sufficiency, sexuality and lifestyle. In the South, as women become income earners in ever larger numbers, this can create, on the one hand, greater freedom for women in control over family income and personal autonomy, and, on the other, tighter control over their life and wellbeing with increasing work burdens and multiple responsibilities (Sen and Correa 2000).

At the *macro level*, the shift in gender orders is being increasingly demarcated by international agreements and restrictive fiscal policies that remove the automatic stabilizers of the Keynesian era that were particularly relevant in the North (Elson 1995). The systems of social insurance and other mechanisms associated with social and family regulation both sustained aggregate demand and were also central to patterns of interests and forms of identification that were central to peoples' lives (Bakker 1997). The attachments to the post-war system of production and reproduction are now being eroded in favor of a privatized system of risk and social reproduction (Gill 1995a). Intensifying individual risk, however, obscures the lines of inequality and the pyramidal structure of income, wealth, power and representation in global capitalism. In the South, the global debt crisis, Structural Adjustment Programs, IMF recovery packages and the decline of direct investment in infrastructure and the "real economy" have led to a "hollowing out" of state capacities and brought into relief the structural lines of inequality (van Staveren 2002). Cuts in budgetary expenditures have adversely affected the education and health budgets of virtually all countries with significant implications for social reproduction (Sen 1997; Vanders *et al.* 2000).

Within this context therefore, we hypothesize a transformation in both North and South that involves three moments in the reconstitution of political order and society; the micro (individual), meso (key social institutions) and macro (state and social formation).

These transformations are complex but can be seen to manifest themselves in two general processes: what we call the *reprivatization of social reproduction* and the *intensification of exploitation*. The latter can be further subdivided into identifiable and quantifiable components. These include: (a) restructuring of the family wage towards its full commodification; (b) growing individual/family indebtedness; and (c) new strategies of survival, including the feminization of survival (see Chapter 6).

These moments and forms of transformation and the phenomena they encompass need to be contextualized. For example, they are occurring in the context of a renewal of primitive accumulation related to the privatization of state assets as well as the enclosure or appropriation of common or social property as it becomes alienated, or potentially alienated to private capital. A very good example of this was the way in which much of the Mexican Constitution was changed in anticipation of the Mexican entry into the NAFTA to allow for the privatization of state firms and negation of rights of peasants and poorer farmers to use common lands. Indeed, these changes allow the *ejidos* or common lands to be bought and sold. The latter measures led to the Zapatistas declaring an armed rebellion on the day the NAFTA came into law on January 1, 1994 (Schneiderman 2000). In other words, the micro and macro (economic) in this analysis are linked structurally. In many respects such constitutional changes in Mexico are similar in this regard to World Bank/IMF reforms in so far as these mandate privatization of land and/or the elimination of subsidies for food and transport, often triggering so-called IMF riots. Another example is how the growing indebtedness of individuals and families is mirrored in the debt crisis of the developing countries and its general disciplinary pressures on governments to exercise expenditure restraint. As has been widely documented, this has often resulted in cutbacks in provisioning for social reproduction.

Thus we suggest that the new historical structures of accumulation/exploitation need to be empirically researched – in ways that connect to the question of shifts in the nature of state, society and social reproduction over the last 25 years. In this regard it is important to note that many socialized forms of provision are still in play. In contrast to the regulation of capital and the financial markets, as well as much trade and investments, many forms of social regulation have yet to be fully liberalized.

For instance, in the former communist countries (and in China), most of the basic conditions of social reproduction were, until very recently, almost fully collectivized. In most of the rest of the world, be it in the developmental state capitalism of Latin America and East Asia or the different manifestations of welfare nationalist forms of state in Europe and North America, there was a mixture of socialized and private provisioning. What was common, however – and is still part of the "common sense" of the political – was the shared notion that the state's role in social reproduction was neither minimalist nor simply confined to the reproduction of the labor force. In other words, the market revolution is a tendency and not a fully worked-out transformation, since resistance to the discipline of capital will mean it can never materialize.

We suggest nevertheless that some if not all of the following specific hypotheses may be plausibly made concerning our three basic moments.

For highly industrialized countries we hypothesize that we can isolate several quantifiable aspects of this shifting order, most notably those relating to the reprivatization of social reproduction, decline of the family wage and the feminization of survival.

Reprivatization of social reproduction involves at least four shifts that relate to the household, the state and social institutions, and finally the basic mechanisms of livelihood, particularly in poorer countries.

The first of these concerns the household, where social reproduction is both naturalized and reprivatized (Brodie 1994). On the one hand, it is returned to its so-called "natural" venue in the household, and, on the other, household and caring activities are increasingly provided through the market and are thus exposed to the movement of money (private forms of home care, elderly care, and so on). A return to a privatized "state of nature" in the household is reinforced by a second transformation whereby societies seem to become redefined as collections of individuals (or at best collections of families), particularly when the state retreats from universal social protection.

The third shift is rather complex but it is analogous to what Marx in *The Grundrisse* called the shift from the formal (market-based) to the real (lifeworld) subordination/incorporation (or subsumption) of labor to capital. What we have in mind here is the way in which capital involves accumulation patterns premised on connected control over wider areas of social life and thus the provisions for social reproduction. This third shift in fact comprises at least two related trends: first, how important social institutions, or more precisely the profitable parts of such institutions, may become subject to primitive accumulation (privatization or reprivatization); for example, how public or socialized health systems are becoming gradually privatized, no longer offering universal coverage. Private health clinics fill some of the gap, although they often concentrate on non-essential treatments or discretionary services such as cosmetic surgery. A second trend would be how the neoliberal attack on social provisioning means that important aspects of social reproduction are necessarily recast in a transnational framework. For example, in poorer countries, the provision of private health services might not be particularly profitable for capital, but might still afford opportunities for profit to be made elsewhere; for example, through controlling the supply of skilled workers (for example, in the health services, that is, nurses and doctors) from countries like India for care and other types of reproductive labor in the developing countries. In the current negotiations to extend the GATS the Indian government, as well as other developing states, is seeking to liberalize access to the OECD labor markets for a wide range of its skilled workers as a means of boosting its exports (that is, remittances), particularly in the context of ageing populations and looming shortages of skilled care workers, especially nurses and doctors, in the OECD. Such migration – as well as other examples detailed in the book – serve to recast the issue of the family wage (see below) and perhaps the social wage in a transnational framework.

A fourth shift relates to basic issues of survival and livelihood. For example, a large proportion of the world's population has no effective health insurance or even basic care, even in affluent countries like the USA where one of its major and intensifying health problems (one that is spreading) is that of obesity and related conditions such as diabetes, as the fast-food culture takes over. By contrast, in many other parts of the world people are starving. The obscenity of this contradiction is reflected in Chapter 9 on the changing structures of agricultural livelihood relative to the world market. As Philip McMichael notes: "the subordination of food to capital has shifted the social provisioning of food from a public necessity to a private right in the marketplace, as neo-liberalism has redefined the meaning of the state and the market." Here the fundamental contradiction is that these "free" markets now exclude or starve previously self-sufficient but now dispossessed populations. People are losing control over their land as food security has been redefined (for example, by international organizations, states and agribusiness), as a problem of market construction and allocation.

With respect to *the family wage* in many of the OECD countries, as well as in parts of the developing world, the key contrast is between the earlier Keynesian welfarist frameworks involving the socialization of risk and some redistribution of income, and today's more market-based system of self-help. During the Keynesian era there was a particular, socialized mediation between production and the needs of social reproduction in so far as the family wage was, to a certain extent, supported by the state to various degrees across countries (Fraser 1997; Young 1999). Today the situation now is one of an individualized wage model (family self-sufficiency). More hypothetically, what may be emerging is a new family wage model where more members of the family are working for the same level of family income, but for much longer hours than during the previous Keynesian regime when family income was supplemented by the state. It may well be the case that this new model is also being sustained by growing indebtedness (based on growing use of credit), and as such it is likely to prove unsustainable (Bakker 1999). By contrast, for the growing numbers of people who have no access to credit or who live in countries with insufficient social welfare provision, poverty is likely to be the result. In the longer term this may imply that there could be a profound crisis of social reproduction not only in the Third World where the bulk of poverty is found, but also in the OECD countries; for example, as the baby-boomer generation retires without adequate savings. Evidence from the USA suggests that more market-based systems of pension provision have not just failed to deliver adequate pension growth; rather they have been associated with a decline in pension holdings.

As we have noted above, one means through which the family wage may be supplemented is on a transnational basis. As noted in Chapter 1, many Third World migrant workers, particularly women, move to the OECD countries to perform labor in domestic service, providing remittances to their own communities in the developing world and supporting their survival: the feminization of survival. This phrase implies much more precarious and increasingly transnational frameworks within which Third World communities can be understood (Young 2001a). The phrase can also act as a conceptual lens through which political discontent concerning globalization can increasingly be viewed (Sassen 1998a, 1998b).

Indeed, new transnational circuits of both profit making and of survival have emerged – profit making by bona fide corporations as well as organized criminal syndicates. Often states foster such circuits (for example, the Philippines' promotion of the export of nurses, domestics and entertainers to Japan and the USA) partly since they both meet domestic labor shortages for the importing country, and may result in emigrant remittances that help to bolster the account balances of sending states. Put differently, some of the indirect and structural effects of shock therapy are its pressure on people to move for reasons of livelihood or simple survival. In this process undocumented workers are even more precarious since they have no protection from either the "sending" or the "receiving" state. The new context for much of global migration also includes the approximately 4 million people trafficked each year during the 1990s to work under conditions of extreme exploitation and abuse. Indeed, many of these victims are trafficked to work in the entertainment sectors of the transnational tourism industries that have expanded in the context of new outward-oriented, market-based development strategies promoted by the international financial institutions and the developing countries. As Sassen observes:

> At some point it becomes clear that the sex trade itself can become a development strategy in areas with high unemployment and poverty and governments desperate for revenue and foreign exchange reserves... When the IMF and the World Bank see tourism as a solution to some of the growth challenges in many poor countries and provide loans for its development or expansion, they may well be contributing to develop a broader institutional setting for the expansion of the entertainment industry and indirectly of the sex trade. This tie-in with development strategies signals that trafficking in women may well see a sharp expansion. (Sassen 2002: 13)

Thus we hypothesize that such patterns of exploitative migration seem to be becoming more systematic and as a result of the interplay between structural adjustment, the growth of transnational organized crime, increasing cross-border ethnic networks and the transnationalization of tourism.[18] The broader conditioning frameworks for such developments are the projects of disciplinary neo-liberalism and new constitutionalism that consolidate and extend the world market. Indeed, Structural Adjustment Policies and shock therapy associated with this discourse are also linked to new patterns of institutionalization with respect to world trade and investment agreements.

In this way, the global restructuring process involves both new patterns of governance and strategies of survival that operate unequally between men and women, between classes and between groups subject to racialization. Whereas privileged professional workers are usually given preferential treatment in international agreements such as the GATS and by immigration and employment regulations, workers who operate lower down the global hierarchy of labor are less fortunate and have less legal and political protection. They are subjected to a global pattern of racialization that discriminates against workers from developing countries and from the former Eastern bloc.

In other words, these new frameworks of governance serve to rearticulate patterns of power and production as well as the spatial reconfiguration of processes and institutions of social reproduction in families, communities and social formations. Such changes in institutions and provisions of social reproduction also involve greater human insecurity, with often the most extreme and insecure conditions attendant upon subordinated women from developing countries (Haddad *et al.* 1995). Indeed, it is widely documented that not only fiscal crisis but also debt and debt servicing problems have become a systematic feature of the global political economy for developing nations since the 1980s. Governments have had to devote ever-larger proportions of their expenditures to debt servicing, resulting in cutbacks in social programs (Rai 2002). What has been less well documented is how, under pressure of greater unemployment, both men and women have struggled to find ways to ensure household survival. Specifically subsistence food production, more work outside the home to earn income as well as emigration and prostitution have all increased in significance as survival options for poor peasant and working-class women. This has emerged in the context of a crisis in the public provision of the basic aspects of social reproduction associated with public health and primary education, institutions that connect directly to the social ontology outlined earlier in this chapter.

These new frameworks and patterns of governance in power, production and social reproduction also raise a broader question: what is being reproduced and for whom? Whose social reproduction matters and reproduction to become what? It would appear that much of the evidence of the past 20 years would suggest that the security of a relatively small minority of the world's population is being protected and reproduced, if need be at the expense of much greater insecurity and deteriorating conditions for creative forms of social reproduction for the vast majority of others.

Notes

1. We thank Barbara Cameron, Matt Davies and Tim Di Muzio for helpful suggestions on this chapter.
2. Marx's concept of species-being was derived from left Hegelian Ludwig Feuerbach's *The Essence of Christianity* (1841). For Feuerbach, human beings are distinguished from animals by consciousness, and in particular that of belonging to a species whose individuals share a similar human essence. For Marx, however, "human essence" or "species character" was something in movement that is free and conscious life-activity, expressed through language and faculties that people developed in society (Marx 1964: 131). Indeed, whilst earlier forms of social

organization separated people from their species-being, under capitalism a condition of "estranged labour" emerged, one where people were systematically alienated from the product of their work, the labor process and their species-character (that is, free, conscious activity) and thus estranged from other human beings. Under the rule of capital, the freedom of workers is reduced to an instrumentality in a process that transformed the advantages of human freedom and its creative objectification into a means to accumulate profit. Thus an alien power manifested itself in the "practical relationship" between "the capitalist and the labourer." Private property was both the means and the result of alienated labor and as such, the emancipation of society from private property was not only the emancipation of labor but also a moment of "universal human emancipation" (Marx 1964: 115–18).

3. This notion of "scattered hegemonies" is derived from Grewal and Caplan (1994: 17). Its expression in the context of this discussion is derived from Bergeron (2001: 1001). Similarly, Alexander and Mohanty argue that: "To talk about Feminist praxis in global contexts would involve shifting the unit of analysis from local, regional, and national culture to relations and processes across cultures. Grounding analyses in particular, local Feminist *praxis* is necessary, but we also need to understand the local in relation to larger, cross-national processes. This would require a corresponding shift in the conception of political organizing and mobilization across borders" (Alexander and Mohanty 1994: xix). As Nesiah cautions: "generalization should always be hesitant and politically grounded" (1993: 203).

4. See Chapters 3 and 4 by Brodie and Bakker. They relate to Polanyi's concept of the "fictitious commodities" of land, labor and capital. The key point is that these were only fictions at a certain moment because they abstracted and subordinated elements of life itself, that is, elements of "species-being" were initially thought of, and then treated *as if* they were commodities in order to serve the purpose of capital accumulation. Thus they became "facts" when legislation was enacted and they were obeyed as if they were social laws.

5. One view of this has been expressed by Hartsock who argues that women are commodities in ways that few men are. They are bought and sold in sex trafficking and as child brides, as well as "consumed physically by enforced childbearing" and emotionally in "caring labour." She adds, "Women also work for wages – which for the majority of women are controlled by men... Commodities do not control their own destinies [or] when to come to market... they have no past and no future. Most fundamentally agency, subjectivity, and history disappear from view" (from Hartsock 2001: 10–11). For an alternative view of the gendering of labor power see Salzinger (2001).

6. Marx argued that "Political Economy confuses, in principle, two different kinds of private property, one of which rests on the labour of the producer himself, and the other on the exploitation of the labour of others. It forgets that the latter is not only the direct antithesis of the former, but grows on the former's tomb and nowhere else" (Marx 1976: 931).

7. For example, new power relations affecting women of different classes and ethnic backgrounds are reflected in changing households, which can no longer be defined as purely private entities. For the "Mistress" it is a private realm, but for the "Maid" it is semi-public workplace. This hybrid space is thus subject to both public and private governance practices. See Young (2001a).

8. Many complex issues that concern how political agency is linked to (transnational) frameworks of collective action. However, evidence is accumulating that

new forms of political agency are asserting themselves in global politics premised upon gender and racial equality goals and on cultural and ecological diversity demands. Some are "practical" demands focused on immediate needs, whereas others are "strategic" and concerned with structural or long-term change. On this see Molyneux (1985). New progressive forces also include Feminists from industrialized countries, more or less associated with organized labor and political parties, as well as subaltern forces from the very bottom of the world social hierarchy such as indigenous peoples and peasant movements. See here Gabriel and Macdonald (1996), Grewal and Kaplan (1994), Nesiah (1993). It may well be that these developments represent a new moment in the redefinition of the political at the global level to counter forces of globalization from above of state power and big capital. Of course, other forces are deeply conservative, anti-modernist and opposed to any conception of the emancipation of women.

9. To deal with all of them convincingly would require a general research program. Here we simply aim to indicate the existence of the dimensions of a social ontology and to link them to our hypotheses.
10. This affects not only the health and well-being of individuals in both North and South (threatened by the growing incidence of epidemics, contagious diseases and viruses) as public health systems deteriorate under pressures of fiscal and debt crisis, but also and fundamentally in the destruction of provisioning systems that allow people not only to subsist but also to live under basic and sustainable economical and environmental conditions (that is, localities of livelihood are undermined by integration into the world market).
11. See amongst others Ahmad (1995), Chatterjee (1986), Fanon and Sartre (1963), Pasha and Samatar (1996), Persaud (1997), Said (1993), Spivak *et al.* (1996).
12. Arrighi (1994), Braudel (1982), Hobsbawm (1994, 1968), Polanyi (1957), Steinmo (1993), van der Pijl (1998).
13. An important discussion from a related theoretical perspective is Peterson (2003).
14. For example in late 1999 the IMF's key Interim Committee urged the following principles to enhance government credibility:

> In many emerging market economies and developing countries, raising growth rates on a lasting basis will require not only sustained growth in industrial countries, but also key structural reforms. These include banking reform, corporate restructuring, tax reform and tax administration, establishment of effective legal systems, protection of property rights, and improved governance. (Communiqué of the Interim Committee of the Board of Governors of the International Monetary Fund, September 26, 1999. Press Release No. 99/46: International Monetary Fund, Washington, D.C.)

15. See Armstrong *et al.* (1985), Bakker (1989), Barrett and McIntosh (1982), Cook *et al.* (2000), Ferguson (1998), Harvey (1990), Jenson (1986), Maroney and Luxton (1987), Molyneux (1979), Picchio (1992).
16. See Bakker (1997), Connell (2000), Young (2001a).
17. See for example Beneria (1999), Cagatay and Ozler (1995), Elson (1999), Gregory *et al.* (1999).
18. The GATS institutionalizes and locks in commitments to the liberalization and transnationalization of tourism – so one of the world's biggest industries is increasingly regulated by the legal regimes of the WTO.

Part II:
Governance and World Order

Governance and World Order: Introduction to Part II
Tim Di Muzio and Alejandra Roncallo

In 1947, Canadian political economist Karl Polanyi wrote an essay entitled "Our Obsolete Market Mentality" that celebrated the end of liberal governance. Polanyi imagined that the war meant that society ended its interwar flirtation with a system of self-regulating markets. He hoped that the post-war period would lead to a rationally planned political economy, operating on a regional rather than a global scale, one that would be premised on social beings rather than an abstract *homo economicus* or the "economic man" of generic Neo-Classical economics (Polanyi 2000). Polanyi's hopes were, to a certain extent initially fulfilled in a variety of more or less planned, developmental and welfarist economic systems. He would therefore perhaps have been surprised at the degree to which liberal ideology has witnessed a tremendous global resurgence. Indeed, as Part II seeks to show, the governance frameworks that have taken shape over the last 20 years have been overwhelmingly liberal in purpose, scope and application.

In this context, Part II begins to explore some of the consequences, contradictions, and paradoxes of the emerging neo-liberal order to uncover how its governance frameworks are reshaping and transforming some of the basic conditions of political economy and social reproduction.

In Chapter 3, Janine Brodie identifies three paradoxes at the heart of neo-liberal globalization and governance structures. This neo-liberal governance project was animated by an unprecedented level of consensus among policy elites who shared common visions on how to achieve global growth and national development through the promotion of a market-based free enterprise system. For Brodie, however, the project of reforming states to facilitate and give greater scope to private enterprise and markets should be understood as a "preliminary experiment in global neo-liberal governance" that is already en route to failure.

Not only has the shift to more market-oriented governance structures coincided with increased levels of human insecurity and "grotesque" levels of inequality and poverty, but also the globalizing elites that previously championed market freedoms are now trying to come to terms with some of its consequences. Indeed, even the World Economic Forum, funded by giant corporations, has altered its tone somewhat from the market triumphalism and stock market bubble of the 1990s to a less sanguine outlook – not least because of corporate governance and other scandals of crony capitalism in the USA. The President of the WEF concluded that there was a collapse in "confidence in the ability of public institutions to govern effectively for the global common good and a lack of trust in the accountability of business towards society" (WEF 2003: 2).[1] As Brodie points out, any reform initiatives on the part of the WEF may prove futile because of three inherent paradoxes in the logic and approach to governance offered by neo-liberals. The first, the *paradox of scale*, identifies a rupture between processes of globality on the one hand, and social problems and political capacities of states on the other. What this means is that while problems of human insecurity are increasingly global in nature, there is a lack of institutional support at the global level for dealing with the negative effects of globalization. The *paradox of necessity* asserts that market-led globalization not only generates human insecurity but it also strips away mechanisms and institutional supports once put in place to mitigate socially destabilizing effects of unfettered markets. This has led to an emerging crisis in social reproduction and gender relations as social supports are dismantled, whereas governments promote self-reliance and the privatization/individualization of risk. The *paradox of sustainability* holds that it may well be impossible for neo-liberalism to reproduce itself as a practical ideology due to the immense social dislocations and popular resistance it engenders.

For Isabella Bakker in Chapter 4, human security is intimately tied to social reproduction and the protection and enhancement of the capabilities that allow men and women to create and shape their own well-being over space and time. She also indicates that neo-liberal governance frameworks that prioritize and privilege the security and rights of large capital over the basic human security needs of the mass of humanity contradict democratic determination of needs and social priorities. Indeed, notions of citizenship are being reconstituted along market-oriented lines, with a number of impacts on gender orders. Bakker links these issues to two aspects of social reproduction – the reproduction of the labor force and provisioning of caring needs in the context of Canada. She uses Canada as an example not only because of its multilevel system of governance and its position in the global hierarchy of capitalist states, but also because Canada has consistently ranked at the top of the UN's Human Development Index. Bakker reasons that if such transformations that threaten human security are found in Canada, logically they are likely to be found in other societies that have embraced neo-liberal governance.

Bakker focuses on new constitutionalism to identify how the Canadian state – always highly permeable to the international – has been restructured away from one relatively attuned to the welfare of its citizens to one premised on facilitating the transnational accumulation strategies of large investors. This process has the effect of insulating economic decision-making from popular democratic pressure and accountability; for example, at the provincial level in Canada, through balanced-budget laws. These laws constrain public spending initiatives and force budgetary cuts – even when state revenues fall off during times of recession. So while such laws may increase investor confidence because disciplined fiscal frameworks are seen as a necessary requirement to control government spending (and thus inflation) such laws tend to exacerbate inequalities and threaten "public initiatives to support the reproductive-care economy." This trend, of course, is not unique to Canada (see also Chapter 10 for discussion of the fiscal crisis of US states which is quite similar). Indeed, as noted by the IMF, the trend is relatively ubiquitous, and since the 1990s has become increasingly prevalent (IMF 2001).

Such efforts to gain investor confidence are not only manifested in balanced budget amendments, but also in recent trade and investment agreements, for example, the NAFTA and in the WTO. According to Bakker, concern with ensuring fiscal discipline, downsizing government services, and governance reforms through trade agreements, coincides with a redefinition of Canadian citizenship. The discourse of citizenship is premised upon individual consumers who pay taxes – as opposed to politically active citizens with the potential to struggle for greater rights and security. The new discourse tends to individualize problems and solutions and displaces collective norms of universal entitlement by emphasizing privatized service provision and individual self-reliance (for example, the reliance on non-profit volunteer organizations).

Bakker concludes that such transformations are associated with a shifting gender order different from that of the era of welfare states. Elements of this increasingly normalized order include: the reprivatization of social reproduction, the decline of the family wage model, the fluidity of public and private spheres of production and social reproduction, and the increasing polarization of women.

In Chapter 5 Seiko Hanochi looks at other issues of governance in the longer historical context of Japan's modern development and insertion into world orders since the nineteenth century. In this context, she explores the complex historical relationship between Japan's constitutional politics, its sex industries, and the changing nature of social reproduction in Japan and the surrounding region. She therefore looks at both legal/formal and illegal/informal aspects of constitutional rights and freedoms, particularly as these have affected undocumented workers in a sex sector heavily shaped by the insertion of the Japanese social formation into the global political economy. Hanochi outlines how three constitutional regimes – each associated with a different relationship between Japan and world order – have governed the sex industries of Japan. Each has a particular governance regime that is characterized by different sets of exploitative power relations, limits and possibilities, and consequences for the insecurity of women and children. Indeed, under a number of military, political and economic influences, the reproduction of sexual exploitation has been hierarchically organized along racist principles. The most recent of the three regimes outlined involves a disciplinary neo-liberal form of accumulation. It is thus associated with an emerging new constitutionalism as Japan seeks to reconcile its internal and external social and political contradictions in the context of its insertion into intensified globalization.

Note

1. Joseph Stiglitz, former Chief Economist of the World Bank and Nobel Laureate, and George Soros, the billionaire financier, have entered the debate against "market fundamentalism" as threatening to human well-being and social development. See Soros (1998), Stiglitz (2002).

3
Globalization, In/Security, and the Paradoxes of the Social

Janine Brodie

The concept of the social draws together many of the core themes of this collection, especially human insecurity, the diminished provision of public goods, and the sustainability of social reproduction in an era of intensifying globalization.[1] Globalization is a contested term perhaps best understood as a set of interactions whose uncertain parameters are, in many respects, historically unique and still unfolding. At a minimum, the many dimensions of contemporary globalization can be subsumed under two related processes – globality, the irreversible forces, many technological, that are breaking down barriers of time, space, and nation and fashioning the planet into a global community, and globalism, a contestable political posture that promotes a transnational worldview, philosophy of governance and institutional structures (Beck 2000: 1–3, 11–15). The prevailing version, neo-liberal globalism, prioritizes economic growth and market logics over all other goals and institutions of governance. With varying degrees of coercion, neo-liberal globalism seeks to enforce privatization, trade liberalization, the deregulation of capital, and the erosion of the public sector and of democratic control on all national polities.

The contemporary world is marked by a deep and perilous gap between the promises of neo-liberal globalism, and the insecurities of daily life for the majority of humankind. For more than two decades, global and national policy elites have shared an unprecedented consensus concerning the most appropriate set of public policies to achieve economic growth and human development on a global scale. Armed with forceful critiques of the national regulation of markets, the welfare state, and big government, neo-liberal economists, housed in the think-tanks and international financial institutions of the globalist North, contrived what can only be understood as a preliminary experiment in global neo-liberal governance. Also termed economic globalization and the Washington consensus, neo-liberal globalism has been imposed on the global South and the former Communist bloc under the terms of Structural Adjustment Policies and Poverty Reduction Strategies and advanced everywhere through the institutional mechanisms of new constitutionalism (Gill 1995b). This legally binding international regulatory regime aspires to create markets where none existed before, to construct an unfettered global market and globally integrated production processes that transcend national boundaries and controls, and to facilitate the spontaneous flow of capital to every corner of the planet.

Almost a generation after its implementation, however, this most recent experiment in unfettered economic liberalism is now widely understood as an unsustainable blueprint for governance in a globalizing era. The unleashing and empowerment of market forces on a global scale as well as the application of neo-liberal precepts on local terrains and cultures have exacted a heavy toll on individuals, families, and communities, intensifying the desperation of poverty, opening a yawning gulf between the rich and the poor, both within and between countries, and fuelling political alienation, insecurity, and violence everywhere (Brodie 2003). The ultimate measures of good governance, human development and security, have never been more elusive for the vast majority of humankind. For example, the 2002 UNDP *Human Development Report* describes worldwide levels of inequality as "grotesque" with poverty deepening among the poorest of the poor and the income gap between countries of the globalist North and the global South widening to record proportions (UNDP 2002: 18–19). In the past two decades, the number of countries scarred by extreme inequalities in income distribution has doubled to include approximately one-quarter of all countries (Culpeper 2002: 3). In record time, neo-liberal globalism has seriously aggravated old social problems such as unemployment and inequality and created new ones; among them, social dislocation and exclusion at unprecedented levels, unsustainable pressures on the fragile processes of social reproduction, and the marginalization of countries and entire continents (Amin 2000: 613). The smug pronouncement of the 1980s that "there is no alternative" to neo-liberal globalism has given way in the early twenty-first century to a belated recognition of the many failures of market-based governance and of the necessity of building a new consensus around a different governing strategy capable of underwriting some measure of human security on a global scale.

As this chapter describes, the current era is not the first time when political communities have been forced to temper the vagaries of market fundamentalism. Threats to human security exacted by the first great era of *laissez-faire* were progressively countered through state regulation, public ownership and the enactment of the social – a shifting terrain of political struggle and public policy focused on individual and societal protection as well as the promotion of social cohesion and political stability (Brodie 2002a). Such critical governing instruments, which facilitated the production and reproduction of capitalist economies and social relations have been progressively restructured and dismantled by the institutions and disciplinary practices of neo-liberal globalism. Moreover, such practices present formidable barriers to a revival of social policies, at least as they have been deployed in the past. Specifically, the forces of globality and globalism have been indicted for fundamentally reshaping both the national and the social terrains of governance. Although there is a growing consensus that "there is no alternative" *other than* to respond to widespread social deterioration and political insecurity, a series of paradoxes that are largely unique to the present period challenge collective interventions in the name of the social. In this chapter, I introduce three paradoxes situated at the heart of neo-liberal globalism. The paradoxes of scale, of necessity and of sustainability draw attention to contradictions and incommensurable foundations that betray globalism as an experiment in governance already stumbling toward crisis.

Globalism and human in/security

The ever-widening cracks in the foundational assumptions of the neo-liberal experiment have not escaped the notice or concern of its architects. Some of the most fervent supporters of the global market, from the World Bank and the IMF to the World Economic Forum, now concede the need for a renewed focus on social policy and other public mechanisms to rebuild communities. In 1998, Joseph Stiglitz, then Senior Vice President and Chief Economist of the World Bank, opened a floodgate of criticism of the Washington consensus. He labeled it as wrong-headed and antithetical to human well-being. In speech after speech and later in a book, Stiglitz methodically dissected the market logic informing neo-liberal globalism, especially its key premise that markets are superior to government in realizing human development, security, and freedom. This premise, Stiglitz argued, was simply misguided because markets systematically fail to develop human capital and increase inequalities both within and between countries. He was especially critical of IMF policies that enforced economic liberalization on countries before they could set in place adequate regulatory frameworks for capital or social safety nets for those dislocated by rapid economic change (Stiglitz 2002: 73). Stiglitz challenged global policy-makers to exercise some humility, to recognize their policy failures, and to begin to contemplate a post-Washington consensus. This new consensus would be charged with the responsibility of promoting human development and security on a global scale (Stiglitz 1998, 2002).

After the Asian meltdown of the late 1990s, many more supporters of the neo-liberal agenda came to a grudging acceptance of the need to formulate a more socially responsive model of governance but this acceptance was sometimes guided by calculated self-interest. Cozy neo-liberal enclaves such as the World Trade Organization (WTO) and the World Economic Forum were increasingly confronted by a diverse coalition of civil society organizations. This anti-globalization movement decried mounting social inequality and environmental degradation and contested the legitimacy of both international financial institutions and their development strategies. The idea that "another world is possible" reverberated in the streets outside the closed meetings of international financial institutions and venues such as the World Social Forum called for deglobalization, sustainable development, and the reorientation of local economies to meet human rather than corporate needs. The growing consensus among economic elites was that, if the mounting social costs of neo-liberal globalism were "not managed intelligently and creatively," the very survival of the project would be threatened by a potential political backlash against free trade, a resurgence of protectionism, and widespread social and political disintegration (Rodrik 1997: 2, 6). Thus, confronted with a growing global resistance to efforts to subordinate society to the laws of economic liberalism, the winners of the globalization game have been convinced gradually of the need to factor the well-being of people back into their accumulation strategies.

The quest for human security, that is, freedom from danger, fear, want, and deprivation, is as old as politics itself. In the 1990s, however, the concept of human security was popularized in ways that fundamentally challenged prevailing neo-liberal discourse and practice. With the end of the Cold War and subsequent optimism about an anticipated "peace dividend," the UNDP and others advanced the argument that the security of states – national security – had diminished in importance in international relations relative to the security of individuals. Throughout the decade, different institutions and actors advanced their own understanding of the meaning of human security as well as different, although often complementary, policy recommendations aimed at promoting this international public good. The human security agenda of the 1990s had three streams: (a) the rights-based approach that sought to advance human security through treaties and covenants; (b) the safety of peoples approach that recommended international crisis intervention and humanitarian relief; and (c) the progressive human development approach that was embraced by the UNDP in 1994 (Hampson 2002: 33–4). According to the UNDP's analysis, human security was multidimensional comprising of economic, food, health, environmental, personal, community, and political security (UNDP 1994).

Each of these approaches challenged the long-held assumption in international politics that the primary object of security was the national state, which, in turn, was responsible for the security and well-being of people, especially citizens, contained within its borders. The emerging human security paradigm had effectively turned this assumption on its head, deeming territorial security of lesser priority than human or individual security. Indeed, the emerging human security agenda entertained the conclusion that, in certain instances, the national state itself posed a threat to the security of individuals. Moreover, the human security paradigm linked the perennial goals of international peace and international security directly to the well-being of individuals rather than solely to the self-interested maneuvering of national states in the international state system: "the world can never be at peace unless people have security in their daily lives" (UNDP 1994: 22). The UNDP Report left little doubt that they considered underdevelopment and growing inequalities between the North and the South as negative conditions for security in people's everyday lives. The idea of progressive human development obviously raised questions about the legitimacy of neo-liberal globalism, especially in light of its failures to realize its promises of trickle-down prosperity for either poor countries or poor people.

The tragic events of September 11, 2001, and their continuing domestic and international reverberations have raised into stark relief the unresolved tensions between national and human security and between international stability and global economic inequality. The attacks provoked a US-led War on Terrorism involving both military aggression against states said to harbor terrorists, such as Afghanistan, and hyper-, if not hysterical, discourses and practices around the protection of borders and the surveillance of citizens and transborder actors. Despite this sadly predictable response to the 9/11 attacks, the growing incidence of international terrorism also has been read by a great many as confirmation that political stability, nationally and globally, can be achieved only through the promotion of human development and security on a global scale.

Subsequently, the War on Terrorism and the USA's emerging doctrine of preventive intervention have been widely criticized for wrongly specifying the problem and, in the process, needlessly threatening the security of countless thousands of people. Prime Minister Mahathir of Malaysia stated this case forcefully at the opening session of the 2003 World Economic Forum in Davos:

> People do not tie bombs to their bodies or crash planes for the fun of it. We have to identify the reasons and remove them. Out-terrorizing the terrorists will not work. But removing the causes of terrorism will... Forces against the axis of evil are not going to win because the target is wrong.[2]

One of the themes informing the contributions to this volume is that neo-liberal governance has failed to provide adequate levels of subsistence and security for unacceptably large populations in both the North and the South. Some analysts, however, consider the current crisis in social reproduction and political stability as a case of *déjà vu* – one that simply repeats the experience of the last great era of *laissez-faire*. Gray, for example, contends that "we are at present in the midst of an experiment in utopian social engineering whose outcome we *can* know in advance" (Gray 1999: 16). Similarly, Ignatieff argues that economic liberalism necessarily intensifies material inequalities, exposes a growing contradiction between political equality and economic inequality, and, eventually, provokes a crisis in citizenship and political legitimacy. In order to forestall this, national states are forced to counter the predictable social consequences of economic liberalism with new welfare policies (Ignatieff 1995). Growing recognition of the looming crisis of neoliberal governance has opened new spaces to rethink the objects and instruments of governance but the means to promote human security in a globalizing era are far from obvious.

In sum, the term "human security" represents one in a long lineage of concepts naming some of the social and political contradictions wrought by various historical configurations of states and markets. As the next section describes, for more than two centuries, many of these contradictions have been defined and managed through the social terrain of modern governance.

(Re-)Forming the social

The image of the pendulum of modern liberal governance swinging between the antagonistic logics of unrestrained capitalism and the demands of human security and social reproduction owes an intellectual debt to Polanyi's influential, *The Great Transformation*, originally published in 1944. This book charted the social and political underside of Western capitalism from the onset of industrialization and the implementation of the first era of *laissez-faire* in the 1800s to the Great Depression, the fascist counter-revolutions, and the world wars of the twentieth century. Polanyi proposed that modern capitalist societies were characterized by an inherent and ongoing tension between the principles of economic liberalism and of societal protection (Polanyi 1957: 136). His thesis was that the ascendancy of free trade and of market-driven public policy was a historically unique approach to governance that was achieved only through the deliberate and sometimes violent interventions of early capitalist states. This untried experiment was predictably followed by a breakdown in the social fabric, erratic manifestations of all kinds of political pathologies, the rise of civil society counter-movements, and, ultimately, a double movement back to the prioritization of social protection in public policy. According to Polanyi, any governing strategy that enabled "the market mechanism to be the sole director of the fate of human beings and their natural environment" invited "the demolition of society" (Polanyi 1957: 173).

Although Polanyi's work is often cited as a case against markets *per se*, it is more accurately read as a critique of market-driven governance and its inherent incapacity to comprehend, let alone manage the complex interplay between forces of economic production and social reproduction. Fervent supporters of *laissez-faire*, he pointed out, first discredited and then forgot "the elementary truths of political science and statecraft... in favour of a mystical readiness to accept the social consequences of economic improvement, whatever they may be," and similar to contemporary critics of neo-liberal governance, he rejected *laissez-faire*'s "uncritical reliance on the alleged self-healing virtues of unconscious growth" (Polanyi 1957: 33). Instead, he argued that the art of modern governance was to moderate the demands of market creation and of capitalist accumulation by inventing "protective countermoves" that blunted the market's destructive impact on individuals and social institutions (Polanyi 1957: 76).

Polanyi's unique intervention was to trace the cultural and discursive designation of the very ideas of society and societal protection as objects of governance. The "social problems" named by early capitalist societies were not self-evident, but rather the product of a specific historical configuration of economic, political, and social forces. For Polanyi, the "discovery of society" and the idea of the "social" occurred "behind the veil" of the market economy, and, especially in the naming of the pauper. "Pauperism," he explained, "fixed attention on the incomprehensible fact that poverty seemed to go with plenty" – a revelation "as powerful as that of the most spectacular events of history" (Polanyi 1957: 84). Contrary to conventional accounts, Polanyi concluded, "social not technical invention was the intellectual mainspring of the Industrial Revolution" (Polanyi 1957: 119).

Also exploring the politics of early industrialization, Himmelfarb drew similar conclusions in *The Idea of Poverty* (Himmelfarb 1984). She described how the social dislocations associated with industrialization prompted the emergence of what she called "the moral imagination" of modern governance – an imagination that named poverty both as a structural problem and as a collective responsibility. Then as now, social problems have discursive, moral, and structural meanings. However, the constitution of the social – the basket of public policies designed to stabilize economies, to reduce the human costs of market logics and failures, and to secure the social stability of increasingly diverse and democratized societies – has been a relatively recent innovation of modern governance (Perez Baltodano 1999: 21). As studies of the welfare state have demonstrated, social policies speak to a number of critical problems of governance posed by capitalist societies. These policies have improved living conditions for the economically disenfranchised, helped reproduce a healthy and educated workforce, reinforced key social institutions such as the nuclear family, and managed class conflict.

Moreover, what are deemed as social problems or, in contemporary parlance, as threats to human security are "articulated in relation to some understanding of the spaces, persons, problems, and objects to be governed" (Rose 1999: 26). As such, social policy embeds deeply, although almost invisibly, in the daily lives of women and men and in popular culture, shaping shared understandings of collective responsibility, social solidarity, and individuality. Because social policies are so centrally implicated in social reproduction, in the generation of labor power and the creation and maintenance of communities, they also help form and re-form the prevailing gender order.

This order, in turn, prescribes a more or less rigid division of labor, social roles, status, and power among women and men (Bakker 2001).

Students of modern governance have provided a rich description of the progressive elaboration and institutionalization of the social terrain of governance in the twentieth century, culminating with the post-war welfare state of mature capitalist economies (Pierson 1998). Social policies, designed to promote the health and safety of workers, the education of children, the condition of mothers and families, and the security of populations with respect to the risks of sickness, old age, unemployment and injury, both blunted capitalism's most destructive tendencies and underwrote the complex and multiple demands of social reproduction and political legitimacy (Dean 2000: 129).

The development of the welfare state is generally portrayed as the postwar settlement between capital and labor that promised more equity and security to societies shattered by the ravages of the depression, political repression and genocide, and world war. However, if welfare state policies emerged partly as a response to market failures, they also addressed what Folbre calls "family failures" – situations where networks of family and kin proved inadequate to the task of providing a social safety net (Folbre 2001: 91). The new industrialism of the early twentieth century generated social costs that surpassed the capacity of the *laissez-faire* state that assigned the weight of responsibility for social reproduction to women, the family, church, and community (Brodie 1997). The welfare state rested on a reconfigured gender order, which remodeled the reinforcing interrelationships between capitalist accumulation and social reproduction as well as between the workplace and the home.

This model enforced a specific sexual division of labor that assumed a stable working-middle-class nuclear family, supported by a male breadwinner, containing a dependent wife and children, and maintained by women's unpaid domestic labor. The state, in turn, guaranteed through progressive taxation, the protection of collective bargaining, and social security and welfare policies that there would be an adequate family wage that combined wage labor with state income supports and collective provision for, among other things, unemployment, misfortune, illness and old age. Although women benefited from public services and income transfers, they were largely tied to the family wage system because of cultural expectations, explicit policy discrimination against women workers, marginalization in the workforce and limited access to childcare. As Feminist scholars have demonstrated, the social citizen was universal in discourse and gendered in practice. While the male breadwinner claimed the entitlements of social citizenship, most women were cast in the role of dependent citizen – dependent on individual men, family, or state-funded and delivered social welfare characterized by surveillance, social stigma, and conditionality (Bakker 1994; Brodie 2002b).

This brief genealogy has identified three dimensions that might inform our thinking about human insecurity in a globalizing era. First, the social was formed and re-formed as a governing discourse within the context of specific historical configurations of states and markets. The development of social policies to ameliorate the worst abuses of capitalism has been profoundly inductive and conjunctural, reflecting the dual role of the liberal state to facilitate capitalist accumulation and to underwrite social solidarity amidst social inequalities. Second, social policies have been deeply implicated in the configuration of the shifting interface between processes of production and social reproduction and are embedded in the daily lives of communities and in gender politics. Finally, since its conception, the social question has been pursued as a national question. The consolidation of national sovereignty in the past two centuries, enabled states to shape, within their formal boundaries, the main determinants of their political evolution and to regulate and condition social relations. The emergence of a "social state" and of social policy resulted from the intersection of national societies, national economies, and national states operating within the legal and territorial boundaries of sovereign national territories (Perez Baltodano 1999: 28–9). The social thus emerged within and has been analyzed through the lens of what Beck terms as "methodological nationalism" – a container theory that assumes, theoretically and politically, that the contours of society coincide with the formal boundaries of the national state and that the state controls this space (Beck 2000: 23).

Globalization and social welfare

Globalization, it is now widely argued, has prompted epochal transformations in modern social organization, not the least because it has progressively shifted power and coherence away from the national state, challenging its status as modernity's pre-eminent political institutional and societal organizing principle (Yeates 1999: 374). Extreme versions of this view, often termed the strong globalization thesis, represent national states as being reduced to a zombie-like presence, living yet dead (Beck 2000: 27) and as "unnatural, even impossible business units in a global economy" (Ohmae 1995: 5). It is also argued that globalization, broadly defined, has permanently eroded the foundations upon which the welfare state was constructed. As Beck bluntly concluded, "all the premises of the welfare state... melt under the withering sun of globalization" (Beck 2000: 1). There is widespread agreement that structural and institutional factors now constrain the capacity of states and national social policy terrains, but whether these factors are fatal is subject to ongoing debate.

Structural arguments take as their point of departure the extraordinary growth of transnational financial flows and transnational corporations. Both are defining marks of the new global political economy that have affected lateral shifts in the sites of economic decision-making, from the public to the private, from national states to corporate boardrooms and money markets.

In varying degrees, all contemporary states are forced to adapt to corporate accumulation strategies, which are formulated to maximize global rather than national outcomes. Transnational corporations may still be headquartered in one country but their operations are increasingly deterritorialized. They can demand subsidies and expensive infrastructure in one state, elect to pay taxes in another, and download the human and environmental costs of production on yet another jurisdiction. It is this deterritorialized logic of capitalist accumulation, it is argued, that drives the global economy and national public policy-making. Accordingly, national states have been forced to bend to the structural power of capital by embracing policies that promise to reduce the most immediate and obvious costs of accumulation within their borders (Gill 2003a: 102–8).

The ability of transnational capital to move relatively unrestrained around the globe is commonly understood to place downward pressure on social policy spending and program development, encouraging national states to engage in a "race to the bottom" to retain and attract capital investment. To the extent that the globalization of production and finance accounts for policy convergence around the lowest common denominator with respect to public provision, regulation and redistribution, states find themselves locked into a permanent referendum – being continuously monitored by international financial institutions, transnational corporations, and bond rating agencies as to their desirability as sites for global capital (Pierson 1998: 68).

It is also argued that national states, confronted with the ongoing threat of capital flight, increasingly tend to discipline themselves according to whether they have got "the fundamentals right," a metaphor for economic policy regimes and taxation strategies designed to protect the value of capital and the climate for making profit, even if this results in residual social welfare regimes (Gill 1995b). In this way, the privileged position of capital constrains the social through indirect mechanisms such as reduced taxation on mobile assets and the shift to consumption taxes that undercut redistribution as well as revenue-raising capacities (Swank 2002: 3). In Canada, for example, the proportion of federal revenues derived from corporate taxes has fallen from approximately one-third in the 1960s to less than 10% today. Personal income tax, payroll deductions, and various forms of value-added and consumption taxes now comprise over 90% of federal revenues.[3]

Clearly, as was noted in Chapter 2, these disciplinary practices weigh most heavily on countries that require or already have high levels of foreign investment and on many Third World countries that need to borrow/repay debts in the international capital markets. The degree of competition among national states to retain investment and to attract global capital nevertheless represents a subtle but important shift in the orientation of states to external capital. Few states can any longer afford to engage in nation-building by adopting tariff or non-tariff barriers or capital controls to pressure corporations to reorganize within national boundaries or to conform with national values and priorities (Soederberg 2003). As Beck has argued, "the threat is no longer of an invasion but the non-invasion of investors, or the threat of withdrawal... There is only one thing worse than being overrun by multinationals," he writes provokingly, "and that is not being overrun by multinationals" (Beck 2000: 2).

A second and complementary argument relates to the capacity of sovereign states to maintain or to expand the social sector in the face of the binding powers of a neo-liberal global regulatory regime. In the contemporary era, the exercise of sovereignty presents a paradox. In effect, many national states have used their exclusive right to act as legal entities in international fora to undermine the scope of their internal sovereignty and policy autonomy. Through membership in the World Trade Organization or as signatories of regional agreements such as the NAFTA, national governments agree to narrow the terrain of state competency by complying with externally derived and binding rules that almost exclusively relate to the deregulation of capital within their jurisdictions (Krasner 2000: 127). Compliance in many of the countries of the global South has been achieved under the weight of international debt repayment schemes, Structural Adjustment Programs and, most recently, poverty reduction strategy papers. This new constitutionalism (Gill 1995b) turns binding control over designated national policy fields to external constitution-like agreements that facilitate the mobility of global capitalism. Such agreements often trump the decisions of national democratic bodies, are binding for an indefinite future, and define a new set of negative freedoms from democratic interventions for global capital operating in national spaces (Schneiderman 2003).

Contemporary globalization studies thus represent the erosion of the postwar welfare state and barriers to the development of social policies as being either *necessary* (a requisite of the inexorable logic of economic globalization and the uncontainable power of global capital), as *mandated* (by the dictates of the new constitutionalism), or as *conditional* (on the effectiveness of these disciplinary practices) (Gill 1998b; Hay 1998: 526). Arguments framed in terms of inexorable logics (strong globalization) have been rightly criticized as being overstated and speculative versions of economic determinism and for misrepresenting globalization as a homogeneous process that affects all national states in the same way (Yeates 1999: 375–6). Indeed there is a growing body of empirical research that questions the widely held view that economic globalization has enforced social policy convergence among all states around the lowest common denominator. Swank, for example, has found that the domestic impacts of international capital mobility are complex and variable, being systematically shaped by national histories, social cleavages, and political institutions (Swank 2002: 5).

Most states have lost some measure of sovereignty and capacity but this erosion has occurred unevenly – horizontally – across the traditional domains of liberal democratic polities. Advanced capitalist states, in particular, have been rolled back on the terrain of the social, specifically with respect to social programs and universal social citizenship rights. The post-war view of the state as protector or insulator is rapidly being erased from popular political discourse and from historical memory (Sbragia 2000). At the same time, state capacity has been rolled forward with respect to institutionalizing the new governing order in the form of privatization, deregulation, and capital-friendly taxation policies, as well as with respect to policing, surveillance, border and population controls. Indeed, policing and criminalization are now all too familiar responses to problems that were previously considered as remedial through social policies.

Deviations from the predictions of the strong globalization thesis should not be taken to mean that the national state has survived unharmed this most recent and unfortunate rendezvous with neo-liberal governance. Neither can it be assumed that countries of the global North can return to the halcyon days of the Keynesian welfare state or that countries of the global South are free to aspire to this model of governance. To the contrary, global and national governance does not exist in isolation or opposition to one another. Nostalgic notions about turning back the clock to relatively closed economies, territorial boundaries, and national sovereignty can be sustained only by ignoring an inescapable fact of daily life in the early twenty-first century – the local and the national are now saturated with, if not constituted by, the global. As Hardt and Negri put it, "the qualitative changes that have blurred the economic and political landscapes of the new millennium are structural and irreversible... superseding the effectiveness of national juridical structures" (Hardt and Negri 2000: 336). While the ongoing political and moral imperative to advance human security cannot be abandoned through the embrace of economic determinism or political fatalism, previous instruments and strategies of governance are ill-equipped to meet the challenges of the contemporary era. They are riddled by a series of paradoxes and contradictions that are difficult, if not impossible to reconcile through the logics and institutions of neo-liberal globalism. The final section of the chapter briefly introduces three of these – the paradox of scale, the paradox of necessity, and the paradox of sustainability.

Three paradoxes

The paradox of scale

The paradox of scale points to a growing discontinuity between the objects and structures of governance as well as between social problems and political capacities. This contradiction has many references in contemporary politics, not the least, globality and the growing separation of the individual from the national state and national citizenship. Globality, as noted in the beginning of this chapter refers to epochal transformations in social, political, and economic organization that have irreversibly altered shared experiences of time and space as well as self and community. The concept focuses attention on new technologies, global interdependencies, social issues that transcend the territorial boundaries and the capacities of national states, and the fashioning of the planet as a relevant space for political action. As Beck explains, globality implies that nothing that happens in the world is an isolated event. All interventions, victories, and catastrophes affect the whole world along a local–global axis (Beck 2000: 11, 15). In the process, social problems and their solutions are increasingly perceived as being global in scope. These epochal changes are understood to disrupt the coherence of national societies, to challenge familiar understandings of society and social protection and to cultivate a new sense of collectivity and shared interest written on a global scale.

This new common sense of who we are is increasingly visible in the explosion of civil society actors that take a borderless world as their first point of reference as well as in contemporary discourses around universal human rights and the emerging human security agenda. Rights once associated with belonging to members of national communities, have taken on new meanings and sources of legitimacy at the global level. The rights-bearing individual, celebrated in numerous human rights codes and discourses since the adoption of the Universal Declaration of Human Rights in 1948, has emerged, independent of consideration of national citizenship, at the level of the transnational as the legitimate claims-maker of contemporary politics (Soysal 2001: 66–7). This transnational subject is clearly the object of the contemporary human security agenda that promotes the idea that the individual's basic social, economic, and political needs supersede the historical status and jurisdiction of the national state (Hampson 2002: 6, 12). As important, threats to human security identified by this agenda are global in scope; among them, population growth, income inequality, pollution, HIV/AIDS, and social dislocation. National sovereignty and national interest are considered secondary points of reference (Hampson 2002: 34).

For a growing number of social policy analysts, conditions of globality suggest that human security and social justice are now best pursued at the level of the transnational (Deacon 1997; Yeates 1999). During the 1990s, the international community invaded national territories riven by internal conflicts. This was done, allegedly, in the name of humanitarian intervention to protect the physical safety of individuals and communities (principally defined in ethnic terms) within those borders (for example, Bosnia and Somalia). However, more inclusive definitions of human security, involving not simply freedom from violence but also acceptable levels of social and political security, demand different instruments of governance that have yet to be developed or perhaps even imagined. Although the historical circumstances are very different, the discontinuities of the contemporary era echo Polanyi's assessment of the liabilities of rights discourses in the years preceding the invention of the welfare state. No mere declaration of rights can suffice:

institutions are required to make the rights effective (Polanyi 1957: 256). The paradox of scale, of course, is that rights, especially social rights continue to rely on national states for their materialization (Soysal 2001: 69).

The paradox of necessity

The paradox of necessity asserts that neo-liberal globalism simultaneously maximizes the need for social intervention in the name of human security while, at the same time, minimizes the political spaces and strategic instruments necessary to achieve this public good. The unleashed forces of global capitalism have generated a full spectrum of human insecurities at unprecedented levels but these same forces have constituted significant barriers to the maintenance or elaboration of social development policies. Under the welfare state, national economic and social policies were linked through demand management policies in a way that enhanced economic stability, individual welfare, and social cohesion. Governments used monetary and taxation policies to stimulate economic activity and social policies to socialize many of the costs of social reproduction, to cushion the human impacts of dips in the business cycle and to maintain a measure of political stability amidst the antagonistic social forces of modern capitalism. The politics of the welfare state forced governments to find balance among key trade-offs, say, between inflation and unemployment and between business confidence and electoral support. These trade-offs comprised what was then understood to be the democratic negotiation of class struggle.

Neo-liberal globalism, however, has largely delinked economic and social policy and subjected each to different rule structures, political discourses, and political hierarchies. From its conception, neo-liberalism indicted the welfare state for being wasteful, paternalistic, and ineffective, recommending instead, the freeing up of old markets and the creation of new ones. Neo-liberalism demands deregulation, privatization, and fiscal austerity, especially in the social policy field. Neo-liberalism, in effect, prescribed a subtle but fundamental cultural shift that would enable the values and the rules of the market to reform and transform virtually every sphere of social organization (Dean 2000: 161). It has forced polities to accept an unsustainable trade-off between economic competitiveness in global markets and social well-being and political stability.

As noted earlier, national states are increasingly locked into constitution-like regulations and structures that limit their capacity either to rehabilitate failed markets, stabilize business cycles or protect their citizens from the worst abuses of capitalism. Previously critical governing instruments such as public ownership, interventionist industrial policies, and various regulatory policies are no longer available to governments. Large portions of the economic terrain are now governed at the transnational scale, while responsibility for social problems remains attached to the national and the local. This denationalization of economic governance is simultaneously outside of the national state and buffered from the demands of democratic governance, yet embedded within national politics and culture (Sassen 1996: 23). The NAFTA, for one, represents a significant barrier to the creation of new social programs such as universal public day care regardless of the need for such a program or a democratic mandate to create one. Before implementing a new social program, the terms of the agreement demand that the initiating government first compensate existing private sector providers of all past and future damages.

At the same time as neo-liberal globalism has shifted power over the economic away from the national state, it also diminished the capacity of democratic institutions to sustain public policies that depart from market conforming principles (Swank 2002: 3). As Gill has explained, the new constitutionalism mandates the insulation of key aspects of the economy from the influence of politicians or the mass of citizens by imposing, internally and externally, binding constraints on the conduct of fiscal, monetary, trade, and investment policies (Gill 1995a: 411). However, this mode of governance fails to anticipate the necessary and historic role of the state to maintain social cohesion and control. This feeds another kind of erosion – an inward push, originating in civil society, that impacts on the legitimacy of the prevailing economic and political order (Brodie 1997). Now marginalized groups are constrained in their struggles for security and equality. As countries democratize, policy sectors that are fundamental to the promotion of social and environmental protection are increasingly deemed immune from the language and logics of democracy. Regulation, decommodification and social spending, three governing instruments that have proved critical to the advancement and well-being of marginalized groups are effectively taken off the political agenda.

As Fitzpatrick notes, scrapping welfare does not eliminate the contradiction between accumulation (economic growth) and legitimization (social expenditure), it merely displaces it. There is actually very little evidence to suggest that the erosion of the public sector or social security programs enhances economic prosperity, at least for the vast majority. But lower social expenditures do aggravate old social problems and, indeed, produce new ones. At the very least, neo-liberalism's retreat from the social terrain tends to undermine the very things that enable markets to work in the first place such as a healthy and educated workforce, political stability, civility, and trust (Fitzpatrick 2001: 122–4). As evidence of the latter, in 2003, a full two-thirds of people worldwide disagree with the statement that their country is governed by the will of the people.[4]

The paradox of sustainability

The paradox of sustainability questions the capacity of neo-liberal globalism, quite literally, to provide sustenance to individuals and communities, to withstand the pressure of growing political contradictions, and, ultimately, to regenerate itself. Beck has enumerated a series of fault-lines whose genesis rests within neo-liberalism's foundational logics, among them, recurrent financial crises, economic disparity and inequality, fragile employment, jobless growth, social exclusion, environmental degradation, and the list goes on (Beck 2002). The foregoing discussion of the paradoxes of scale and necessity clearly expose contradictions that betray the neo-liberal experiment as a flawed system of governance, one that, echoing Polanyi's admonition, "has forgotten the elementary truths of political science and statecraft" (Polanyi 1957: 33). Governing systems that fail to provide for a population's basic needs or develop and sustain spaces for political mediation may not have a long shelf life.

The final focus of this chapter – and a major focus of Chapter 4 – is the emerging crisis in social reproduction and gender relations. Neo-liberalism is largely silent about gender as well as social reproduction but it is, nonetheless, a profoundly gendered philosophy of governance that has significantly disrupted gender orders in the globalist North and the global South. Two axes of change are particularly significant: (1) the *simultaneous erosion and intensification of gender* and, (2) the *autonomization and responsibilization of individuals and families*. Combined, these contradictory tendencies betray neo-liberalism as an unsustainable governing project, not least because, as Feminists have long argued, it fails to successfully anticipate the necessities of social reproduction in the contemporary era.

In a challenging essay written more than a decade ago, Haraway characterized contemporary discourses and practices as being marked by the *simultaneous erosion and intensification of gender*, both literally and metaphorically (Haraway 1991: 166). These contradictory tendencies are clearly embedded in the logics of contemporary governance. Since the 1980s, the ascendancy of neo-liberalism has virtually erased gender from policy making and as a legitimate grounds for making claims on the state (Brodie 1997). This worldview constructs individuals as genderless and rational market actors in the pursuit of self-interest and disregards the unpaid work of social reproduction as irrelevant for its calculations. Women's reproductive labor is bracketed out as having no market value or, at best, existing as an externality. The erosion of gender as a homogeneous social category also is revealed in the growing racial and class-based disparities among women themselves, enabling some women to buy and exploit the domestic services of other women, a phenomenon that increasingly has taken on global proportions. Domestic workers are a primary export from many countries of the South and remittances from these same workers have become integral to the functioning of many local economies (Young 2001a). Paradoxically, the imprint of gender also has intensified in everyday life, as governing and popular discourses have put renewed emphasis on the so-called "feminine sphere of the home" and the "feminine" qualities of selflessness, nurturing, and care-giving as well as on the sexualized and commercialized female body.

The contradictory status of gender is clearly demonstrated in the welfare reforms implemented by Anglo-American democracies in the 1990s. In Canada, for example, the child has been designated as the object of social and redistribution policies that are increasingly delivered through the tax system (Harder 1999). The 1996 US Personal Responsibility and Work Opportunity Reconciliation Act requires that mothers on welfare, overwhelmingly single, either find jobs or participate in state-run workfare programs in order to collect benefits. The rationale behind these programs is that women on welfare must take financial responsibility for their children and break the cycle of dependency that they allegedly pass down to the next generation. Workfare programs are largely blind to the time and monetary constraints of childrearing, casting mothers as potential workers in need of discipline. Reformed programs, however, also encourage these same women to marry and, in effect, enter into private dependent relationships. Both state and federal welfare/workfare programs in the USA now offer a marriage bonus to program participants with the expressed aim of reprivatizing the costs of social reproduction on the traditional nuclear family form. However, the male breadwinner family model is disappearing and, some would argue, is an unsustainable institution considering that most families require two wage-earners to stay above the poverty line (Philipps 2002: 22).

Contemporary paradoxes of gender appear everywhere, as a recent UNIFEM report recounts. For example, more women are obtaining higher education, but they continue to receive fewer financial rewards than men. More women are in paid employment, but the quality of the jobs and the degree of protection and rights attached to employment has dropped precipitously, and more women are entering legislative assemblies while power is moving elsewhere (UNIFEM 2002: 82). Most critically, however, there has been a marked increase in the feminization of poverty. Gender is the strongest predictor of poverty in both developed and developing countries.

The second contradictory axis of sustainability involves simultaneous demands for *autonomization and responsibilization*. This double movement points to the progressive detachment of individuals from social networks and supports while, at the same time, responsibility for systemic problems is being downloaded onto the individual (Rose 1999: 154–5). Beck refers to this process as individualization that has a different meaning than individualism understood either as self-actualization or as self-seeking behavior. In sharp contrast with the experience of previous generations that located social problems in structures, neo-liberal individualization places steeply rising demands on people to find personal causes and responses to social problems – what Beck describes as the contemporary compulsion to find biographic solutions to the contradictions of the system (Beck 2002). Poverty, for example, is conceptualized and deemed remedial at the level of the individual through various self-help strategies or skills enhancement. Common problems cease to be additive – they do not add up to a common cause. The paradox is that the individualization and fragmentation of inequalities into separate biographies is our collective experience. Social inequality is on the rise precisely because the demands of individualism feed myopic and often antagonistic conceptions of public welfare and human security (Beck and Beck-Gernsheim 2002: 16, 169).

The tension between autonomization and responsibilization is especially germane with respect to gender and social reproduction. Women have been drawn, by choice or by necessity, into the workforce, in effect, to become genderless workers and rational economic actors precisely at the same time as the social supports for reproductive and caring work have been progressively dismantled (Bakker 2001). Women, although obviously in varying degrees, find themselves squeezed between growing demands for their paid labor in order to support households and growing demands on their unpaid domestic and care-giving work as government austerity programs erode various forms of collective support and provision (see Chapters 4 and 6 in this collection).

In this pincer movement, demands for unpaid caring work have increased substantially due to cutbacks in social programs. Those with special needs, the elderly, children and the sick rely on the unpaid labor of women. Domestic labor and caring work may be purchased on the market but these costs are prohibitively high for most families. More commonly, the decline of the family wage in the North and economic instability and pervasive poverty in the South have pressured women to undertake paid labor or to participate in the informal sector to bolster family income, no matter how poor the pay, how degrading the activity, or how distracting from the care of dependents (Peterson 2003). Neo-liberal governance has meant fewer state services, especially for the poor, while the burdens of care have fallen to communities, households and, ultimately, women. From the perspective of many observers, the capacity of individuals and informal networks to provide for basic human needs already has been surpassed. Thus one prediction is that the crisis in sustainability promises to intensify in coming decades as families take on ever more fluid forms, populations migrate and age, social infrastructures continue to erode, and the spread of HIV/AIDS takes on horrific proportions (Daly and Standing 2001: 4–6).

Conclusion

The three paradoxes of the social outlined in this chapter present unique challenges to the institutions and practices of governance in a globalizing era. The neo-liberal experiment that has reshaped patterns of politics and human security for the past quarter century has been simply that – an experiment. And, as with all experiments, experimenters can achieve their intended results or "things can go terribly wrong" (Ruggie 1997: 9). By most measures of human security, neo-liberal globalism has been a failed experiment in governance for the vast majority of humanity. The premise that "we can choose to have a market economy without some form of state provision of welfare is no more compelling now than it was twenty or even one hundred years ago" (Pierson 1998: 169). The contemporary period thus invites a revival of our moral imagination and a reform of the tools of statecraft that stretch the goals of governance beyond short-term calculations of economic efficiencies to embrace the meaning of human well-being and security in a globalizing era. Our imaginations may very well demand that the solutions to persistent social problems of poverty and inequality be explored beyond the boundaries and capacities of national states. Reform also may demand that the processes of production and reproduction be reintegrated in entirely new ways. For example, the recognition in public policy of care work as real work and as an integral contribution to human security could both help alleviate one of the major causes of women's poverty as well as generate economic demand and stability (Daly and Standing 2001). It is certain, however, that any meaningful pursuit of human security in a globalizing era will require the redistribution of income and opportunity, both horizontally, through borders and across geographic and cultural expanses, and vertically, from those who have benefited disproportionately from globalism to those it has forgotten.

Notes

1. I thank Susan Minsos, Susanne Soederberg and Malinda Smith for their careful reading and very useful comments, as well as the Social Sciences and Humanities Research Council for support of my research.
2. Statement made to the opening session "Trust and Governance for a New Era," World Economic Forum, 2003.
3. *Edmonton Journal*, February 19, 2003.
4. Reported at the 2003 meeting of the World Economic Forum. The poll by Gallup International and Environics included 34,000 people from 46 countries. <www.weforum.org> Downloaded 25 January 2003.

4
Neo-liberal Governance and the Reprivatization of Social Reproduction: Social Provisioning and Shifting Gender Orders

Isabella Bakker

The convergence of capitalist values and liberal conceptions of democracy is a global phenomenon, remaking notions of citizenship in the image of the market. The vehicle for this totalizing, conservative movement to a market-oriented model of citizenship is neo-liberalism. Here, I will trace the gender dimensions of this shift in industrialized countries with particular reference to the Canadian federal system. The Canadian case is an interesting one as it represents a multilevel system of governance and a political economy that is highly permeable to the effects of globalization.

Although I argue that the restructuring of state forms and citizenship norms is occurring on a gendered terrain and, in fact, is fashioning a new gender order, I am not suggesting that all women are losers and all men winners in this process. Rather, it should become clear that complex and contradictory gender relationships and alliances are being produced under neo-liberal economic governance, resulting in both an intensification and erosion of gender difference (Haraway 1991). That is, while neo-liberalism promotes – indeed, depends upon – a feminization of the workforce, it also exposes more women and men to market forces, in the process producing a similarity of experience for some of them. And, as Brigitte Young illustrates in Chapter 6, the transnationalization of motherhood and care work is also creating more profound differences among women, partly due to race and class differences. Yet women's relationship with commodities remains more complicated than men's since they are at the crossroads of production and reproduction, producing and reproducing commodities (including labor power) and yet can be and are consumed as commodities themselves (see also Chapters 5 and 8).

Thus in this chapter I illustrate how the macroeconomic framework of neo-liberalism and its attendant governance structures expose fundamental contradictions between the formal gender neutrality of market citizenship and its unspoken reliance on women's unpaid work in social reproduction. The nature and conditions of the not directly waged work of social reproduction vary among women according to place, class, ethnic, racial and sexual status (Daly and Standing 2001; Rai 2002). Here social reproduction is defined as the social processes and human relations associated with the creation and maintenance of the communities upon which all production and exchange rest. This involves not only the social wage, that is, state provisions associated with health and welfare and socialization of risk (pensions, unemployment insurance, social safety nets, kinship networks), but also structures associated with the long-term reproduction of the socioeconomic system such as education. These processes, institutions and ideas shape the way that individuals, families and communities view the social, political and indeed moral order.

No economic system can sustain itself without an appropriate set of social, cultural as well as economic values. Yet the elements of social reproduction change across time and space. Indeed, state transfers and benefits directed at sustaining social reproduction are being reconfigured in both quantitative and qualitative terms. One hypothesis that has been put forward is that in the context of neo-liberal restructuring, social reproduction is being both privatized through the erosion of the social wage and pushed into the informal sector. The latter refers to that sector of the economy which is not directly subject to market regulation by the state or international treaties and which is therefore outside of the framework of national economic accounting. Of course, some individuals, families or groups are simultaneously engaged in formal and informal economic activities making the dividing line less clear, more fluid. For example, organized crime syndicates make profits in informal activities such as sex trafficking and narcotics, but need to launder this profit into the formal, that is, legal economy, through the financial system. The same is true for undocumented foreign domestic workers (for instance, nannies and gardeners) who are often employed in wealthy households and who send a portion of their wages as remittances to their hometowns and villages in Mexico, the Philippines, and so on.

The purpose of this detailed outline is to indicate to the reader some of the social terrain for considerations of human security, for example, as it was defined in 1994 by the UNDP, that is, in multidimensional terms to include many of the social provisions that provided social security. However, the UNDP did not elaborate in detail on links to social reproduction as we define it in this book, and it was less concerned to highlight issues of power and capabilities associated with human security and human development (UNDP

1994).[1] This is significant because one argument that comes from new work within Feminist Political Economy is that informalization of social reproduction constrains the expansion of people's capabilities – a cornerstone of people-centered human development (Nussbaum 2000).[2] It is these capabilities that enable individuals to participate in processes that affect their well-being, that is, their *voice*. Hence, protecting and extending capabilities becomes a key element of human security. Yet for capabilities to be maintained, people's command over resources must be protected particularly during crises (Aslanbeigui and Summerfield 2001). However, evidence is accumulating that neo-liberal governance structures, its laws and institutions are characterized by unequal representation and a decreasing availability of public goods required for the maintenance of capabilities and basic human security. By contrast large capital has not only *voice* in its dealings with governments but also *exit* possibilities (often guaranteed by states in international agreements, for example, freedom to move capital). By contrast, the poor – many of whom are women – tend to have only *voice* since they tend to be place bound and hemmed in by unresponsive domestic structures and a restrictive international migration and refugee regime.

A full investigation of these issues would require a detailed consideration of the privatization and informalization of social reproduction. This chapter takes a narrower scope out of necessity. Focusing on two aspects of social reproduction – the reproduction of the labor force and of provisioning and caring needs – I will use the example of a country that has consistently ranked at the top of the UNDP's Human Development Index (HDI): Canada. My underlying assumption is that if arguments about the informalization and privatization of social reproduction hold here, they are likely to be plausible elsewhere.

I will begin by outlining a series of new constitutionalist initiatives of the Canadian federal state in fiscal policy that underscore the privatizing thrust of public policy and reshape how social reproduction needs are met. The next section explores how the shift at the level of world order from embedded liberalism to disciplinary neo-liberalism marks a shift in the gender order. The latter refers to the gender division of labor and the structures of power that shape the symbolic and material representations of gender relations. I argue that the qualified social citizenship of women in the post-war order is being eroded in favor of a market citizenship based on a possessively individualist notion.

I then focus on four aspects of the current transformation that are propelling the formation of a new gender order in Canada and other industrialized economies:

1. the reprivatization of social reproduction which represents a dual movement: one that returns the work of social reproduction to where it "naturally" belongs, the household; simultaneously, we see women's

traditional caring activities increasingly performed in relationships that are commodified and societies that are being redefined as collections of individuals;
2. the decline of the family wage model in many OECD countries that assumed some collective responsibility and resources for social reproduction and that is now increasingly externalized by capital in its cost calculations;
3. the fluidity of the public/private and production/reproduction which highlights that the strict boundaries demarcating the gender spaces of liberal democracy have always been shifting and contested cultural constructions;
4. the increasing polarization among women which is an outcome of greater reliance on market-based sources of income and provisioning resulting from the withdrawal of states from these functions and/or the reconstitution of states themselves to operate according to market principles and criteria.

Neo-liberal governance and conceptual silences

The responses of nation-states to transnational accumulation are increasingly circumscribed by a neo-liberal consensus which imposes identical conditions on all governments: reduce state spending and regulation, maximize exports, and facilitate market forces in the interest of restructuring national economies as part of transnational or regional trading blocs. Neo-liberalism rests on several premises that hearken back to the nineteenth century. First, institutions such as the state and market should be premised on the primacy of individual self-interest as the fundamental form of motivation. This is because, second, the most efficient allocation of resources and maximization of utility and welfare is said to occur through the market mechanism. And third, therefore the role of states should be to provide public goods that will underpin and underwrite market frameworks.[3] This is the reason why neo-liberal discourse separates economics from politics – in order to maximize the freedom of private economic forces from significant democratic accountability and public oversight. Indeed, it is in this context that Gill refers to the dominant framework of accumulation as disciplinary neo-liberalism. This framework relies on markets – especially the capital market – to reward and to discipline economic agents. It does so in ways that tend to privilege investors, who are seen by governments as central to the process of economic growth (Gill 1998a: 25). Thus new liberal constitutionalism involves the creation of a "quasi-constitutional framework for the reconstitution of the legal rights, prerogatives, and freedom of movement for capital on a world scale," thereby insulating dominant economic forces from democratic accountability (Gill 1997: 12). Gill identifies several components of new constitutionalism, two of which are directly relevant to my discussion:

1. strategies for reconfiguring state apparatuses so that governments themselves become the facilitators of market values and discipline; and
2. measures to construct markets through legal and political structures, which both redefine and internationally guarantee private property rights (for example, the World Trade Organization).

Reconfiguring state apparatuses

Reconfiguring state apparatuses involves liberal re-regulation and a dramatic shift in government commitments from securing the welfare of citizens to facilitating the flow of global capital. This has often been accomplished through a depoliticizing discourse of deficits, competitiveness, and balanced budgets, surrounded by an aura of technocratic neutrality. Playing the numbers game, and by deploying the apparently neutral language of stability, efficiency, and system preservation, has served to partly legitimize neo-liberalism. It has thereby avoided the deeply political question of what kind of system we want. In this way, technical discourse plays an active part in normalizing and sustaining the social and economic inequalities produced by fiscal law and policy. For example, an alarming new trend in Canada has been the passage of balanced-budget amendments, which will likely exacerbate social and economic disparities and prevent equality-seeking public initiatives to support the reproductive-care economy (Philipps 1996).

Thus new statutes and laws constrain governments in their fiscal policy decisions by establishing caps in spending and taxation. They also discourage proactive policies to promote equality and full employment since for a number of reasons, provincial (subnational) balanced-budget legislation, in particular, is likely to generate increased pressure for regressive spending cuts (as opposed to tax increases) whenever revenues decline. The political costs of spending money to eradicate poverty or to address the human impacts of restructuring will tend to be perceived as high if it entails significant provincial tax hikes. In this way, balanced-budget laws undermine the crucial role that flexibility in government spending can play in stabilizing the economy during private-sector recessions. Without the ability to engage in counter-cyclical spending, governments will have to meet a fall in levels of demand through spending cuts, a strategy which might well postpone recovery as well as tending to hit the most vulnerable (Philipps 1996: 718).

In terms of civil society, the counterpart of this reconfiguration of government is to shift towards a citizenship based on individuals as consumers and taxpayers rather than one characterized by citizens who are politically engaged and active. Indeed, rather than civic, political, and social rights, the neo-liberal consensus emphasizes individual solutions to what are seen as individually determined problems, not social, common ones (Bakker 1996b; Brodie 1996). Further, the new welfare/workfare frameworks are premised on a gender-neutral, human resources model in which joblessness and poverty are treated as an individual rather than a highly gendered social and structural problem. They adopt a radical individualism that roots social problems in character defects, and requires solutions directed at motivating and disciplining individuals to become self-sufficient. Its discourse speaks of "clients" rather than "citizens." Importantly, this new discourse tends to obscure the gendered underpinnings of poverty and social assistance receipt, as well as the constraints that unpaid reproductive and caring work place on women. In fact, gender is rarely even recognized as a variable in social assistance policy reform.

An increasingly relevant example that is linked to the provision of welfare functions in the OECD countries is the reliance on the voluntary sector and its active promotion by governments as a privatized substitute for the provision of public goods. For example, in Canada, the federal government has enriched the tax benefits provided to charitable donors (Philipps 2002). Yet the state has not simply relinquished its role in social reproduction to the voluntary sector. The changes in tax rules that have taken place since the mid-1990s require the active intervention of law makers and public servants who determine which non-profit groups and which donations are worthy of public support. In Philipps' words, they "police these boundaries." She has found that the combination of cutbacks in direct government funding of non-profits and the enhancement of charitable breaks is in effect favoring a subset of voluntary agencies that qualify under the current *legal* definition. According to Philipps:

> As a consequence, non-profits that are characterized by Revenue Canada as advocacy groups, because they call for legal or policy changes, or publish literature that is deemed propagandistic rather than educational, are routinely denied charitable status... This excludes the work of many equality seeking groups, including women's organizations, from the definition of charity, and precludes their access to tax subsidized private donations. (Philipps 2002)

A number of privatizing effects result from the movement away from direct funding of non-profit agencies towards subsidizing philanthropy through the tax system. First, government's role in welfare is less visible and accountable since these tax expenditures are not explicitly stated in the national accounts (Philipps notes that the cost to the federal government of providing income tax concessions to charities and donors was estimated at $1.015 billion in 1994 and was projected to increase by 67% to $1.693 billion by 2001).[4] Second, the decisions made about services to be funded become individualized. Third, service provision becomes decentralized, spread unevenly across the country and not necessarily accountable to those who need the social services. Fourth, the distribution of the tax benefits tracks the distribution of market income since the value of donations and tax credits tends to rise with income. Finally, such privatizing effects operate on both the distribution of resources and on the construction of social norms (Philipps 2002).

Yet at the same time the capacity of the private sector to take up many of these functions also needs to be established. Governments in Canada have continually called on the voluntary sector to fill the gap made by cuts in outlays for social infrastructure and transfer payments. Indeed, the very invisibility of the voluntary sector in conventional accounting means that the assumption that communities will fill gaps left by government service reductions has yet to be properly tested. However, the 1997 National Survey on Giving, Volunteering and Participating by Statistics Canada allowed for a first-time trend-line analysis of formal volunteer work in Canada. The numbers concerning formal voluntary activity (work through non-profit organizations) reveal that voluntary hours per capita have declined by 4.7% in the last ten years. If voluntary work had continued to be offered at the same rate as ten years ago, Canadians would have received 110.2 million more hours of formal voluntary services than they actually did. In consequence the decline in formal voluntary work is estimated to have cost $1.83 billion in lost services in 1997 (GPI Atlantic 1998). Thus the GPI survey suggests that the new reliance on the unpaid sector as being able to respond to contractions in public sector expenditures is unlikely to deliver the services needed. Other studies are needed, then, to measure how far and whether this gap is being filled by the voluntary sector, and thus whether this sector is underfunded for the tasks at hand.

An additional gender-based effect of the switch from direct funding of public services to indirect subsidization of charities and their donors is that more resources are shifted towards those who flourish in the market. For instance, Philipps found that for 1997, 67.5% of charitable credits benefited men versus 32.5% for women. Overall, she concludes that these tax benefits shift the tax burden away from the more affluent whilst facilitating greater control by them over the programs and services that their donations finance (Philipps 2002). The privatization of social services through changes in the tax system therefore changes both the nature of the services provided as well as the kinds of claims that citizens can make on them.

In this way, citizenship norms are being restructured so that collectivism and universal entitlement is displaced by a privatized system of service provision, in which social power (and with it the ability to influence the distribution and forms of social provision) is reallocated towards those with higher income levels.

Redefining/guaranteeing private property rights

As for measures to redefine and guarantee private property rights, the restructuring of states has involved both downsizing and a change in how remaining public goods and services, such as education, health, and environmental standards, are delivered to citizens. Not only have states withdrawn from much of the public economy, forcing people to rely on the private sphere of the family, but remaining public sector activities are also being reshaped according to private sector rules and criteria. This is often a function of both national political decision-making and international trade agreements. The North American Free Trade Agreement, for example, treats the private sector as the norm, referring to anything in the public sector as a "non-conforming measure." The underlying assumption in the NAFTA is the less government, the better (Cohen 1997: 31).

Such a sweeping homogenization and privileging of market forces over democratically organized decision-making obscures the historically specific form of the state in different countries. Canadians are rather sensitive about this because of the different historical role the Canadian state has played versus that of its largest and most important economic partner, the USA. This is not to assert that states are always good, the market always bad. Rather, two issues are raised here: that historically, states have played different and often supportive roles in creating societies that are prosperous and egalitarian, and that many states (not all) offer the possibility of public debate about fundamental decisions affecting the economy and social system. Trade agreements have strong implications for democracy, since many critical issues affecting people's lives are being removed from the domain of national government precisely by trade agreements. Many aspects of international trade law are interpreted and enforced by people on supranational panels who are not responsible to citizen nationals anywhere. The conditioning framework of international trade agreements enshrines neo-liberalism, which asserts the superiority of private international law in the regulation of commerce and removes questions of legal regulation from national and democratic controls (Cutler 1997). Indeed, some possibilities for collective action through multilateral regimes may increase, but these operate at least one step removed from democratic accountability (Cerny 1993: 618).

Restricting the scope of the public sector through trade initiatives has strong implications for women, minorities, and disadvantaged male and female workers, who have historically struggled for the expansion of that sector to attain equality. The public sector is important for women as both users and providers of services – in Canada, one in three women works in the broader public sector. Trade harmonization has affected the policy environment in areas like environmental and labor-market regulation as well as problems such as pay equity – the cost of which, it is argued by employers, is an obstacle to competitiveness and must therefore be abolished (Bakker 1991).

To summarize the argument so far: the current transformation in liberal-democratic states corresponds to important changes in the broader global political economy. In the industrialized countries, this shift is one away from the welfare state and corporate capitalism toward a neo-liberal state underpinned by globalization. This rewriting of modern history is, however, highly gendered. As the next section illustrates, these processes are transforming states, markets, and citizenship as well as the impositional claims upon which these categories have rested (Brodie 1997).

The shifting gender order

The shift at the level of world order from what Ruggie (1982) has called "embedded liberalism" towards disciplinary neo-liberalism involves shifts in production, the state and civil society (Gill 2000b). It also marks a shift in the gender orders of North and South, that is, in the gender division of labor and the structures of power that shape the symbolic and material representations of gender relations. As noted in Chapter 2, a gender order is a dynamic process of symbolic and material representations of gender relations that is more or less institutionalized. Gender orders coexist with, serve to shape and are shaped by world orders. Thus, recent shifts in the governance of social reproduction and provisioning – propelled by new constitutionalist reforms – can also be analyzed in terms of three dimensions or levels of analysis to be explored below: the micro (individual), the meso (institutional) and the macro (world order) levels.

The idealized gender order of the post-war welfare state in the industrialized economies rested on a specific model of the workplace, home, and family. The family consisted of a male breadwinner who supported a dependent wife and children. The wife's unpaid domestic labor was a crucial component of this stable model. The state, in turn, guaranteed a family wage through policies like progressive taxation, collective bargaining, and social welfare. Tax policies, to varying degrees, were designed to impose more of the costs of reproduction on the owners of capital through the social wage. The paid labor of many (not all) women was seen as secondary to that of their husbands (Brodie 1997). The state, through the tax system and expenditure policies, was an active agent in constructing a gender order based on assumptions and incentives around the availability of unpaid caring labor in the household, the economic sharing within family households, the ability of primary caregivers to access a social wage, and the definitional boundaries of who constitutes a family (Philipps 2002).

This is not to say that women did not benefit from this client relationship. For one thing, it encouraged Canadian women to make claims as women vis-à-vis the state, to push and elaborate the links between social rights and liberal-democratic citizenship. Many policy initiatives like childcare, pay-equity legislation, and women's shelters developed out of this politics of expanding welfare states and liberal democracy.

At the same time, Canada's post-war order ensured that most Canadian women had a very different relationship to the safety net than typical working men. Most analysts draw a distinction between what is termed "institutional" and "residual" social welfare policies. Institutional policies are usually tied to workforce participation, take the form of insurance or an entitlement, and generally have no stigma attached. Unemployment insurance is an example. Residual social policies, in contrast, provide assistance in the last resort. They tend to take the form of minimum, temporary assistance, often offered at the discretion of welfare bureaucracies and only after need is established and evidence provided that all other avenues of help have been explored (Guest 1985: 1). Welfare assistance is an obvious example.

The point to be stressed here is that, because most of Canada's institutional social policies were tied to wage labor-force participation, these became entitlements primarily for working men (Bakker 1996b: 6). Women who remained in the home could only resort to residual social policies if, for whatever reason, they no longer had access to the family wage. This fundamental difference in how most men and women accessed the welfare state has led some observers to argue that the post-war welfare state, in Canada and elsewhere, consisted of a gendered, two-tier system of social provision. Men, through their labor-force participation, gained entitlements as citizens to social security, whereas women, tied to unpaid labor in the home, became clients of social welfare agencies. For them, social assistance was not a right but, instead, intrusive, conditional, inadequate, and often punitive.

Despite Feminists' critical stance toward this dual system of social citizenship, they nevertheless recognized the importance of social policies that maintained women's well-being. During the last 15 years or so, the foundations of both the economic and political aspects of this citizenship and its related gender order have been eroded. Social citizenship has given way to market citizenship as the role of government and the rights of citizens have been redefined at the micro, meso and macro levels of society.

We elaborated in Chapter 2 how, at the micro level, this involves a reconstitution of the self and the subject at the deepest level. As Altvater suggests, this is "the way in which bourgeois individuals are constituted; in their interaction they produce market-constructed rationality and therewith themselves" (Altvater 1993: 61). At the micro level, the neo-liberal approach rests on the strong protection of liberty and property rights, premised on a Lockeian possessive individual and civil society that exemplifies how each person is the proprietor of his own person and capacities and does not owe society. This Lockeian notion is now increasingly reinforced through constitutional and fiscal means that protect individuals from expropriation of private property (Gill 2001b). Even those individuals outside or at the margins of formal circuits of capital – poor men and women, informal sector workers – are socialized through social and cultural references to markets. At the meso level, it involves the reconstitution of labor markets, including their feminization and informalization, with resulting reconstitution of the family and of the sites and nature of the provisioning of subsistence. At the macro level, the shift in gender orders is being increasingly demarcated by international agreements and restrictive fiscal policies that remove the automatic stabilizers of the Keynesian era, as well as tending to reinforce a tendency towards fiscal austerity and thus cuts in budgetary expenditures that have adversely affected the education and health budgets of virtually all countries in recent decades.

All of these factors suggest a new redistribution of social reproduction work among women based on their class, ethnic origin and citizenship. The next section will explore further the concept of social reproduction and link it to the changing spatial and temporal context of neo-liberal restructuring.

Social reproduction and neo-liberal restructuring

Drawing on the work of Young, I want to focus on four aspects or dimensions of the current transformation that are propelling the formation of a new gender order in the industrialized economies (Young 1998).

Reprivatization of reproduction

Reprivatization implies that social reproduction will once again be assigned to the private sphere in various guises. For instance, social reproduction can be offloaded to households and women's unpaid work. It can also be shifted to paid domestic workers within the household or substituted through bought services and commodities via the market. Reprivatization of reproduction represents a dual movement: one that returns the work of social reproduction to where it "naturally" belongs, the household; simultaneously, we see women's traditional care activities increasingly performed in relationships that include the explicit movement of money (Folbre and Nelson 2000: 134). This suggests a disembedding process of the social from the economic that evokes an earlier period of regime change.

Polanyi noted that pre-capitalist social and economic relations were embedded within the structures of production and reproduction. With the advent of industrialization, the division of labor (and the increasing physical separation of labor from its sites of production and sites of consumption), and commodification, a disembedding of these aspects of social reproduction occurred. However, this disembedding process – along with the process of commodification – encounters its own limits. For Polanyi, labor, land and money are in fact "fictitious commodities" that can only be considered to be commodities at the risk of threatening social cohesion: for "the postulate that anything that is bought and sold must have been produced for sale is emphatically untrue in regards to them" (cited in van der Pijl 1998: 15). Polanyi argues that the discipline of the market premised on these fictitious commodities forces social forces to press for state interventions to curb the destructive effects of market forces on society, nature and money (Polanyi 1957: 76). Thus social struggles generate social protection, which is mobilized periodically to keep market forces in check. Van der Pjil notes that:

"Social protection" in Polanyi's sense largely equals this form of socialization of labour, i.e., the collective organization of its regeneration. This includes both day-to-day and generational reproduction of labour power – the physical, psychological, and qualification requirements which the family and other community forms cannot (fully) provide any more and which are accordingly taken up by the state. (van der Pijl 1998: 21)

Under neo-liberal restructuring, this has been attacked and partly reprivatized, thereby reducing the socialization of risk for the majority and privatizing risk at the level of the individual (Gill 1995b: 21; van der Pijl 1998: 21).

Here, then, we begin to discern other key components of social reproduction:

1. biological reproduction;
2. reproduction of the labor force;
3. reproduction of provisioning and caring needs.

Biological reproduction or procreation refers to childbearing and, although a basic component for the reproduction of the labor force, can be differentiated from the latter as referring strictly to the physical development of human beings (Beneria and Sen 1997; Jenson 1986). This creates a situation wherein many women are consumed and used up like other commodities (Hartsock 2001). Enforced childbearing consumes women physically and the leading cause of death for women globally remains pregnancy and complications from childbearing.

The reproduction of the labor force refers to the daily maintenance of workers and potential labor and the process by which they become workers. This aspect of social reproduction was the focus of a great deal of debate within Marxist Feminist Political Economy in the 1970s and formed part of the "domestic labor debates." The object of these debates was to specify women's contribution through their unpaid labor (hence "exploited" labor) to the functioning of capitalism and the perpetuation of patriarchy within the family, in other words, to uncover the material conditions of women's oppression. More recent accounts link questions of the reproduction of the labor force to the systemic contradiction between capitalist accumulation and the necessary reproduction of different strata of labor power and consumers (see Chapter 10). Here the focus is on the changing conditions of both women's and men's contribution to the reproduction of labor power and the mediating relationship of the state via the social wage.

A third component, which comes out of the Feminist economics literature, is I believe different from the other two as it recognizes that certain aspects of social reproduction are intrinsically different from other labor processes; that is, the cooking of a meal, the caring for one's children has a functional value for the reproduction of the system, but these activities also have an intrinsic value that goes beyond a strict labor process (Folbre 2001; UNDP 2000). Demographic changes in the industrialized economies suggest that there may be a reduced aggregate burden of child raising and an increasing burden of elder care (Folbre and Nelson 2000). The personal and relational nature of women's domestic activities means that labor has its own motivations rather than being defined by a distinct product (Himmelweit 1999).

Thus a gender-sensitive notion of provisioning would capture, in addition to the state and voluntary sectors, the provisioning through the domestic sector of both human capacities and the provisioning values that distinguish the domestic sector (largely comprised of households) from the commercial values of the private sector and the regulatory values of the public sector. The circulation of values adds to an analysis of flows of money and real resources. By incorporating provisioning values of the domestic sector, this introduces the idea that the moral order is something produced in part by activities within the state, public and domestic sectors and transmitted between them. Hence it does not remain as an assumed parameter exogenous to Political Economy (Elson 1998).

Several conclusions follow from this discussion of social reproduction. First, the sphere of social reproduction is articulated to the sphere of production and is an integral, interrelated part of the economy. Secondly, the relationship between these spheres can only be understood historically and goes beyond a functionalism for capital or patriarchy once the affective relations of social reproduction are introduced (Humphries and Rubery 1984: 339).

The decline of the family wage model

During the past decade, like most modern Western democracies, Canada has experienced a number of significant economic and social changes that have challenged the assumptions underlying post-war social policy and placed additional and growing pressures on the social safety net. The globalization of industry, corporate restructuring, and rapid technological innovation have brought persistently high levels of unemployment (indeed, the highest since the Great Depression of the 1930s), decelerating economic growth, increases in part-time employment, and growing inequalities that have created a "polarization" among working people (Banting and Beach 1994: 1).

One effect of these changes has been that the family wage, the cornerstone of the post-war economy and gender order, has been shrinking, along with the economic prosperity of the middle classes who provided the economic base for taxation and income redistribution during the 1950s and 1960s. Indeed, throughout North America real wages have fallen in the past two decades. In Canada, between 1989 and 1991 alone, the median real Canadian family income declined by approximately $2,500 in constant dollars (Banting and Beach 1994: 14). At the same time the structure of families is changing, with many more single-parent families. In the mid-1990s women constituted approximately 90% of the growing numbers of lone parents in Canada. And 69% of lone parents received some income from welfare programs (Woolley 1995: 1).[5]

Fluidity of public/private in production/reproduction

Contrary to classic liberalism, the strict boundaries demarcating the gender spaces of liberal democracy have always been a shifting and contested cultural construction. The economic distinction between public and private goods, for example, is not organic but a product of politics (Brodie 1997: 230). Neoliberal Political Economy contributes to a marked fluidity between the public and private spheres, or the sites of production and reproduction, in several ways. Increasing informalization in advanced urban economies reconfigures not only economic relations between men and women, but also the sites where marketized labor occurs (Sassen 1998b). Homework and other forms of subcontracting of labor, for instance, are not gender-neutral because it is mainly women who adopt homework as an income strategy, and because men and women adopt homework for very different reasons and under different circumstances. Traditionally, homeworking has been used by capital as part of its accumulation strategy, but recent fiscal constraints and shifts in the perceived role of the state have led to the introduction of homework as a new public sector strategy (Boris and Pruegel 1996; Leach 1996). The displacement of public sector functions either to the market or the home as the unpaid caring work of women is a process of "reprivatization" and contributes to the permeability between public and private (Brodie 1997: 235). This sets in motion a process in which aspects of production are naturalized (that is, public goods and services are returned to where they "naturally" belong) and reproduction is made invisible by informalization.

The privatization project is simultaneously placing greater demands on women as caregivers in the family and community as workers in the labor market (Bakker 1996a). Reprivatizing the costs of social reproduction is intensifying women's labor in the provision of needs and individualizing the risks of lifetime income streams through private savings and pension funds. Documentation of unpaid work in Canada since the 1970s shows that overall, Canadians spend more time in unpaid work (that is, work of economic value which produces a set of marketable goods and services) than in paid work (Bakker 1998: 20). Women spend more time on unpaid labor at virtually all stages of the lifecycle than men (about 1.0 hours more per day). Yet at the same time as the material conditions of the traditional family are being eroded, more and more women are providing a vital contribution to the living standard of their family through waged income.

In this double movement, reprivatization is intensifying the material and discursive claims made on the family while undermining the very material and discursive conditions that could support these claims – greater responsibility for care-giving and women's financial contribution through labor-force activity is assumed and encouraged, yet dependency, particularly women's dependency on the family (or the state) is pathologized.

Increasing polarization among women

Some authors have argued that shifts in employment away from manufacturing and toward services are contributing to income polarization. As a result, wages and earnings are no longer clustered around the middle of the wage distribution, but are moving toward an hourglass configuration in which wages tend to be clustered at the top or bottom. Emerging jobs are polarized according to earnings and skills, a situation favoring the feminization of employment (Standing 1989). This may represent a gain for women in terms of overall economic participation, but produces more precarious, low-wage forms of economic activity. Conversely, for certain categories of male workers the feminization of employment and its restructuring of labor markets has meant a downward trend in their wages and working conditions, leading to a convergence between male and female employment conditions at the lower end of the hourglass in some OECD countries.

Another implication of earnings, skill, and job polarization is that as women continue to be drawn to either pole of employment, the disparity among them will increase. This has economic as well as political implications. Pay equity (equal pay for work of equal value) and equal employment-opportunity legislation, for example, assume a commonality of interests among women, but economic restructuring appears to be creating both material differences and skill divisions within female ranks. The increasing polarization or segmentation among women signals, for some analysts, a class-based divergence of interests among women in the labor force (Bakker 1991). Finally, the very conditions of social reproduction are being reconfigured by neo-liberal dynamics to create a polarization among women – the "mistress and the maid" phenomenon (Young 2001a). Thus it creates a stratification of social reproduction needs in the sense that the needs of the employer are emphasized over the needs of the domestic worker. Domestic workers are also stateless, unable to make claims as citizens in the way their employer might (Arat-Koc 2003).

Conclusion: neo-liberal governance and human security

The emerging gender order is not only unequal in terms of effects on human security, but it also contains elements of a new regime of moral regulation. For example, the new moral order privileges the private over the public and the individual over the collective, and reasserts the family as a gender-neutral self-sufficient unit of care-giving and reciprocal obligation. This market-oriented conceptualization of social citizenship rests on a growing emphasis on citizenship obligation, what some have called a "duties discourse" (Lister 1997: 31, citing Maurice Roche).

For Feminists, a key issue is how care and reproduction fit into this new configuration. Will social risk be completely privatized with deleterious effects for the human security of the poor and intensified inequality among women (as well as between women and men)? Or else is there a possibility of social forces resisting commodification in the Polanyian sense as attempts to sever controls over market forces from the nation-state are countered and as the global economy is brought under renewed and broad-based social control? Here contradictory tendencies highlight the paradoxical nature of globalization. Social mobilizations such as Eco-Feminism, environmentalism, and the peace movement have developed in response to the way unregulated markets impact negatively on human security. However, social movements of a less progressive nature such as ethno-nationalism, racism, and neo-fascism also have been strengthened by reaction to a globalizing trend.

As we move into this century, moreover, a paradoxical gender order appears to be emerging. We are witnessing, concurrently, intensification and an erosion of gender. Key factors and forces suggest that gender is central to neo-liberal transformations. Neo-liberal economic and social policies have had the effect of integrating large groups of women into employment. This so-called feminization of work varies greatly across the globe. For example, elite women in OECD countries may be integrating into the new market structures of the service or knowledge-based economies at a faster rate than men. The increasing employment of women in manufacturing industries in newly industrializing countries in particular, those that receive large inflows of foreign capital, is also an outcome of globalization. This means, paradoxically, that both men and women experience problems of human insecurity in similar ways, that is, in a class-based manner.

Thus at the same time as global forces have pointed to the centrality of gender relations, increasing commodification and individualization have created new class, race and ethnic differences. Increasing commodification allows some women to buy and exploit the domestic services of other women who are often from a poorer region of the world. Canada, for instance, has seen successive waves of women first from the Caribbean, now the Philippines, coming to work as nannies for middle- and upper-middle-class families.

So as women and men become increasingly exposed to market forces, as both producers and consumers, there may be a convergence of experience. However, unless the work that occurs in the household becomes less gender-specific (that is, done mainly by women), the perceived erosion of gender difference and the convergence of male–female conditions is merely a mirage. Whether done by one group of women or another imported for that purpose, domestic labor is still fundamentally private, women's work. In that sense, the domestic worker and the woman who employs her share a common condition: they both experience their paid work as incompatible with their social reproduction needs. Furthermore, both are raising children in societies where childcare is seen as a private, individual matter (Arat-Koc 2003). Reprivatization of social reproduction is a neo-liberal policy strategy that individualizes the provision of human security. How individuals are able to cope with such a strategy depends on their market and citizenship status (or lack thereof), and their capacities for collective action become increasingly atomized.

If we are to prevent the increasingly unequal gender and world orders of neo-liberalism, we must challenge the emerging notions of citizenship which are shrinking public spaces and marginalizing equity-seeking groups as "special interests." This order of human security also places the onus on domestic workers (many of whom are "non-citizens") who fill the provisioning needs of an increasing number of middle- and upper-class households. The state in Canada, as we have seen, plays a critical role in negotiating the public/private boundaries of production and reproduction, and policing the boundaries of citizenship. At the same time, fiscal policy is shifting the risks of adjustment and neo-liberal restructuring downwards: down to subnational and local levels of government (often without increasing their resource capacity to meet these new functions) and down to communities and households, particularly economically and socially vulnerable women. The questions posed by these trends are: is a democratic and progressive form of human security possible in a more privatized and more commodified world order? And is this gender-order really stable, or will its fragility be revealed not only through social dislocations but also through the increasing number of financial crises that have marked the last decade?

Notes

1. The UNDP is now dealing with issues of accountability and power but tends to separate these from specific questions of social reproduction and bases its premises on liberal individualism. The latter does not provide a convincing framework to address problems involving collective action, unless this is explained as the aggregate actions of individuals in response to incentives from the "political market," that is, from a methodological individualist perspective. Also, such an approach constructs a theoretical language that may be alien to multiple frameworks of thought in the non-Western world that are not embedded within economic rationalism and notions of representative democracy. See Bakker (1997).
2. Nussbaum identifies ten capabilities, among which are: the ability to live a long and healthy life, free of abuse, and to have control over one's political and material environment. See Nussbaum (2000: 78–80).
3. Friedman and Hayek exemplify this discourse. See Friedman (1962), Hayek (1944).
4. All dollar sums referred to in this book are in US dollars unless noted otherwise.
5. Social assistance payments were cut in Canada in the 1990s so that by 2000 the average family on welfare had only half the income needed to live above the poverty line. It is thus little surprise that, despite a sustained economic expansion during the decade, child poverty in Canada has been growing. In 1989 one child in seven lived in poverty, whereas by 1999 one in five children, or 18.5% of all children, lived in poverty. See Campaign 2000 (2001).

5
Constitutionalism in a Modern Patriarchal State: Japan, the Sex Sector, and Social Reproduction

Seiko Hanochi

This chapter offers a critical gender perspective to explore some of the effects of international constitutional politics on the patriarchal forms of the modern Japanese state. The approach I take assumes that the state develops, in general, a legal and political framework which accommodates two of its major purposes: to develop the production system for its economic prosperity and to guarantee the security of its social reproduction within given international contexts. And in turn the social reproduction in modern states has historically involved the regulation of moral and ethical life, which includes the regulation of social institutions such as the family as well as associated sexual mores and what today is called the sex industries or sex sector. All of these elements form part of a particular gender order within the context of a particular social formation and pattern of power relations, in ways that have unequal implications for human security.

In the Japanese case, the sex sector is a largely hidden part of the state, regulated on the basis of the economic and political interests of the ruling classes as they are understood and defined within a given international context (for example, as defined by colonial, Cold War and post-colonial and neo-liberal globalization frameworks). In this context, one of the aims of this chapter is to bring to light the hidden nature of the state form and to show how the sex sector and its regulation serves to constitute important aspects of power and authority, production and market forces, and not least the patterns of social reproduction in the Japanese system, at the expense of its principal victims, women and children who are trafficked into bondage or ostensibly "free" prostitution. In this context I will also highlight some of the implications of the interaction between Japan and patterns of regional development in terms of these fundamental dimensions of social and political life and their implications for poor communities throughout the region.

In this context this chapter will explore evolving relationships between the sex industries or the sex sector and the forms of political rule in modern Japan that have marked its transition from the Old Meiji State form to what Gill calls the new constitutionalism. Japan has had three constitutional regimes since it joined the international community in 1868. Since Japan became a modern state, it has adopted two formal constitutions and is now considering whether to abrogate the second. The first was the Meiji Constitution pronounced in the name of Emperor Meiji in 1890. The second was the Constitution of 1946, promulgated in the name of the people of Japan, under the guidance of the US Occupation Authorities. And in 2000 the Lower House of the Diet set up a Commission for the Study of the Constitution in response to growing majority demands to abrogate the 1946 Constitution.[1] Indeed, although there is as yet no formal new constitution that corresponds to the most recent globalized regime, there is nevertheless a *de facto* constitutional revision underway that involves the increasing use of neo-liberal social and economic regulation in Japan and the redefinition of the sex sector by market forces that operate at the interface between the criminal and legal frameworks of power and production (see also Chapter 7 on this issue).

In what follows I discuss:

1. Japan's constitutional development and its origins in the old Meiji constitution;
2. shifts in the ways that the modern Japanese state has legislated and regulated its sex industries;
3. new conditions and contradictions arising from the interaction between disciplinary neo-liberalism and new constitutionalism, on the one hand, and the sex industries, on the other.

Finally I reflect on the racist nature of today's global sex industries.

In each phase of the exposition, I will relate my argument and evidence to issues of human security and the social reproduction of Japanese society, and to its direct and indirect effects on the victims of international sex trafficking, mainly women and children from Asia.

Japan's constitutional development

Let me first summarize some of the basic principles of the two formal Constitutions of the modern Japanese state (1890 and 1946) and relate them to some of the issues associated with a new constitutional politics that emerged in the late 1990s.

Emperor Meiji proclaimed in the Preamble of the 1890 Constitution that the Constitution is to lead descendants of his subjects on the basis of principles inherited from his ancestors, principles that would ensure his subjects would support him as the symbol of the nation, in facing the external world, and thus to strengthen the glory of the Empire inside and outside of the nation. This discourse of the "Emperor-system" defines the framework within which constitutional politics, that is, the political decisions regarding the fundamental principles of all national institutions, were made in Japan before its defeat in 1945 at the hands of the Allies. Its principles refer to the (mythical) ancestors of the Emperor and the descendants of his subjects, and they establish the familial, patriarchal and imperial framework of all the social institutions governed by the Meiji Constitution. This framework was meant to strengthen the glory of the Empire especially in the face of the international pressures from Western powers.

The old constitutionalism represented by the 1890 Constitution attempted to build a familial state where all the "subjects" were to be united in their efforts to develop the productive and reproductive activities and powers of the Meiji State, under threat of Western colonization. At the same time, however, the Meiji State itself developed into a colonial expansionist state by mobilizing its subjects and forming an aggressive Imperial Army.

By contrast, during the Occupation following the defeat of Japan's imperial-militarist state, Japan moved towards a more open, post-colonial and outward-looking constitutionalism, aimed at building an internationally competitive, liberal, but centrally guided economy, with a production and reproduction system based on a well-integrated corporate sector. Japan also renounced both the development of armed forces other than for purposes of self-defence and the deployment and use of nuclear weapons. This second modern constitution of 1946 was created under pressure of defeat in war although it was promulgated in the name of the people of Japan. And despite US pressure to democratize the central constitutional principles, its first clause declares that the Emperor is the symbol of the unity of the Japanese people. This meant that it singled out Japan from the outside world as a unified nation, under the Emperor. At the same time the Preamble of this Constitution states that, "All peoples of the World have the right to live in peace, without fear and want" (Oishi 1995: 262–3). Thus the idea that Japan was re-entering the now post-colonial international system was combined with the idea that Japan is a unified nation. Unity was narrowly interpreted to mean that the State of Japan should guarantee the peaceful life of its people, eliminating fears of invasion and providing freedom from want. This principle of unity was implemented by establishing a strong state, one that was externally peaceful and dissociated from international (military) conflicts. Internally it would eliminate some of the fears of Japanese people by excluding foreigners and maintaining internal peace and order through efficient institutions of policing. The strong state would satisfy the wants of the Japanese people through efficient guidance of the corporate sector, supporting weak sectors in its mobilization of the economy.

It appears that a third Constitution is now being formed partly through a process of abrogation and reform of the 1946 Constitution. Japanese Diet debates during 2000 are indicative of the way in which developments are moving, although there was radical disagreement between the witnesses over the introduction of new Articles and whether to abrogate some of the older clauses and Articles. For example there were divisions as to whether to scrap Article 9 on Japan's rights to expand its armed forces and over Article 29 on property rights. Here there was fundamental disagreement over the right of the state to nationalize key sectors and thus a debate took place about which mechanisms could protect private property rights. The more reactionary critics of the 1946 arrangements criticized how they ignored the important role of the family and how the family question was effectively suppressed by the individualism of the 1946 Constitution. Indeed some of these witnesses supported a return to the Meiji Constitution and the familial state form. Others, however – indeed, a strong force that supported the abrogation of the 1946 Constitution – were attempting to remove the restrictions it puts on private property, economic freedom, and the free market. These critics reflected the influence of neo-liberal globalization of the end of the twentieth century, and efforts to lead Japan towards a new type of authoritarian-liberal state. The latter perspective defines the role of the state as a protector of neo-liberal economics, combining "deregulation" of the "guidance" aspect of the post-World War II state with efforts to strengthen its security and surveillance role against the anti-social and anti-systemic forces caused by globalization.

The rest of this chapter will show how this transformation of the Japanese state created different types of policies towards the sex sector. Each transformation had implications for the insecurity of women and children from the countries under the political, military and economic influence of Japan (Oishi 1995: 268–85).

Meiji constitutionalism as a reaction to international colonialism

Let us now direct our attention to the world situation within which Japan began to build a "modern state." During the nineteenth century a public brothel system was adopted throughout Europe and this system spread as the colonial rule of Western powers expanded. However, this system was largely abandoned in Europe at the end of the nineteenth century as a consequence of the "social purification" campaign of feminists who led an international movement against "white slavery."[2] Nevertheless, the major powers, such as France and Germany as well as Great Britain, maintained this system in their colonies even after World War I. The USA, which had never adopted a public brothel system on the federal level, had adopted such a system in several states and it was institutionalized in the Philippines when colonizing that country. Following its regulation of military prostitution, the US Army established the public brothel system to protect its forces from venereal diseases, that is, it was viewed as a means to guarantee the health of occupying armed forces of the imperialist powers.

Feminist movements in Europe and North America fighting for abolition of public brothels gave birth to an international anti-trafficking regime, which was completed by the League of Nations in the 1920s through several conventions forbidding the exploitation of the prostitution of women under a certain age. It thus divided the trafficked women by age into minors and adults, and in terms of their mode of exploitation into forced and free workers. The League of Nations thus legitimized sexual exploitation of free adult women in prostitution, whilst in effect permitting the increasingly international and clandestine sex sectors to exploit trafficked women from the colonies in a system that was based on exploitation of the natural and human resources provided by colonies and semi-colonies of non-Western regions (Hanochi 1998a). This system linked traditional impoverished sectors of these societies to the world commodity market through domestic migration to the industrializing urban regions and to metropolis countries. It often meant for many women of the developing regions an increasing pressure for self-commodification through "prostitution," for example, in the sex sectors of the industrialized countries.

This pressure was experienced in the context of a particular patriarchal, racist and colonialist discourse. Thus a widespread perception arose in the West that colonization had become a burden of "superior" white men, since it caused increases in criminality and "social unrest." These social ills were portrayed as partly a consequence of the influx of non-Western and uneducated people, including the "immoral" trafficked women in prostitution from the colonies. This legitimized a structure of racist and sexist discrimination. In effect women from the non-Western colonies and semi-colonies were treated as "racially retarded" immoral women, to be excluded from civil society, and at best kept in the informal sector of society under the control of the criminal organizations. It was this colonialist framework and supremacist discourse that Japan joined in 1868. This meant that Japan had to adjust all its pre-modern institutions to the new conditions. This included its traditional sex sector, which had been regulated by the policies of the Tokugawa Shogunate through the *kuruwa* institution of the Edo period that lasted from the early 1600s to the 1860s.

The *kuruwa* public brothel system of the Edo period was not only an outlet for sexual energies and exploitation but also a cultural mechanism that provided a free space in feudal Japan where an emerging bourgeois culture flourished. *Kuruwa* was based on bonded slavery of young women (*oiran*) from poor regions that were trafficked into the urban centres of Edo (Tokyo), Kyoto, Nagasaki and other key administrative/commercial centres. Patriarchal benevolence was expressed in *kuruwa* culture where *oiran* were regulated by special codes of promotion that permitted them to aspire to respectable status as *tayus*, that is, master entertainers (known abroad as *geisha*). This institution thus did not suffer from the Western stigmatization of prostitutes as immoral women. The Meiji State maintained the *kuruwa* institution as it had been under the Shogunate until it faced major international criticism following the so-called *Maria Luz* Incident of 1872.[3]

The response of the Japanese government was to change the *kuruwa* into a new regulated brothel system separating the *okiya* from the *zashiki* saloons where prostitution was practiced (Fukuda 1993). This abolished the formal distinction between the owners of the *okiyas* who were the creditors of the bondage contract, and the owners of the saloons who exploited the prostitutes and who paid the women. The women in turn passed on their compensation immediately to their *okiya* creditors. However, in spite of this formal separation, fundamental practices of the *kuruwa* culture were maintained, whilst the national regulated brothels became integrated into the state.

The Meiji form of state involved a self-contained legal and political framework that cemented a cohesive bloc among the different sectors of the ruling classes: the Emperor, the traditional elite, national and local, including the military and the landlords, the bureaucrats and the modernizing intellectuals, planners, engineers, and so on; and the business elite. In this sense the old Meiji constitutionalism was the legal expression of a state project based on a set of institutional and moral principles of mobilizing the people, workers, peasants, and military in order to maximize their productivity. The Emperor was the paterfamilias of a familial state composing families whose task was the social reproduction of a cohesive workforce, and a strong army.

In this context, the Meiji state emphasized a division of labor between the factory as the locus of production and the home as locus of reproduction, using the national brothel system as a complement to the factory and the family. This is because the sex sector, under this framework of social reproduction, served the purpose of detaching the satisfaction of the sexual drives of the male members of the family, so that maximum efficiency in production and social reproduction was achieved in the factory (by men) and in the family (by wives and mothers). The public brothel system became an institution that was therefore tolerated officially and utilized informally in effect to guarantee the security of the core institutional complex of Imperial Meiji society: its state–family–factory complexes.

The modernization of the Japanese political economy led to its internationalization around the 1920s. Economically this took the form of more labor-intensive production, for example, in textiles, accompanied by commercial activities in East and Southeast Asia selling cheap textile products. Migration into neighboring Korea and China was also a consequence of Japan's economic underdevelopment combined with demographic pressure.

This international economic expansion led to political and military expansion. The colonization of Korea and the northeast region of China (Manchu-Guo) led to the war in China and the Pacific (1931–45), referred to in Japan as the Fifteen Years War (Suzuki 2002: 138–63).

The internationalization of modernizing Japan was closely accompanied by the internationalization of its sex sector. The demand for female prostitutes in the colonies of Southeast Asia caused Japanese women from poor regions of West Japan to be trafficked into this region. They were called the *kara-yuki-san* (those who go to Kara or Asia) and acted as pioneers for Japanese peddlers and commercial interests to move into this region, facilitating the latter's adaptation into local communities as they competed with overseas Chinese who were well rooted there. *Kara-yuki-san* acted as a Trojan horse for Japanese traders in the 1920s and 1930s, paving the way for military invasion in the 1940s. *Kara-yuki-san* symbolized how the internationalization of Japanese modernization is a forerunner of the contemporary North–South relations where women from poorer countries are the objects of commercial and sexual exploitation by men of richer status. Whilst Japan succeeded in avoiding colonization as a state, its poor female citizens were sold, not only within Japan to the brothels of the richer urban modernizing centers, but also to richer foreign brothels where the colonial rulers and rich overseas Chinese and other subaltern colonial strata fueled the demand for female prostitutes. As will be explained later, the women trafficked into Japan were later called *japa-yuki-san*, descendants of these *kara-yuki-san* (Morisaki 1976: 17–57, 99–132).

During the 1910s and 1920s, the first phase of the economic internationalization of Japan, Japanese women were sold to the sex market of Southeast Asia. The second, military expansion phase of the Fifteen Years War saw women from colonial occupied territories as the victims in the military sex-slave institution known as the "comfort women" (Mori 1999: 63–102). This violent institution was based on both the *kuruwa* and the *kara-yuki-san*. It created public brothels, often run by the Japanese army who forcefully recruited its sex workforce to service invading armies of Japan in China. After the Nanking Massacre and the mass rape incident that intensified anti-Japanese sentiments of the local peoples, the Japanese army opted to open "comfort stations" for its occupation forces. This was intended to avoid further mass rapes of women in the occupied territories albeit in the context of an expansionist military policy involving the systematic exploitation of foreign women and children. This type of military institution was entirely different from the public brothel system of the Japanese domestic sector, not only by virtue of its international composition but also by the violent means used in it. As noted, the informal role of the sex sector under the Meiji Constitution was to strengthen the Japanese family system in the service of increased economic and military productivity. This meant that it excluded foreign women and children.

From the Anti-Prostitution Law to the global sex trade

The Meiji colonial empire was defeated by the US. During the US Occupation, Japan developed a new constitutionalism (Dower 1999: 52–78, 100–9). This placed the patriarchal Emperor system within a democratic framework supporting the development of an internationally competitive economy. The new form of state was expected to help the US in developing the regional economy, buttressing the bilateral military agreements and, in time, acting as a bulwark against Soviet expansionism. The economic base of this system was an emergent "civil society" committed to economic recovery in the 1950s and the goal of "doubling income" in the 1960s. This economic orientation was strengthened by a massive rural to urban migration and the emergence of a consumerist culture with a strong sex-orientation. These trends helped Japan to build a state dedicated to national unity and economic growth, and integrated Japan into the international market, with sex industries an important part of the post-Occupation society.

Indeed, the sex sector became an integral part of the "Emperor System of Democratic Constitutionalism," not, however, in recreating its role in the familial state complexes, but rather in reproducing the emergent consumerist civil society. Sex industries became important in the accumulation of wealth for the corporate sector not only in the productive economy but also in the service economy.

The Occupation period (1945–51) prepared this trend (Hosoya and Nagayo 2001: 132–48). A combination of extreme impoverishment of the Japanese people, combined with the presence of a rich foreign military's bases occupying the country, led to the proliferation of the sex districts in urban Japan during the ten years following the defeat of 1945. Combined with Japan's decision to sign the 1949 UN Convention Against Trafficking as a proof of its decision to adopt world standards of morality, this led the Japanese government to adopt a new Anti-Prostitution Law (*Baishun Boushi Hou*) (Fujime 1998). Under pressure from US Occupation forces, public brothels were finally abolished through this law and new regulated zones were created for sex industries under strict regulation (criminalizing solicited prostitution). However, women in prostitution organized themselves in opposition to this new law and demanded social security and provision of financial support to women leaving the sex sector. Their movement, which was part of the post-Occupation labor offensive, was crushed. Women in prostitution were turned into individual "immoral women" thus practicing prostitution became illegal after the Law becoming effective in 1957.[4]

In this way the abolition of public brothels left Japan with "modern" sex industries, which had developed during the Occupation to service the Occupation forces and were also receiving Japanese customers. This opened up the Japanese sex industries to non-Japanese women who could not have been integrated into *kuruwa* culture. During the Occupation, "comfort stations" opened by the Japanese government evolved into new sex institutions where GIs were serviced. These "modernized" women in prostitution were known in military slang as *panpan* – for the Japanese public an especially derogatory term, combining anti-American feeling with contempt for the women in prostitution who were breaking traditions of *kuruwa* culture. Indeed, strong opposition to closing the *kuruwa* came from political forces associated with anti-Western and anti-modern conservative sectors in Japanese society, resulting in some concessions by the abolitionists who emerged in the 1950s thanks to the support given to them by the Occupation forces. Indeed, *Baishun Boush Hou* was the result of a compromise between the two forces: it abolished formal prostitution institutions but permitted the development of sex industries, provided that they did not practice prostitution openly. The abolition of the traditional public brothel system left the Japanese sex districts with only the modern institutions of clubs, bars, and cabarets and the sex sector was open to foreign women. This meant that Japan of the 1970s and 1980s developed its sex industries with a sex workforce composed of the *japa-yuki-san*, women trafficked from East and Southeast Asian countries and later from outside Asia (Fujime 1998; Hanochi 1998b). Here one of the legal and administrative measures developed by the Japanese state to support the competitiveness of Japanese firms, the *Fuzoku Eigyo Hou* (Law Concerning Sex Industries) plays an important role. On the other hand, Japanese ODA policy included the development of tourism, and this involved a sex aspect. One of the first economic assistance projects to South Korea included the development of the tourist facilities in Chejuu Island, which then became a major target of Japanese sex tourism. In this way, Japanese government assistance to sex tourism and domestic sex industries helped to prepare the globalization of the Japanese economy by internationalizing its economy including the recruitment and reproduction of the workforce of its sex industries. In effect modernized sex industries have become the object of a neo-Keynesian investment policy in so far as they help in creating effective demand for sex tourism and domestic sex industries. The laws mentioned above regulate the sex industries in such a way that different sex services (except sexual intercourse) are legalized, provided that they are reported and taxed. Laws and regulations established in the 1960s provided the basis for the introduction of trafficked foreign women and children into the Japanese sex workforce. They guarantee security, law and order whilst building international competitiveness of Japanese industries, including sex industries, provided that they do not trespass the limits of public decency.

Foreign sex workers became more easily exploitable, first by Japanese sex tourists during the 1960s and 1970s and second, in the late 1970s and 1980s when women and children from neighboring Asian countries began to be massively imported (trafficked) into the sex districts of Japan, often under highly insecure working and social conditions. Thus post-Occupation Japan involved a transformation from an economically closed state that was militarily expansionist (exploiting foreign women and children as military sex slaves) into an internationally exploitative state-directed economic expansionism, appropriating trafficked women and children from Asian and other developing countries, that is, reproducing legally a sex workforce that has been illegally trafficked by criminal organizations (Hanochi 1996).

Globalizing new constitutionalism and the sex industries

A globalizing new constitutionalism represents the onset of a third, new form of state for modern Japan. It emerged in the 1990s, after being prepared by the increase of "illegal" or undocumented migrants and trafficked victims during the "bubble "economy period of the 1980s. This new constitutionalism is combined with active cooperation with US international security efforts (expressed by the New US–Japan Defense Guidelines) and a strong effort to reaffirm the national identity of Japan, for example, reflected in the National Flag and National Anthem Law. In this context, the new Japanese state stresses the reproduction of national identity values, while cooperating with US dominance and the global standards of disciplinary neo-liberalism to help protect the security of the global market.[5]

From the end of the twentieth century, a stress on threats from transnational criminal organizations has combined with a fear of terrorism. In the Japanese case, the concern about maintaining the homogeneity of Japan is linked to a strong fear about the intrusion of foreign criminal elements. Some see such homogeneity as Japan's only guarantee of security in the face of globalization, which forces it to open its borders to dangerous tendencies of pluralism and other threats. Indeed, this search for security in homogeneity is threatened by the infiltration of different trends of immigration in the civil society of Japan, especially in its sex sector. During the 1990s, a new subculture emerged in big cities, especially in Tokyo. It was created by Asian migrant workers, including the sex-workers, who began to migrate to Japan in the 1980s followed by relatives and their friends in networks crossing the national boundaries of Japan (Mushakoji 2002: 186–205).

Kabuki-cho in Tokyo was one such sex district where women from Korea, China, Thailand, the Philippines, Colombia, Russia and Eastern Europe created "international" subcultural communities. New "ethnic stores" appeared in these communities as a consequence of the new demand for imported food and goods, as well as information (newspapers, magazines and rental videos), from the diverse home countries of the new migrant workers during the 1980s and 1990s. Survey results show sudden increases of ethnic business and ethnic entrepreneurs in the 1990s in Shinjuku and Ikebukuro, two multiethnic districts of Tokyo associated with the Kabuki-cho sex district (Okuda and Tajima 1998: 17–27). Most of the foreign inhabitants of these multicultural districts have migrated and settled in Japan in the 1980s. Trafficked women constitute an important proportion of them. Japan's major cities have become more global cities with the emergence of cross-border ethnic networks that have begun to transform urban identities. However, this transformation took place silently without drawing the public attention of the Japanese majority, who continued to believe in the homogeneity of Japanese culture. When increasing numbers of Japanese realized what had occurred there was a widespread sense of uncertainty and insecurity. Majority opinion sought a return to the "good old days" before globalization, or even before modernization, to recreate a reassuringly homogeneous society where everybody shared the same nationality, the same language, and the same ethnic origin, reflecting the prevailing sentiment in Japanese politics that rejects the emerging multiethnic subcultures as threatening the integrity and security of Japan. This sentiment is also at the base of the appeal made in 2001, with widespread popular support, by the Mayor of Tokyo, Shintaro Ishihara. As is also noted in Chapter 8, Ishihara called for the Self Defense Forces (the Japanese military apparatus) to be ready to control "illegal foreign workers" who might disturb public order during earthquakes and other natural calamities. This type of sentiment was also reflected in the recent declaration of Premier Mori about the necessity to re-educate the young generation in the belief in Japan as a "divine nation" (Amano 2001) Ishihara and Mori are two sides of the same coin: in the face of globalization and multiethnicization, it is believed essential for the state to defend the human security of the Japanese. The way this is reflected in the sex industries is through intensified surveillance and control of "illegal" (undocumented) migrants who are conflated with the transnational criminal organizations exploiting them.

At the same time the sex industries and the transnational criminal organizations not only profited from the prosperity of the Japanese "bubble" economy in the 1980s, but also from the stagnation of this economy in the 1990s after the "bubble" exploded. This is due to the widening economic gap between the rich Japanese urban centers and the poverty of local communities in East and Southeast Asian countries. This poverty forces women into the structures of exploitation of the sex industries, especially in the rich countries, in the hope of earning sums of money unavailable to them in their country of origin. Thus Asian women, due to the lack of other means of earning money, are forced to commodify their bodies for the gratification of Japanese bourgeois men. The transnational criminal organizations exploit them and turn the global sex industries into one of the most lucrative service industries, channeling the profits they make into other sectors of the global criminal economy (Lim 1998). In this context, the sex industries maximize their profits by incorporating different systems of exploitation, from pure slavery, to bonded slavery, to unprotected and unorganized labor (and indeed organized labor in Europe). These different power relations and social modes of exploitation are applied in the context of a racist hierarchy in the sex industries. The free women of industrialized countries, white or Japanese, are at the top, and the trafficked women from Asia (and Latin America) are at the bottom as slaves, bonded slaves or hyper-exploited unprotected wage labor.

This combined system of exploitation in the sex industries may in fact be the typical mode of exploitation more generally in the post-colonial era of disciplinary neo-liberal globalization, although it is very difficult to establish the real profit made by the joint exploitative activities of the sex industries and the criminal organizations. Its gain comes not only from the taxed legal earnings of the sex industries, but also from illegal, unreported prostitution activities of women in sex industries under the control of criminal organizations in the so-called "informal" sector. There is, however, one place in Japan where participation of the global criminal organizations in the sex districts has been partially disclosed by police campaigns: Kabuki-cho, in the Shinjuku "entertainment" zone of Tokyo, which is one of the most concentrated of Japanese sex districts. In a narrow area, about one square kilometer, Kabuki-cho contains about 5000 pubs, cafes, cabarets and other clubs, and other institutions out of which about 45% belong to the sex industries involving foreign women and children. In Kabuki-cho, the official statistics records 20,000 foreign citizens, which is about 10% of the local population, a great concentration of foreigners in Japan where the official percentage of foreigners in the population is less than 1%.[6]

The foreign women and children working in these sex industry institutions are in effect mostly bonded slaves, that is, women who are forced into financial dependence ("debt") by organized crime, incurring high charges for their food and shelter and placed in situations from which they cannot leave (a situation similar to serfdom). Consequently, these women must accept the conditions imposed by the criminal syndicates. However, in some rare cases women succeed in repaying their so-called "debts" and begin to save money and send money to their home communities as remittances, although this is becoming less and less realizable under the continued economic crisis in Japan. Kabuki-cho still prospers, but in other sex districts of Japan, most of the women and children are unable to pay their "debts" and some have difficulty even in gaining enough money to be able to eat. Many become sick before repaying "debts." At the same time it is known, but difficult to prove, that unlike many of the Japanese women and children who are exploited but not bonded, the women and children from less developed countries are trafficked and continue as bonded slaves, in the strictest sense of the term.

Exploitation of such prostitution generates enormous money, divided among the legal and illegal exploiters. In most sex districts of Japan, the Japanese Mafia controls the local sex industries paying their foreign criminal associates. In 1994 four murders in Kabuki-cho prompted the Tokyo police to conduct an investigation. They failed to catch the real criminals, but at least it disclosed their existence and that Kabuki-cho was found to be under the control of a transnational criminal network that ruled over the Japanese *yakuza* organizations. The Triads, one of the three major Chinese Mafia groups with strong connections in Hong Kong and Taiwan, was trafficking women and children from South and Northeast Asia, Latin America and Russia into Shinjuku to work in Philippine bars, Taiwanese cabaret clubs and Colombian parlors, and so on. In response the Tokyo police organized a "Center for the General Environmental Cleansing of the Shinjuku District," an initiative that eliminated for a few months the so-called "illegal migrant workers" from the sex industries institutions and streets. Very soon newly trafficked women and children replaced them, and the local sex industries were able to resume normal business after the police had concluded that they had successfully "cleansed" Kabuki-cho. In the cleansing process it was neither the Chinese Mafia nor the Japanese *yakuzas* who were arrested, but the foreign victims of trafficking, usually charged with "illegal overstay" (which was easy to prove) rather than soliciting and other criminal acts forbidden by the Anti-Prostitution Law (Hanochi 1999).

This is a typical example of how the women trafficked into Japan have no rights or legal protection. The Japanese police and immigration authorities are not interested in protecting the trafficked victims. They only try to minimize the negative effects of the presence of foreign criminals on the "law and order" of the Japanese society. They thus meet the policy goals of the Japanese state, which ignore the security of non-Japanese women and children. This situation of insecurity of women and children from the poorer countries in Asia and elsewhere, from where the victims of trafficking come to enrich the globalizing Japanese sex industries, is not in itself a problem for disciplinary neo-liberalism and new constitutionalism since it increases the competitiveness of the Japanese service industries in the global mega-competition between corporations and states from different jurisdictions.[7]

The racist nature of the global sex industries

At the turn of the twenty-first century the Japanese state form is characterized by a growing free market orientation combined with a strong surveillance/control policy. In this sense it is not different from previous forms in combining production with security. However, it differs from its earlier forms in that it adheres to an externally defined disciplinary neo-liberalism that combines global financial competitiveness with cooperation with other industrial powers to fight against transnational criminality. The new globalized Japanese state plays a contradictory role in the regulation of the sex industries. It participates in the global campaign against the transnational criminal organizations whilst encouraging the globalizing of Japanese sex industries and the way that they increase their capital accumulation through the exploitation of women and children trafficked from poorer countries by the criminal organizations. It is thanks to the bonded slavery imposed on the women and children from poorer countries that the sex industries have become a more lucrative source of income, not only for the criminal organizations (more so than narcotics) but also for the sex industries and indirectly for the state (through taxation). By contrast the old constitutionalism of the Meiji State did not make foreign women a source of income, but rather made them the victims of military sexual slavery in its final expansionist stage. Of course the new sex industry structure of Japan is "preferable" to state-run military sexual slavery. It is nevertheless reprehensible. It protects only the security of the global market and bolsters the social reproduction of the national values and identity discourse of the Japanese state, at the expense of foreign women and children, and indirectly their families and communities. Indeed, such racism is inherited from late nineteenth- and early twentieth-century practices. However, in place of colonial rulers and military forces, it is transnational sex tourism and the search for "exotic sex" from the customers of the North that sustains the sex in and from the South – that is since the US "rest and recreation" facilities, linked to US bases, began to disappear. This pattern is intensified by the global competition of video-sex and cyber-sex industries, whilst the sex sectors of OECD countries are increasingly legalized and deregulated, allowing the reproduction of exploitation according to a racist hierarchy of "free" women, bonded workers and slaves in the sex industries. The contrast between the liberal attitude towards the legalization of sex industries and the criminalization of trafficking (that is indispensable for the competitiveness of the global sex industries) typifies the contradictions built into the disciplinary neo-liberalism of the trilateral "industrial democracies." In effect the governments of these societies reproduce racist exploitation and violence against women whilst claiming to promote women's rights as an integral part of their global "good governance" project in the developing world (Hanochi 2001).

In conclusion, the three constitutional regimes of the Meiji State under colonialism, the post-Occupation Showa State under post-colonialism, and the new globalized state under disciplinary neo-liberalism were all patriarchal under the authority of the Emperor. However, the social reproduction of its modes of gender (and racial) exploitation changed. The different moments in this process involved national familial, international commercial, and finally global disciplinary neo-liberal forms of gender exploitation. These transformations were most clearly reflected in the regulation and disciplining of the sex sector by the state, which took first the form of public brothels followed later by sex industries reproducing their sex workforce by international trafficking of women from developing countries. Finally we now see a more globalized sex sector, under neo-liberal discipline that promotes in a number of contradictory ways the global sex industries in the commodity form – whilst strengthening some forms of international cooperation and surveillance to control transnational crime, including efforts to control some of the trafficking of women by transnational criminal organizations.

Notes

1. Forms of authority over the sex sector illustrate both change and continuity not only in terms of their regulation but also in how they have affected the security of the women and children working in the sex sector.
2. The abolitionist campaign started in Britain, led by Feminists such as Josephine Butler. Butler did not attack "prostitution" *per se*. She criticized the double standards that forced women to be exploited by men, either as "virtuous wives" at home or as "depraved whores." The leadership of the abolitionist movement fell into the hands of the Christian conservative moralist Feminists in their campaign to "cleanse" society. It developed into an international campaign to combat trafficking as "white slavery," a racist project based on a class-based concept of prostitution. The "white slaves" trafficked from Europe to the colonies were meant to serve in brothels, where the colonial rulers needed (working-class) white women to complement the coloured women in prostitution to satisfy their sexual appetites. This campaign against "white slavery" was diametrically opposed to the approach of Butler who called for solidarity across classes and peoples. See Butler (1898).
3. The *Maria Luz* was a Peruvian slave ship carrying trafficked Chinese women. During a stopover in Yokohama some women escaped to the refuge of a British ship. A Meiji court heard the demand from the *Maria Luz* to return the women to bondage. Judge Ohe Taku ruled that the slaves had to be freed, and that the treatment they received on the *Maria Luz* was an abuse of their rights. However, the ruling caused an international outcry that pointed out that the *kuruwa* system in Japan was itself based on the same form of bonded slave trafficking.
4. In the 1920s Japan cooperated with the League of Nations' abolitionist efforts and participated, even after having left the League, in the Bandung Conference of 1937 called by the League to abolish trafficking in the Orient. The 1949 UN Convention continued the anti-trafficking efforts of the League and gave Japan the opportunity to improve its international image which had been tarnished by the militarist expansionism.
5. This was manifested in the new laws adopted in 1999, for example, new Guidelines for US–Japan Defense Cooperation, the National Flag and National Anthem Law, and a third statute legalizing telephone tapping by the police as one measure to develop a surveillance system against transnational criminal organizations. See Kang and Yoshimi (2001).
6. Cited in the newspaper *Asahi*, April 15, 1999.
7. In the 1990s, OECD governments became concerned at how criminal money was disturbing the (legal) global financial markets, reflected in the agendas of the 1995 Halifax G7 Summit and the 1998 Birmingham G7 Summit. In December 2000, 148 countries gathered in Palermo, Italy to attend a high-level UN conference. 121 of the countries present signed the new UN Convention Against Transnational Organized Crime, and over 80 countries signed one of its supplementary protocols – the Protocol to Prevent, Suppress and Punish Trafficking in Persons, especially Women and Children. Other supplementary Protocols Against the Smuggling of Migrants by Land, Sea and Trafficking in Firearms were also widely adopted at the end of 2001. The new UN Convention and its supplementary protocol on Trafficking in Persons have to be ratified by 40 countries before they become instruments of international law. See Ramond (2001).

Part III:
Crises, Tensions, and Contradictions

Crises, Tensions, and Contradictions: Introduction to Part III
Tim Di Muzio

The themes of Part III involve the social consequences of financial crises, new forms of flexible accumulation, the constitution of global labor regimes, deepening processes of commodification associated with sex trafficking and the informal arrangements and legal orders that sanction their existence. A common thread is that a more disciplinary neo-liberal world order corresponds with more precarious forms of social reproduction, intensified exploitation and human insecurity. This is a world where, for example, Gandhi's ethical imperative to provide security to the most vulnerable is far too frequently, perhaps increasingly, ignored.[1]

Chapter 6 by Brigitte Young bridges the themes of Parts II and III by linking questions of governance to financial crises. She seeks to go beyond economistic understandings of financial crises by focusing on their social dimensions and consequences for human security in recent Asian and Latin American crises. While many writers have sought to explain recent financial crises from a macroeconomic standpoint – chiefly concerned with why and how fixed exchange rate regimes collapse – Young suggests an alternative approach. Financial crises create massive social upheavals that impact the daily lives of the most vulnerable members of society, as well as simultaneously generating strategies for cultural and moral resistance.

In this context, Young highlights the impact financial crises have on the role of women in communities and shows how economic meltdowns not only worsen insecurity but also intensify the exploitation of women's work as one manifestation of strategies for human/household survival. For example, in Argentina the crisis increased disenchantment with the free market model of development. The popular mood in Argentina has been reflected in recent novels, television plots and plays. A Buenos Aires production, *Los Albornoz*, is a tragicomedy about a middle-class family that has sunk into poverty during the era of neo-liberalism. Its unemployed father finally turns his children to prostitution as a survival strategy.[2]

Such issues are not unique to Argentina. A recent study on the social/gender consequences of the Asian financial crisis, whilst admitting that "too little is known" about how financial crises impact the lives of the most vulnerable, nevertheless noted that women and children were "disproportionately hurt" by economic contractions. In Asia, the financial crisis has gone with increased (female) unemployment, domestic violence and prostitution. It has reduced food intake for women in the home and caused children to go looking for food in garbage dumps. It has been linked to a proliferation of the narcotic drug trade whilst there has been a decrease in vaccination and medical use drugs to combat illness (Atinc and Walton 1998: 14–23).

In this regard, Young emphasizes how precarious and gendered conditions of survival for the many are associated with security for the few. Indeed, crises are partly caused by the neo-liberal governance frameworks either externally imposed by international financial institutions or adopted by states in order to attract, maintain and protect the interests of capital and thus of financial investors. Thus societies undergoing economic crises are subject to massive unemployment, impoverishment, reduced social spending and new forms of insecurity, while capital is treated to publicly arranged bailouts.

Chapter 7 discusses aspects of the general social reproduction of the labor–capital relationship. Here Randolph Persaud draws attention to racialized aspects of the social construction of labor power as a commodity. He shows how an emerging regime of global labor supply corresponds to new forms of flexible accumulation that rest on "historically embedded racialized practices of labor exploitation." He argues that an accurate understanding of the modern global division of labor must take account of the history of specific social formations and labor market hierarchies constituted along racial, ethnic and gendered lines. Understanding racialization of labor relations allows for a more accurate reading of the power relations of production that exist between employers and workers. Indeed, the world's workers can be roughly divided between relatively "protected" privileged workers of the "primary labor market" and the many gradations of "unprotected workers." The latter experience unprotected, disposable and contingent forms of employment in the "secondary" or more primitive labor markets. In the USA the latter form of exploitation relies heavily on undocumented Third World immigrants, women, and those workers historically marginalized from secure conditions of employment.

Persaud's primary concern is, however, with how racialization of workers has operated as a device to legitimize exploitation while simultaneously creating the global labor supply required for more flexible accumulation patterns. He seeks to show how, while social reproduction and racialization of labor power is undergoing more precarious transformations, the chief beneficiaries of this emerging regime of global labor supply seem to be the new labor intermediaries and capitalist employers. This imbalance might help us explain why, in February 2002, the International Labor Organization formed the World Commission on the Social Dimensions of Globalization with an ambitious agenda to explore the impacts of globalization "on the life and work of people, on their families and their societies."[3]

Part of this dialectic of inclusion and exclusion is explored in Chapter 8, on social reproduction, human trafficking and the informal sex sector in Asia (see also Chapter 5). Again it should be emphasized that the illegal yet highly profitable trade in human beings is not unique to Asia – it is a global problem of staggering human proportions involving over 4 million people (mostly women and children) trafficked each year as victims of commercial sexual exploitation or other forms of forced labor.[4] The severity of the problem is evident not only in the number of humans trafficked each year, but also in the growing numbers of governmental and non-governmental organizations that have focused their resources and energies on combating this alarming trend. It is of course also reflected in the growth of transnational criminal syndicates, corrupt government officials and banks and financial houses that benefit from what some have called a crime against humanity.[5] According to a recent UNICEF report perhaps the most disturbing of these developments is the rapid increase in commercial sex trafficking of children "bought and sold like chattel, trafficked within and across borders, thrown into such situations as forced marriage, prostitution, and child pornography." Thus these children suffer "profound and sometimes permanent damage" (UNICEF 2001, quotes are from the Preface).

Kinhide Mushakoji's contribution also helps us to identify some of the cultural, political and economic mechanisms associated with these trends. Mushakoji focuses on the Philippines–Japan bilateral networks to explore how formal and informal mechanisms of exploitative migration and social exclusion bear on the social reproduction and human security of trafficked sex-workers. Using data from the Toyota Project/DAWN research he directed, Mushakoji argues that the *formal* mechanisms of power and production in the labor market, civil society and the state conceal the sex sector and thereby allow transnational criminal syndicates to *informally* control the sex workforce. The contradictory tension between the rule of law and informal social realities occludes these forms of exploitation from official reality. Furthermore, such patterns of exploitative migration and the complex dialectic between informalization and counter-informalization must be understood within the context of neo-liberal globalization: neo-liberal policies have served to exacerbate conditions of inequality and poverty and thus make it easier for criminal syndicates to exploit women and children from the global South.

Notes

1. Kinhide Mushakoji put this position well in his "Open letter on Human Security," sent to the United Nations in September 2001:

   Human security should refer to all human persons and all human groups. However, preference should be put on eliminating the roots of insecurity of the most vulnerable peoples, individuals and groups, as has been formulated by Gandhi as "the smallest child walking on this Earth"... It may be recognized that the justness of a society is measured by how it cares for the vulnerable, but it is not noted that the security of the society is also dependent in the long run on making security possible for the vulnerable. This concept is one that links positive and negative aspects of human security in ways that indicate they cannot be sustained without the maintenance of the most vulnerable life forms in the complex ecosystem and human civilization.

2. Anthony Faiola, "Argentina Doubts Market Wisdom." *Washington Post*, August 6, 2001.
3. A backgrounder to the Commission notes:

   Concerns and issues are often raised about the impact of globalization on employment, working conditions, income and social protection. Beyond the world of work, the social dimension encompasses security, culture and identity, inclusion or exclusion and the cohesiveness of families and communities. (ILO 2003)

4. Paula Dobriansky, "Tackling the Sex Slave Trade." *Observer*, March 2, 2003. She is US Under-Secretary of State for Global Affairs.
5. According to Article 3, paragraph (a) of the Protocol to Prevent, Suppress and Punish Trafficking in Persons, especially Women and Children, which supplements the United Nations Convention against Transnational Organized Crime, trafficking in persons:

   shall mean the recruitment, transportation, transfer, harbouring or receipt of persons, by means of the threat or use of force or other forms of coercion, of abduction, of fraud, of deception, of the abuse of power or of a position of vulnerability or of the giving or receiving of payments or benefits to achieve the consent of a person having control over another person, for the purpose of exploitation. Exploitation shall include, at a minimum, the exploitation of the prostitution of others or other forms of sexual exploitation, forced labour or services, slavery or practices similar to slavery, servitude or the removal of organs. (<www.undcp.org/odccp/trafficking_human_beings.html>)

6
Financial Crises and Social Reproduction: Asia, Argentina and Brazil

Brigitte Young

"Anti-globalists see the 'Washington consensus' as a conspiracy to enrich bankers. They are not entirely wrong."[1]

This chapter sketches a methodological approach to explore aspects of intensified globalization that relate to the spatial and temporal reorganization of social reproduction. It is intended to point towards the need for further research and indicate some of what this research might look at.

Why is this important? The International Monetary Fund has identified 158 financial crises in the period 1975–97 (IMF 1998). This number does not include the 1997/98 Asian crises and its contagion effects on Russia and Latin America. Such crises have profound implications for human security and social reproduction. Indeed, financial crises are thus neither new nor a rare occurrence, and they have come to help characterize the recent period of intensified globalization. Whether they emerge in the form of the debt crises of the 1980s, the currency crises in Europe at the beginning of the 1990s, the financial crises in Mexico, Asia, Russia, Brazil, Argentina, and Turkey in the 1980s and late 1990s, and the ongoing banking crisis in Japan, these crises underscore a growing and pervasive instability of the global financial system. When Asia, seemingly the last bastion of stability, succumbed to exchange rate problems in 1997 and financial instability spread to countries with seemingly favorable economic and monetary conditions (Eichengreen 1998), it surprised even those economic pundits who had championed the "Asian miracle." As David McNally points out, these pundits believed "that open markets and the free flow of capital would be the salvation of humankind" (McNally 1998: 1).

With such issues in mind, this chapter explores transformations in the structures of power, production and social reproduction in East Asia and Latin America. Financial crises have unequal effects across the social spectrum. They accelerate shifts in gender orders towards more marketized forms shaped by disciplinary neo-liberalism.[2] They invoke new mechanisms to reconfigure social reproduction in both OECD and developing countries. Financial crises are linked to dislocations, particularly in care and provisioning in ways that have undermined the human security of many millions of people. Such crises and dislocations are not simply the results of economic forces but can be traced directly to political decisions and the state forces that implement regimes of fiscal austerity. State policies have been locked in by new constitutional mechanisms such as fixed exchange rates and in the case of Argentina, a currency board. Such policies involve expenditure restraints and cuts in social provisions with unequal effects and burdens across the population. This chapter will therefore highlight how disciplinary neo-liberalism, despite offering some new freedoms for women (for example, to sell their labor power in the marketplace), has not brought about transformations designed to provide equal justice and emancipatory power for women. Indeed, for many people in developing countries, recent financial crises have brought economic immiseration, creating greater human insecurity and struggles for survival for both women and men. Thus some of the evidence in this chapter suggests that increasingly insecure conditions at the bottom of the world social hierarchy are consequences of, as well as conditions of existence for, the globalization from above of the elites and professional classes.

Intensified globalization, financial crises and social reproduction

When Argentina was hit in December 2001 with strikes, street battles and looting of stores, with 20 dead and hundreds injured, it signaled the failure of the neo-liberal model of intensified globalization – a process punctuated by frequent and intense economic and social crisis and a general sense of human insecurity (Gill 2003b). The crisis in Argentina, affecting also neighboring countries, was more than an economic crisis and more than a political crisis. Citizens lost trust in the viability of their political and social institutions and social cohesion was in danger of collapse (Huffschmid 2002).

The Argentine crisis – much like the Asian crisis – was not supposed to happen. After all, Argentina was the "*Wunderkind*" of the IMF and of the G7 (the seven big Western industrial countries that effectively constitute a directorate for the world economy). Argentina adhered to the IMF's prescribed market-oriented reforms, which included consolidation of the state budget, privatizing and deregulating the public sector, lowering tariffs and, crucially, fully opening its capital markets to the free movement of funds. Thus when

President Menem introduced these policies he radically broke with the interventionist and inflationist policies of the past, and in 1991 created a currency board system to create a quasi-constitutional mechanism to strengthen external discipline over macroeconomic policies and thus inspire the confidence of investors.[3] A currency board is a monetary institution that issues bills and coins fully backed by a foreign reserve currency. Thus pesos became fully convertible into the reserve currency (US dollars) at a fixed exchange rate: that is, each peso issued in Argentina would have to be fully backed by one US dollar. The aim of this was to create a policy that would be credible in the eyes of foreign investors since, because of the fixed exchange rate, such investors would reasonably perceive no threat of currency devaluation. They would thus feel protected from any possible depreciation of their capital (property and assets) caused by changing monetary conditions. This arrangement was intended to prevent capital flight (it assumed that currency and capital controls caused capital flight, rather than vice versa). Thus the aim was not only to retain capital but also to encourage foreign investment and reverse the economic stagnation that Argentina had experienced for much of its modern history.[4]

This scheme in effect abdicated Argentina's monetary independence to the policies of the US Federal Reserve but under formal IMF supervision. As a result, the domestic money supply became completely dependent on foreign capital flows (Flassbeck 2002). In the short term, hyperinflation disappeared and Argentina was able to draw in huge amounts of foreign capital, for example, to buy up its relatively cheap, newly privatized state assets. However, its currency became overvalued, partly because the American dollar appreciated considerably relative to the currencies of Argentina's major trading partners (for example, Brazil devalued its currency by 40% in 1999; the euro depreciated considerably after its introduction in January 1999). This meant that Argentina was losing competitiveness, its exports stagnated and its economy went into recession. At the same time, its national elite, the Washington financial institutions and foreign investors closed their eyes to a simple truth: whoever borrows in hard currency has to repay in hard currency, or risk a debt default. Argentina experienced a severe currency crisis in 2001 and at the beginning of 2002 it was forced to abandon its fixed exchange rate of one peso to the dollar. The ensuing crisis that now grips Argentina exceeds in its magnitude and social effects those of 1975, 1981, and 1989. Argentina is now confronted with huge increases in poverty, a destruction of its industrial base, and the breakdown of governmental functions at the national and regional levels, and an inability to service its foreign debts (Becerra *et al.* 2002).

While Brazil has not quite slithered into the economic morass like Argentina, nevertheless it also faces huge economic problems, many caused by its adoption of disciplinary neo-liberalism as its policy framework during the 1990s. In fact, the $30 billion loan that Brazil received from the IMF in September 2002 was the largest credit the IMF has ever provided for any single country. The impact of this huge financial transfusion seems to have been negligible. The Brazilian currency (the real) sank further, at times reaching record lows. That the candidate for the socialist working-class party (PT), Luiz Inácio Lula da Silva, won the recent presidential election in Brazil by a landslide and took over political power on January 1, 2003, is in no small part based on the rejection of the neo-liberal policies of President Cardoso during the 1990s. Lula's promise that fighting hunger will have priority over servicing the international debt had made him the symbol of hope for a different kind of globalization in Latin America (ATTAC 2003).

Of course, there is much more to these questions than the conventional discourse of orthodox Political Economy would allow. To explain the scope and the depth of financial crises means we need to look beyond relatively narrow "economic" questions linked to the credibility of government policies and the confidence of foreign investments. Indeed, largely absent and silenced in the orthodox academic discourses involving economic and financial crises is the social question, and specifically issues of social sustainability and social reproduction. As the editors note, many critical approaches analysing the mechanisms of the new global political economy have sought to explain crisis and transformation from the perspective of power and production. Gill has gone farther than most critical theorists challenging the intellectual community to understand globalization not only in narrow economic terms but also in terms of social and cultural transformations. Also important in his analysis are changes in economic governance – for example, currency boards, fixed exchange rates or independent central banks with low inflation targets – all intended to lock-in commitment of *future* governments to a neo-liberal framework of accumulation. These new disciplinary frameworks over macro-economic policies have as their counterpart the new bilateral, regional and multilateral trade and investment treaties (for example, the WTO) that lock in liberal policies and strong protection of property rights. In this context Gill suggests that the restructuring of global capitalism involves the restructuring of states and political power, and of society and culture (Gill 1999, 2003a).

In sum, missing in most critical theories is an understanding of how the restructuring of the world economy connects to the process of social reproduction. Partly at issue therefore is the degree to which the disciplines and competitive pressures of the new global market order tend to fragment human communities, increase social inequality and intensify human insecurities. Also at issue is the role of women. Indeed, women play a particular role in the global political economy because of their location at interstices between production and social reproduction. Their relationship to the market is more complicated than men's since they are at the crossroads of production and social reproduction.

The increasing threat to human security in the form of financial instability, income inequality, poverty and unemployment, domestic violence, civil war, environmental degradation, ethnic cleansing, and human trafficking calls for new theorizing that includes the complex layering of human concerns ranging from local and short-term needs to global and long-term requirements for human survival. In the aftermath of the Asian crises, a cornucopia of studies appeared on the academic market focusing on the macroeconomic environment leading up to the financial turmoil, but few studies link the financial instabilities to the everyday insecurity of vulnerable people. If we look from "the bottom up," we see that the financial turmoil has destabilized the conditions for survival for the mass of unskilled workers and those living at the margins. Job and income insecurity, health insecurity, environmental insecurity, and political and community insecurity have all worsened in the aftermath of the financial meltdown (Grown *et al.* 2000). But the social fragmentation, disintegration and poverty are not evenly spread across countries, classes, genders, and ethnic groups. In fact, the impacts are highly unevenly distributed.

Thus this chapter attempts to provide a Feminist and Radical Political Economy perspective. It illustrates how global financial turmoil with its devastating impacts on human security and human development is a striking example of the emerging global contradiction between the extended power of capital on the one hand, and the viability of social reproduction for most of those living in the crisis-ridden regions on the other. The first section focuses on social reproduction and how gender regimes and gender orders have been reconstituted. In the second section Asian financial crises and the human security dimensions of gender relations are analysed relative to relationships between finance, paid reproduction work and the feminization of survival. Finally, my focus is on how regional economic crises have created dislocations affecting social reproduction and provisioning of basic needs for the most vulnerable in Argentina and Brazil.

Changing governance frameworks

The current global transformation corresponds to important changes in the governance frameworks of production and social reproduction. As noted in Chapter 1, social reproduction refers to the ongoing reproduction of the commodity labor power and the social processes and human relations associated with creating and maintaining the social order.

In this context, a particular separation between "private" and the "public" was the hallmark of the industrial age. What was considered productive work was confined to the public sphere and the "economy." Work in private homes, subsistence work and to a lesser extent small artisan production for use value were generally characterized as "unproductive work." This division of labor was gendered, with specific roles for men and women. Men were expected to be breadwinners in the formal public labor market, women to be subordinated to men as care-givers carrying out unpaid "unproductive" work of social reproduction in the home. The conceptual separation between private and public of the industrial age also formed a key assumption of liberal-democratic Political Economy after World War II, despite its decreasing adequacy in an era of increasing flexibilization of women's work. Indeed, recent increasing integration of women into labor markets has also led to new definitions of gender roles. Women are now working in larger numbers as wage labor in a flexible, marketized, more individualized framework. New patterns of work challenge the public–private dualism, as do changes in family activities in the context of neo-liberal restructuring. Whether women in the Caribbean, in Asia, do such work or by those in the "global cities," its common feature is that it is a combination of activities in formal (transnational) production, in informal sector work, and in the subsistence economy of the family. The borders of these economic spaces are quite fluid for women, but relatively rigid for men (Young 2001a, 2001b).

As a result of these changes in production and social reproduction, the gender orders and regimes associated with intensified globalization are also being transformed. The concept of *gender regime* refers to institutionalized practices and forms of gendered systems of domination that are constituted as social ordering principles in all societies. Social norms, rules, regulation, and principles are not gender-neutral entities, but are inscribed with specific norms for the roles men and women are designed to play in the polity. The networks of overlapping social and cultural mores then become embedded in the institutional structure of a particular governance framework. These institutionalized but varied gender-practices are continuously reproduced. *Gender orders* are the aggregate of these gender regimes at the level of macro-politics. The interaction between state powers that bear on gender relations, cultural definitions of gender, and the historical possibilities in gender relations make up these orders. As Chapter 4 shows, they are stabilized through various micro and meso practices that ensure the reproduction of these gender orders within and across countries (Connell 1987; Young 2001b).

One hypothesis is that in the context of neo-liberal restructuring, gender orders and regimes are being radically transformed suggesting that in the process the social reproductive work is being reconfigured. However, these transformations are not the same across and within countries and regions. Instead they depend on various aspects. First we need to explore the degree to which social reproduction and the conditions for human security have been redefined as a result of the new political economy and juridical frameworks of disciplinary neo-liberalism. One would expect social transformations to be much greater in Argentina than in Brazil, given the power of capital in concert with the IMF to impose fiscal austerity and thus deflation on Argentine society. Indeed, because monetary policy was externally determined, fiscal policy became the means of economic adjustment through expenditure reductions that reduced outlays for social provisioning and the care economy. So whilst Argentina's monetary policy was effectively subordinated to US financial and political interests, and whilst Brazil was also dependent on loans from the IMF to service its international debt, Brazil still retained some sovereignty over its monetary policy, partly because it did not opt for a fixed exchange rate with the US dollar. After 1991 this was never the case for Argentina because of the currency board system it created.

Secondly, it is important to emphasize that effects of economic restructuring on social reproduction depend on the historical sexual division of labor, class divisions among women and racialized hierarchies and norms in particular social formations. For example, in my analysis of the shift of gender orders from Fordist production to intensified, disciplinary neo-liberal globalization, I have identified three major transformations:

1. the end of the family wage model and increasing feminization of the labor force;
2. reconfiguration of the public/private and production/reproduction towards changing boundaries and fluidity between the monetized and non-monetized economies;
3. increasing inequality among women due to privatization of social reproduction and its different impacts on women of different classes, races and nationalities (Young 2001b).

While these specific characteristics were originally identified as relevant to the Western industrial countries, the restructuring of the global political economy and the increasing power of capital force countries from Asia to Latin America to privatize, deregulate and liberalize their economies thereby increasing the commodification and informalization of social reproduction around the globe. The Structural Adjustment Policies (SAPs) of the IMF and the World Bank in countries that are experiencing liquidity problems have invariably shifted the costs from the paid to the unpaid economy and have increasingly exposed women to direct market forces. The Fund's policy has usually required reductions in government expenditures, cuts in real wages, reduction in domestic demand, and emphasis on trade liberalization and increasing exports. All of these measures influence gender relations by altering the relationship between the productive and unproductive (that is, re-productive) spheres, and the state's role in defining and expanding the "private" (Bakker 1994). In response to budgetary austerity, countries seem to invariably impose disproportionate reductions in the provisions for economic and social services, in attempts to avoid cutting the civil service and/or the military budget. Cuts in education, in health services, food and transportation subsidies, sanitation facilities, water access services and other care provisions hurt most those "who are members of a subordinate class, gender or ethnic group, tend not to be fully owners of their own labor, but are subject to the control of patrons, landlords, chiefs, community 'bosses', village 'headmen', husbands, fathers, to whom they have obligations which are enforced, in last instance, by overt violence" (Elson 1997: 55).

Structural Adjustment Programs have led to an expansion and deepening of the market in the countries affected and have squeezed the resources available for the maintenance of care, both unpaid care and also care services provided by the public sector (Beneria 1999). As Grown, Elson and Cagatay pointed out, the squeeze on care happens through several channels: "a squeeze on unpaid time available for care as men and women allocated more of their time to paid work; a squeeze on public provisions of care, as public expenditure was cut back in response to international economic pressures; and a squeeze on quality of care services provided by the private sector as a result of competitive pressures to cut costs" (Grown *et al.* 2000: 1147). These cost-cutting measures may in the short run increase the competitiveness of the countries by making labor cheaper and help to consolidate the state budgets. In the long run, however, the erosion of education and health care services and other public goods may lead to more crime, violence against women and children, to a decline of educational opportunities for girls, increases in HIV infections, an erosion of social solidarity, and ultimately it may lead to lower economic growth and productive potential for the country as a whole.

Exploring how regional financial crises create dislocations with unequal gendered, racialized and class-based effects in Asia and Latin America, I will focus on four key components of social reproduction (Hartsock 2001; see also Bakker in this collection and Truong 2000):

1. Biological reproduction refers to procreation and childbearing, a process of physical development of human beings. But biological reproduction refers also to the international trade in body parts (organ trade), in which humans are commodified and broken down into body parts and sold as pieces on the market.
2. Reproduction of the labor force refers not only to the sustenance of (male) workers so that they can sell their labor power in the marketplace, but also to the maintenance of women's and children's labor power either in the formal, informal or subsistence economies.
3. Reproduction of the care economy includes aspects such as cooking meals, caring for children, the elderly, community work, volunteering in NGOs, and providing a psychological "cushion" for family members as a result of economic insecurity (Truong 2000).
4. Paid "reproduction work" refers to work in the sex sector, prostitution and entertainment, including domestic work. Unique to this kind of labor power is its disposal of and control by others. Women and children are commodities in "that they are consumed, used up like other commodities" (Hartsock 2001). The existence of slave labor conditions often combined with violence, the absence of legal status, the cross-border circuits of trafficking of women and children played out in the shadow and offshore economies has remained largely invisible (Sassen 2000; Truong 2001). Exploitative sex work must also be theorized and understood as a failure

of the state to provide protection for women and children in intensified globalization, as well as part of an active state strategy linked to exploitation of women (see also Chapters 5 and 8).

East Asian financial crises and their impact on social reproduction

Singh and Zammit use "meltdown" as a signifier of what happened to the currency and stock markets in the five East Asian countries most affected by the financial crises (Indonesia, Malaysia, Singapore, South Korea and Thailand). Between July 1, 1997, and February 1998, the Indonesian stock market fell by over 80% and the currency depreciated by over 70%. In Thailand, prices fell over the same period nearly 50% and the value of the exchange rate against the US dollar declined by more than 40% (Singh and Zammit 2000: 1266). This meltdown in the financial sector generated a deep economic crisis. Gross domestic product declined in Korea and Malaysia by more than 5% in 1998; in Thailand it fell by nearly 8%, and in Indonesia by a staggering 20%. The effects of this economic downturn on poverty, real wages and employment have been equally catastrophic. According to World Bank estimates, cited by Singh and Zammit, 17 million more people in Indonesia fell below the poverty line in 1998, 2.3 million more in Thailand, more than half a million (665,000) in the Philippines, and just under half a million in Malaysia. In sum, approximately 20 million more people were added to the 30 million who already lived below the poverty line in these nations, simply as a result of the effects of the financial crises (Singh and Zammit 2000).

In most of the economic studies analyzing the East Asian financial instabilities, geopolitical factors do not play a role. Discussions are confined to the controversy of whether the crisis was due to endogenous forces (weak banking system and crony capitalism) or to the huge foreign capital movements (Eichengreen 1998; Huffschmid 2002). But as Gill has pointed out, geopolitical factors have been at work in so far as the US used its strategic power to impose a specific neo-liberal model of restructuring on Asia (Gill 1999). This point is important because it involves a shift away from state-directed capitalism in Asia toward a free market system with its emphasis on deregulation, liberalization and privatization. Once the crisis swept across the countries, the IMF moved in not only to deal with macroeconomic restructuring, but also to impose deep structural reforms that in turn removed the fragile social safety net that had been put in place during the "Asian miracle" growth period.

"Globalization from above" in the form of transnational capital and international financial institutions created the conditions that made these countries hospitable to disciplinary neo-liberal governance. The resulting dislocations in social reproduction, care and provisioning in Asia was thus not just a result of economic forces. Due to the neo-liberal strategies of state consolidation and fiscal austerity, public goods necessary to serve as safety nets have been cut intensifying the human insecurity for a large part of the population living at the margin. However, the increase in human insecurities is a topic that has vanished from the media and academic discussions. Five years after the crisis, the IMF still views the financial turmoil in Asia as a short-term phenomenon. Using aggregate data, financial analysts have stressed the positive economic growth trends, moderate inflation and the strengthening of the exchange rates in the Asian countries, when in actual fact, this macroeconomic "prosperity" has been very unequally distributed and is particularly fragile (Furtado 2000; Lim 2000; Singh and Zammit 2000).

Before we present some data on the gender dimensions of the East Asian crisis, it is well to heed Truong's warning that a Eurocentric perspective does not sufficiently come to grips with how gender differences were reconfigured during the development process of the "Asian miracle" (Truong 2000). She argues that neither the Asian miracle nor the Asian crisis and its aftermath can be understood without focusing on the "embeddedness" of gender norms that have guided much of the growth and conversely have made women more vulnerable in times of crises. She identifies a four-tier gender order for Asian countries:

1. the wage earner, constructed along male norms with a formal wage system and protection;
2. casual workers constructed along female norms and confined to temporary, part-time contracts, piece rates and irregular work. Such norms can be applied irrespective of the gender;
3. the dependent housewife – responsible for the maintenance of the workforce and care work – which may or may not combine unpaid care work with paid work;
4. paid "reproductive workers" who take up either different forms of sexualized services in prostitution and entertainment, or domestic services (Truong 2000: 161).

The particular gender ideology Truong refers to is based on the glorification of subservience and sacrifice as female virtues that are manifested in the particular gender-orders of East Asia. Indeed, the World Bank East Asia Environment and Social Development Unit also cautions about the use of aggregate statistics which do not reflect the cultural, legal and institutional differences faced by men and women. Analyzing men's and women's labor force participation in Korea, one analyst cites Confucian traditions and patriarchal family systems as the institutional basis for gender discrimination that pervades all social, and political and economic structures (Slok 2001).

East Asian gender ideology of female subservience was crucial in how women were integrated into the labor force during the period of the "Asian miracle." The shift from import-substitution to export-oriented strategies in

Asian economies led to a vast increase of women into the labor force. In Korea, women's rate of employment increased from 36.3% in 1963 to 48.7% in 1996 (Yoon 1998). However, as recent Feminist economists have demonstrated, the integration of women was based on a form of gendered wage inequality. In a fascinating study, Seguino argues that such gender inequality helped to stimulate growth in the East Asian economies. Low female wages have spurred investment and exports by lowering unit labor costs, providing the foreign exchange to purchase capital and intermediate goods that raise productivity and growth rates. These discriminatory practices were made possible by gender norms forcing women to accept their low status and low pay (Seguino 2000: 27).

It is not surprising that when the Asian financial crisis unfolded that women were more disadvantaged by the cyclical instability and economic depression than men. This in turn had devastating repercussions on the sustainability of social reproduction affecting women, children, families, and also entire communities and regions. If we look at some specific countries, we note that there are variations in how the crisis affected the gender roles in sustaining social reproduction. The unemployment rate for women in South Korea was steeper than it was for males; in Thailand and the Philippines, the burden of layoffs fell more heavily on men, but women's average wages fell more than men's. In the Philippines, women were pushed out of the relatively well-paid manufacturing sector and forced into the service sector with longer hours and lower wages. Male unemployment worsened due to the bigger declines in the industrial sectors. At a time when women were forced to shoulder greater domestic care duties, their working hours as wage earners also increased relative to men. One central coping strategy during the crisis was to increase the working hours of women, leading to more "idleness" for men due to underemployment, unemployment and shorter working hours (Lim 2000).

The case of the Philippines gives some insights into how women's working time both in regard to the labor market and the household was extended beyond physical capacity. Not only were women responsible for the reproduction and sustenance of (male) workers, they also had to carry a heavier burden to maintain their own labor power whilst spending more time caring for their families. As the state rolled back many of its public services, it was women in the home who had to make up for the goods that were no longer provided by the state. Inherent in the social norm of making women responsible for the care economy is the idea that there is an unlimited supply of unpaid female labor to compensate for macroeconomic instabilities (Elson 1997). Since economic models do not take into account production in the family unit, the private sphere counts only as an externality and women's time is assumed to be infinitely elastic. Reproductive caring was even further threatened when the Philippines were simultaneously struck with the natural calamity of the El Niño (a climate-affecting warm surface current) setting in motion an agricultural crisis with subsequent steep rises in food prices (Lim 2000).

The impact of the crisis not only manifests itself in the form of reduced employment and wages. Women are caught in a "pincer movement": "the amount of caring and unpaid household duties may increase when family members become unemployed or sick, while the economic pressures increase for women to undertake paid labor to contribute to family income, no matter how poor the remuneration and disagreeable or degrading the activity" (Singh and Zammit 2000: 1260).

In Korea, the unemployment rate was higher for women than for men. In particular, women's employment experienced a drop of 7% in the formal economy. At the same time, female daily and temporary work increased (66% of employees), whereas among male workers this figure was 35%. In addition, Korean women were substituted in the labor market at three different levels: male workers were substituted for female workers; young women were substituted for older women, and workers in insecure jobs were substituted for workers in secure jobs. The unemployment rate of Korean women fell between 1996 and 1998 by 2.8% (0.5% for men). Despite the higher unemployment rate of women, the state appealed to women to provide a psychological cushion for males who lost employment. With the slogan "Get Your Husband Energized," the state invoked the traditional norms of the men as breadwinners and women as care-givers (Singh and Zammit 2000; Yoon 1998). The World Bank's East Asia Environment and Social Development Unit concluded that the crisis did not create a new gender order, but deepened the discriminatory trends that existed before the crisis (Slok 2001).

The same asymmetrical gender effects can be seen in Thailand, Malaysia and Indonesia. In Thailand and Indonesia women were particularly hard hit by the reduction of income in the informal economy and the homework sector, and the virtual collapse of petty traders and street vendors. In the Indonesian weaving sector alone, the income of women declined by more than 75% (Singh and Zammit 2000). In Thailand, rural employment declined sharply and this decline was largely among women. It appears that many of these women had to return to housework. These changes also had very negative implications for the consumption rate of the poor. For the average poor household, food accounts for 71% of household expenditure in Indonesia and about 55% in Thailand. Zhiqin predicts that if one person per household were affected by unemployment, an increase in unemployment in Indonesia of 9 million workers since before the crisis would affect 21% of all families. Not only did the sharp decline in family income have a negative impact on the basic consumption needs of women and children. The soaring prices of medicine and health services and the reduction in employer-provided health facilities meant that women were forced to neglect their reproductive health. The availability of contraceptives has sharply declined and the health status of pregnant women has been particularly threatened, leading to a higher maternal mortality rate than prior to the crisis (Zhiqin 2000: 7).

Other authors studying the effects of the crisis have noted an increase in suicide rates, family abandonment by household heads, rising domestic and community violence, and women and children in poor households suffering from depression and delinquency (Floro and Dymski 2000). There is also some case study evidence that families pull their daughters out of school before sons. Even before the economic turmoil, girls in Indonesia were far more likely to drop out of school than boys. Once girls have left school they rarely return. Keeping girls out of school will have long-term negative consequences not only for young women, but also for the economy as a whole (Singh and Zammit 2000).

In many respects, the rigid application of austerity policies under the tutelage of the IMF that followed the East Asia financial crisis made it much more difficult for those living at the margins to survive and indeed to regain their pre-crisis economic and social position. Indeed, following the crisis an even larger number of East Asian workers have become more vulnerable and unprotected. The human effects of this increased insecurity are reflected in the huge increase in "paid reproductive work," which I discuss below.

Financial crises and paid reproductive work

Most accounts of human trafficking, prostitution, and the trade in human organs fail to link these economic activities to the financial crisis. Truong has pointed out that even many Feminists have focused only on biological and labor force reproduction and caring work, but have not included sexual work and paid reproductive work in the realm of social reproduction. As a result, the political accounts of trafficking and prostitution have been left to criminologists, human rights activists or analyzed within migration studies rather than theorized within Political Economy frameworks (Truong 2000).

But, as Sassen has pointed out, the growing presence of women in the shadow economy of prostitution, housemaids, tourism, and entertainment has become an important source of livelihood for women themselves, a source of profit for the traffickers and traders, and provides the debt-ridden governments with the much-needed foreign exchange (Sassen 2000). Two points are important in this regard. First, research does indicate that economic need is a fundamental entry point into prostitution. Second, the heavy debt burden of many developing countries plays an important role in this triangle of the feminization of survival, profit-making, and government revenue enhancement. Intensified globalization has made the conditions possible for "systemic connections between, on the one hand, the mostly poor and low-wage women often considered a burden rather than a resource, and, on the other hand, what are emerging as significant sources for illegal profit-making and as important sources of convertible currency for governments" (Sassen 2000: 524).

In the development of this new "global service industry," states are key actors. As a result of economic restructuring, and the significance of capital mobility, states derive a large part of their legitimacy today not from their own citizens but from the players in the international financial markets. No longer are welfare concerns of citizens necessarily the primary interests that drive state policies. Due to liberalization, states have been forced to enter the ring of international competition, in which they compete with other states to offer the most flexible conditions to attract foreign investment and corporations. In this reconfiguration, "competitive states" (Hirsch 1995) replace welfare states, and governments become like market actors, judged solely on narrow efficiency criteria.

As developing countries seek to become attractive "courtesans" to global capital, they often also become more dependent on remittances from migrants. If we take the case of Indonesia, for example, there are currently 1.95 million Indonesians working abroad, of which 65% are women. Already prior to the Asian crisis, remittances of these overseas workers amounted to approximately $4.8 billion. Indonesia is also notorious for its engagement in illegal trafficking. We know little about the relationship between illegal trafficking and male unemployment. Nevertheless, it is instructive to note that manufacturing wages declined in 1998 by a staggering 25.41% from the previous year.[5]

Taking another example, the remittances from migrants in the Philippines have become that country's third largest source of foreign exchange earnings. In terms of migration flows, there is an important change in gender composition since the Asian crisis. Male Philippine migrants declined after 1997, but the deployment of workers to Japan and Hong Kong, mostly women working as entertainers and domestic workers, has increased (see also Chapter 8). While there was a dramatic decline in 1998, the remittances between October and December 2000 helped to prop up the Philippine economy by strengthening the purchasing power of Philippine households and sharply boosting the gross dollar reserves of the country during the Christmas season. According to the OECD, the Central Bank of the Philippines reported the country's US dollar reserves at $14.9 billion by December 28. This was $420 million higher than the $14.5 billion at the end of November. Earnings of overseas workers from the Philippines at current prices grew by 26.4% for the year 2000 (OECD 2001).

A similar story can be told for Thailand. The number of regular emigrants rose only slightly in 1999. However, female migration has increased after the Asian crises while decreasing for males. Of the total female migrants, the number increased to 20.5% in 2000 (11.9% in 1997). We find exactly the reverse with males. Their rates had declined to 79.5% in 2000 from a high of 88.1% in 1997. One study for the period 1993–95 had already shown that the illegal economy in Thailand – including drugs, trafficking, prostitution, gambling – was estimated to have generated between $11 billion and $18 billion. This corresponds to about 8–13% of GDP (Phongpaichit and Piriyarangsan 1998). It is no wonder that the United Nations has warned that human trafficking is the fastest-growing criminal trade in the world. Profits from these criminal activities are estimated to amount to about $10 billion a year.[6]

If we return to the question of sustainability of social reproduction in the light of intensified globalization, we find the rebirth of a transnational economy of domestic labor. As pointed out above, paid reproductive work also includes domestic servants and nurses. If we take again the case of the Philippines, the Philippines Overseas Employment Administration has been active in exporting Philippine women as nurses and maids to the US, the Middle East and Japan. High foreign debts and unemployment made this a lucrative strategy for the Philippine government. Philippine workers have sent on average nearly $1 billion a year to their home government. This human export strategy coincided with the demand of the labor-importing countries. Demand for domestic workers increased in the Middle East oil-producing countries after OPEC price increases in the 1970s (Sassen 2000). In the US, the demand was great for nurses due to domestic labor shortages, a result of low wages and low prestige in the nursing sector. And in Japan, the demand for female "entertainers" increased unabatedly despite – or because – the economy was stagnating and men looked for comfort from paid reproductive workers (see Chapters 5 and 8).

However, there is another reason for the export of Asian women that has received little attention. The growing labor force participation of professional women in industrial countries is accompanied by the largely "invisible" development of paid work in the private household. Growing numbers of migrant women are employed in undeclared jobs in the household-oriented service industry, in cleaning, and as child carers, allowing more women to have professional careers. An invisible link has thus emerged between women's increasing participation in the protected, upper professional echelons of the formal labor market in industrial countries and the informal unprotected labor market roles of migrant and immigrant women.

On the one side is the "mistress" and on the other stands the "maid," separated by different racial, ethnic, class and national belongings and backgrounds (Young 2001b). It is important to recognize, however, that this development is directly linked to the neo-liberal character of globalization as this is reflected in state policy. As long as most welfare states are reluctant to provide, and are in the process of scaling back, the support structure for working women, the conditions upon which women enter "male work structures" are not just gender- but also class- and race-specific. Professional women in industrial countries, but also in developing countries, have the advantage of falling back upon mostly cheap, often undocumented migrants, to perform household tasks and childrearing. Without adequate public childcare services, and without being able to fall back on the services of women from developing and transitional countries, educated women would be less able to climb professional ladders that demand great personal mobility and flexibility. These activities are performed by (mostly) overqualified Eastern European women in Germany, or by African-Americans or Latin and Central American immigrants in the US, or Filipina women in Italy and Canada in a new international division of labor. We witness a polarization between the feminization of work for most, unprotected labor, and the emergence of a new professional class of global "workers" that includes well-educated women. Intensive globalization has increased flexibilization and individualization in the labor markets. Due to the gender norms and gender ideology of both industrial and many developing countries, reproductive work is *shared among women*. As a result, we witness a rebirth of a transnational economy of domestic labor and the rise of a privileged professional class of women and the growth of an ethnically defined female underclass (Young 2001b).

In the next section, a brief account will be given of the financial crises in Argentina and Brazil and how they created social dislocations and caused job and income insecurity, health insecurity, environmental insecurity, and political and community insecurity. This section will be kept brief. In essence, many of the factors found in Asia are replicated in Latin America. Unfortunately, there are very few studies in English about the crises and their gender dimensions. What is missing is an exploration of gender orders and gender norms in Latin America connected not only to the immediate financial crisis, but more importantly to how gender orders were transformed in the process of neo-liberal restructuring of Latin America in the 1990s. Connecting intensified globalization to the reconfiguration of gender orders in Brazil and Argentina is an important future task for Radical Political Economists and Feminist Economists. However, this is a task that cannot be accomplished in this chapter.

Argentina and Brazil: the shift to a neo-liberal governance framework

On the heels of the debt crisis of Latin American countries and the subsequent decline in *per capita* income in the 1980s followed a radical turn to neo-liberal restructuring of the import-substitution governing framework in the region. Fernando Henrique Cardoso won the election in 1994 promising monetary stability, hoping thereby to attract foreign investment and modern technology to turn around the economic malaise of the 1980s. On coming to power, Cardoso implemented the central aspects of the Washington Consensus: liberalization, privatization, deficit reduction and fiscal austerity, and deregulation. By the end of Cardoso's second term, he was faced with a financial crisis and Brazil was forced to borrow two major credits from the IMF ($10 billion and $30 billion). When the IMF granted Brazil the $30 billion loan in September 2002, it was the largest loan any single country had ever received from the IMF. Despite the financial infusion, the promised economic boom never happened. Brazil instead confronted an economic crisis and staggering social inequalities (ATTAC 2003; Huffschmid 2002).

This leads us to the choices and questions posed for Brazil in the light of the election of a left-wing president for the first time in its history. Although the new president, Lula da Silva, campaigned on a platform to fight hunger as his first priority, he nevertheless nominated Antonio Palocci, a known champion of austerity policies as Finance Minister, as a means to allay any fears that the international financial community might have of a fundamental shift in macroeconomic policies. This shows the limited room for macroeconomic maneuver that the new president feels his country has in the context of neo-liberal globalization. Thus his goals will be more difficult to finance, even with minor changes in the Washington Consensus that may allow for poverty reduction: financial markets operate on the basis of the perception of future profits flows, not the needs of the hungry. Pursuing a restrictive fiscal and monetary policy whilst claiming to fight hunger may be seen as further evidence of the contradiction between intensified globalization and the sustainability of social reproduction.

Argentina has come close to a human catastrophe in the aftermath of the economic reforms of market opening instituted by Menem in the early 1990s. Argentina declared default and in effect its bankruptcy in 2001, and the economy spiraled into depression far exceeding any recent economic crisis (for example, 1975, 1981, and 1989). Under Menem, the country initiated an extensive privatization drive of state-owned firms: telecommunications, petrochemicals and banks, earning the country about $40 billion and state surpluses in the early 1990s. By 1994, with public assets sold, such surpluses turned into budget deficits. Despite following the program of the IMF in deregulating, liberalizing and privatizing the public sector, Argentina slid into financial chaos. The international financial community hesitated for over a year to provide any new credits.

In the meantime, the country has sunk deeper into economic crisis, half of the population lives in poverty, the industry has been dismantled, and there is a general breakdown in the elementary functions of governments. Becerra *et al.* (2002) argue that it is too simplistic to put the sole blame on the "convertibility" scheme (the currency board than was in force since 1991). A better explanation these authors suggest is in the model of trade opening "imposed alongside the fixed dollar exchange rate with no regard for the effect of periodic convulsions of world capitalism, the country's peripheral position in the global economy, and above all, the last decade of neo-liberal policies" (Becerra *et al.* 2002).

A new IMF credit was finally granted for 2003, but only to allow Argentina to spread its repayments over a longer time period. At the same time, the country had to agree to very stiff new conditions. It had to achieve a budgetary surplus of 2.5% of GDP (prior to debt service), reach a 3.0% economic growth rate and a reduction of the inflation rate to 22%. Unlike the huge loan Brazil received in 2002, the IMF and the US Treasury Department refused to provide further aid to Argentina, arguing that its political class had not done enough to create the conditions for adequate (neo-liberal) "reforms."[7]

These macroeconomic instabilities, over which ordinary people have little control, have had devastating impacts on the population both in Argentina and in Brazil. If we focus on the four major aspects sustaining social reproduction (biological, reproduction of the labor force, reproduction of the care economy, and paid reproduction work), then the simple task of sustaining human life at all four levels is seriously in danger. The effects in Argentina are particularly devastating given the overall wealth of the country. Of the 37 million inhabitants, it is estimated that 53% live at the poverty level, and 15 million live under extreme poverty (set at an income of $2 a day). According to a *Washington Post* article on May 3, 2002, an estimated 8,000 people were falling into poverty on a daily basis. To make matters worse, the discrepancy between poor and rich has increased. According to one commentator, the richest 10% in Buenos Aires have 54.6% of the total income while 50% of the population with the smallest income have 8.7% of total income. In terms of gender, 7 out of 10 of the lowest-income inhabitants in the city of Buenos Aires are women (Spieldoch 2002: 14).

Particularly devastating has been the impact on educational opportunities for adolescents. For a country that has achieved one of the highest literacy rates (96% in 1999), 50% of Argentine adolescents aged 13–17 have not completed high school. Riley has pointed out that girls are the most deprived due to cultural restraints, household poverty, child labor and social roles (Riley 2002). Depriving children of schooling will certainly have long-term consequences for economic growth in Argentina and will widen the discrimination between males and females.

With increased unemployment and a stagnant economy, food security in Argentina is developing into a national crisis. The death rate of children has risen quite dramatically. The director of the local children's hospital in the Northern province of Tucumán commented that three or four more hospitals are needed to take care of all the undernourished children. While the Argentine government spent $650 per capita on health services in the province of Tucumán in the past, the amount spent today is $140.[8] Although the country produces 99 million tons of food each year and is capable of feeding a population ten times its size, Argentina has to rely on food assistance from Spain (Spieldoch 2002).

The situation for Brazilians living at the margin is no less catastrophic. The IMF "rescued" the Brazilian economy in 1999 with additional loans tied to conditions that forced the country to reduce the state's role in the economy, open internal markets to foreign investors, make the labor force more "flexible" and to deregulate investment controls. Placing the interests of international investors above social concerns resulted in a social expenditure cut of 23.7% of total costs in 1999, affecting such programs as the fight against poverty; support for needy children, senior citizens, and the disabled; the eradication of child labor, and land reform. The Brazilian *Social Watch Report* concluded: "The social situation of Brazilians is profoundly marked by one of the highest rates of social inequality in the world and by an absurd level of concentration of wealth" (Carvalho *et al*. 2000).

Added to the existing inequality of income and opportunity between men and women in Brazil is the high degree of inequality *among* women based on race and class. In 1998, the average monthly income for black and brown men was 46% of the average white male income. In contrast, a black woman earned only 40% of a white male income. White women were able to close the wage gap between males and females from 68% in 1987 to 79% in 1998. Black women were not able to close this gap. In fact, black women earned 39% less than white women in 1998 (white 79%, black 40%, measured as a percentage of income of white males). This inequality has largely to do with how black women are integrated into the labor force. Overwhelmingly, they are segregated into doing paid reproductive work in white households. In 1995, domestic workers represented 19% of the female economically active population. This represents in absolute numbers some 50 million of which 56% are black (Carvalho *et al*. 2000). This racialized and class-based division of labor between a white "mistress" and a black "maid" is not new to Brazil. What is new is the increase and pervasiveness of informal work as a survival strategy for many women segregated by different racial, ethnic, class and national belongings and backgrounds.

One of the very few English studies on the gender implications of the Argentine crisis argued that even this survival strategy of (women doing women's work) has been threatened in Argentina (Spieldoch 2002). When the government decided to freeze the bank accounts of everyday citizens, the middle class was hurt most directly by this action since they no longer had access to their money.[9] The *corralito*, as the freezing of people's savings account has become known, has also had indirect negative repercussions for the poor, since they are driven from formal into informal work, or those already in informal domestic reproductive work have lost even this meager source of income.

What is to be done?

The brief account of financial turmoil and those dependent on government social provisions in Argentina and Brazil has similarities to the Asian situation. The problem is not just one of consolidation of the budgets and fiscal austerity. More important is the political change associated with disciplinary neo-liberalism and how this is locked-in by new constitutional devices. As governments are forced to consolidate the state budgets and to strengthen the legal protection of private property in order to attract foreign investment, they are also forced to comply with IMF and World Bank reform initiatives that involve the privatization of social services – irrespective of whether it endangers the very fabric of social life or threatens the survival of the most vulnerable. Once privatized, these public goods are transformed into entities that are simply judged by profit criteria and no longer provided on the basis of human needs. This may be giving rise to a new global situation where the human insecurity of most of the world's population is increasing.

Women play a particular and precarious role in this interstice between production and social reproduction. The manufacturing sector is often the first to lay off workers (both men and women). It seems to be that women who lose their jobs in this way find new employment either in the more precarious, low-paid service sector or as paid reproductive workers. Longer working hours and the lower wages then coincide with increasing demands of caring for their families. This caring refers not only to cooking, and caring for children, the disabled and the old; it also refers to the psychological "cushion" that the traditional gender norms ascribe to women. As men lose jobs and fail in their socially prescribed roles to function as providers for the family, "there is a loss of pride and a sense of shame" (Spieldoch 2002: 17). Many studies have documented that under such circumstances domestic violence increases, men abandon families or are forced to relocate to find new work, and women have become heads of households. These shifts disrupt traditional social and gender roles and orders.

As we indicated earlier, one has to be careful not to make normative judgments about the disruption of traditional gender orders that are often highly discriminatory and abusive towards women. However, the change in gender orders has not resulted in greater emancipatory power for women to demand equal justice, largely because it is the result of greater economic immiseration for both women and men, leaving both worse off in the process. Having been robbed of the social safety net and the traditional protection of families and men, women and children seem to bear the brunt of the consequences of intensified globalization.

Nonetheless, ever more voices for radical policy change can be heard. Even the "masters of the universe" at Davos can no longer ignore demands for "deglobalization" (Bello 1999). New forces proclaim that "a different world is possible." Indeed, in countries affected by these economic dislocations, new forms of democracy are in the making. Women workers in South Korea, paid reproductive workers and landless peasants in Brazil, workers in the informal sector of Argentina together with the middle class, whose wealth has diminished – all find themselves in popular protest against "globalization from above." So rather than seeing the present situation only in negative terms, popular protest in Argentina is a historic moment that represents an opportunity for change. The protests are not restricted to large urban areas but also occur in the provinces, in farming areas and in former natural-resource depletion areas (Spieldoch 2002). Women are important actors in these protests. The Madres de la Plaza de Mayo have a 20-year history in Argentina of non-violent protests against the human rights abuses of the military government and are also involved in the recent protests. Other groups such as the local assemblies and the youth movement (including young women) have joined in. Women have called for a National Truth Commission, modeled on the South African experience, to bring those responsible for the intensive economic mismanagement and corruption to account (Gago and Stzulwar 2002; Spieldoch 2002).

In sum, looking at the present battle between the globalization from below challenging the globalization from above, we seem to witness a "clash of globalizations" (Gill 2001a) between owners of capital with their shareholder-dominated society against those who wish to see a wider range of stakeholders participating in crucial social, political and economic decisions. This counter-movement itself serves to form political limits to intensified globalization and gives rise to new forms of democracy.

Notes

1. "A Plague of Finance." *The Economist*, September 9, 2001.
2. Of course one should exercise great caution in making any normative judgments about the virtues of traditional social relations since many of these are frequently abusive towards women.
3. A currency board system is similar to a fixed exchange rate that unifies two currencies. However, unification would only have been complete if Argentina had accepted full dollarization and effectively eliminated its own currency, allowing only US dollars to circulate, an option contemplated by President Menem in 1999.
4. Editors' note: in this perspective Argentinean policy would only have been fully credible if the spread of interest rates between loans issued in pesos and those issued in US dollars had been close to zero, indicating identical levels of currency risk. In reality the spread (that is, the risk premium) was often much wider than this during the 1990s, indicating less than full confidence by mobile investors in the credibility (sustainability) of the currency board system. They were to be proven correct in 2002 when the system collapsed.
5. Asian Migrant Centre, 1998, <migrantnet.pair.com/files/Rindonesia98.htm>
6. "Das Zehn-Milliarden-Dollar-Geschäft." *Frankfurter Rundschau*, February 27, 2002.
7. "Atempause für Argentinien." *Frankfurter Rundschau*, January 18, 2003.
8. "Die Klinikbetten für sterbensschwache Kinder reichen. Längst nicht mehr." *Frankfurter Rundschau*, November 23, 2002.
9. Editorial note by Tim Di Muzio and Alejandra Roncallo: while most Argentines could not access their money in banks after the capital control decree of December 3, 2001, on the day before it came into force the security of capital was protected by 385 armored trucks filled with money driven to the International Airport outside Buenos Aires and US$20 billion in cash is said to have left the country bound for the US, Paraguay and Uruguay by plane. A further $10 billion is also said to have been moved offshore *after* the controls were implemented. See Marcela Valente, "Argentina: Food Emergency as Gov't Looks into Capital Flight." Inter Press Service, January 16, 2002.

7
Power, Production and Racialization in Global Labor Recruitment and Supply

Randolph B. Persaud

This chapter analyzes the racialized dynamics of general social reproduction to explore ways in which the labor–capital relation as a totality is reproduced, albeit through different configurations of social relations, institutional forms, and ideological frameworks. Considerable emphasis is placed on the strategies of securing labor supply. Studying historical tendencies of labor supply affords an opportunity to examine various regimes and patterns of accumulation. Since all processes of accumulation have socially necessary objective conditions for stable reproduction, the analysis carried out here is also about those very conditions.

According to Marx, value is produced through a process where the direct producer sells his/her labor power to capital. The transaction, that is, the labor power sale, however, is not an arbitrary act outside of a general system of social relations with definite institutional cohesion. In fact, setting up such a general system is what takes place in the process of the *subsumption of labor by capital*. Indeed, capitalist accumulation has historically been dependent on extending the scope of the labor–capital relation by drawing in more and more labor power. Thus Marx writes:

> The *process of accumulation* is itself an intrinsic feature of the capitalist process of production. It entails the *new creation of wage-labourers*, of the means to realize and increase the available amount of capital. It does this either by extending its rule to sections of the population not previously subject to itself, such as women and children; or else it subjugates a section of the labouring masses that has accrued through the natural growth of the population. (Marx 1976: 1061)

Marx further states: "Capitalist production is not merely the reproduction of the relationship: it is its reproduction of a steadily increasing scale" (Marx 1976: 1062). Two things should be clear so far. Firstly, subsuming labor power hitherto outside of capitalist commodification brings about the labor–capital relation. Secondly, the reproduction of the said relation is achieved by the diffusion of the conditions of subsumption itself. What this chapter does is to show how the internal subjugation of an (internal) accrued laboring mass, and the "steadily increasing scale" has each involved processes of racialization. The first process has involved internal racialization of labor power, an example of this being the racialized status of Irish labor. The second process refers to both the outward expansion of capitalism on a worldwide scale, plus securing labor power by voluntary and involuntary movement of labor. So three general forms of labor supply receive sustained attention here; namely slavery, indentureship, and modern labor migration, with the last given most attention.

Slavery relied on coercion, the use of physical force, in combination with legal instruments, as a means of guaranteeing the stable reproduction of such labor power. Indeed, labor systems are rarely if ever formed outside of the political and legal frameworks that constitute who are deemed to be political and legal subjects, and (in the case of antiquity) those who are not, such as slaves. Thus ancient slavery involved not only violence and dehumanization, but also deprived slaves of legal personality and citizenship, and slaves were treated as mere instruments of labor. Slaves were not considered to be legal persons, whereas of course, their owners, as citizens, were. Perry Anderson has noted that "in Roman theory, the agricultural slave was designated an *instrumentum vocale*, the speaking tool, one grade away from the livestock that constituted an *instrumentum semi-vocale*, and two from the implement which was an *instrumentum mutum*" (Anderson 1974: 24–5). Agricultural slavery in antiquity was built on a notion of beast of burden, and urban slavery involved "the reduction of the total person of the labourer to a standard object of sale and purchase..." (Anderson 1974: 25). Labor power in modern slavery was also formulated and reproduced in the emerging capitalist world economy through juridical reification of the slave. *Indentureship* was employed both before and after modern slavery. The ingenuity of this system of labor supply was that it took the legal form of the *contract*, but maintained extensive use of coercion as an instrument of reproduction. In both instances, as this chapter shows, "race" became an element in the "discursive economy" that "allowed" a simultaneous claim to rationality/modernity and juridical/substantive inequality.

The issue of modern *labor migration* takes up the bulk of the analysis. Here the argument is that labor supply in the modern world economy involves complex dynamics at the level of social formations, states, and world orders. The argument has two components. Firstly, while the world economy has increasingly required foreign labor, cultures of racism at the level of social formations have acted as fetters on foreign labor supply. The task of the state has been to negotiate between these two forces. This has required states to be innovative because the foreign labor is often doubly discounted – partly because of supposed lesser worth, and partly because foreigners supposedly take away jobs from domestic workers. States dealing with these pressures successfully might be described as *slick states*: they have negotiated the twin pressures of global and local forces with acumen. A second component of my argument pertains to how global labor migration is a conduit for the emergence of a new development in labor subsumption and availability. The development is occasioned by the rise of hyper-flexibility of labor *and* the coexistence of both relative and absolute regimes of exploitation in the same social structure of accumulation. The relative (intensive) regime is built on increased rates of exploitation, while the absolute regime (extensive) is built on supplying the daily operational needs of the intensive sector of the "new economy."

In order to proceed more systematically, it is necessary to map out some of the broad structural developments that underpin the new economy. The most important of these developments are:

(a) the rapid transformation of modes of social relations accompanying shifts towards ideas-based value production and, more broadly, the consolidation of service oriented economies in the Western industrialized states and Japan;
(b) the simultaneous immigrantization, racialization, and feminization of the processes of labor market segmentation, which themselves have been deepening since the onset of global monetarism;
(c) the production of a new hegemonized common sense about the "proper place" of diasporic populations in advanced countries; and
(d) the extent to which these latter phenomena, when combined, form the basis for a new global culture founded on racio-cultural and marketized notions of worth, value, and identity.

An understanding of these phenomena might be fruitfully pursued through analysis of what is clearly called an emerging regime of global labor supply. This chapter therefore demonstrates the ways in which this emerging regime is built upon historically embedded racialized practices of labor exploitation. Specific attention is paid to forces governing the movement of immigrant labor.

The growth in use of immigrant labor has as much to do with questions of control of the labor process, as with problems of labor shortage or price (in the form of wages). The labor control thesis, however, cannot be divorced from the assumption (or probability) that foreign labor of certain national, racial, ethnic, or cultural background is either more accepting, susceptible, or vulnerable to outrageous exploitation. This is a special kind of exploitation, different from the technical definition of extraction of surplus outlined by

Marx. It involves extreme economic exploitation *and* conditions of work that involve forms of dehumanization, near or complete industrial and political disenfranchisement, and racio-cultural quarantine. Quarantine implies a complex of practices, which involve the spatial regulation of foreign laborers, as well as debarment from any claims to the privileges of citizenship. In liberal democracies such debarment is the formal legal expression of a culture of *containment*. A culture such as this is not the logical preserve of any nation or people, but at the same time it is not without an ancestry.

Today more than 100 million people live in countries in which they were not born, and there are about 54 million migrant laborers in foreign countries. While these numbers are statistically insignificant in terms of the global labor force, the actual impact of immigrant labor can only be properly appreciated in terms of its sectoral locations, the countries where it is concentrated, and the social, political, and cultural responses which its presences elicit. But beyond these ways to analyze immigrant labor, there are in fact other aspects of the question that are distinct and that must be carefully examined to allow for an understanding of the deep imbrications of racio-cultural dynamics and labor supply. Before this is done we need to look at explanations of why people migrate.

Migration theory

The most widely accepted understanding of migration is articulated through "push–pull" theory: people move on account of unfavorable conditions in their home country, combined with favorable conditions in the host or receiving country: "'Push factors' include demographic growth, low living standards, lack of economic opportunities, and political repression, while 'pull factors' are demand for labor, availability of land, good economic opportunities, and political freedom" (Castels and Miller 1993: 19). Push–pull explanations are underpinned by the assumption that migrants are rational economic beings who make a cost-benefit analysis of their life-chances. This links to Neo-Classical price equilibrium theory, that is, such rational individuals will move from low-wage areas (or sectors) to places which offer higher remuneration.[1] In the long run the mobility of labor (and capital) is supposed to equalize severe price distortions for labor, thereby bringing an end to labor migration. This assumes perfect knowledge, free mobility, and actual markets in labor, conditions that are difficult to meet on account of cultural and political reasons.

Labor recruitment theory offers a similar explanation for migration, but places emphasis on the process of recruitment, and the considerable organized effort of employers to obtain labor (Repak 1995: 11). The process of recruitment is dynamic and cumulative in that initial migrants, once settled, are expected to generate chain migration. The latter is supposed to ensure a constant supply of (cheap) labor. Some scholars have modified labor recruitment theory by adding the variable of gender. The argument is that labor recruitment is not gender-neutral since evidence indicates that many employers prefer to hire women, particularly if the tasks they are brought to perform are socially, economically, and culturally *constructed* as "women's work."

Push–pull and labor recruitment theories are micro-theories in the sense that they tend to focus on the personal attributes of the migrants, and in some instances, on the proximate circumstances of recruitment. However, these theories are weak because of what they omit from their explanations. They are behavioral theories built essentially on *individual* actions, except when gender is factored into the analysis. An alternative approach is to take cognizance of behavioral factors but situate them in a more structural analysis. Two theoretical perspectives attempt to do this: migration systems theory, and historical structural theory.

The structural approach focuses on the institutional structures that generate and sustain migration flows. The movement of people on a large scale may be seen as a collective phenomenon tied to developments in the world economy (Castels and Miller 1993: 22). In migration systems theory, specifically, the sending and receiving countries are units of an international system. Castels and Miller put it thus:

> Another way of stating the migration systems approach is to say that each specific migratory movement can be seen as the result of interacting macro and microstructures. Macro structures refer to large-scale institutional factors, while microstructures embrace the networks, practices and beliefs of the migrants themselves. This type of analysis presupposes an historical approach based on a concept of global interdependence. (Castels and Miller 1993: 22)

A major claim of systems theory is that despite the variability of migratory movements, certain patterns and regularities are decipherable. The most prominent of these are that young, economically active men migrate (first), usually to save money for personal and family betterment. Some of the migrants return home, but others stay and in due course send for spouses and/or other relatives. Permanent settlement occurs as a result (Castels and Miller 1993: 24–5).

Historical structural theory is remarkably similar to systems theory in that it considers the macro structures and institutions critical to an understanding of migratory flows. The key difference between the two is ontological. Whereas systems theory characterizes the global system as one of interdependence, historical structural theory sees a world capitalist system defined through a global division of labor, with its structures, institutions and social relations, including gender relations, fundamentally informed by the dynamics of accumulation and social reproduction. Historical structural theory argues that the key issues involve how the requirements for accumulation, expansion and reproduction are secured. Methodologically, this entails analysis of both the intended actions of the relevant agents *and* the underlying structures and tendencies extant in the global capitalist economy. The behavioral elements of migrants matter only if objective conditions occasion migratory flows. For the purposes of this chapter the most important condition is the problem of "scarcity" of cheap controllable labor.

Historical structural theory places emphasis on the early development of the world capitalist economy which relied heavily on cheap and/or free labor. Thus according to Sassen there were two predominant systems of labor supply in its formative stages: (a) forced movements of people from one area of the periphery to another, and (b) the subjugation of indigenous and hitherto autonomous populations and their forced transformation into laborers (Sassen 1988: 31–2). In the colonization of the Americas this involved various means of forced labor, including slavery, *mita* (citizens were obliged to work for part of the year for the colonial state), peonage (servitude based on indebtedness of the laborer or *peon* to the creditor), *encomienda* (compulsory tribute paid by natives to the conquerors from the product of their lands), and tribal contract labor (Bannon 1966; Simpson 1929). Labor "scarcity" as used by Sassen means "Any situation in which the characteristics of the labour supply threaten existing or foreseeable levels of accumulation..." (Sassen 1988: 27). Absolute and relative scarcities may be delineated, but more importantly the form that the labor supply system itself takes must be differentiated on the basis of the extent of development of the productive forces, and specifically on the organic composition of capital: "In areas where the surplus-generating possibilities exceeded the local labour supply and there were economic or technological constraints upon the substitution of labour by capital, the new enterprises imported workers" (Sassen 1988: 29).

In this framework therefore migratory flows are seen partly as the result of foreign investment, generally from the industrial economies to the developing countries. Foreign investment tends to disrupt the material bases of economic and social reproduction, usually through the commodification of social relations of production, restructuring of land tenure, and the gradual transformation of culture.

Despite their various strengths, a common weakness of these perspectives on migration is that they tend to either miss or under emphasize the raciocultural factors *governing* and *regulating* labor migration. Secondary status accorded to racial factors in part stems from treating labor as a dehistoricized and abstract category: either as a factor of production in Neo-Classical theory, or as a producer of value in Marxist perspectives. What is suggested here, however, is that the cultural history of the modern global division of labor and of specific social formations within the world system has constructed labor market hierarchies which are essentially defined by race and ethnicity. Race and ethnicity, combined with gender, therefore, are *generative* of the patterns of labor practices, that is to say, who does what, where, the rewards that appertain, and the worth conferred on particular kinds of labor activity. These patterns are direct descendants of various forms of racialized labor regimes, colonial practices, and practices of sovereignty.

Indeed, new patterns of accumulation have been increasingly built on a deepening of labor segmentation, both in the global division of labor and in national social formations. The most generalized aspect of this segmentation is to be found in the crystallization of core (protected, established) workers in the primary labor market, and contingent (unprotected, non-established) workers in the secondary labor market (Harrod 1987: 1–43). These are not simply different categories of workers delineated only on the basis of skill, income, or sectoral location (Cox 1987: 55–63). Whilst both may belong to the "enterprise labor market," different social relations separate them. Protected workers are an integral part of an organization and receive relatively privileged conditions and remuneration. They have greater job security, better working conditions, higher pay, scheduled merit reviews, benefits such as health care provision, retirement packages, liberal leave of absence arrangements, and so on. They also often have formalized representation, usually through unions. They might also have performance bonuses, stock options, and other instruments of non-salaried compensation.

These conditions contrast with those of "unprotected" workers. New immigrant workers usually from Third World countries are a fundamental part of this stratum, as are African-American workers in the USA. The attributes of this sector are: low wages, considerable insecurity, poor or even dangerous working conditions, little or no benefits, and virtually no representation.[2] Perhaps most telling, these workers are considered *disposable*. Their employment is precarious not only on account of market fluctuations, but also because workers in an entire operation have to accept such terms and conditions of work. Efforts aimed at representation are met with swift retribution, for example, withholding pay, firing, reporting undocumented workers to the authorities, violence, or, in extreme situations, relocation of the operation.

Non-established workers in this enterprise mode straddle a fine line between the primary and secondary labor markets. Indeed, workers in this category are getting closer and closer to those that are in the primitive labor market proper. The latter is characterized by informality and exaggerated contingency. Whilst they are not in a formal market, there are in fact principles, norms, and expectations governing their recruitment, compensation, and conditions of work. Their malleability is in fact part of their attraction to employers.

To grasp the totality of the new forms of labor practices it is important to take account of the interconnectedness of workers' vulnerability and disposability on the one hand, and the new patterns of labor market flexibility, on the other. Labor market flexibility is one component of a new structural configuration of state–society relations, modeled after some notion of abstract liberalism. A complex of material, juridical, and political elements have fused together producing a new hegemonized common sense which articulates the abstract logic of the market with the historically embedded property rights expressed in *menum et tuum*. The political aspect has its origins in the undoing of the post-war industrial consensus and the sustained attack against not only organized labor, represented as an impediment to market efficiency. Flexibility has a double existence, as a new institutional form of labor procurement, control and discipline, and as a nodal point of an emerging macro-cultural system of inside/outside.

As noted above, there is a recursive relationship between disposability and flexibility, and the imbrications of these two "instances" has given rise to various institutional forms of labor supply. Thus labor recruitment companies sell not only the labor power of the laborer, but also the disposability of his/her labor power. Disposability itself is thus part of the commodity. Again, the crux of disposability is not restricted to adjustment of the quantity of labor power, but to a larger project of separating the worker from the employer. This is clear if one takes even a cursory look at recruitment/supplier companies. Cumberland Labor, a supplier of temporary labor, for example, informs businesses that among the reasons for contracting with them are: (a) "The rising cost of legislated and other employee benefits, especially health care"; (b) "An alternative to ease the reluctance of full-time hiring."[3] A Texas warehouse manager who contracted with Labor Ready (another major supplier of labor) observed: "It's convenient to get some people when you need them, and then when you don't need them, they go away." And again, "You don't have to worry about laying them off."[4]

Labor Ready was founded in 1989 and it bills itself as the "McDonald's of temporary labor" in the USA. The company has close to 500 offices and "employs" over 50,000 people. Labor Ready has also opened offices in Europe and has plans for further expansion. By contrast, Pt. Orienta Sari Mahkota Labor Services of Indonesia must be the mother of all such enterprises in Asia, supplying labor to Malaysia, Singapore, Australia, Japan, Korea, Arab Emirates, Kuwait and many other countries. It expects to "develop the next years together with the globalization era" (*sic*). Companies such as these specialize in light manufacturing and low-skill services such as cleaning and gardening. Others provide "body shop" operations: "high-tech" and highly skilled workers, especially in computer software and health care. In many instances these workers are simply "leased" to the company that requires the labor service. This form of labor supply may be called *deployment*, since in essence labor contractors simply gather, organize and move the laborers.

Secondly, there is a rising *spot market* form of labor supply.[5] This form is pervasive in the USA, and if the pattern of exporting the US model continues, may become a worldwide phenomenon. Its workers gather at places of convenience and await labor contractors who turn up and, depending on their "labor orders" for the day, select those desired. Despite its informality this method of labor recruitment and supply is actually quite structured.

Information for and on the market concerning wage rates, working conditions, treatment by the bosses, and security vis-à-vis the immigration authorities, work availability, and so on, is not only provided by "word and mouth" but also the "hire" is also done without written transaction. In the USA the vast majority of these workers are recent immigrants (mostly from Central America and Mexico), with a substantial amount being undocumented. This form of unprotected labor is located in the primitive labor market.

There is also an additional form in which the worker is deemed "self-employed," in the sense of the self-employed owning his/her own labor. In this instance there is no employer and employee, only a contract *administrator*, such as Odco, the firm that may well have invented this form. In the Odco mode, a contract administrator performs some but not all the functions that "traditional" employment agencies undertake. Agencies contract the workers and then hire them out for a profit. One thing that is clear in this "arrangement" is that it is essentially a legal invention and indeed the system got its legal sanction from an Australian High Court ruling in 1991. The key finding of the court was that this system is not based on a contract either "of" work, or "for" work, but "to" work. The worker is "self-employed" because the agency claims to be simply "administering" the contract between the end user and the contractor – who in this case is what we usually call a worker.

A third form of labor supply follows more established patterns of employment, defined here as a direct transaction between employer and worker. In this instance there is an "*immigrant pool*" of laborers who constitute a flexible reserve of labor, living close to the places where their labor services are usually required. The immigrant pool form may be delineated also on the basis of their conditions of entry, stability of residence, legal status, property ownership, and political representation. An immigrant community must be distinguished from an *immigrant pool*. The latter is part of the former, but the reverse does not hold.

The developments described above may be understood within a broader context of not so much the disappearance of work, but the *disappearance of employment*. These developments have their origins in a long and sustained effort by capitalists and political forces associated with their interests, in beating back any organized form of action, representation, or even thinking on the part of those who sell their labor power for a living. The record of union-busting activities is well established. But the developments that are emerging seem to go beyond the more general erosion of organized labor. Entirely new "models" are emerging equipped with new juridical frameworks and legal sanctions. In an immediate sense, these developments do not have any necessary relationship with processes of racialization, but, as will be shown shortly, leaving the latter out would be to misunderstand the process and its associated historical conditions of emergence. The connections have to do with questions of control and disposability in ways that need to be reformulated and theorized.

Racial and cultural aspects of disposability

Our attention thus far has been focused principally on transformations in labor markets, with an emphasis on deepening segmentation. References have also been made to race, gender, and immigrants, but the relationships of these to transformations need to be linked systematically. When this is done it will become obvious that the developments generally understood as globalization are simultaneously practices of racio-cultural exploitation and marginalization.

Recall that liberal economic theory, and specifically push–pull theory, suggested that labor moves from low-wage to high-wage areas. There is considerable evidence for this. Millions of people have moved across borders in search of better economic rewards. But that is, so to speak, only half the story. The question to ponder is, how do we explain that some people have been allowed to follow the logic of the "price mechanism," whilst others have not? In a world system which prizes sovereignty as the salient value, control of borders is both an expression of that value and an instrument of its instantiation. At one level, government, in the form of policy-making and enforcement, practices this sovereignty. At another level, sovereignty has to be understood in terms of the cultural assumptions and the balance of social forces in the social formation.

In some societies there are comprehensive and deeply embedded systems of racio-cultural taxonomies. These are essentially macro systems of inside/outside in which the claims of authentic belonging to the national space are restricted to a dominant group. The criterion of inclusion simultaneously inscribes those who are not allowed in. Race *works* in constituting these systems of inside/outside. Race is thus a verb, a kind of *action*, active in the *making* of social phenomena. The important question to ask, therefore, is not "What *is* race?" but "What does race *do*?"

Responses to the first question have shown that it is difficult if not fruitless to attempt an answer. The general consensus is that "race" is more than a set of morphological features, and has very little to do with questions of intelligence or other kinds of abilities which are explainable as natural. It is now widely accepted that "race" is socially constructed, and that just about any attribute can be made into a racial signifier. In this view the signs of race are, therefore, arbitrary, and the meaning of race is contingent. However, the answer to the question "What does race do?" needs to be answered with less focus on the fluidity of meaning, and more on the *making* of "society." Indeed, in answering the question "What does race do?" it is also necessary to ask, "For whom, and for what purpose?"

These issues will become clearer as we look at labor supply practices. As a general observation it might be noted that, in part, what permits labor disposability and other forms of control is how those deployed, for example, in the spot markets or labor pools, are (with major exceptions) largely people who have already been reduced in the cultural hierarchy of the receiving nations.

Labor supply and labor control: colonies and elsewhere

Labor supply developments have strong connections with previous patterns of movement, although, of course, there are distinct elements of the current conjuncture. Two specific points need to be underlined here. First, the onset of major migratory flows coincided with structural turns in patterns of capitalist accumulation. Secondly, each turn produced its own hierarchy based upon some combination of racio-cultural, ethnic, and economic characteristics. Slavery developed essentially as a form of labor in an extensive regime of accumulation, and it was controlled and disciplined through the preponderant use of coercion. Whilst there were juridical frameworks governing the slave mode, these were essentially concerned with the slave as a form of property, rather than as a person. The 1857 Dred Scott decision in the USA, which denied that slaves were citizens, was symptomatic of this. But how could slave-holding societies maintain discourses of freedom, democracy, individual rights, and so on, whilst denying these principles in the predominant form of labor supply; namely the slave trade, and bondage? This contradiction was resolved (for the slave holders and their defenders) by reducing the enslaved to a position below the status of human. Race was invented as a comprehensive system of equivalences through which "whiteness" and various othernesses were produced. The discursive formations emphasized the supremacy of the white Christian in ways that were often expressed as philosophical knowledge, history, and law, and these helped to provide the cultural infrastructure where in which forcible confinement, corporal punishment, torture, and various other forms of violence were legitimized.

Slavery had not even ended when attention was focused on developing a new form, or at least a reinvention of an old one: indentured servants. In the Caribbean, the dawn of the end of the slave trade in the early nineteenth century with the commitment to abolish slavery had by 1834 raised anew the question of the scarcity of the supply of "controllable" labor. It was with a view to resolving this problem of labor supply that John Gladstone wrote to Gillanders, Arbuthnot & Company in Calcutta on the subject of Indian labor: "It is of great importance to us to endeavour to provide a portion of other labourers, whom we might use as a set-off, and when the time for it comes, make us, as far as possible, independent of our Negro population" (quoted in Scobie 1840: 4). The impulse to become "independent" of the Negro population was because in the late Caribbean slavery era, the control of the planters started to weaken, beaten back time and again by labor revolts. The slaves had begun forming Task Gangs through which they negotiated some aspects of their work. This is what Gladstone and other planters wanted to avoid. The solution was "bound labor." Gillanders replied that they had been in the trade of indentured labor with success in Mauritius and they went on to identify the Hill Coolies of Bengal within their larger global racial ideology that legitimated the institutionalized subjugation of supposed "lesser peoples." The coolies, wrote Gillanders, have "hardly any ideas beyond those of supplying the wants of nature... [They are] more akin to the monkey than the man. They have no religion, no education, and in their present state, no wants, beyond eating, drinking and sleeping; and to procure which, they are willing to labour" (Scobie 1840: 5).

Laborers from India were, however, not the first indentured servants. As far back as the seventeenth century poor whites made up a sizeable indentured class of workers in the Caribbean, and in Virginia as well. The racial dialectics in the two periods, however, were different. In the earlier episodes of indentureship the poor whites were split away from the other laboring classes on the basis of their whiteness. In Virginia, for instance, white indentured servants often joined with freed blacks or even slaves in agitating against the planters. The planters responded by passing a slew of laws which reinvented the colony along racial lines. In 1661 all whites were required to bear arms, a law clearly intended to give some distinctive privilege to whites, as a way of separating them from the "Negroes" and "Indians." A series of other laws were enacted, culminating in 1705 when the Virginia legislature determined that "all horses, cattle, and hogs, now belonging, or that hereafter shall belong to any slave, or of any slave mark... shall be seized and sold by the church wardens of the parish... and the profit thereof applied to the use of the poor" (Takaki 1993: 67–8). The poor in this instance were poor whites. Early white indentured servants therefore were drawn into "whiteness" – they became white.

This labor supply regime was distinctive because the laborers were neither "enslaved" nor free. The laborers had *contracts*, which specified the terms of their work and remuneration, and the conditions under which the contract would be ended. The laborer was thus a legal person, and the techniques of control and discipline were constructed bearing that in mind. Whilst these forms of control and discipline show similarities with those in slavery – namely, control of movement, political disenfranchisement, physical violence, and so on – the difference is that "the law" was often invoked, and those found resisting employers' designs were often charged and prosecuted in a court of law.

At about the same time that Chinese and East Indian indentured laborers were being deployed to several parts of the world, nearly 50 million Europeans came to America (Ignatiev 1995: 38). Analysis of this massive movement of people reveals a close relationship among labor needs, changes within American capitalism, and definite patterns of racialization and ethnicization of labor markets. The racial assumptions of labor supply in this instance have to be understood through immigration policy. The US, as well as other settler colonies (for example, Canada, New Zealand, and Australia) all adopted what amounted to a whites-only policy. On the surface this seems rather clear-cut.

However, the fact of the matter is that whiteness itself was not a stable and incontestable category.

In the case of the United States, the nineteenth century saw increasing diversification of the sources of immigrant labor. The new entrants came from Ireland and settled in the industrial Northeast. Mexican and Chinese laborers were concentrated on the West coast, particularly concentrated in gold mining, agriculture, and railroad building. Japanese immigrants would also settle in the Western part of the US, though in much smaller numbers. In the Northeast, the Irish were inserted in the lower rungs of factory work, and Irish women became the quintessential housemaids. Towards the end of the nineteenth century, there was another switch in sources, this time, from Southern and Eastern Europe, and Italy in particular.

The first wave of Irish workers preceded the potato famine. These immigrants displaced workers from depressed industrial areas, who came to America on account of the rise of manufacturing industries during and after the Napoleonic Wars (Ignatiev 1995: 38). According to one view, the displaced Irish were "scooped up" by America, which "made them its unskilled labor force" (Ignatiev 1995: 38). Douglas' observation that "White men are becoming house servants, cooks, stewards, common labourers and flunkeys to our gentry" spoke to the double identity of these immigrant laborers; white in skin colour, but placed outside of the economic and cultural privileges of "whiteness." Ignatiev has shown how many "Irish" immigrants were in fact Scots and their subordinate "Irish" identity was a racial category already constructed in Britain (Ignatiev 1995: 35). The key point is that their *inferiority* in Britain, produced through practices of racialization, made them available as objects of vicious economic exploitation within the racially configured US political economy. "Yankees" regarded the Irishman "as one made to work," a quality that had already been formulated for African slaves. This "beast of burden" notion was itself situated within a larger framework of assumptions:

> The Irish were imagined as apelike and "a race of savages," at the same level of intelligence as blacks. Pursuing the "lower" rather than the "higher" pleasures, seeking "vicious excitement" and "gratification" that was merely animal," the Irish were said to be "slaves" of "passions." (Takaki 1993: 149)

These supposed innate qualities had proof in external, observable features, such as those noted by an 1851 piece in *Harper's Weekly,* which pointed to "Celtic physiognomy" – "the small and somewhat upturned nose [and] the black tint of the skin" (Jacobson 1998: 48). Assumptions of the "natural features" of the Irish were combined with supposed behavioral tendencies, and it was here that the relationship between nature and labor was established. The Irish were thought to be *submissive*, and this, when articulated with ignorance and inferiority, implied that the work they did and the squalor in which they lived were the natural results of who they were as a people. They were, in other words, personally responsible for their situation.

The Chinese, Japanese, and Southern/Eastern Europeans came to the USA, as it needed labor for the assembly line as noted. Immigrants from Western Europe were now well established in the USA and both the labor market and the general social structure reflected their privileged position. They formed the economic core both in terms of private property ownership, and for those who labored, the leading sectors of industries. The Irish, who since the early nineteenth century had been struggling to wrench themselves out of ethnic compartmentalization, were relieved of their status as the pre-eminent immigrant object of derision by the end of the century. The Irish had joined "white" America, with their credentials accumulated, in part, through sustained confrontation with the African-American population, and in the Western USA, with the Chinese.

Two points need to be underlined here. Firstly, the racialization of the "Irish," Chinese, Japanese, Italians, and other people from Southern and Eastern Europe was central to constructing their vulnerability within the society, making them more exploitable as cheap labor. Secondly, people subjected to racialized marginalization and exploitation tended to occupy inferior positions in the social structure of accumulation. Specifically, they were almost always confined to the secondary labor market; or as in the case of slavery, and indentureship, no market at all. And in the early and mid-twentieth century, demand for labor power was driven increasingly by the rise of assembly line production, which had a double consequence. First, the nature of such work meant it could be learned with little training. This inherent deskilling meant that it was possible and desirable to displace craft workers organized in guilds (Rupert 1995). A second consequence was a tilt towards "cheap foreign labor" as a priority of industrial concerns. This shift was informed by embedded racial practices in the culture and political economy, including a racial "common sense" and a widely disseminated doctrine of scientific racism.

Globalization and labor supply

The distinctive characteristic of slavery, indentureship, and quasi-indentureship (such as in the case of the Chinese) was that these labor regimes were configured around coercion, strictly *controlled movement* of the workers, and supremacist positions constructed around race. The slave and the indentured servant had to have a pass to move from one plantation to another; there were strict guidelines regulating assembly, the distance one was allowed from one's place of labor service or ownership, and so on. Both slave and indentured societies had elaborate laws governing movement. Elaborate legal systems were formulated to regulate the spatial characteristics of these societies. Included were not only the controls of physical movement *per se*, but also the wider topography of social relations. National sovereignty was inscribed by *keeping out* foreign powers but simultaneously *keeping in* a substantial part of the laboring population. Similar regimes based upon controlled movement have existed outside of slavery and indentureship. A notable case was apartheid in South Africa and Rhodesia.

Current developments in the global political economy seem to indicate that exploitation based upon confinement has not ended but is in fact now exported outside of Europe and North America. The reverse seems to be happening in the developed and other industrialized countries; namely, what we might describe as hyper-mobility of labor. The racio-cultural and gendered dynamics in these developments should not be underestimated. There are also forms of supply that are combinations of restriction and mobility.

Some countries secure their mobile workers through highly organized means, often involving both private sector and state interests. A number of Asian economies fall in this category, with Japan and Singapore almost permanently requiring foreign workers. The issues affecting Japanese labor supply "... begin with Japan's economic competitiveness and end with its cultural identity" (Papademetriou and Hamilton 2000: 5). Much like Europe and North America, the segmentation of the Japanese labor market reflects patterns of racialization. The dilemma of this nation has been how to have available labor supply without fundamentally altering the racial composition of the society. Previous labor shortage pressures were in part strategically solved through taking production to where the labor is available. This took the form of direct foreign investment. The same might in fact be said for some other Asian countries, such as Chinese Taipei, Hong Kong, the Republic of Korea and Singapore (Kim 1998: 33). There are limits to that strategy, however. The joint impact of demographic pressures and movement towards services has meant more of that labor is needed in Japan itself. With an ageing population and longer life expectancy, service for the elderly has become a major industry, but one dogged by shortages. The construction industry has also suffered shortages.

Japan's strategy to solve this problem is almost a textbook case of the racialization of labor supply. A strategy consisting of three different components of labor supply has been adopted. The first has a long history and relates to Japanese-born workers of Korean origin. These Japanese-Koreans form part of a pool of cheap, available labor, and most are still vulnerable on account of lack of full political rights. The second is based upon disposability, organized through so-called trainee programs. In this instance visas are offered to foreign workers, but, unlike the USA where many people with work visas are able to adopt residency, and eventually citizenship, this is not the case in Japan. The very disposability of the labor power forms part of its qualification. The third component in a sense "proves" the racialization of the whole strategy, since it is based on the active recruitment of persons of Japanese ancestry. In this regard, thousands of persons of Japanese ancestry from Brazil and Peru have "returned" to Japan with privileges based solely on the fact that they are of Japanese blood. The repatriation program seems to be geared towards broadening the base of Japanese stock for purposes of population replenishment, given the low birth rate. The trainees and Korean labor pool are disposable.[6]

Other Asian countries are also dependent upon cheap, foreign, and "docile" labor as an important aspect of their economic development. Malaysia is especially dependent on Indonesian labor, through both official state programs of intake and a system of unofficial movements. The Malaysia case is one of hyper-mobility par excellence, since periods of economic downturns are partly handled by deporting foreign labor. This is precisely what happened when the Malaysian economy began to be buffeted by the Asian contagion of the late 1990s. In 1998 the Malaysian government put in place "Operation Get Out," which was intended to drive mostly Indonesian foreign workers out of the country. The scale and importance of this operation cannot be overemphasized since foreign laborers make up as much as one-fifth of the Malaysian workforce, and of the 1.2 million foreign workers, 800,000 are illegal or undocumented Indonesians.

Malaysia is much in the same company as Thailand, which had been using about 1 million foreign workers (mostly from Myanmar) in good times, but started its own expulsion campaign after the disastrous financial collapse of 1997. In 1998 alone, the Thai government expelled nearly 300,000 foreign workers. While workers from Myanmar have been subjected to sustained rounding up, it should be noted that the undocumented and overstays from Western countries and Australia move with relative impunity in Thailand. In part this might be explained by the demand for English-language skills, which has resulted in a concentration of Western foreign illegals. But preference does seem to be given to the (foreign) whites and or/Westerners. Singapore, which came at the top of a recent world competitiveness ranking, has long depended on foreign labor, but again, that labor is disposable in times of economic malaise. In 1998, the government of Singapore also declared "war" on the foreign illegals. Workers caught without proper documentation were put in jail and given "six strokes of the cane."[7]

Developments in the European labor supply system share many of the strains and contradictions of the Asian situation, but with real differences. In the Asian case, the limits put in place recently are less for cultural reasons and more explainable in terms of a major economic downturn. The Asian clampdown, therefore, is more a matter of demand and supply for labor. With regards to Europe, the limits also come from intense efforts by anti-immigrant forces, including neo-Nazi and skinhead groups. The differences between Asia and Europe also reflect the different labor supply systems in place. In the case of Asia, the movement of labor is more akin to the way Mexican labor moves to the USA in time of demand and returns home either after harvest time (for seasonal labor), or after amassing some financial resources. But in Europe the situation is rather more like the Japanese case, but less so when compared to the rest of Asia. Europe, like Japan, has historically met problems of labor requirements by immigration intake. This is clearly evidenced by British policy towards the Commonwealth countries after World War II when there was need for general labor. West Indians, Indians, Pakistanis, Bangladeshis, and some immigrants from Sub-Saharan Africa took up jobs in Great Britain. In a sense they had replaced the Irish in that historic role of cheap labor. France took in millions of immigrants from North Africa, and especially from Algeria, Morocco, and Tunisia. This was no small matter for the French who, since the end of World War I, had sought to replenish their staggering wartime losses by bringing immigrants preferentially from Spain, Belgium, and Italy (Simmons 1996: 147). In the early 1920s French business interests formed the General Immigration Society which "... took as its mission to organize the recruitment and placement of immigrant... labor" (Hollifield 1994: 146).

Like Britain, France had tapped its former colonies in times of need in order to create a labor pool, but as early the 1960s began to experience severe resistance from civil society groups.[8] French capital wanted cheap, controllable labor, but the local population working within a long tradition of xenophobic resentments mobilized against the state and, of course, the immigrants themselves. As far back as before World War II, the French right had accused the government of allowing the invasion of France by foreigners (Simmons 1996: 149). Laws were put in place that debarred foreigners from various "privileges" such as holding government jobs, and in 1974 labor immigration came to an end. Simmons has shown how the temptations of cheap labor were contradicted by systemic racism, especially after the 1962 independence of Algeria: "On the one hand, French authorities feared the economic and social consequences of the large number of Algerians who wished to enter France; on the other, business leaders wanted to ensure a continued supply of cheap, docile labour" (Simmons 1996: 152). But President Pompidou perhaps registered the contradiction in the clearest language, stating in 1963: "Immigration is a way to create a certain freeing up of the labour market and of resisting social pressure" (Simmons 1996: 152).

Developments in France in the 1960s through the 1980s mirrored those in Britain in key respects, particularly the rise of organized movements against foreign labor, and against that rather more abstract "thing" called "immigration." In both cases these movements became attached to political machines, with leaders catapulted into positions where they could significantly affect electoral outcomes. In the case of Britain, Enoch Powell built his movement through a complex articulation of civilizational threat, cultural decline, job losses, crime, and neighborhood destruction, among other things.

> Powell's representation of the English nation as the self-sustaining, invulnerable, eternal and essential source to which Britain can always return operates as a phantasmagoric construction. Like all fantasies, his

image of England is a purely non-contradictory space, which is absolutely purified of all subversions and interruptions. (Smith 1994)

Powell's anti-immigrant exclusionary discourse was later skillfully combined with an aggravated homophobia, Thatcherite monetarism, and global anti-communism. Back in France, Jean-Marie Le Pen would take the quasi-fascist and anti-immigrant National Front to "great" electoral heights. Le Pen would move the Front from less than 1% of the votes in the 1974 presidential election, to 15% in the 1995 and 2002 presidential races. Indeed, in 2002 Le Pen sent shock waves across European politics by advancing to the presidential run-off with Jacques Chirac.[9]

While the British and French dealt with their labor requirements by creating labor pools (that is, vulnerable but settled supply) out of former colonial subjects, the German strategy has been more like that of the Japanese. The antipathy towards people of other races in Germany (which once led to the Jewish Holocaust and racial crimes against other groups) put in place an amalgam of institutional and knowledge infrastructures which were dedicated to racial domination. According to Lee:

> The coddling of ultra-right-wing offenders dated back to the early years of the Bonn Republic, which stacked its courts with hanging judges who were responsible for dispensing Hitler's justice. Virtually the entire West German judiciary had served the Nazi state, but these arbiters of racial hatred hardly got a spanking after the war, even though they had ordered the execution of forty-five thousand people for dubious reasons. Reinstated in West German courtrooms, they polluted the climate of German jurisprudence throughout the Cold War and later. (Lee 2000: 269)

There seems to be a general sense that Nazism and its teachings are things of the past, and that once Germany "joined" the West, it abandoned institutions that produced racial persecution. Nothing could be further from the truth, and nowhere has this been more visible than in labor intake policy, institutionalized in immigration policy. For a long time Germany essentially maintained a policy of restricting citizenship to people of German blood, a policy that is similar to that of Japan. The core of the policy has been that "Germany recruited workers but got human beings, and the settlement of probationary migrant workers in Germany transformed a narrow labour market policy into a much wider immigration phenomenon" (Martin 1994: 192). German reconstruction and the subsequent economic boom required a massive infusion of foreign labor power. The infrastructure of racism, however, shaped that policy so workers would be disposable, and, once finished with their assignments, would return home. The German "guest worker" program was developed to satisfy the labor needs whilst at the same time avoiding a commitment to citizenship. What is interesting here is that the notion of "guest" has a profoundly racist place in modern German history; Jews were considered "guests" although they had been born there and were in fact citizens. But these types of connections need not be made in order to establish the point. The evidence of racial assumptions of foreign labor came from the German government itself, which has applied techniques of racial science even in the post-war period:

> New rules implemented by the German Interior Ministry required non-EC (European Community) and non-US citizens applying for residency to have their skull and nose size measured. Official immigration questionnaires specifically asked what type of nose a person had. A German nose was identified as a "normal" nose, and the "abnormal" nose shapes of various non-Germans were coded accordingly. (Lee 2000: 270)

This cranial approach to residency demonstrates the deeply embedded supremacist assumptions governing post-war German policy. The "guest workers" like the "trainees" in Japan were not supposed to have stayed, but they did. This threw the whole regime of population replenishment and labor power into crisis. According to Martin:

> Most of the foreigners living in Germany are the legacy of the failed guest worker policies of the 1950s and 1960s. Guest workers from Southern Europe helped sustain Germany's "economic miracle" but they did not follow the plan and leave their manufacturing, mining, and construction jobs to make room for fresh temporary workers. (Martin 1994: 192)

The rotating labor system, which the German government had touted, began to collapse by the early 1970s, and as once *workers* stayed, so did their families:

> In parts of many German cities, including Frankfurt and Berlin, foreigners soon outnumbered Germans. The presence of Yugoslav and Turkish children in German schools revealed that many "guests" had decided to stay. The reaction of most Germans was negative. Politicians told xenophobic Germans that the migrant workers were necessary to assure economic growth, but many Germans believed that "over-foreignization" was too high a price to pay for economic success. (Martin 1994: 202)

The xenophobic infrastructure has recently produced violent outbursts against immigrants. In 1992, there were 1500 documented cases of far-right violence, including killings. While the violence has abated in comparative terms, developments in the world economy have led to a renewed call for foreign workers to work in some sectors, and especially in the computer software industry. The response from one major political party, the Christian Democrats, is *"Kinder statt Inder"* ("Children instead of Indians").[10]

In the USA the labor supply system is more complicated, in part because there are several systems at work, and also because past methods of supply have left indelible imprints on who is allowed in, in what numbers, and who their sponsors are. Since the early 1980s the USA has witnessed a swelling of the ranks of non-established workers. In part this has to do with globalization and pressures of global competitiveness stemming from strong manufacturing economies in Asia that force US capitalists to reduce cost by introducing more flexibility in labor. But another dimension has to do with the computer revolution and with deindustrialization. Further, sustained growth of the US economy through the 1990s created a tight labor market with unemployment falling to historic lows (Persaud and Lusane 2000).

With threats of wage driven inflationary pressures, the USA has, for all practical purposes, tolerated illegality as the medium through which labor would be taken in for the millions of jobs at the lower end of the economy. This became necessary on account of upward social mobility of a significant portion of the African-American population. In most places in the USA, Mexican and Central American labor have become central to maintaining the lifestyles of the middle classes. This is so because these workers provide all the services (at affordable prices) necessary for two parents to work. These workers are temporary in terms of length of stay in the USA, or in terms of the duration of their job. For the many who are in the USA illegally, their undocumented status makes them vulnerable to institutionalized exploitation, both in terms of working conditions and pay. Their vulnerability is important to the toleration of their presence, and part of that vulnerability lies in the political ease with which the "illegal alien" can be dispensed with. Again, the foundations for this disposability were laid much earlier in American history. Mexican labor occupies a special part of that history. A 1951 Presidential Commission described the system with great precision. In part, it said:

> When the work is done, neither the farmer nor the community wants the wetback around. The number of apprehensions and deportations tends to rise very rapidly at the close of a seasonal work period. This can be interpreted not alone to mean that the immigration officer suddenly goes about his work with renewed zeal and vigor, but rather that this time of the year cooperation in law enforcement by farm employers and townspeople rapidly undergoes considerable improvement. (U.S. President's Commission on Migratory Labor 1951: 78)

The current labor supply system for the peripheral sectors of the US economy is very much a continuation of the system that was used in the 1940s and 1950s.

Conclusion

In conclusion, it appears that the logic of foreign labor is thus very much the same worldwide, whether one is "recruiting" for the high- or low-wage sectors. There is no debate that a low-wage labor shortage exists in the USA and has existed for some time. By contrast the same cannot be said for jobs which are associated with the computer (software) industry, and the general e-economy. In fact, some scholars, politicians, and labor activists have been straining to make the point that what is in shortage is not labor, but cheap, "docile" labor. Most of the intake for this industry and other skilled/technical areas (such as in the health industry) is facilitated through H-IB visas, which are granted for up to three years. The quota of H-IB skyrocketed by 352% between 1990 and 1995, with a substantial number of these workers coming from countries such as India and the Philippines. The workers must remain at their employer at least until when they have applied for permanent status. This could take a couple of years, since various Justice Department regulations, and documentation from other departments of government, must be obtained prior to submission of application for permanent status benefit. The criticism is that this makes the workers "vulnerable," since, for one thing, they have to be sponsored by the employer and accordingly must not "rock the boat" too much. One writer suggests that foreign nationals earn 15–30% less than local workers for the same job. The incentive for the employers then is two-fold: namely, lower wages and tighter control of the work process. Moreover, once these immigrants come in they will initiate more migration of people with similar skills, which in the medium and long term would hold wages down even more structurally.

In sum, this chapter has examined various regimes and patterns of accumulation as they relate to historical tendencies of labor supply and control. In particular, the racialization of workers was linked to the creation of a global labor supply for more flexible accumulation during different historical moments. The current moment suggests an emerging regime of global labor supply that is more precarious and that will benefit the new labor intermediaries and capitalist employers.

Notes

1. Data from Asia show this pattern clearly. In 1993 the median income of the highest sending countries (Myanmar, the Philippines, Indonesia, Sri Lanka, China, Pakistan, India, Bangladesh, Cambodia, and Vietnam) was $460, while that of receiving countries (Japan, Singapore, Brunei, Chinese Taipei, and the Republic of Korea), was $16,215. Malaysia and Thailand are transition countries that both send and receive foreign labor. They had, respectively, per capita incomes of $3160 and $2040 (OECD 2002).
2. In September 1991 a fire at Imperial Foods, a chicken processing plant in Hamlet, North Carolina, killed 25 workers and injured more than 50. Investigators found

a long list of safety violations, including emergency exits, which failed to open. For a penetrating analysis see Harvey (1996: 334–46).
3. "Why Use Cumberland Labor?" <www.cumberland.com/why.htm>
4. L. M. Sixel and Jenalia Moreno, "A Bunk and a Job." *Houston Chronicle*, August 30, 1998. Cited in "Research Reports and Polls: Industrial Temps," <www.labor research.org/ind_temps/big_thing.html>
5. I would like to thank Stephen Gill for suggesting this point.
6. Medium-sized manufacturing firms in Japan are increasingly reliant on foreign contract labor from Korea, China, Brazil, and Philippines.
7. Seth Mydans, "As Boom Fails, Malaysia Sends Migrants Home." *New York Times*, April 9, 1998.
8. Groups such as the *populationnistes*, which explicitly pushed for the "ethnic selection" of immigrants. See Hollifield (1994).
9. "Shock French Election Result Sparks Protests." *Guardian*, April 22, 2002.
10. Peter Finn, "A Showdown With Extremism: Germany Considers Banning Right-Wing Party as Violence Spreads." *Washington Post*, August 5, 2000.

8
Social Reproduction of Exclusion: Exploitative Migration and Human Insecurity

Kinhide Mushakoji

This chapter tries to show how the socioeconomic security of the victims of exploitative migration is violated by states and criminal organizations. It explores, for example, how governments exercise formal (legal, publicly regulated) control over the national labor market and Mafiosi exert informal (illegal, unregulated and often violent) control over the workforce in the sex industry. These two agents thus give formal and informal support to exploitation within the sex industries and thus, directly and indirectly, reproduce particular and extreme forms of social exclusion and economic exploitation of the victims of coercive migration who form part of the workforce of the sex industries. Indeed, what I call exploitative migration highlights wider issues connected to the movement of people in the context of neo-liberal patterns of globalization, as well as pointing towards ways to understand wider world order problems such as the "terrorism" of anti-systemic movements at the start of the twenty-first century. The criminal organizations can be best viewed as part of the "anti-social" movements.[1]

Specifically, neo-liberal globalization involves a widening gap between the formal regulation of the world market and the informal realities in the life-worlds and everyday reality of people within modern capitalism. A process of informal migration forms an integral part of globalization. Such informalization involves particular, exploitative and exclusionary networks that link the fates of North and South. These networks are partly regulated by the formal authorities and corporations, and partly regulated by organized crime syndicates. For example, the Philippines–Japan bilateral networks explored in this essay are linked to larger networks of trafficking and reproduction of the workforce of the global sex industries. This is complemented by a general lack of interest in the receiving countries in the human security and human rights of the sex workers trafficked from the South. As the global economy expands, they are both more exploited by informal forces and more socially excluded by conventional/formally legal forces of the state and civil society. This is the dialectical, transnational process of the reproduction of exploitative migration and social exclusion in neo-liberal globalization.

This chapter discusses mechanisms for the social reproduction of this system of exploitative migration and social exclusion. It will focus on the case of the entertainers/sex workers who come from the Philippines into Japan. The analysis is based on accounts given in a study of the survivors and promoters conducted within the framework of the Toyota Project/DAWN research.[2] The interviews and Focus Group Discussion helped ascertain how notable gaps existed between the perception of the survivors and the official treatment of trafficking in ways that reflect the two dimensions of the world market: the formal and informal. In this context we will show that the informal control of the sex workforce by transnational criminal organizations is made possible by a mechanism of *occultation* of the sex sector within the formal mechanisms associated with power and production in the labor market, civil society and the state.[3]

Socioeconomic insecurity: Filipina "entertainers" in Japan

The International Labor Organization originally articulated a concept of socioeconomic security/insecurity defined broadly in terms of production and social reproduction. The ILO's definition can be criticized for lack of precision yet it is useful because it emphasizes that socioeconomic security is a condition *sine qua non* of decent work, that is, work that is not dehumanizing and that is based on reasonable conditions for the reproduction of communities. So if human security in a negative sense consists of a guarantee that one feels secure about not facing danger of dehumanization in one's work (as well as freedom from violence), socioeconomic security in a positive sense involves having access to decent, productive work today and tomorrow in the wider framework of social security. Socioeconomic insecurity, then, becomes the insecurity faced by a human being when her/his role in production and social reproduction is in danger of being dehumanized, subjected to coercion and her/his livelihood and home are threatened. And of course, labor migration may lead to socioeconomic insecurity if and when migrants face these dangers.

With this in mind, we will now explore the case of the Filipina "entertainers" who are exploited by the Japanese sex industries in reproducing their labor force. This is a typical example of socioeconomic insecurity caused by the social reproduction of exclusion under conditions of exploitative migration.

How does this process occur? On the one hand the state reacts to informal control of the sex sector by criminals, developing efforts to maintain formal law and order, whilst in effect turning a blind eye to many practices and failing to protect the victims of violence and trafficking. Filipinas who have migrated to Japan, especially between the 1970s to 1990s, experience a deep sense of insecurity caused by the gap between their expectations to work as "entertainers/artists" in clubs and other "respectable" institutions of the Japanese leisure industry, and the fact that they are forced by owners of their workplaces to prostitute themselves. Japanese sex industries use a hierarchy of sex workers from less developed countries, with different modes of exploitation, going from pure slavery, to indentured labor, to unregulated or unprotected labor (Mushakoji 2001). The Filipinas, working formally as "entertainers," are near the top of this hierarchy, since until they decide to remain in Japan after the expiration of their contracts, they are not under bondage by the criminal organizations, as are most other foreign sex workers trafficked into Japan (see also Chapter 5).

The specific mode of exploitation of the Filipinas is based on a system of "escorts" called *dohan* which puts them in a state of insecurity due to their lack of legal protection against threats of physical reprisals, for example, if they protest at the low proportion of their earnings from clients they receive from their employers.[4] *Dohan* is a Japanese word meaning to accompany someone, and refers to the prostitution of sex workers who "accompany" male clients to "love hotels" outside their workplace. This avoids clubs risking legal penalties for selling prostitution. Laws that concern acts performed outside of the workplace govern any penalties that might be imposed. It is an informal institution in the sense that it is not part of the formal "work" of the sex workers who "entertain" their clients in the clubs but who do not prostitute themselves. The system of *dohan* also involves Japanese sex workers who are freer and better paid. For the Filipina entertainers *dohan* is not at all part of the formal contract they have signed with their Japanese agent.

In analyzing the system of exploitation of the Filipina entertainers, we must first describe how the formal system was established, and combined with the informal *dohan* system. An agreement was concluded in the 1970s between Japan and the Philippines to regulate the migration of "entertainers/artists" whose qualifications are guaranteed by the Philippines. Their workplace, that is, the clubs, and so on, are regulated by Japan. The formal aspect of this migration is to supply Filipina "artists" to clubs in Japan; the reproduction of the artists' workforce in Japan is thus to be guaranteed by the immigration of Filipinas. This formal system continues today with small modifications. It became, *de facto*, however, a system reproducing the workforce of the Japanese sex industries as a result of Japanese sex tourism to the Philippines. Its rapid expansion convinced criminal organizations that large profits could be made by introducing Filipinas who suited the tastes of Japanese male tourists.

According to an "inside informant" the "entertainer" system changed its nature around the end of the 1970s.[5] This person is still working today as a promoter sending Filipinas to Japan, following a period in the early 1970s as an "entertainer/artist" on the stage of several of the most expensive clubs in Tokyo, such as the Mikado (a night club famous for its exclusivity, one that does not officially practice *dohan*). In response to our questions she expressed dismay that the institution of "entertainer" had become a pretext to send Filipinas into the Japanese sex industries during the 1980s. Up to the end of the 1970s, the genuine artists that were sent to Japan were authorized to visit for six months and were regulated by strictly observed contracts on the part of the Japanese side that hired them.

Migrating Filipinas' expectations that they would find security and relative affluence in Japan were based on the fact that they were officially recognized as "entertainers/artists" by both their home and receiving countries. The Philippines and Japan signed an agreement where the former was screening and sending "entertainers" with mutually agreed qualifications, and Japan was guaranteeing a decent workplace, where the stage was of adequate size, with separate toilets for men and women, and so on. Thus the expectation of decent work and guaranteed security seemed to be based on firm legal and institutional grounds. However, the Filipinas who had passed a test proving their qualifications as artists, found that the workplaces they were sent to were not the "decent" clubs they hoped to be hired by, but sex clubs where *dohan* prostitution was practiced. Once in Japan, they are allocated to a variety of workplaces, many not meeting the standards specified. A recent survey indicates that in 90% of the cases the entertainers are placed by Japanese agents in sex clubs, snack bars and other sex industry workplaces which do not meet the standards and conditions specified in the agreement between the Japanese and the Philippine authorities (Immigration Office: Ministry of Justice 1996: 36–40). In reality, such institutions were receiving commission for lending their names to the real workplace assigned to the incoming Filipinas. In these clubs they were not "entertaining" customers on the stage but sitting with them, and being forced to take on additional *dohan* prostitution outside their workplace.

In sum, this form of sex work is discriminatory, exclusionary and hyperexploitative in the sense that workers are forced to live together under surveillance of the criminal organizations controlling their workplace. They receive smaller percentages of the money they would otherwise get in full from clients if they were "free" prostitutes. At the same time they are effectively excluded from the Japanese "civil society," stigmatized as foreign sex workers. The only place they can find some physical security is in a Catholic church, if their master or *mama-san* (madam) allows them to go.

Informalization, occultation and reproduction of the sex industry workforce

It is important to realize that the Filipina entertainers are not at the bottom of the sex industry workforce hierarchy. Thai sex workers are trafficked into Japan without any legal protection (the Thai government has no agreements with Japan). Filipinas on the other hand are governed by a migration system that was bilaterally agreed to by the Philippines and Japan.[6] The system is justified by the Philippine side as a legitimate labor export, beneficial to the workers and to the Philippine economy. On the Japanese side, the agreement is perceived as being part of its development assistance. The Philippines' authorities who promote Filipina entertainers' migration are aware that *dohan* prostitution exists but take the view that entertainers themselves should decide whether to accept additional work, and if they do, it is to be regulated by Japan.[7]

Clearly a central interest of the Philippine authorities is to increase national income through substantial remittances of the entertainers, which are difficult, for obvious reasons, to measure exactly. It is not only difficult to obtain information on remittances sent by informal means (sex industries report only earnings from legal activities) but also money for *dohan* remains part of the unreported informal economy.

On the Japanese side, it was only in the late 1990s that the Japanese immigration authorities began to express some concern about "entertainers" not abiding by the agreements. Forced prostitution in Japanese sex industries does not seem to have been the most serious concern of the authorities. Rather, as good bureaucrats, they did not like deviation from the immigration rules agreed bilaterally and thus they sought to tighten procedures and authorize migration to Japan only to genuine entertainers. It is interesting to note that tightening Japanese control over Filipina entertainers corresponded to worldwide concern about transnational criminal organizations, for example, in G7 deliberations in the 1990s. Until this time, the Japanese police sought, at best, to control criminal organizations exploiting the Filipinas and victims of trafficking; they seldom succeeded in arresting the illegal exploiters of the entertainers.

This lack of enthusiasm of the Japanese police may be linked to the reproduction of the workforce of the sex industries, under conditions that are indispensable for their competitiveness. The Japanese government supports its service industries in global market competition and as such has tolerated informal exploitation of the sex workers, provided that the regulations of the *Fuzoku Eigyou Hou* (Law Concerning Sex Industries) are at least formally observed.

On the other hand, if *foreign* criminal organizations are involved in the Japanese sex industries, wider concerns are expressed in Japanese politics and society. It is well known in Japan that the case of the Kabuki-cho multinational sex district, now under the control of the Chinese Mafia, was a cause of serious concern for the Mayor of Tokyo, Shintaro Ishihara. This district was singled out in 1999 by Ishihara, who declared in a speech to a regiment of the Self Defense Forces (the Japanese military) that they had to be prepared to take action, in the event of natural calamities like earthquakes, against any possible uprising of "illegal migrants" or "third country people" (a derogatory expression used for Koreans belonging neither to the Japanese colonists before 1945 or to the occupying Americans after 1945). Ishihara specifically mentioned Kabuki-cho where he said that even Japanese *yakuzas* (Mafiosi) could not walk in the streets at night. This reflects a growing fear within the Japanese ruling class about multiethnic migrants breaking up the traditional homogeneity of Japan and the Japan-specific problem of xenophobia behind the public authorities' discriminatory treatment of Philippine entertainers and other foreign sex workers.

However, xenophobia in Japan should not make us lose sight of the more general structural problem connected to exclusionary factors in South to North patterns of exploitative migration. There is a global trend in the sex industries, exploiting women migrants from the South in general. In the sex industries of the industrialized countries, all the sex workers are exploited, but the women and children from developing countries are much more exploited than their colleagues. Of course the *dohan* system exploits not only Filipinas and foreign sex workers but also Japanese "entertainers." However, the Japanese receive more generous commission, and the proportion of the remuneration for their *dohan* they have to give to the master or the *mama-san* is smaller. By contrast Filipinas are also often bound by debts, and forced to live together in boarding houses under constant surveillance by the *yakuzas*, whereas their Japanese colleagues are living separately and can leave more easily when they so decide.

Thus the Japanese sex industries, as a system, involve double standards. On the one hand sex industries are permitted and recognized by the public authorities as a "decent" leisure industry, under the name of *fuzoku-gyo* (where *fuzoku* means sex-related social practices). On the other hand, the state condemns prostitution, but accepts its clandestine practice provided that it is performed informally, that is, in situations where formal evidence cannot be obtained, and hence outside the legal control of the state. Informality is indispensable to maintain cheap foreign labor in the sex industry. Thus a double standard combines formally "decent" with informally "indecent" work involving the discriminatory exploitation of trafficked sex workers.

Such a double standard is also made possible by the "occultation" or occlusion of the sex sector in the discourse of civil society and public authorities. The informal work of the Filipina migrant workers is partly maintained and reproduced by this occlusion, that is, its invisibility in the eyes of society and officialdom. Its reality is concealed under the cover of the legality of the "entertainer" institution. Occultation here is based on the shared interest of the governments of the sending and receiving countries, in maintaining the "entertainer" institution. For Japan it allows some male citizens to satisfy their extramarital sexual drives, and it provides a considerable tax income to the state and the prefecture (regional authority). For the Philippines it generates considerable remittances to help with the nation's balance of payments. Thus whilst civil society and the state welcome female migrant workers into the formally legal sex/entertainment industries, legislation does not prevent the authorities from closing their eyes to informal prostitution. Once out of their working place, the authorities consider such sexual activities to be only personal "love affairs" with their customers.

In this way, the social reproduction of the workforce of the Japanese sex industry is supported by the informalization of the work of the Filipina entertainers. In this context, their involvement in the reproduction process directly influences their biological reproduction activities and develops for them an additional source of socioeconomic insecurity. The next section of this chapter looks into this important aspect of the social reproduction of exclusion: the question of the so-called Japan Filipino Children, or "JFCs."

Insecurity, biological reproduction and provisioning of care

In general, victims of exploitative migration have insecurity built into their biological reproduction as well as in provisioning for their caring needs. This is an important aspect of the insecurity that many trafficked women and children experience. The international human rights community represented in the United Nations Commission on Human Rights overlooks it. The latter has long been concerned with violation of the rights of trafficked women and children, and the violence they endure. However, these legal experts ignore reproductive security, because their attention is focused on criminal organizations, and human rights violations. They also overlook not only the biological reproductive rights of the victims of trafficking but also the rights of their children.

In the case of the Filipina entertainers in Japan, much of the insecurity of the survivors is caused by the fact that many have had relations with Japanese customers and other Japanese men, sometimes marrying them formally, and have had their children. Their insecurity increases due to the lack of legal protection for themselves and their children. The latter are discriminated against as "mixed blood" JFCs. Also, fathers (frequently) fail to live up to their obligations to offer parental support. JFCs are deprived of protection by the state. They also become the object of discrimination by their society. This is why the problem of JFCs has become so serious that it is now the object of support and caring activities by civic movements both in the Philippines and in Japan.[8] Cooperation between NGOs and politicians of the two countries began in 1993, and since then joint activities have been developed to find the Japanese fathers and to have them recognize their responsibility toward their partners and their children. Quite a number of lawsuits have been successfully conducted, but more cases continue to come up. Voluntary legal support and fundraising to permit the entertainers to return to Japan to testify in court is currently conducted by NGOs in both countries.[9] The Philippine government has paid increasing attention to this problem, to the point of making it a matter of interstate negotiation with Japan.

However when the problem is addressed it is mainly in terms of private law, or of humanitarian interstate cooperation, and not connected with the rights of reproduction and of socioeconomic security of the victims of exploitative migration. To develop an adequate legal regime covering this aspect of exploitative migration is indispensable. The JFC case is not unique and other cases are ignored because of the occultation process that surrounds this aspect of exploitative migration. There are many cases of Japanese-Thai children lacking any support – in spite of growing attention by civil society and the governments of both Thailand and Japan about trafficked women and children.[10] Their right to reproduction and socioeconomic security is entirely ignored. It is very likely that similar cases exist in other regions.

It is important here to realize that this type of insecurity is a direct consequence of their exclusion from the institutions associated with welfare and other forms of care in both their country of origin and in the country where they are exploited. In addition, they are often treated as "illegal migrants" devoid of civil rights, as both the sending and receiving society reject them. Their children suffer from social stigma and racial prejudice.

Formal, informal and the "quotidian"

A key hypothesis of this chapter up to this point has been that exploitative forms of globalization are creating a widening gap between the formal texts and regulations of the world market ("the rule of law") and the more violent, exclusionary informal realities not codified by them. Now we must go one step further and interrogate what this means through use of a concept borrowed from Betty Reardon in her definition of human security: the "quotidian" or everyday lived reality.[11] By this is meant the social context of and moment when a person experiences security/insecurity.

The quotidian world of the entertainers involves an ambivalent, or more precisely a polyvalent treatment by clients who enjoy their company and who exploit them, sexually and economically, often justifying their actions as helping poor women and children. The *mama-san* cares for their everyday needs, sometimes with kindness, sometimes using coercion and physical violence, often calling in the *yakuzas* to punish the recalcitrant. The *yakuzas* are feared, but they are also the protectors of the sex workers. The police, who are supposed to protect the sex workers, often treat them as culprits or accessories of the criminals.

The survivor entertainers interviewed and involved in the Toyota Project/DAWN Focus Group Debate (FGD) made a variety of candid statements reflecting on their everyday experience.[12] Of their clients, they agreed that they "generally find it pleasurable to be pursued and courted by Japanese men." In their everyday world, "the line between 'work' and 'pleasure' can be sometimes blurred." When asked about their experience in the clubs some expressed repugnance against being forced into *dohan* dating with certain men. However, they also find some clients with whom they have *dohan* relationships attractive. The *mama-sans* and the *yakuzas* are both seen as sometimes good, sometimes bad. *Mama-sans* who have favorites and who become jealous are seen as bad, not necessarily as exploiters but as women with power. The younger *yakuzas* are sometimes violent, older ones are "gallant" and protect the entertainers when clients harass them. Some of them report cases where their resistance to the *yakuzas* led to being locked in their boarding house. The entertainers make positive and negative assessments of about their recruiters, promoters and Japanese agencies.

The ambivalence/polyvalence of the entertainers vis-à-vis their everyday world reflects the fact that the reproduction of the workforce of the Japanese sex industries cannot function alone, or indeed very well, by brute force. A minimum acceptance of the system by the entertainers and other recruited sex workers is indispensable. This, however, should not be interpreted just as voluntary support, since any human person develops a psychological protective complex or coping mechanism in such circumstances. This mechanism is based on the tendency to assess reality in terms of perceptions of relative security, even where they are in conditions that perpetuate their basic state of exploitation. Thus the above example of *yakuzas* protecting the entertainers from the clients' harassment shows the fact that the *yakuzas* are perceived as agents reducing the insecurity of the entertainers in the face of violence from clients. The *yakuzas* are not agents of human security as we have defined it throughout this chapter.

Another psychological mechanism that needs to be taken into account is linked to the social anatomy of the sex districts where the entertainers live and work. Here the formal institutions of the state and civil society do not provide very much of a sense of security to them. The police, and the NGOs, are perceived as remote agents, foreign to their world, whereas their owners, and the *yakuzas* behind them, are the proximate agents of everyday life and on whom their insecurity and security depends.

This narrative does not always corroborate with formal records and texts, including reports by the NGOs and researchers. The latter tend to generalize on the basis of public images, which classify the different agents into binary categories of good and bad. This does not mean that the agents perceived as good or bad by the entertainers themselves are "objectively" good or bad, since they are part of an intricate exploitative system reproducing the workforce of the global sex industries.

Moreover it is incorrect to dismiss as subjective the everyday experience of the entertainers. Their sense of security/insecurity determines their attitude vis-à-vis both *yakuzas* and the police. Indeed the exclusionary reproduction of the workforce of the sex industries takes place both in the everyday world of the informal sex districts, where migrant workers are exploited, and in the global structures of power competition between the public authorities and the criminal organizations. This is a competition between forces of informalization and counter-informalization.[13] The competition is engaged at different levels, from the informal everyday level to the formal global level where the sex industries operate and where elements of their structure are quoted on the world's stock markets. It is important to have a holistic understanding of how the different levels are interlocked. In what follows, I will try to present a rough picture of this multilevel power struggle.

Encounters: forces of informalization and counter-informalization

Now we move towards a bottom-up analysis that starts with everyday realities where the entertainers interact with the agents of the criminal organizations, the sex industry, and the public authorities.

The everyday world where the Filipinas live is an informal community, the sex district, where sex workers under different systems of exploitation compete with each other, and provide a choice of services, prices, and exotic attractions to Japanese clients. The system reproducing this hierarchy of sex workers is selectively exclusionary, in the sense that all sex workers of different nationalities and status of exploitation are excluded from the hope of performing decent work. However, they are more or less exploited, as unorganized workers without any legal protection, as bonded slaves, or as pure slaves. In this hierarchy of exclusion and exploitation, the Filipina "entertainers" are, as we saw above, in a relatively favorable position. This is so, however, only until the time their contract expires, when they become illegal migrants forced to work under harsher conditions, often becoming bonded slaves due to their indebtedness to the agents or the *yakuzas*. Beside the entertainers losing their formal status due to their overstay, there are also the Filipinas who do not obtain the status of entertainer, failing the required state examination. Many decide to rely on informal channels provided by the criminal organizations and migrate to Japan often under bondage contracts. They are forced to pay an exorbitant sum for the illegal services provided by the criminal organizations of both the Philippines and Japan, and they become indebted to them when they cannot pay these sums.

Whilst sex districts are the loci of intense competition, often violent, among criminal gangs exploiting (and protecting) sex workers of different nationalities, the districts also are informal communities. Filipina entertainers perceive their security/insecurity within this predominantly informal community where sex clubs are legally registered, but where most of the income comes informally from the commission to the sex workers by *dohan* clients. Here owners, *mama-sans*, *yakuzas* and sex workers have informal personalized relationships of a *Gemeinschaft* type in ways quite different from formal rules and regulations prevailing in bureaucratic, corporate and civil society (*Gesellschaft*).[14] This is one of the reasons why survivors interviewed gave positive evaluations of *mama-sans* and *yakuzas* – they were effectively the only people with whom they had human contact. Thus despite internal conflicts and competition, this *Gemeinschaft*-like informal community, where the entertainers live together with other sex workers and their exploiters, forms an alliance against interventions from the police. Indeed this form of socialization extends to the trafficking networks and forms part of the globalization of the reproduction of the sex industry workforce. In this context there is, to a certain extent, a struggle between what I call forces of informalization and counter-informalization.

Filipinas have always represented the majority of the foreigners entering Japan using the "entertainer" institution. The Ministry of Justice of Japan eventually decided to make standards for "entertainers" more stringent after having received reports from the foreign entertainers, their friends, and the NGOs concerned with their welfare that many of them were in reality working in sex clubs, bars and cabaret clubs where they were forced to prostitute themselves, and were forced to give the club owner a great part of their commission, and were under constant surveillance without any freedom of movement. Official surveys showed that more than 90% of the entertainers were becoming "illegal" migrants by "overstaying" their visas.

This high rate of informalization of the formal entertainers was met by different measures of counter-informalization by the Japanese immigration authorities, that consisted of adding stricter conditions both on the clubs inviting entertainers, and on the entertainers' qualification as performing artists. On the other hand, the new standards simplified invitations by Japanese institutions genuinely interested in artistic performance, such as the ethnic restaurants inviting Filipina musicians and dancers.

Efforts to control the foreign criminal organizations dominating the sex districts like Kabuki-cho have been made by the Tokyo police. They conducted several *te-ire* (round-ups) of the sex clubs, snack bars and cabaret clubs known to be under the control of criminal organizations. They have not been successful beyond arresting as "illegal" foreigners a few sex workers whose visas had expired. Rumors attribute the failure of these round-ups to tip-offs by some police interested in keeping good connections with the criminal organizations. What is clear is that the police cannot penetrate into the informal realities of the sex districts without the support of informants. At the same time the Japanese police, whilst in some respects making praiseworthy efforts, often treat the crimes of the transnational criminal organizations as "crimes by foreigners" and reflect a xenophobia that sees foreigners as more violent than the Japanese. Partly as a result, no efforts are made to protect the foreign sex workers, although the Ministry of Justice knows that their rights are violated.

On the international level, the United Nations, with the active support of the G7, has developed a powerful counter-informalization instrument, the UN Convention Against Transnational Organized Crime. It has three Protocols; the Protocol against the Smuggling of Migrants by Land Air and Sea, the Protocol to Prevent, Suppress and Punish Trafficking in Persons, especially Women and Children, and the Protocol against the Illicit Manufacturing of and Trafficking in Firearms, Their Parts and Components and Ammunition. The first two Protocols are closely related to exploitative migration. Thanks to the interventions of the High Commissioner for Human Rights supported by concerned human rights NGOs, their text focusing on preventing, arresting and punishing transnational organized crime have been largely improved in referring more to the human rights of the victims, trafficked women and children and smuggled migrants and refugees. Yet the emphasis of the Convention and of the Protocols is placed on control of the transnational criminal organization because they affect the public safety and the security of capital.[15]

This is partly why efforts of the forces of counter-informalization do not necessarily increase the socioeconomic security of the women migrants. This is mainly due to the fact that the experts who have drafted the international counter-informalization instruments were unable to see the quotidian realities and could not deal well with structural informalization, in their definition of the rights of the victims of trafficking. This is a most unfortunate case of occlusion, where the formal agents responsible for international law-making cannot perceive the informal complexities of the everyday life of the "entertainers." Even more seriously, the complex interactions between two forces, one of informalization allied with the transnational criminal organizations, and the other of counter-informalization allied with the governments, together dialectically reproduce exclusion, exploitation and socioeconomic insecurity of the excluded women migrant workers. This is partly the consequence of a cat-and-mouse interaction: tightening of the formal control by the former leads to further informalization by the latter. It is natural that the latter tries to escape from the tightening grips of the former.

The power struggle between the two opponents is accompanied by increased exploitation of the migrants and trafficked women and children, and increased surveillance on them by both the criminals and the authorities. This is accompanied by intensified exclusion: the victims of trafficking, including the entertainers, as well as all women migrants, become the objects of international surveillance by the authorities and of increased suspicion by Japanese citizens. Both sides disturb the socioeconomic security of the victims caught between the two.

The above process of informalization and counter-informalization is structurally an integral part of the process of globalization of the world market.

As a consequence of the neo-liberal policies of the formal agencies, migrants, especially women, have increasingly strong incentives to leave the developing countries, because of the lack of decent jobs and the growing gap between rich and poor. This is combined with the demand for their labor from the affluent industrial economies. In the case of the Japanese economy in the 1980s, the increasing relocation of subcontracting small manufacturing enterprises from Japan to neighboring countries increased the reliance on the service sector. This is one reason why the sex industries have continued to play an increasing role compared to the other sectors of the productive economy – even in 1990s Japan after the "bubble" economy had burst. On the other hand, the restrictive immigration policies of the government of Japan, rejecting unskilled labor, especially that of women, forces the migrant to choose the sex industry. Filipinas profit from the formal "entertainer" institution, and other women and children use informal channels. This generates a process of expanded reproduction of the informal migrant labor force.

This informalization of migrant labor is also a consequence of the accelerated globalization of the criminal sector. This process, being neo-liberal, creates an offshore and unregulated system favorable to the growth of global criminal organizations. This leads to an expansion of the workforce of the criminal organizations, especially those with a large offshore base, such as the Chinese Mafia with Hong Kong. This is one reason why the Triads controled important sex districts in East Asia such as the Kabuki-cho in Tokyo. Counter-informalization is but a reaction to such global trends by the OECD supported by the United Nations as they seek to preserve the capital security of the formal global corporate sector. Governments tighten their formal control of trafficking in order to protect capital security from the financial threats caused by the transnational criminal organizations.

The sex workers in general, and the "entertainers" in particular, are consequently the victims of neo-liberal globalization. As the global economy expands, they are both more exploited by the informal forces and more excluded by the forces of counter-informalization. This is the underlying dialectical process of the reproduction of exclusion of exploitative migration, which follows neo-liberal globalization.

Concluding reflections: insecurity and Global Political Economy

Let us broaden our perspective beyond the case of exploitative migration and look more generally at the problem of the socioeconomic security of vulnerable groups, facing globalization and informalization.

What we found in the case of the Filipina entertainers can be applied, *mutatis mutandis*, to different situations. The case of terrorist organizations, which is a typical example of anti-systemic informalization, can be compared with transnational criminal organizations, which represent a case of anti-social informalization.

The "terrorists" or more precisely the Mujahiddin engaged in an indiscriminate terrorist *Jihad*, are working through a network of communities quite similar to the criminal networks trafficking women and children into the informal communities of the industrial countries. The terrorists seem to use informal routes, leading from developing to industrial countries, similar to the traffickers in their communication and their financial transfers. They find refuge in informal communities of migrants, similar to the ones composing the sex districts. Their informality makes it difficult for the formal authorities to obtain information. Even when they are informed, the message the authorities receive is often distorted by their occultation of informal realities.

The informality of the everyday world of many *Gemeinschaft*-like communities in both the developing and the industrial countries provides a sanctuary, difficult to access from the formal *Gesellschaft* world, for the reproduction of its workforce. It is on this informal ground that the terrorists build their informal networks, which expand across borders into the industrial countries.

The superior surveillance and information-processing capacity of the formal technocratic apparatus used by the dominant alliance of the anti-terrorist states is unable to detect such activities because of its occultation of the informal everyday realities, which are viewed as irrational, unrealistic and effectively incomprehensible in their eyes.

Of course the development of the terrorist informalization is met by the counter-informalization of the dominant forces, which build formal arguments to justify the use of brutal force against the "terrorists." This produces "collateral damage" among the vulnerable people in the informal communities, but has the effect of also dissociating them from any formal efforts to control the terrorists.

As in the case of the Filipina entertainers whose socioeconomic security had to be guaranteed more broadly within the context of the security of everybody living together in the same informal everyday world, the expanded reproduction of the terrorists' workforce will be interrupted only when the socioeconomic security of the vulnerable people in the informal everyday world, in both the developing and the industrial countries, is adequately guaranteed. As long as extreme patterns of exclusion and exploitation are reproduced in the global economy, the reproduction of the workforce of terrorism will be unavoidable.

To propose this overextended hypothesis on the basis of a quite specific case of the Filipina entertainers may seem to be trespassing the borders of this chapter. However, I want to stress the fact that the ongoing process of neoliberal globalization is accompanied by the informalization of the labor force of marginalized social categories both in terms of extreme inequalities of gender, class and race, and in terms of culture and ethnicity. This situation facilitates the goals of the forces of informalization (anti-social criminal organizations and the anti-systemic terrorists) as they seek to develop their control over the marginalized dwellers of the informal and socially excluded world.

The forces of counter-informalization (for example, the states and ruling elements of the OECD and to a certain extent elsewhere), with their overwhelming military and police means, their cyber-surveillance technologies, and their powers of conviction and media control, wage a "war" against the two faces of informalization and seek to tighten the formal constraints on the marginalized people living in the informal world. As already mentioned, this world is often where a great number of collateral victims are created in the "war" against terror, many of whom are innocent victims wrongly arrested or civilian casualties. This exclusionary reproduction of victims in the widening sphere of marginalized peoples in the neo-liberal global political economy is one of the most serious threats to the socio-economic security of humankind.

This is why I close this chapter by stressing the urgent need to develop a comparative research agenda on globalizing anti-social criminal organizations and anti-systemic terrorist organizations and their relationships with the hegemonic forces of counter-informalization, analyzing the power, reach and frameworks of thought of the formal institutions of the latter, especially the military, the police, and immigration authorities. More knowledge of this aspect of the global dialectic will illuminate our understanding of the structures of everyday life and their links to frameworks and processes of power, production and social reproduction in disciplinary neo-liberal globalization.

Notes

1. We use this term for any movement, violent or non-violent, which puts into question the existing formal political-economic order and attempts to replace it. We define anti-social as any movement, violent or non-violent, which seeks to profit from the flaws of the existing formal political economic order to obtain illegal profits.
2. The Toyota Project is called "Trilateral Comparison of the Impact of Globalization on the Human Security and Human Rights of Women: With special emphasis on women migrant workers, transnational organized crime and international security cooperation." It involved cooperation with DAWN Philippines July–August 2001 in a study focused on a group of former Filipina entertainers. This chapter is based largely on testimony of these sex-industry survivors to DAWN, July 30–31, 2001 in Manila.
3. On "occultation" see Mushakoji (1996).
4. Survivors who participated in the Toyota/DAWN study reported they were not told about *dohan* before beginning work. All expressed embarrassment, but some mentioned they accepted *dohan* as an additional source of income, even when they had to hand to owners a major part of their commissions. Others reported violent treatment when they refused to practice *dohan*. This indicates the ambiguity of survivors' perceptions of this institution, which is exploitative, both sexually and monetarily.

5. The anonymous witness was a president of a firm promoting Philippine-Japanese cultural exchange, sending performing artists and entertainers to Japan. She claimed to operate within the framework of labor conditions agreed by authorities of both countries. Her narrative is based on her own experience, as artist and then as promoter.
6. Since there is no formal legal agreement, it remains a diplomatic-administrative bilateral agreement where the office promoting migration of workers (Philippines) and the immigration office of the Japanese Ministry of Justice establish standards about qualifications of "entertainers" and the workplace assigned to them. On the Japanese side the relevant legal regulation is the *shutsunyukoku-Kanri oyobi Nanmin Nintei Hou* (Law on Immigration and Refugee Qualification) and the Ministry Directive on the Standards Regarding paras 1–2 of the above law.
7. This is a position shared by several Philippine government officials responsible for the promotion of Filipinas migration (interviews, Manila, July 31, 2001).
8. Masako Owaki, member of the Upper House, stated in interview that she became aware of the problems of the JFCs in 1993 when invited by Philippine parliamentarians to a meeting on the topic in Manila to establish closer bilateral cooperation.
9. Batis Center and DAWN Philippines in the Philippines and several NGOs are working together under the Coordinating Center for the Support of JFCs in Japan.
10. Mrs. Owaki, who has visited Thailand several times and who has taken up the case of a Japanese professor prosecuted for child prostitution in Thailand in the Japanese court in 1997, is certain that there are quite a number of Japanese-Thai children but that their case has attracted the attention neither of civil society nor of the governments in sending and receiving countries. This is despite close cooperation between the NGOs in combating the trafficking.
11. See the Open Letter to the Chairs of the UN Commission on Human Security (September 2001, <humsec@yahoogroups.com>) signed, among others, by Betty Reardon where the concept of the "quotidian" is explained.
12. See the Report of the Toyota Project/DAWN FGD (Tokyo 2001, unpublished).
13. On "informalization" see Altvater and Mahnkopf (2002).
14. On the concepts of *Gesellschaft* and *Gemeinschaft* see Toennies (2001).
15. The Convention indicates its concern about capital security in its definition of criminalization of money-laundering. Its requirements include participation of criminal groups (Art. 5), money-laundering (Art. 6), corruption (Art. 8), and obstruction of justice (Art. 23). The Protocols on Trafficking and Smuggling show a bias for security of the industrialized countries by not giving rights of asylum to trafficked persons, and they do not permit smuggled persons to stay in the countries to where they have been smuggled.

Part IV:
Human In/Security on a Universal Scale

Human In/Security on a Universal Scale: Introduction to Part IV
Isabella Bakker, Stephen Gill and Tim Di Muzio

Whilst Part II questioned the sustainability and legitimacy of neo-liberal structures of governance, and Part III highlighted tensions and contradictions for human in/security relative to intensified exploitation of labor, Part IV directs our attention to questions of what is being secured, how this security is achieved, and for whose benefit in the global political economy. In other words, the questions posed in Part IV link together issues connected to imperatives of capital accumulation (including how large corporations seek to maximize control so as to augment their pecuniary worth) to *how the rule of capital is secured* socially, politically and militarily in the face of global resistance to human insecurity, intensified exploitation, and threats to sustainable, progressive forms of social reproduction.

Issues such as these pose the question of whether capital is, or is not, productive. And whilst we cannot enter into this enormous debate at this juncture, we realize it needs to be fully confronted in any subsequent research programs connected to questions this volume has addressed.

Some of the positions in such a debate might be very crudely identified as follows. A particular radical view, derived from Veblen (reflected in Josephson's work on the robber barons, noted below) is that capital is a fetter on the productive powers of society. Capital is a form of power, and more precisely an institutional means to exert control over social production and if need be to exercise sabotage over society so as to maximize its extraction of social surplus. A second view, still held widely on the left, is based on an orthodox reading of Marx. For Marx, the ultimate source of capital's productivity and power is seen as the exploitation of surplus labor. Thus capital is also seen as a form of power as well as a social relation (involving capital and labor). Despite its contradictions, however, capital is generally viewed as a historically progressive, transformative force that tends to augment the productive powers of society. A further argument developed along these lines by Marxist Feminists is that provisioning labor in the sphere of social reproduction acts as a buffer that facilitates the exploitation of surplus labor in formal production, responding to the expansions and contractions of demand for labor, perhaps supplemented by the state's provision of a social wage.

In this volume we take a somewhat different position: that any complete understanding of the productivity of capital requires an integrated analysis of production/social reproduction. We have also emphasized shifts in governance frameworks for production/social reproduction, and how these are shaped and conditioned by new constitutional mechanisms and disciplinary neo-liberal forces, in ways that are both productive of a certain set of power relations, but that might be destructive for human security and broad-based and progressive forms of human development.

A final set of views is widely held and based in Neo-Classical Economics and Neo-Liberal Political Economy, and most of the debates over global governance that emanate from the international financial institutions are located within this context. Here capital is seen as the most important, creative and directing productive force (factor of production). Thus neo-liberals in this tradition call for maximum freedom for capital to accumulate, seeing concentrations of capital and wealth as both productive and justified as means to maximize welfare and efficiency. A modified Neo-Classical view would be that capital is only fully productive and socially efficient if it is subject to redistribution. For example, a research network funded by the Ford Foundation argues that:

> Unequal distribution of assets... denies the poor access to factors of production... [and] facilitates the exploitation of the excluded by perpetuating unequal economic power relations... This scarcity allows the asset holders (for example, home owners) to generate a higher income (such as rent). The same would apply to other forms of assets, such as credit and financial assets, where if people had access to abundant credit, the ability to charge high rates of interest would be compromised. Therefore contrary to orthodox economic theory, the distribution of income is not related simply to the productivity of the assets, but also to its scarcity. Clearly, asset distribution must form part of a broader analysis of poverty, and policies of asset redistribution must be considered as a core element of a strategy to reduce poverty.[1]

So it is with these debates in mind that we draw the reader's attention to a little-noticed footnote in *Capital*, where Marx quoted the Secretary to the London Consolidated Society of Bookbinders, T.J. Dunning:

Capital eschews no profit, or very small profit, just as Nature was formerly said to abhor a vacuum. With adequate profit, capital is very bold. A certain 10% will ensure its employment anywhere; 20% certain will produce eagerness; 50% positive audacity; 100% will make it ready to trample on all human laws; 300%, and there is not a crime at which it will scruple, nor a risk it will not run, even to the chances of its owner being hanged. If turbulence and strife will bring a profit, it will freely encourage both. (Marx 1976: 926, fn 15)

So whilst Marx generally thought that capital was both a productive as well as a destructive force in transforming social conditions of existence, he never lost sight of the violence associated with not only original or primitive accumulation but with accumulation more generally. In this regard, Marx thought Dunning's words revealed how the central, indeed ultimate interest of owners of capital was the greatest possible augmentation of pecuniary values. Marx thought that capital would go to extreme – if need be, illegal – lengths to multiply the size of these values, including control over the infrastructures that underpin the very material basis of general social reproduction. Examples in economic history of this are legion, for example, the nineteenth-century US robber barons who, operating from Wall Street, gained control over the railroads in order to exploit the vulnerability of both producers and consumers across the growing, far-flung continent as the frontier expanded (Josephson 1934).

A similar and more recent process took place recently in California where after the very deregulation for which giant energy firms had lobbied, a number of these very firms colluded to exert full control over the entire California energy sector. The firms were then able to massively increase prices, whilst businesses and citizens in California faced higher bills, blackouts and brownouts, and not least, the most vulnerable who were unable to pay bills were denied service altogether, in a society which, as is noted in Chapter 10, is dependent upon intensive uses of energy for its social identity and social reproduction. Indeed, reflecting the tactics of the earlier robber barons, energy prices were rigged to meet the profit expectations of Wall Street investors.[2]

Thus in Part IV, the three chapters consider the dialectic between the expansion of capital, that is its universalization, and the conditions for human security and social reproduction in both affluent and poorer societies. So in evaluating the evidence concerning global inequality and structures of exploitation and in/security, we would note that of the perspectives we have sketched on the question of whether capital is productive, only a particular neo-liberal perspective would see the present distribution and use of capital in an especially positive light. Moreover, this perspective separates the economic and political aspects of capital accumulation, in ways that depoliticize what are in fact deeply political questions – such as redefining of food security by connecting its provisioning through deeper integration into the world market.

By contrast, and noting that "food security is ultimately a political relationship," Chapter 9 by Philip McMichael seeks to understand how and in what ways the discourses and practices associated with "food security" have changed since World War II and what consequences these transformations have for social reproduction, particularly in the developing countries. McMichael argues that with the onset of neo-liberal globalization, food security has been redefined from one based on notions of national self-sufficiency to one premised on the production and delivery of food by private market forces. This process is encouraged and increasingly locked-in by new constitutional multilateral legal mechanisms that privilege large agribusiness and facilitate their ability to gain control over the global food commons. Such control by the corporate food giants is achieved through horizontal and vertical integration and increasingly protected by intellectual property rights in trade and investment agreements. However, such developments are leading to a reduction in biodiversity, an increase in monoculture, the loss of local knowledge systems, the concentration of farming and agro-export platforms, and a rapid decrease in food self-sufficiency with a corresponding increase in hunger. In other words, the accumulation of profit seems to take precedence over any wider concern for human life, human security and notions of local, sustainable social reproduction. As McMichael notes, "the social reproduction of affluence rests on a foundation of starvation."

Nevertheless McMichael notes that globalizing forces "from below" are increasingly combining to challenge corporate power under the banner of "food sovereignty." For example, the Brazilian landless-workers' movement seeks to offer an alternative to corporate agriculture founded on principles of ecology, democracy, education and cooperation, and thus politically redefines the issues of social reproduction in a progressive way.

Chapter 10 by Stephen Gill focuses on the social reproduction of affluence, and its representation in US culture, society and political economy. Gill situates his analysis in a sketch of the hierarchy of social and political forces in a global order configured by disciplinary neo-liberalism. For Gill, this world order is characterized by growing inequality and human insecurity, on the one hand, and by concerted efforts to guarantee the security of capital, on the other, for example, through the institutionalization of new intellectual property rights and other governance frameworks. These frameworks are elaborated in Chapter 11, which also indicates that if legal and governance frameworks are not enough to secure the US-led project of globalization (and with it the power of capital), surveillance and military power is also threatened or is actually used against those who may oppose it.

Thus according to Gill an exploration of the US political economy is crucial to understanding contemporary world order, partly because the dominant stratum of its capitalist class is highly organized and conscious of its strategic position in the project as well as the process of globalization. With this in mind, Chapter 10 identifies fundamental elements in US society, culture and political economy to help explain what motivates US foreign and domestic policy. American lifestyles are increasingly energy-intensive, consumerist, individualist and premised on forms of social Darwinism that have entailed restructuring of social institutions and patterns of social risk. This, along with the shock associated with the mega-terrorist attacks of 9/11, as well as violence within US society, have led to generalized and growing perceptions of increasing insecurity on the part of the various components of the American social formation. In this context, Gill points out that one of the paradoxes of intensified globalization is that there may be an inverse correlation between the amount of wealth held by individuals and their sense of personal security. Despite the trends for affluent people to invest in the construction of panic rooms, to live in gated communities, and to hire private protection for their personal security, high net worth individuals seem to be increasingly concerned that they live under a state of siege. Gill links this to what he calls social enclavization, in which both the spatial and social coordinates of social inequality and the associated new insecurity are undergoing redefinition.

By contrast, whilst the rich seek to construct new means of security, and have their social reproduction underpinned by hiring workers from the new service classes and receiving subsidies from the state that socializes their risks (corporate welfare), the US poor see a reprivatization of social and economic risks, they endure punitive regimes of workfare, criminalization and surveillance, and they are situated amid racialized patterns of incarceration in a society that is increasingly atomized and violent. This is also reflected in racialized employment conditions as well as in remarkably high US incarceration statistics and the use of capital punishment.

Paradoxically, many black members of the working classes of the USA seek to escape from the violence of contemporary American society by enlisting in the US Armed Forces. In many respects, the US Armed Forces act as a surrogate system of socialized provision, providing social structure and a sense of duty, meaning and inclusion, albeit paradoxically one that operates globally to secure the interests and investments that tend to benefit the US plutocracy and the affluent "culture of contentment" of the USA.

Recent evidence on the new, "all-volunteer, professional" US military and its role during the war in Iraq in 2003 have indicated how important enlistment in the armed services has become, especially for black women and men, particularly those who have some educational attainment and who have little opportunity for advancement in their fragmented communities. The military provides them with structures that civilian life denies them: training, education and career possibilities. In a society riven by racial discrimination, for working-class blacks and Hispanics, the military is increasingly seen as an "equal opportunity employer."

Thus members of the US working classes provide much of the personnel for the Pentagon's global power projection. As Chapter 11 shows, such projection has been recently linked to new doctrines of "democratic imperialism" involving strategies to secure the world for an expansion of American-led corporate globalization as well as its energy security. Indeed, this was recently codified in a new National Security doctrine of "preventive" war and unchallengeable military superiority (US Government 2002). Such superiority is premised on "full spectrum dominance." Full spectrum dominance means that the US now intends to dominate any adversary, or indeed potential group of adversaries, across the entire spectrum of military capabilities (land, sea, air and space), backed up by dominance in information processing, cyberwar, intelligence and propaganda. Since 9/11 this new imperial vision has become increasingly asserted in US strategy, for example, as reflected in the Bush Administration's offensive to promote "regime change" and threats to "pre-empt" potential adversaries.

Despite divisions within the ranks of the American leadership, elements from the Bush Administration have stated that the purpose of American strategy is not only to make the world safer for globalization but also to extend it, eliminating threats not only from rogue regimes and religious fundamentalists, but also those that might stem from the widening gap between what the Pentagon calls the "haves" and "have-nots" in world society. As one Pentagon strategist put it, justifying the anticipated war in Iraq and its extension throughout the Middle East and elsewhere, "If gated communities and rent-a-cops were enough, September 11 never would have happened... [The threats to the USA] will not go away until we as a nation respond to the challenge of *making globalization truly global*" (Barnett 2003: 7, emphasis added). It is statements such as this, along with bellicose noises coming from Washington prior to and indeed after the fall of Baghdad in April 2003, that have unnerved many people throughout the world. This new juncture seems pregnant with intensified global conflict, as states and social forces will undoubtedly seek some means to resist or indeed to countervail American hyper-power in the new world order.

Notes

1. Capital Ownership Group: <cog.kent.edu/grppoverty.htm>, accessed April 21, 2003.
2. Richard A. Oppel, "Panel Finds Manipulation by Energy Companies." *New York Times*, March 27, 2003.

9
Food Security and Social Reproduction: Issues and Contradictions[1]

Philip McMichael

Food security, like development, is a universal ideal. But like development, food security is ultimately a political relationship, with consequences for who decides what is produced for whom and under what conditions. This chapter examines the circumstances under which the food security relation expresses changing conditions of social reproduction, focusing on the tensions arising from the undermining of national provisioning by corporate globalization. The central thesis is that while the patterns of social reproduction of the current neo-liberal regime and its social-democratic predecessor have not been independent of capitalist social relations, they diverge sharply in support of public versus private rights, and structures of public accountability and social sustainability and security.

In the past half century, "food security" has functioned as an enabling concept in the development arsenal. Its changing meaning reflects the transformation of development ideology, from a public project deploying foreign aid to support the ideal of the "development state," to a private project of marketing of the state and deepening the commodification of food. That is, food security has been incorporated into the privatization of public functions associated with corporate globalization and its neo-liberal regime. Here, the fundamental contradiction is that "free" markets are progressively excluding and/or starving populations already dispossessed through the very implementation of markets in the name of food security. The consequences are that despite conditions of food abundance, a growing proportion of the world's population is experiencing an increasingly unsustainable form of social reproduction as capital reorganizes relations of production and consumption of food on a world scale.

This chapter traces the reframing of the food security relation in the process of subordination of developmentalism to neo-liberalism. Within this movement, the privileging of corporate agriculture has led to a syndrome of "food from nowhere," where agro-exporting by transnational food firms has turned the natural world into a giant chessboard of corporate comparative advantage at the expense of rural communities and biodiversity. As states accommodate to the appropriation of food security by corporate interests, subject communities and their counter-movement supporters are reappropriating the initiative via the explicitly political ideal of "food sovereignty." Through an examination of the changing meaning of food security, this chapter illuminates the political-economic relations of the corporate assault on farming, biodiversity and food quality, and the counter-movement alternatives of "food from somewhere."

Food security in the development project

Food security as an ideal emerged in the post-World War II world as a programmatic thrust of the international development project. Food shortages were endemic to the colonies, resulting from their conversion to export agriculture and the use of market infrastructures to channel grains out of rural communities into metropolitan centers. At the turn of the twentieth century, for example, "Londoners were in effect eating India's bread" (Davis 2001: 26–7). Subsequent colonial independence movements seized on the issue of food security, and, with European grain harvest failures threatening post-war reconstruction plans: food security became part of the development agenda globally.

The development project was framed within the terms of the Bretton Woods regime of "embedded liberalism" (Ruggie 1982) whereby international trade and financial flows were politically contained and managed by multilateral institutions such as the General Agreement on Tariffs and Trade (GATT) and the International Monetary Fund (IMF). Even though post-war neo-colonial relationships sustained the colonial division of labor, and a corporate-led process of transnational integration of economic relationships matured under this regime (Lacher 1999), sovereign states in the UN system were supposed to develop national economies. The GATT sought to reduce barriers to trade, but agriculture was excluded from the original GATT agreement (1947), giving force to the principle of national food self-sufficiency. This principle took its bearings from the US path of development, which modeled the national articulation of manufacturing and farming sectors (Friedmann and McMichael 1989). However, the model of national development was inevitably subordinated to the global power relations of Cold War geopolitics.

The USA's strategy of containment of communism partly depended on elaboration of the development project as an international relation (including aid) framed in national terms. Designed to stem communism by promoting free enterprise, the development project was backed by a massive military and economic aid program, including food aid (McMichael 2000). In fact, the USA managed to override the United Nations multilateral program of international relief, centered in two of its agencies: the Food and Agricultural Organization (FAO) and the UN Relief and Rehabilitation Administration (UNRRA). President Truman ignored the UN's proposal for a World Food Board to organize reserves and regulate international trade in food. Instead he chose to pursue bilateral programs. US food aid replaced UNRRA aid in the Far East, bolstering Chiang Kai-shek's anti-communist forces in China, and in Europe via the Marshall Plan (Cleaver 1977: 16). By 1953 the Marshall Plan had transferred $41.3 billion to the First World, and $3 billion to the Third World, as part of the containment strategy of the Cold War.

Under these historic conditions, food security through aid was indelibly linked to the doctrine of development through containment (and vice versa). The US food aid program, facilitated by the 1954 Public Law 480, institutionalized a pattern of channeling government subsidized food surpluses to strategically located Third World countries (Friedmann 1982). Wheat imports into the Third World rose from a base of practically zero in the mid-1950s to almost 50% of all world food imports by 1971 (Friedmann 1990: 20). While this program's strategic rationale was geopolitical, in subsidizing the development of urban-industrial sectors in select Third World states with cheap American food, the post-war food regime linked American farming prosperity to growing food dependency in the Third World.

In a parallel development, the green revolution deepened food dependency on US bio-technology, as hybrid crops (mainly wheat and rice) were introduced into irrigated areas of the Third World, from Turkey to Brazil, to complement the flow of grains from the USA, and increasingly European, "breadbaskets." Green revolution farmers were weaned from a seed sharing culture of mixed farming to a monoculture of staple grains marketed in urban areas. Food security, again, was constructed as a commercial operation geared to supplying relatively cheap foods to urban consumers. This model, stemming from the emphasis of the development project on elaborating national economies (supplemented with foreign aid and technology transfer), displayed its urban bias, privileging the centralizing forces of government-sponsored industrialization and residualizing rural culture.

Reframing "food security" as a market good

The 1990s shift from a nationally-centered development project to a corporate globalization project marked the subordination of public to private interests, as neo-liberal ideology identified the world market as the vehicle of development. Food security was redefined in market terms. This formulation framed the GATT Uruguay Round (1986–94), laying the groundwork for the

1994 WTO Agreement on Agriculture. The US representative to the Uruguay Round articulated the redefinition thus:

> The US has always maintained that self-sufficiency and food security are not one and the same. Food security – the ability to acquire the food you need when you need it – is best provided through a smooth-functioning world market. (quoted in Ritchie 1993: fn 25)

The 1986 Uruguay Round initiated the most recent phase in the liberalization of agriculture, when the Cairns Group of agro-exporters and a powerful US-centered agribusiness lobby pressed for agricultural reforms in the GATT (the US proposal was drafted by the former senior vice-president of Cargill, which shares 50% of US grain exports with Continental). Reforms included reductions in trade protection, farm subsidies and government intervention. Free trade was the ostensible demand, but the underlying agenda was an informal US mercantilism of constructing a "comparative advantage" through deregulating a highly unequal world market. The Agreement on Agriculture was designed to open agricultural markets by imposing minimum import requirements and tariff and producer subsidy reductions. The effect was to open markets for Northern products, strengthening the position of the OECD countries in the international division of labor in agriculture. From 1970 to 1996, the OECD share in the volume of world cereal exports rose from 73% to 82%; the USA remained the world's major exporter of commercial crops such as maize, soybeans and wheat; and the share of Africa, Latin America and Asia in world cereal imports increased to nearly 60% (Pistorius and Wijk 1999: 110–11).

The elevation of food security to a market good substitutes the price form for political calculus in determining the possibility and extent of national food self-reliance. This is not to say that nation-states uniformly can attain food self-sufficiency, since in addition to varying ecological and spatial endowments the post-colonial state system remained embedded in a division of world labor, where some countries depended disproportionately on tropical exports. However, the marketization and the privatization of food security intensify such dependence as it removes the capacity of all states to build and/or protect national farm sectors.

While this may appear phenomenally as a movement from state to market, as the organizing principle of the political economy, it is actually a more profound shift, with far-reaching implications for the conditions of social reproduction. Modern capitalist states are instantiated within private property relations, such that markets are political institutions, underpinned by contractual and other regulations ultimately enforced by state power. As political institutions, markets have been structured by the balance of social forces, which in turn depend partly on the prevailing conditions of capital accumulation. As these conditions have incorporated increasing dimensions of social life, through commodification, markets and states have been transformed to facilitate and reflect this process. Thus the subordination of food to capital has shifted the social provisioning of food from a public necessity to a private right in the marketplace, as neo-liberalism has redefined the meaning of the state and the market. Food, formerly a basic necessity and a mere wage cost to capital, has become increasingly a consumer product and a frontier of profit as capital has incorporated consumption relations into the accumulation process itself (Friedmann and McMichael 1989). Incorporation stems from two complementary strategies: first, agro-industrialization and the reconstruction of food as a consumer product (Barndt 2002; Dixon 2002), premised on the abstraction of agriculture from its ecological and cultural foundations (Goodman *et al.* 1987); and, second, the deepening of this process through the elaboration of multilateral rules to decompose public securities and recompose market relations favoring corporate rights over public/civic rights (such as land and seed access, and food self-sufficiency).

The political recomposition of market relations as corporate property, authored by states via neo-liberal rules, depends on a variety of often quite contradictory tactics – such as trade controls, subsidized exporting, market deregulation, farm subsidies, intellectual property rights, and so on. The global South, under pressure to open markets, bitterly opposes the current hypocritical intensification of agricultural protections in the global North, reducing the South's market access. While these political tactics may contradict neo-liberal rhetoric, they collectively undermine the coherence of farm sectors, rural cultures and civic rights to food security, by enhancing corporate control. In this sense, the privatization of food security relations expresses the shift from the welfare/development state of the mid-twentieth century to the privatizing state of the twenty-first century, with the Uruguay Round as midwife.

The GATT agreement, which included anti-dumping protocols and provisions to avoid exporting of food surpluses, was soon subverted by US and European practices. In 1955, the US government instituted protection of its farm supply policies of price supports and production controls to establish a price floor. While tariffs protected farmers specializing in single products (wheat, corn, rice, sugar, dairy products), price subsidies encouraged overproduction, generating the food surpluses exported under the auspices of the PL-480 program. By the early 1960s, the European Common Agricultural Policy (CAP) negotiated border protection of its domestic food system with the USA, in return for free entry of American feedstuffs. The CAP then generated surpluses of animal protein supplied by cheap imported feed, which in turn closed local outlets for domestic feed grains. Both sets of policies, in generating food surpluses, led to an intensifying competition for world market outlets via export dumping (Friedmann 1993).

World agricultural prices fell 39% between 1975 and 1989. In this context, the US Agriculture Secretary, John Block, confirmed the neo-liberal definition of food security, observing in 1986 that:

> The idea that developing countries should feed themselves is an anachronism from a bygone era. They could better ensure their food security by relying on US agricultural products, which are available in most cases at lower cost. (quoted in Schaeffer 1995: 268)

In the same year, US corn-dumping forced Zimbabwe's grain marketing board to cut domestic producers' prices almost in half and to reduce its purchase quota from these producers (Watkins 1996: 43). In other words, the food source switched from domestic farmers to the international grain traders.

The Uruguay Round targeted US and European Community agricultural policies (Dawkins 1999), attempting to discipline the destabilizing impact of US/EU export competition, and the growing cost of farm subsidies, which contradicted neo-liberal doctrine. The Round was committed to liberalization of agriculture and services, paying lip service to market access for Southern exports, but essentially shaped by American and European needs to regulate Northern trade competition and lower the farm bill, and, arguably by an American attempt to weaken the CAP's export apparatus. Anticipating the outcome of the Round, the McSharry reform of 1992 enabled the EU to drop its original CAP farm price support policies and embrace the government subsidy system adopted by the USA in the 1980s (Dawkins 1999; McMichael 1994). Such privileging of the price form synchronized EU policy with the US policy (formalized in 1996) of favoring traders over producers by removing the floor on farm commodity prices, establishing a "world market price" for agricultural commodities. Grain traders were now able to purchase commodities through farm contracts at prices below the cost of production (including public subsidies), and dump them on the world market. Farm prices for the major commodities in world trade fell 30% or more in the first half decade since the WTO agreement was signed in December 1994 (Ritchie 1999), and *The Economist* has noted that commodity prices are at an all-time low for the last century and a half.[2]

The privileging of the price form was anticipated by the Agreement on Agriculture, which mandated universal reductions in trade protection, farm subsidies and government intervention. The mechanisms included converting protections such as import quotas to fixed tariffs, subject to progressive reduction; a standard of minimum market access for every agricultural product (5% for the global North and 4% for the global South); "decoupling" of farm support from production volumes; and export subsidy reductions (Einarsson 2001: 5). Such deregulation of farm price supports has compromised the ability of many countries to meet their commitments to the WTO's Agreement on Agriculture, as their farmers have been unable to recover the cost of their production in the face of collapsing prices. Countries with capacity to pay have retained subsidies.

The establishment of a world market price (expressing corporate relations) reflected an ongoing capitalist restructuring of Northern agriculture, in turn enabled by the GATT reforms. In effect, this price reflected corporate dominance in world agriculture. For example, by the mid-1990s, 80% of farm subsidies in the OECD countries concentrated on the largest 20% of (corporate) farms, rendering small farmers increasingly vulnerable to the vicissitudes of a deregulated (and increasingly privately managed) global market for agricultural products. In 1994, 50% of US farm products came from 2% of the farms, and only 9% from 73% of the farms (Lehman and Krebs 1996). Between 1998 and 1999, UK farm income fell by about 75%, driving 20,000 farmers out of business; and US farm income declined by almost 50% between 1996 and 1999 (Gorelick 2000: 28–30).

In other words, privileging the price form is not so much a method of freeing trade, as a strategy favoring agribusiness: consolidating corporate production and processing and cheap food to enhance agro-export power. The US/EU Blair House Agreement – essentially a WTO-normalized protection racket – legitimizes Northern agro-export advantages. The Agreement pegged reductions in domestic support and export subsidies to a baseline from 1986, when stocks and subsidies peaked. This allowed the EU and the USA considerable flexibility in meeting their obligations, and established a "peace clause" regarding action against farm support programs and export subsidies (Dawkins 1999). The legitimization of export subsidies (25 of 132 WTO members) has, perversely, allowed the USA and the EU to intensify export dumping such that "just 3 (members) are responsible for 93% of all subsidized wheat exports and just 2 of them are responsible for subsidizing 94% of butter and 80% of beef exports" (Dawkins 1999).

Through the Agreement on Agriculture, the WTO institutionalized an historic shift in the meaning of food security, presaged by US Agriculture Secretary Block at the opening of the Uruguay Round. Under this regime, states no longer have the right to full self-sufficiency as a national strategy. Rather, the minimum market access rule guarantees the "right to export" and this "applies to developed and developing countries alike, and even when the lower prices is made possible through export subsidies" (Einarsson 2001: 6). Southern states signed onto the Agreement on Agriculture expecting to improve their foreign currency earnings from expanded agro-exports, in order to retire foreign debt. However, since Northern commodities are cheaper on the world market because of export subsidies and economies of mechanized scale, and corporations' internal transactions account for 70% of the international food trade, the overall impact of expanding minimum market access requirements and tariff lowering is likely to promote exports from North to South, rather than in the opposite direction (Einarsson 2001: 7).

Substantively, then, food security has involved growing dependence on food importing for a large minority of Southern states. By the mid-1990s, half of the foreign exchange of the FAO's 88 low-income food deficit countries went to food imports (LeQuesne 1997). FAO analysis has shown that food dependent states' food bills grew on average 20% between 1994 and 1999, in spite of record low prices in the late 1990s (Murphy 1999: 3). Meanwhile, Northern states continue farm support, with effective subsidies, by one estimate, of 49% and 30% for US and European farmers, respectively (Malhotra 1996: 2). In the absence of public capacity in the South, unprotected farmers are exposed to a structure of unfair trade. As Oxfam asks: "How can a farmer earning $230 a year (average per capita income in LDCs) compete with a farmer who enjoys a subsidy of $20,000 a year (average subsidy in OECD countries)?" (Bailey 2000).

This "food security" relationship is consistent with a corporate conceptualization of "comparative advantage," formulated thus:

> The Agreement on Agriculture prescribes a model for agriculture that has basically only one dimension: increasing agricultural production for exports, importing what cannot be produced without tariff protection or subsidies to producers. (Murphy 1999: 2)

Thus, for India, Sharma observes: "whereas for small farmers the subsidies have been withdrawn, there is a lot of support now for agribusiness industry... The result is that the good area under staple foods is now shifting to export crops, so we'll have to import staple food" (quoted in Madeley 2000a: 79). In Chile, between 1989 and 1993 the food crop area fell 30%, as beans, wheat and other staples were replaced by fruit, flowers and other export crops – a pattern repeated across the South under the neo-liberal regime. While 90% of agricultural research expenditures in Latin America were devoted to food crop research in the 1980s, during the 1990s 80% focused on export crops (Madeley 2000a: 54–5).

While the substitution of export crops for domestic crops is only an approximate measure of the dismantling of national farm sectors, or of the "commons," as the foundation of rural life, nevertheless it symbolizes the subjection of agriculture to the commodity form, via neo-liberal institutional dictates and the corresponding privatization of food security relations. As local producers and markets are scuttled by removal of public protections, marginalized by the privileging of export cropping, and swamped by artificially-cheapened food imports, the conditions of social reproduction in the countryside are reconstituted within new circuits of capital enabled by the corporate globalization project.

"Food from nowhere"

The WTO's regime of liberalization is distinguished by a process of conversion of parts of the world into a series of agro-export platforms – as an alternative model to a world of states with farm sectors as anchors of self-sufficiency. This gives rise to a "food from nowhere" syndrome (Bové and Dufour 2001: 55), which symbolizes a food security relation based on the abstraction of agriculture through its incorporation and reproduction within global capital circuits. At the core of this process is the appropriation of farming, which takes several forms – expulsion of rural populations through land dispossession and concentration as farming is rendered unviable by withdrawal of public supports and exposure to world market prices for food, or the conversion of farmers to contract farming, or hired/plantation/migrant labor, depending on context and crop. In a 1997 FAO study of 16 Southern countries, the overall impact of liberalization was identified with:

> A general trend towards the concentration of farms, in a wide cross-section of countries. While this led to increased productivity and competitiveness with positive results, in the virtual absence of safety nets the process also marginalized small producers and added to unemployment and poverty. (quoted in Madeley 2000a: 75)

A Honduran farmer, in Seattle, noted:

> WTO regulations have extremely destructive effects on small farms in Honduras. Import barriers have come down, permitting the import of cheap food produce from Europe, Canada and the US. Today, we cannot sell our own farm products on the markets because of these imports. Free trade is for multinationals; it is not for the small peasant farmers. (quoted in Madeley 2000a: 81)

While the FAO study did not provide data on expulsion, conservative estimates are that between 20 and 30 million people have lost their land from the impact of trade liberalization (Madeley 2000a: 75).

Structural Adjustment Programs (SAPs), implemented by the IMF and the Bank under the auspices of the management of the debt crisis, provided a dress rehearsal for the wholesale trade liberalization associated with the establishment of the WTO. SAPs, applied on a case-by-case basis, used currency devaluation, privatization, wage reduction and trade liberalization measures to discipline and stabilize indebted states and their currencies. Not only did SAPs decompose national economies (Chossudovsky 1997: 78), but also they reinstated a new, and dramatic, cycle of de-peasantization (Araghi 1995).

In Peru, for example, the IMF conditions for debt rescheduling in 1990 reportedly almost halved real wages, reduced those with adequate employment to 15% of the workforce and drastically impoverished 4 million people. Structural adjustment, supplemented by cheap corn imports, resulted in inflated prices for fuel, farm inputs and agricultural credit, bankrupting small farmers and enriching agro-industrial monopolies. The impoverishment of staple food producers and the enrichment of commercial, export agriculture was anchored in new laws in 1991 privatizing and concentrating landownership, polarizing the countryside around new areas of peasant subsistence (and coca cash-cropping) and agro-export production (Chossudovsky 1997: 206–7). By 1995, food insecurity was measured in a ten-fold decline in corn cultivation while coca production had risen by 50% (Ismi 1998: 10).

In Southern Africa, where 15 million face starvation currently, the official "famine" threshold has been crossed (for definitions of this threshold, see Patel and Delwiche (2002: 2)). Structural adjustment policies have contributed to this condition, through promotion of export agriculture and the replacement of state marketing boards with private buyers, whose purchasing decisions are governed by profit and speculation, both of which discriminate systematically against small producers (Patel and Delwiche 2002: 4). In Zambia, those living below the poverty line rose from 69% to 86% between 1996 and 2001. Across Lesotho, Malawi, Mozambique, Swaziland, Zambia and Zimbabwe, 51% of the population live below national poverty lines. In Lesotho, two-thirds of the population live below the poverty line, and yet the World Food Programme has declared there are adequate food supplies in the market (Patel and Delwiche 2002: 2). This fundamental contradiction, whereby "free" markets exclude and/or starve populations dispossessed as a result of their implementation, characterizes food security under the neoliberal regime.

As suggested above, markets are political institutions, and their behavior is a function of the policies and forces constructing them. India is a seemingly counter-intuitive case of national food self-sufficiency with a government-managed food supply, currently stockpiling 53 million metric tons of surplus wheat. And yet 350 million Indians starve. In a manner reminiscent of the US government's relationship to powerful farm lobbies in the 1950s, the Indian central government has privileged large Punjabi farmers (green revolution beneficiaries) through purchasing their grain at increasingly inflated prices. Government exporting of surplus grains at lower prices maintains the high domestic price of grain. This practice has inflated wheat prices 30% since 1997, pushing consumer prices beyond the reach of the poor, at the same time as international lenders have pressured the government to reduce food subsidies. Meanwhile, the inflated market has intensified corruption, stimulating informal marketing of at least a third of the grain that should be available to the poor through the half a million "ration shops," representing a Public Distribution System that is gradually deteriorating. In the Punjab's neighboring state of Rajasthan, villagers unable to purchase wheat are forced to eat boiled leaves or discs or bread made from grass seeds, which hastens rather than slows the march of famine-induced death.³

Indian agriculture, the home of tens of millions of small farmers and source of livelihood of 75% of the population, is steadily being undermined by the neo-liberal policies introduced in 1991. An Indian Ministry of Agriculture booklet stated in 2000: "The growth in agriculture has slackened during the 1990s. Agriculture has become a relatively unrewarding profession due to an unfavourable price regime and low value addition, causing abandoning of farming and migration from rural areas" (Paringaux 2001: 4). Corporate seed prices have inflated ten-fold; cheap imports (notably of rice and vegetable oils) have undercut local farmers and processors. Meanwhile, policies promoting agro-exports of affluent commodities like farmed shrimp, flowers and meat in the name of food security increase human insecurities. Every dollar of foreign exchange earned on meat exports destroys 15 dollars' worth of ecological capital stemming from the use of farm animals in sustainable agriculture (Shiva 2000: 14). In these overall circumstances, the social reproduction of affluence rests on a global foundation of starvation, destitution and destruction of social and ecological sustainability.

The leading regional component of WTO liberalization is the North American Free Trade Agreement (NAFTA). Public Citizen's *Global Trade Watch* documents a common process of elimination of small farmers across the whole North American region as the legacy of the NAFTA (implemented in 1994).⁴ While US dumping of subsidized corn in the Mexican market has displaced millions of Mexican *campesinos* (not to mention the associated genetic contamination of landraces), US crop farmers in turn face an intensification of competitive imports from Mexico and Canada. Since 1994, 33,000 US farms with under $100,000 annual income have disappeared (six times the decline for 1988–93). Meanwhile, during the 1990s a massive demographic shift occurred in Mexico, where population growth overall was 20%, urban population grew 44% and rural only 6% (Public Citizen 2001: ii–iv). In Canada, meanwhile, although the agro-export trade surplus has grown, farm incomes have declined by 17.6% and farm debt has spiked by 53% (Public Citizen 2001: 12).

Under NAFTA, the Mexican government followed the US/EU policy of privileging the price form by eliminating the floor price for, and obligation to purchase, under the *Compania Nacional de Subsistencia Popular* (CONASUPO), staple crops such as maize and beans, replacing these guarantees with direct-assistance to farmers under the *Programa Nacional de Solidaridad* (PROCAMPO). Removal of price supports exposed *campesinos* to commodity markets controlled by the transnational grain traders, reducing real market maize prices to *campesinos* by 46.2% between 1993 and 1999 as US corn shipments to Mexico grew 15-fold (Public Citizen 2001: 17, 24).

From a food security perspective, NAFTA is the culmination of a longer process of conversion of Mexico from a food self-sufficient nation (formally relinquished in 1982 when the Mexican Food System, *SAM*, was dismantled) to one that imports one-third of its food needs. The food security relation has been reconstituted, as elsewhere across the global South, through a new division of agricultural labor whereby Mexico specializes in horticultural exports to North America (fruits and vegetables) and imports a proportion of its staple grain requirements. Displaced maize farmers (especially women) find their way either to the new *agro-maquilas* in Mexico, or to North American orchards or plantations, where what they may earn in a week in Mexico equals what they earn in a day in the USA (Barndt 2002: 45). Either way they have entered the global circuits whereby they are producing food for (socially) distant consumers under the control largely of transnational corporations. Barndt chronicles the increasingly common conditions of social reproduction of the global labor force:

> [T]he only Mexican inputs are the land, the sun, and the workers... The South has been the source of the seeds, while the North has the biotechnology to alter them... [T]he workers who produce the tomatoes do not benefit. Their role in agro-export production also denies them participation in subsistence agriculture, especially since the peso crisis in 1995, which has forced migrant workers to move to even more scattered work sites. They now travel most of the year – with little time to grow food on their own plots in their home communities... [W]ith this loss of control comes a spiritual loss, and a loss of a knowledge of seeds, of organic fertilizers and pesticides, of sustainable practices such as crop rotation or leaving the land fallow for a year – practices that had maintained the land for millennia. (Barndt 1997: 59–62)

The corporate relation

The deepening of the food from nowhere pattern, via the political reconstitution of markets, expresses and enhances the power of food corporations. The WTO ethos is that universalizing the export model would render agricultural protections unnecessary because of expanding global food flows – recasting food security as a global relation. With respect to US policy, Public Citizen notes:

> Proponents of the [NAFTA] legislation contended it would make farming more efficient and responsive to market forces; in reality it essentially handed the production of food to agribusiness... Ironically, to counteract the predictable failure of NAFTA and the similar farm deregulation policies embodied in the Freedom to Farm Act, Congress has had to appropriate emergency farm supports – in massive farm bailout bills – every year since the legislation went into effect. (Public Citizen 2001: 16)

As states that could afford farm support ran up huge relief bills, agribusiness corporations took the opportunity to restructure, with input industries and output industries consolidating "within and across their narrow sectors and [creating] alliances with other food industries to encircle farmers and consumers in a web... from selling seeds and bioengineering animal varieties to producing the pesticides, fertilizers, veterinary pharmaceuticals and feed to grow them to transporting, slaughtering, processing and packaging the final 'product'" (Public Citizen 2001: 19). The Canadian National Farmers Union testified in 2000 that "almost every link in the chain, nearly every sector, is dominated by between two and ten multibillion-dollar multinational corporations" (quoted in Public Citizen 2001: 20).

Once NAFTA sanctioned 100% foreign investor rights in Mexican agriculture, Pillsbury's Green Giant subsidiary relocated its frozen food processing from California to Mexico to obtain cheap wages, minimal food safety standards, and zero tariffs on re-export to the USA; Cargill purchased a beef and chicken plant in Saltillo, and Cargill de Mexico invested nearly $200 million in facilities such as vegetable oil refining and soybean processing in Tula. Meanwhile, anticipating the Free Trade Area of the Americas, Tyson Foods has cross-border operations in Mexico, Brazil, Argentina and Venezuela; ConAgra processes oilseed in Argentina; and Archer Daniel Midlands crushes and refines oilseed, mills corn and flour, and bioengineers feeds in Mexico, Central and South America; and Wal-Mart sells in Argentina and Brazil (Public Citizen 2001: 21). Cross-border operations enable corporations to exploit food market asymmetries between North and South, undercutting Northern entitlement structures and their institutional supports by optimizing the strategy of global sourcing, and keeping control over processing and distribution where most of the value added in corporate agribusiness is to be made.

Ultimately, global sourcing is a relationship dependent upon the political reconstitution of markets by trade rules. As Public Citizen observes:

> Multinational agribusinesses were positioned uniquely to take advantage of trade rules that force countries to accept agricultural imports regardless of their domestic supplies. The companies utilized their foreign holdings as export platforms to sell imported agriculture goods in the US, and by thus increasing supply, put negative pressures on US agriculture prices. (Public Citizen 2001: 13)

Bové, referring to the pervasive influence of the regime of world prices resulting from the nexus between agribusiness and WTO rules, claims:

> Less than 5% of agricultural production goes on to the world market. Yet those responsible for that 5% of international trade dominate the other 95% of the production that is destined for national consumption (or

neighbouring countries), and force this sector to submit to their logic. It's a totalitarian exercise. (quoted in Bové and Dufour 2001: 147)

In privileging market prices as the criterion of farm survival, free trade rhetoric thereby justifies the use of institutional means (trade rules, free trade agreements) to extend markets for agribusiness at the expense of small farmers across the world. The human consequence of this process of displacement is reflected in the transformation of conditions of social reproduction, whereby populations and rural cultures once embedded in relatively local, or even nationally-managed, circuits of food are disembedded and/or reincorporated, often on tenuous terms, into global commodity circuits, where access to food is no longer socially or politically guaranteed.[5] In addition, the tens of millions of uprooted and migrant laborers circulating the world foreshadow a future of redundant populations with no place to go. As the website of the international farmers' movement, Via Campesina, remarks in relation to liberalization of agricultural trade: "the massive movement of food around the world is forcing the increased movement of people."

Biotechnology and food security

The latest twist in the reconstruction of food security is associated with transgenic technology. Just as the mid-twentieth-century development project derived its legitimacy from its claims to address the widespread Third World poverty and food scarcities (Escobar 1996), so the biotechnology industry draws on images of world hunger today to justify its claims to having the means to resolve the food security question. Thus Monsanto corporation's website proclaimed in 1998: "Guess Who's Coming to Dinner? 10 billion by 2030." It warned that low-tech agriculture "will not produce sufficient crop yield increases and improvements to feed the world's burgeoning population," declaring that "biotechnology innovations will triple crop yields without requiring any additional farmland, saving valuable rainforests and animal habitats" and that "biotechnology can feed the world... let the harvest begin" (quoted in Kimbrell 1998: 294).

Today's biotechnology public relations offensive in many ways repeats the green revolution formula in that it proposes a technological solution to hunger in abstraction from the real conditions of agriculture and rural populations across the world. The green revolution may have been successful in quantitative terms, in producing bumper crops of macronutrient staples, but it privileged wealthy, well-endowed farmers, introduced alien seeds and their variety of inputs into local ecologies, and intensified the urban bias of development planning. In short it overrode alternatives such as more democratic use of farmland and natural resources, and more diverse farming styles, crop systems and diets likely to be more appropriate to local ecological and community sustainability. The difference with transgenic technologies is that they are privately owned (whereas the green revolution was a publicly-supported project), they are unproven, and most important of all, the world is *not* currently in a situation of food scarcity as it was in the green revolution era.

The application of transgenic technology to food production across the world would arguably deepen the crisis of social reproduction that has accompanied the shift towards a more globalized and commodified development paradigm. In the first place, technological solutions usually obscure the variety and complexity of the social relations associated with unequal land ownership and control. As a farmer in Pampanga in the Philippines observes:

> I don't even have land. I am renting some land together with my husband where we are planting rice. Sometimes, I work as a farm worker for other farmers. What can I do with these new seeds? I'm sure they are expensive... Who will pay for them? We cannot. And even if we would be able to plant them, any surplus they would create would go to the landlord and to the traders. We would still be as poor as ever. Poor farmers need land in the first place so they can reap the fruits of their own work. (quoted in Kuyek 2000)

Further, approximately 1.4 billion people in the global South depend on farm-saved seeds as their main source, and of course crop genetic diversity is part of their centuries-old ecological adaptation. In addition to corporate control of technology, food quality and markets, ownership of transgenic seeds would accelerate the reduction of global biodiversity and the diverse local knowledge embedded in the cultures of the world's remaining peasant farmers.

While the biotech industry has other possibilities on the horizon, especially pharmaceutical, or functional, foods, it is also speculating on a future of transgenic agriculture, conducting a "hunger crusade" to widen public acceptance of its market. The five largest "gene giants" (AstraZeneca, DuPont, Monsanto/Pharmacia, Novartis and Aventis) together account for 32% of the global seed market and 100% of the transgenic seed market (Shiva 2000: 9). The transgenic seed market is a new market frontier. In addition, there is a total of at least 132 genetic patents on crops that evolved in the global South but which are now grown worldwide: 68 for maize genes, 17 for potato, 25 for soybean and 22 for wheat, indicating that staple foods (and feeds) are increasingly targeted for corporate patenting (Madeley 2000b: 9). Corporations are buying up local seed companies in the global South, assuming growing dominance in national seed markets.

The reconstitution of markets as corporate property via the WTO includes the attempt to institutionalize gene patenting via the discourse of intellectual property rights (IPR). The discursive struggle is carried out in both multilateral and national arenas, where the concept of gene patenting is juxtaposed with the concept of biopiracy. Gene patenting, a universal standard of scientific practice and private rights, discounts traditional knowledge(s) and sustainable agricultural and cultural practices. Biopiracy is foreshadowed in the WTO Trade Related Aspects of Intellectual Property Rights (TRIPs) regime, which draws its legitimacy from a synthesis of European and US patent laws and their claims to protect and promote innovation. The TRIPs protocol requires states to establish protection of biological resources either through patenting or an effective *sui generis* system, established through the 1992 Convention on Biological Diversity (CBD) confirming national sovereignty over genetic resources. Although the protocol has yet to be implemented universally, states that choose the latter are still under pressure to earn foreign exchange on access to their genetic resources.

TRIPs arose to stem intellectual property pirating of Western products (watches, CDs, and so on) in the global South, but, ironically, now appears to sanction a reverse biological form of piracy on a disproportionate scale, threatening livelihood, rather than simply commodity, rights. An intellectual property rights regime has enabled seed legislation to force farmers to use only registered varieties, challenging farmers' rights to plant crops on the grounds of patent infringement, and creating dependence on corporate seeds (Shiva 2000: 90). This regime, which only recognizes governments and corporations as legal entities, sanctions the expropriation of genetic resources developed by peasants, forest dwellers and local communities over centuries of cultural experimentation. The economic, political and cultural (not to mention environmental) implications are profound. As Shiva points out:

> The seed is, for the farmer, not merely the source of future plants and food; it is the storage place of culture and history. Seed is the first link in the food chain. Seed is the ultimate symbol of food security. (Shiva 2000: 8)

In the view of the biotechnology industry, however, food security is increasingly linked with a transgenic future. Already the US food aid program has incorporated transgenic foods into its original program of food surplus disposal. Unsold transgenic crops (Japan and the EU currently ban GM food for human consumption) have been, since 1996, recycled through government-managed stockpiles to be delivered as food aid to the global South, via the UN World Food Programme. In this context, US Secretary of Agriculture Glickman encouraged agribusinesses to donate transgenic food through food aid programs, arguing "If they took the longer view they might see the benefit of focusing on the developing world not just as a gesture of corporate citizenship, but because such an investment will ultimately pay dividends as developing countries mature into reliable customers" (Food First 2000). At the end of 2002, the Zambian government defied the US attempt to dump GM corn there via the aid program, choosing instead to purchase grain domestically and regionally for redistribution to victims of famine (Patel and Delwiche 2002: 5). This choice affirmed the UN Biosafety Protocol that requires members to evaluate the impact of GM crops before choosing to import them. As an alternative, the EU sponsors a program to subsidize aid recipients' choices to purchase food regionally.

The combined effect of market liberalization flooding the South with cheap grains, the potential normalization of GM food in food aid, and the centralization of the biotechnology industry, poses a long-term threat to the biodiverse system of intercropping of farmer varieties across the world, and to farmers who will either lose their land or enter into new relationships termed "bioserfdom." Should transgenic technology prevail, its genetic reductionism forecloses an agro-ecological future by denying the possibility of existing food cultures or reformed land relations to resolve hunger via forms of social reproduction embedded in democratic arrangements. The corporate bid for control in the name of global food security is premised on the elimination of *extant* agricultures and alternative agro-ecological models, currently mobilizing against corporate globalization.

Food sovereignty and food from somewhere

Resistances to the global interpretation of food security are mushrooming. They are often framed not only in terms of protecting local farming, but also in terms of revitalizing cultural, ecological and democratic process. The Charter of Farmers' Rights issued by the international Seed Satyagraha Movement for biodiversity asserts the rights to land, to conserve, reproduce and modify seed and plant material, to feed and save the country from food insecurity, and to information and participatory research (Nayar 2000: 21). The transnational movement Via Campesina asserts that "Farmers Rights are eminently collective" and "should therefore be considered as a different legal framework from those of private property." Via Campesina, which unites landless peasants, family farmers, agricultural workers, rural women and indigenous communities, claims that:

> Biodiversity has as a fundamental base the recognition of human diversity, the acceptance that we are different and that every people and each individual has the freedom to think and to be. Seen in this way, biodiversity is not only flora, fauna, earth, water and ecosystems; it is also cultures, systems of production, human and economic relations, forms of government; in essence it is freedom.[6]

Food sovereignty, in this vision, would subordinate trade relations to the question of access to credit, land and fair prices, to be set politically via the rules of fair trade to be negotiated in UNCTAD and not at the WTO, and as a radical alternative to the current corporate regime, with active participation of farmers' movements in building democratic definitions of agricultural and food policies. The specificity of this politics is that, whilst the consumer movement (and some post-modern social scientists) have discovered that "eating has become a political act," Via Campesina adds: "producing quality products for our own people has also become a political act... this touches our very identities as citizens of this world."[7] Access to land is a first step, and Via Campesina declares:

> Access to the land by peasants has to be understood as a guarantee for survival and the valorization of their culture, the autonomy of their communities and a new vision on the preservation of natural resources for humanity and future generations. Land is a good of nature that needs to be used for the welfare of all. Land is not, and cannot, be a marketable good that can be obtained in whatever quantity by those that have the financial means.[8]

Exemplifying this principle is the Brazilian landless-workers' movement, the Movimento dos Trabalhadores Rurais Sem Terra (MST), and a member of Via Campesina. The Cardoso government (1995–2002) model, subordinating the Brazilian political economy to global financial capital, occurred in a context where 1% of landowners own (but do not necessarily cultivate) 50% of the land, and 4.8 million families were landless. An extensive system of agricultural subsidies has been withdrawn, yet OECD member states' agricultural subsidies continue at $360 billion a year. As the MST website notes: "From 1985 to 1996, according to the agrarian census, 942,000 farms disappeared, 96% of which were smaller than 100 hectares. From that total, 400,000 establishments went bankrupt in the first two years of the Cardoso government, 1995–96." Between 1985 and 1996 rural unemployment rose by 5.5 million, and between 1995 and 1999 a rural exodus of 4 million Brazilians occurred. While in the 1980s Brazil imported roughly $1 million worth of wheat, apples and products not produced in Brazil, from "1995 to 1999, this annual average leapt to 6.8 billion dollars, with the importation of many products cultivable... in Brazil."[9]

In the past 17 years, the MST has settled over 400,000 families on 15 million acres of land seized by takeovers in Brazil. The landless workers' movement draws legitimacy from the Brazilian constitution's sanctioning of the confiscation of uncultivated private property: "It is incumbent upon the Republic to expropriate for social interest, for purposes of agrarian reform, rural property, which is not performing its social function..." (Article 184, quoted in Lappé and Lappé 2002: 70). The MST is organized in 23 states of Brazil and, whilst dispossessed farmers comprise 60% of its membership, it also includes unemployed workers and disillusioned civil servants. Land seizures are followed, gradually, by the formation of cooperatives, which involve social mobilization "transforming the economic struggle into a political and ideological struggle." Beyond the task of settling hundreds of thousands of families on recovered land:

One of the great novelties that the experiences of the struggle and the organization of the MST have introduced is combining a political program for getting more land released with a program for the land already secured. It is precisely in linking up what it calls the struggle for the land with the struggle on the land that the MST reveals an extraordinary potential for a confrontation with capitalism. (Flavio de Almeida and Sanchez 2000)

The MST "model of social appropriation" (Dias Martins 2000) deploys democratic decision making to develop cooperative relations among workers and alternative patterns of land use, financed by socialising a portion of settlement income. Participatory budgeting allocates funds for repairs, soil improvement, cattle feeding, computers, housing, teachers' salaries, childcare, mobilization, and so on. Fundamental to this social project is the Freirian dictum that "a settlement, precisely because it is a production unit... should also be a whole pedagogic unit" (Dias Martins 2000), which the MST refers to as a "work and study" method of education. Joao Pedro Stedile, president of the MST, observes:

Under the objective economic conditions, our proposal for land reform has to avoid the oversimplification of classical capitalist land reform, which merely divides up large landholdings and encourages their productive use. We are convinced that nowadays it is necessary to reorganize agriculture on a different social base, democratize access to capital, democratize the agro-industrial process (something just as important as landownership), and democratize access to know-how, that is, to formal education. (quoted in Orlanda Pinnasi *et al*. 2001: 51)

The MST's 1600 government-recognized settlements include medical clinics and training centers for health care workers; 1200 public schools employing an estimated 3800 teachers serving about 150,000 children at any one time. A UNESCO grant enables adult literacy classes for 25,000, and the MST sponsors technical classes and teacher training. MST cooperative enterprises generate $50 million annually. They produce not only jobs for thousands of members, but also foodstuffs and clothing for local, national and global consumption. As one commentator notes:

These collective enterprises show why the MST is considered a leader in the international fair trade movement. The movement is supplying a real, workable alternative to corporate globalization, putting community values and environmental stewardship before profit making. MST co-ops offer a glimpse of what environmentally sustainable and socially just commerce would look like. (Mark 2001)

Conclusion

In relation to the changing discursive context of food security, it is important to note that "hunger has assumed a uniquely global character. 'Hunger amidst scarcity' has given way to 'hunger amidst abundance'" (Araghi 2000: 155). This shift in the character of hunger is mirrored in the reformulation of conceptions of food security – from a national/bilateral to a global/multilateral issue. It also registers the shift from national/public commitments of universal forms of social reproduction through citizenship rights, social wage, welfare and developmentalism, to privatized and exclusive forms of social reproduction depending on consumer rights to corporate-managed delivery of goods and services. While neither form of social reproduction is independent of capitalist social relations, the difference between the two models is that the latter privileges private over public rights, where working classes and other minority or marginalized social groups (including peasantries) have declining or no claims on public assistance.

The redefinition of food security as a market relation dramatizes the distinction between formal market rights, and substantive social rights, licensing the global institutions to lock-in the competitive advantages of corporate agriculture, and legitimizing industrial agriculture's purchase on feeding the world. This view seeks to render invisible the alternative, agro-ecological model used throughout the world, which produces considerably more, more diverse and more sustainable, outputs of food than high-input industrial agriculture (Norberg-Hodge *et al.* 2001: 61).

Ultimately the question of food security is not simply about the corporate model displacing the agro-ecological model; rather it is about the corporate model attempting to suppress the alternative agro-ecological model in a strategy to secure the rights of capital and the profits of agribusiness. It is in this sense that "food security" discourse plays the role of midwife to capital and its attempt to impose its will through the protocols and rules associated with the WTO regime. But it is also in this sense that the various counter-movements to corporate globalization are reframing the discourse around the question of "food sovereignty," as a substantive political, social, cultural and ecological program to restore and revitalize forms of social reproduction anchored in democratic community organization.

Notes

1. I thank Stephen Gill for useful suggestions and Alicia Swords for research support.
2. "A Raw Deal for Commodities." *The Economist*, April 17, 1999.
3. A. Waldman, "Poor in India Starve as Surplus Wheat Rots." *New York Times*, December 2, 2002.
4. Global Trade Watch is a division of Public Citizen, the Washington D.C.-based national consumer and environmental group founded in 1972 by Ralph Nader.

GTW <www.citizen.org/trade> was created in 1995 to promote government and corporate accountability in the globalization and trade arena.
5. The tenuous nature of social existence is fundamentally related to the casualization of labor, resulting from the degradation of the institution of wage labor, which is no longer guaranteed under global neo-liberalism, and it has receded as a political and social goal as the rights of capital have expanded. See McMichael (1999).
6. <ns.rds.org.hn/via/theme.biodiversity.htm>
7. Posted on <ns.rds.org.hn/via/>, accessed December 3, 1999.
8. See <ns.rds.org.hn/via/theme-agrarian.htm>
9. See <www.mstbrazil.org/EconomicModel.html>

10
Social Reproduction of Affluence and Human In/Security[1]

Stephen Gill

Chapter 2 posed issues concerning the security of capital, the security of states (national or state security) and human security, with the latter understood as a basic condition of existence for not only sustainable but also progressive forms of social reproduction that allow human beings to express their species-being as defined in Chapter 2. So in Chapters 10 and 11, I address the question: What type of security and what institutions for social reproduction are being most protected in the emerging world order, by what and for whom?

To answer this question the two chapters will explore aspects of the global dialectic between the historical structures and processes of globalization from above and from below, and will deal with two sets of issues, mainly relative to the USA:

1. Who are the main beneficiaries of disciplinary neo-liberalism, their social and ecological outlook, and how is their security protected; for example, within the USA (discussed principally in Chapter 10).
2. How the American social order and political economy is secured – not only nationally but also globally (discussed mainly in Chapter 11).

I will argue that the reproduction of this social order in a global context is contradictory since it involves both the social reproduction of the affluence of a minority of the world's population and human insecurity for a majority. It is linked to new US state strategies premised on securing the USA as the epicenter of disciplinary neo-liberal patterns of intensified globalization. In making this argument I highlight what is perhaps one of the main paradoxes of globalization. Material conditions and human security are widely thought to be correlated with social status and levels of affluence (for example, UNDP

1994). However, the reverse seems to be the case, at least in the USA. There, the wealthier that people become, the more insecure they perceive themselves to be – a paradox that has very important implications for American global strategy and world order.

Thus Chapter 10 deals with the context and conditions for human security and social reproduction from two vantage points: the power relations of production and the unequal forms of provisioning for social reproduction and socialization of risk. Here I address concerns that were raised in Chapter 1 where it was pointed out that human security and progressive, sustainable forms of social reproduction presuppose a collective sense of confidence about the future and minimum social conditions where unnecessary dangers, risks and crises are minimized or eliminated in everyday life.

The global hierarchy of socio-economic in/security

The emerging world order is characterized by intensified and growing inequalities of income, wealth, ownership and control, in a context where capital has become an increasingly universal force, manifested in liberalization of not only trade but also of finance. In sum, the recent development of the global political economy has involved a process shaped by disciplinary neo-liberal frameworks of power and accumulation. And we have seen, for example in Chapter 6, how rapid movements of capital in the new liberalized frameworks of accumulation have coincided with increasing incidence of financial crisis and social dislocation.

It is in this context that I initially address questions of global inequality. Indeed, in the past two decades, whilst aggregate world income has increased, inequality *between states* may have declined (largely because of economic growth since 1980 in the two most populous and poorest countries, China and India). However, if one examines the distributional aspects of restructuring of the political economy *within* states, we can see a global phenomenon, one more pronounced in certain countries than others: intensification of the inequality of income between rich and poor people. The result is that many countries are gravitating towards the Brazilian patterns of extreme socioeconomic inequality, in many cases accompanied by associated racialized patterns of social stigmatization and stratification. Indeed, measured within countries, inequality of income and especially of wealth has clearly increased very rapidly in recent decades, and this is very significant given that the vast majority of people never leave their country of birth – something that is acknowledged not only by the UN but also by the World Bank and the IMF.[2] Thus inequalities of wealth, income and provisioning at the national level have great impact on social reproduction and human security. So in what follows I give a simplified sketch of what such issues may mean for different social strata in a more globalized social formation.

I start with those strata associated with globalization from above. At the very top of the global social hierarchy are the elites, ruling classes and plutocrats who account for a very small proportion of the world's population, and who are highly mobile across different jurisdictions, often possessing several homes ("properties") and a range of assets and bank accounts, some of which may be offshore.[3] The globalizing elites (intellectuals and political leaders) form the brains of corporate capitalism and manage its global strategy. They comprise several hundred thousand or perhaps, if one includes the managerial and scientific strata, about 1 million in number. For many of these people their worldview is shaped by their privileged class position, educational formation and socialization (for example, many are educated at ruling class universities, such as the Ivy League schools in the USA, Oxbridge in England, and so on). These elites are part of sophisticated networks of communication and social power. Such powerful people are, of course, represented within the leadership of many of the mainstream political parties and institutions in each of the countries to which they are connected, and in which their corporations may be registered (many corporations are in fact registered in offshore centers for reasons of control and to avoid "onshore" taxes and regulation, as mentioned in Chapter 2). However the powerful also possess influence in a range of international institutions and private organizations, some of which comprise what might be called prototypical transnational political parties. The main examples of such transnational political parties of corporate capital include the World Economic Forum in Davos, and the more exclusive Trilateral Commission.

It has often been claimed that the members of the globalizing elites operate with a consciousness associated with what Braudel called "world time" (Braudel 1980) and what Harvey and others have called "time-space compression," an awareness of the possibilities that are open to them in networked, interconnected globalization (Harvey 1989).[4] Nevertheless, one might suggest that this cosmopolitan consciousness of the world is not only instrumental (it views the world as a potential stage for corporations and associated forms of statecraft) but also can be breathtakingly naïve, with an inability to grasp how different forms of (global) consciousness are a feature of intensified globalization. For instance, in a discussion of global governance, Joseph Nye recently observed "cosmopolitan consciousness may be common at Davos, but it is present in only a small fraction of the world's six billion people."[5] Nye is the current Dean of the Kennedy School of Government at Harvard, a former Pentagon Official in the Clinton Administration and an Executive Committee Member of the Trilateral Commission.

The economic titans bestriding this stratum are the plutocrats (super-rich billionaires) and the wealthiest parts of the aristocracy (who enjoy inherited wealth and power). In the celebrity culture that has swept the world in recent times, the lifestyles of the rich and famous become the objects of commodified desire, whilst the true political connections and preferences of the plutocracy are shrouded in mystery. Indeed the life-world of this stratum is subsumed in folklore and social mythology. The majority of the super-rich is American. In the most recent *Forbes* magazine survey of the world's richest people, 222 of the 400 billionaires in the world in 2003 came from the USA, including seven of the ten wealthiest people on the planet – an issue I will return to below when I discuss US policy towards global economic governance.[6] In this context, a major proportion of the globalizing elites should be thought of as the best brains that money could buy in the service of capital. Indeed, as was noted in the introduction to Part IV, capital accumulation does not necessarily mean that capital, or the key individuals that direct its activities are becoming any more productive (or productive at all). For example, in 2002 a *New York Times* op-ed focused on a work that reported, amongst other things, on the compensation of America's ten most highly paid CEOs between 1981 and 2000. In 1981 they were paid an average of $3.5 million. By 1988 their average remuneration was $19.3 million, but in 2000 this jumped to $154 million, despite the fact that several top earners were implicated in scandals and bankruptcies. Thus whilst US real wages stagnated, earnings of top executives rose 4300%, partly due to stock options and other more or less legal ways of augmenting compensation (Phillips 2002).[7] Such executives straddle, of course, the plutocratic and elite strata.

And of course a fuller understanding of the globalizing elites, would have to encompass the intelligentsia, cultural and scientific elites, as well as the technocrats and bureaucrats in key governmental and other international organizations, all of whom are internationally mobile, but many may be, or are critical of the prevailing order, and as such much less attuned to, and subordinated by corporate capital.

Under the elite level, lies a stratum closely associated with what I have called the normalizing frameworks of market civilization with its cultures of consumption: "the culture of contentment" (Galbraith 1992). In the USA such relatively affluent urban and suburban dwellers are crucial in providing a mass basis driving current American security and economic policy. Globally, this stratum includes perhaps 300–500 million relatively secure workers, mainly in the OECD, and about 80–100 million of them work directly or indirectly for transnational corporations. These people not only provide labor for corporate capital, they also are the main consumers for the global brands. Such workers are a protected labor aristocracy fully incorporated into the reproduction of corporate capital: better remunerated and more secure in their employment than the vast majority of workers in the world. The political rationality of such workers is largely revisionist and reformist, and opposed to revolutionary action. Nevertheless, middle management and skilled workers have become much less secure in their employment than 20 years ago – partly as a result of strategies of flexibilization of labor control and remorseless trends towards corporate downsizing that have been a characteristic of a restructuring process driven by the need to deliver "shareholder value." Such restructuring has been used to justify massive increases in the remuneration of leading executives that have typified American corporate life during the past two decades.

With respect to the strata that constitute globalization from below, we would include the vast numbers of much more economically and politically insecure people, consisting of at least two-thirds of the world's population (that is, over 4 billion people). During the boom years of the 1960s unprotected, proletarianized and marginalized workers were found mainly in the developing countries but they are now located in all parts of the world. Such workers enjoy the fruits of consumer society, although their ability to consume is conditioned by relative lack of income, and the need to sell their labor in order to survive (they are more likely to wear cheap counterfeit copies of global brands). These workers suffer from unequal representation and are less likely to receive equal treatment before the law enjoyed by members of the culture of contentment. With respect to the power relations of production, such workers are highly subordinated. They are subject to labor market forces that are largely unconstrained by unionization, and their subordination is increasingly associated with primitive labor markets and employers that simply treat them as objects, rather than as human subjects. In this context many such workers are disciplined by antediluvian labor controls associated with the (so-called) new forms of slavery and debt bondage (see Part III for discussion of the racialized and gendered aspects of these forms of hyper-exploitation). However, it is worth noting that these workers are absolutely crucial for the production of global brands, particularly in clothing and apparel, as well as in electronics and other mass consumer products, which is why companies like Nike are so sensitive about the many campaigns to boycott their products on the grounds of maltreatment of workers. Indeed, it may well be true that such transnational corporations actually provide better working conditions than their counterparts in developing countries, but the key point here is that these new proletarians provide much of the cheap labor inputs into the national and transnational circuits of production and exchange dominated by the sourcing strategies of the brands controlled by giant corporations. They are thus crucial to the new frameworks of what Marx called the expanded reproduction of capital.

Indeed, coastal regions of China provide much of this labor, disciplined not by capital as such, but by the power of a communist state apparatus. In the Pearl River Delta region north of Hong Kong, millions of migrant workers work in factories to produce goods to fill the shelves of OECD retailers. Many of these workers are not allowed to unionize. They live in large dormitory buildings, often sleeping ten or more to a room, and work to send income back to their home villages and families. In China, introduction of the price mechanism in agriculture and local services, replacing free, socialized provisions, has meant that basic education and health care are now too costly for many people. To supplement the family wage, men and women are forced to move to work in the coastal factories to obtain income.[8] A recent report by the Union of Needle Trades, Industrial and Textile Employees described many of the modern sweatshops in countries like China where workers produce the goods sold by major retailers such as the Hudson's Bay Company in Canada, and Wal-Mart throughout North America: "These workers, mostly women, work exhausting hours for shockingly low pay, often in unsafe conditions. In China, for example, 3 million young women work for wages as low as 12 cents an hour to make sporting goods and toys sold in the US and Canada" (MacAdam 2003: 1).[9]

Finally, there are subordinated, marginalized people living in subsistence economies in rural communities. The latter have often been viewed as neither significantly articulated into the productive system and exchange circuits of global capitalism, nor into market civilization, although this is less and less the case. Because of TV and other linkages they no longer lie outside global frameworks of consciousness and action. Indeed, as the examples of Chinese labor in the Pearl River Delta and elsewhere demonstrate, these communities are being dragged into the modern social struggles associated with primitive accumulation as they are dispossessed of their livelihood in a wrenching process with its origins in the enclosure systems of the fifteenth and sixteenth centuries in Western Europe. As Chapter 9 illustrates, increasing control over local agricultural systems and social reproduction by giant agribusiness and life science corporations generates pressures on individuals and communities to struggle for their survival, and as such, it generates resistance. At the same time, whilst deprivation and dispossession push peasants off the land, the need to survive forces these people into wage labor and draws migratory movements from countryside to city within North and South, and from South to North. Thus such people change the configuration of power relations of global capitalism (for example, there are signs of significant efforts by Chinese workers to assert their collective rights and to organize). It remains to be seen whether this will be the case for others drawn into the transnational circuits of labor supply, for example those working as maids, gardeners and care workers, as well as in the sex industries of the OECD.

Thus, whilst each of these broad categories of workers seems to be relatively divided in terms of their political perspective, as Chapter 9 reveals, some of them are beginning to forge their own revolutionary consciousness. Indeed, a growing organized and innovative social movement of the subaltern forces has come into being involving an alliance with disaffected members of protected workers and other sections of civil society heretofore divided by labor segmentation and political fragmentation (Gill 2000a). This revolutionary perspective is now connected to the beginnings of a transnational political party, the World Social Forum, which is organized from the working-class industrial city of Porto Alegre, Brazil. The WSF is opposed to the parties of the globalizing elites, for example, the World Economic Forum of Davos Man. Of course the latter is organized from one of the world's wealthiest nations, Switzerland, a country well known for being a principal offshore center, tax haven and center for private banks and banking secrecy.

The social reproduction of affluence: the US case

In the sections that follow I suggest that the social forces that benefit most from, and that largely consent to the frameworks of accumulation and social reproduction associated with the US-led project of globalization (its plutocrats, the globalizing elites, and more broadly its culture of contentment) are protected by coercive panoptic (surveillance) and carceral systems and ultimately by military power. The latter is exercised in a hierarchy of global military power that has the USA at its apex, its expenditures massively dwarfing those of most of its main rivals combined.[10]

Holding such issues in mind we first pose a crucial question: what motivates US policy in support of disciplinary neo-liberalism? And how does this relate to the questions of human security and social reproduction?

The former President, George H. Bush, offered one answer to this question. Bush declared in 1992 before the UN Conference on the Environment in Rio 1992, that "Our lifestyle is not negotiable." The implications of this for US politics are crucial. By analyzing what this lifestyle entails we can get a sense of what is being secured by the exercise of American supremacy in the emerging world order. What President Bush referred to was the unwillingness of the most politically significant segments of the US population to give up their attachment to energy-intensive patterns of production and consumption. This lifestyle is reflected in its middle classes' liking for large suburban houses with enormous heating and air-conditioning systems, an apparently insatiable appetite for cheap consumer goods and food, and not least a socially constructed dependence upon the automobile.[11] In this sense, given that the US dependence upon imported oil is growing, a consistent categorical imperative of American foreign policy has been to secure access to and control over relatively cheap foreign oil, particularly Middle Eastern oil. In this sense the war on Iraq in 2003 is entirely consistent with the main justifications for and motivations in American foreign policy.

A good example of this energy-intensive lifestyle that also connects to issues of personal security is the mania for gas-guzzling sport utility vehicles (SUVs) that has swept North America in recent years. These huge, relatively expensive four-wheel drive vehicles are rarely used for off-road purposes. Rather they have become the contemporary mobile equivalent of body armor as people typically use them to travel to work, the shopping mall, to take the children to school or to play sports.[12] A recent and representative instance of this mania involved a middle-class mother discussing her transportation needs. She lives in a (very affluent) dormitory community (in Marin County, just north of San Francisco across the Golden Gate Bridge). Based on an interview, the journalist reflected her outlook on society and the environment as follows: "Encased in a massive black Toyota Land Cruiser, Shirley Collenette admits feeling a little guilty about her gas-guzzling, smog-inducing, planet-warming, road-hogging 'armor' as she calls her sport utility vehicle. But need is stronger than guilt."[13] Of course her neighbors may be much less assertive (or conscious) of their own self-regarding interests than is this Marin County resident, and indeed many of her neighbors may have no intention to directly or indirectly harm the security of others or to endanger the planet, although in effect they may do so, in so far as this pattern of behavior is generalized from an individualist frame of reference and therefore becomes structural.[14]

It needs to be added here that over the last ten years the average gas mileage of vehicles sold in the USA for all manufacturers has been going down, in large part because of the shift towards the production of SUVs and pickup trucks by the Japanese, as well as by the Detroit producers. In a recent survey compiled by the USA's Union of Concerned Scientists, we see that Japanese manufacturers tend to have by far the best gas mileage, whereas the US-based big three have by far the worst. The best performance of the big global producers is Honda with an average of 30 miles per gallon for vehicles sold in North America. By contrast DaimlerChrysler now produces vehicles for the same market that average a mere 22 miles per gallon, down from 24 miles per gallon in 1990. Needless to say, this decline in fuel efficiency coupled to the consistent expansion in the numbers of vehicles is bloating the already huge North American appetite for oil.[15]

The dialectic of need and guilt, noted above, is also reflected in trends in home construction as the affluent seek greater exclusivity and security. In affluent locations such as those in Marin County, the homes get bigger and bigger, with a typical middle-class house now comprising well over 5000 square feet, usually with a three- or four-car garage to house the proliferation of vehicles (as well as lawnmowers, mini-tractors and various other machines and gardening devices). These houses are often built in communities that resemble medieval fortresses, surrounded by fortifications, gated and patrolled by armed security guards who use surveillance cameras to police these privatized spaces.

The background to these developments involves how Americans understand and perceive issues of personal security, since they exist in a society with over 200 million handguns, and a proliferation of exotic weaponry of all kinds. Indeed, since the US Constitution gives individuals the right to bear arms, if need be against the state, it allows for the growth in the trend towards a wider privatization and militarization of personal security, which has become a feature of the lifestyles of the rich and famous, and more generally the affluent strata in US cities such as Los Angeles (Davis 1990). There is a growing sense amongst the affluent that they are living not only under threats of environmental and other forms of generalized risk (Davis 1998). There is also a growing perception that the rich are under a form of siege, from the threat of both foreign terrorism (that is, perceptions of threat and insecurity stemming from world order structures), and violence from within the USA itself.

This may explain why there has also been a further trend for the very wealthy to build panic rooms in their mega-homes (reinforced cells to protect them against intruders) just in case their outer moats and fortifications are breached.[16]

A recent *Financial Times* article noted that, "Executives and high net worth individuals" in the USA have come to fear not only terrorism but also kidnapping. Whereas celebrities drawn from the world of entertainment can normally choose where they work and live, this is not usually the case for business executives. Thus those wealthy executives who cannot avoid going to business centers seek to protect themselves in various ways; for example, by varying their commuting routes and the vehicles they use. When they arrive at work their offices have come to resemble fortresses. In New York, for example, "Wall Street has increased security at office buildings since September 11, with increased surveillance at banks and brokerages ranging from electronic security, guards, metal detectors and even sniffer dogs." Particularly since 9/11, demand for the services of elite security firms such as Kroll has risen. Indeed, a Kroll survey completed shortly after September 11 not surprisingly showed that concerns over "physical security and emergency planning have dramatically increased." Kroll provides its wealthy clients with personal protection and physical security in workplaces and when they travel so as to "avoid problems such as emergencies, dangerous neighborhoods and airline strikes." Kroll advises its clients to have their properties (homes and the grounds surrounding them) surveyed for "any type of exposure" and to install better security lighting and cameras, as well as "microwave beams and other devices to make a residence impregnable." They counsel their clients who have to venture overseas to "avoid air travel if possible, and to stay in hotels with American affiliations, such as the Four Seasons, Ritz Carlton and St Regis." Kroll also offers an international travel intelligence service to help their clients navigate the intricacies of this more dangerous world.[17]

By contrast over the past decade, "the proportion of Americans living in poverty [has] risen, and income for middle-class households [has] fallen."[18] Thus not all Americans are "contented" since in a fundamental sense they are almost all implicated into the uncertainties associated with the neo-liberal political economy of insecurity that has driven the flexibilization of labor. This is a strategy of capital that in effect denies security to workers whilst fragmenting the latter's ability to provide for their livelihood. Flexibilization of labor takes a variety of forms, including a tendency to increase the number of part-time, or limited contracts (many Americans have several jobs in order to earn sufficient income, and partly as a result the hours worked by average Americans have gone up very dramatically in the past decade). In this framework, workers are denied, "the existential security without which neither freedom nor the will to self-assertion are conceivable, and which is the starting point of autonomy. Work in its present shape cannot offer such security even if it manages... to cover the costs of staying alive" (Bauman 2001: 118–19). The wider point is of course that the past two decades have entailed acceleration in trends towards greater economic uncertainty. This also helps to explain why many Americans are "discontented" and why many are far from enamored with the new conservative forces, embodied in the Bush Administration, forces that are seeking to intensify class warfare. Thus liberal commentators such as Paul Krugman and Bob Herbert speak for many Americans when they point out how the policies of the current Bush administration involve fighting wars on two fronts: abroad, for example, one against Iraq and the other at home. The latter is in effect a class war, designed to redistribute wealth upwards, and undermine federal programs designed to benefit the most vulnerable members of society:

> Bush... sounds the alarm for war and blows the trumpet for tax cuts [that principally benefit the wealthy.] Congress cuts domestic programs... Those who object are effectively silenced by the war propaganda and the fear of seeming unpatriotic... Last month the President offered a plan to make it more difficult for low-income families to obtain government benefits, including tax credits and school lunch assistance... The Administration proposed changes in the Medicare program that would make it more difficult for elderly people, many of them frail, to appeal the denial of benefits like home health care and skilled nursing care... Billions of dollars in cuts have been proposed for food stamp and child nutrition programs, and for health care for the poor. Collectively, these are the largest proposed cuts in history. Even cuts for veterans' programs are on the table – in the midst of a war![19]

Indeed, the US working classes and poor not only get badly funded federal social programs, but also they seem to be paying much more of their income in taxes than was the case 30 years ago, and they are also much more likely to be tax-audited in the US than the rich. The Internal Revenue Service is underfunded and unable to force taxation on the rich who are able to hide their wealth and/or take advantage of tax loopholes.[20] This is part of a general shift whereby American corporations contribute less and less of their profits into general taxation. In 1973 the effective tax rate on profits of US corporations was 32.4%, and this fell to 25.8% in 1999. However, one analysis has shown that whilst corporate profits are officially taxed at 35 cents on the dollar, the 10,000 *largest* corporations only pay about 20 cents of tax on each dollar of profits, mainly due to legal tax shelters and frauds that are too complex for the IRS to understand. By contrast the average effective tax rate for Americans who pay federal income tax rose from 21 cents on the dollar in 1973 to 28 cents in 2000.[21]

As taxes for the wealthy and for corporations are cut, the US states experience their worst fiscal crises since before World War II, whilst their hands are tied by new constitutional balanced budget laws. This means that not only federal, but also programs at the state level are being drastically cut back:

> Last year brought the storm warnings: some layoffs, the inconveniences of libraries closing early and roads without fresh asphalt. Now, as states scramble to find ways to cut nearly $100 billion this year and next from *budgets that must by law be balanced*, the cuts are much larger, and their effects profound. It is not just that states are withdrawing health care for the poor and mentally ill. They are also dismissing state troopers, closing parks and schools, dropping bus routes, eliminating college scholarships and slashing a host of other services that have long been taken for granted... in Texas, 275,000 fewer children will receive health care. The state already ranks first in the number of children without medical coverage. Ohio is planning to cut 50,000 people from health coverage, which would be the largest increase of uninsured Ohioans in history.[22]

Thus another way to widen consideration of such issues is to consider governance frameworks for social welfare and socialization of risk at a number of levels – both federal and provincial (for example, US states) as well as regional and global frameworks. In this regard with respect to welfare and health care, most OECD social security ministries have shifted to intensified monitoring of recipients of "assistance," that is, those outside of the disciplines of the labor markets. The new workfare schemes are designed to "produce" and police a pool of low-wage workers for capital to exploit, whilst in effect introducing differential forms of political treatment (for example, citizens become "clients") and social entitlements among citizens (see Chapter 4 on this question). Here it will be remembered that Jeremy Bentham's management schemes for disciplining paupers and prisoners in his Panopticon Plan was designed to transform paupers and inmates so that they would become profitable to the sponsors of his scheme, the shareholders in a giant private joint stock company: the National Charity Company (Bentham 1995). Indeed, the panoptic aspect in the governance of the present disciplinary neo-liberal social order is reflected not only in the widely documented expansion of state surveillance but also in the explosion of private collection of information about populations by capital for purposes of market power (for example, construction of consumer profiles). Moreover, this information can be and is consistently used to discipline individuals *within* market forms, for example by denial or provision of private credit, or in the US case, private health care and insurance, which in any case is not available to over 40 million Americans who are deemed too risky to insure by the private insurance corporations. In the USA such data is also used in hiring workers and health information seems to be a criterion in whether to eliminate from employment those who might be potentially "risky," that is, costly to corporate health plans (Gandy 1993).

Thus new patterns of social discipline involve a complex dialectic of uncertainty/insecurity and governance frameworks that either privatize or socialize a range of risks, in ways that differentiate between different class strata. In the USA, professionals and other affluent workers often get considerable socialized protection against financial risks. For example, the US Federal Deposit Insurance Corporation, created after the Great Crash in 1933, insures depositors for $100,000, and "deposits maintained in different categories of legal ownership are separately insured," thus allowing individuals to have "more than $100,000 insurance coverage in a single institution."[23] By definition this is a subsidy to and a socialization of the risk of the relatively wealthy, since by definition the poor will not have much in the way of savings. Another example is "corporate welfare," that is, the way that major US corporations receive enormous subsidies and tax write-offs from the states and federal government. Finally, the mid-1980s bailout of the Savings and Loan industry involved the largest socialization of private debt in history, to the tune of approximately $500 billion.

With this social and political landscape in mind, recent demographic research on the USA indicates that in a social and spatial sense there is a new politics of inequality, a process that has been attributed mainly to race, thus obscuring its class dimensions (Massey 1996: 403–4). However, this is a global phenomenon, where the affluent are increasingly not only economically, but also socially, spatially and politically segregated from the rest of society and especially from the poor of the world's population (unless of course the poor are their domestic servants) in a process I call *social enclavization*. Whilst the affluent hold all the important tokens of economic citizenship, such as platinum credit cards, and have access to credit at the lowest rates of interest, the poor have little access to credit, and when they do they pay usurious rates of interest. At the same time, as we have noted, social programs that support the family wage and the basic mechanisms of social reproduction are under attack, as welfare is replaced by punitive regimes of workfare – akin to those imagined by Jeremy Bentham and the Victorian "reformers" in nineteenth-century Britain.

In addition, one of the primary indirect effects of what might be called a new medievalism that separates and segregates rich and poor communities is to undermine the material capacities for the social reproduction of less affluent communities. The trends towards suburbanization have meant that affluent taxpayers have left the inner-city areas for their far-flung gated communities where they monopolize political representation, with the result that the urban tax base, mainly constituted by sales and property taxes, is eroded. Demographic researchers have shown that this has left poorer communities caught in a vicious cycle, where the poor inner-city areas get worsening services (Massey 1996). On the other hand, the rich, in their suburban, dormitory communities, get better services than they previously enjoyed, although they end up paying a smaller proportion of their income in property taxes, since their taxes no longer have to subsidize provisioning for the poorer neighborhoods, which by definition no longer exist in their new *heimat*.

Massey has argued that such developments in the USA have been connected to a new form of increasingly nihilistic, violent social ecology in many cities (Massey 1996). It may be no accident, therefore, that in order to contain the repercussions of this violent "social ecology," the major growth industry in the USA over the past 20 years has not been high-tech, dot.com corporations, but private forms of crime control and the development of the so-called prison industrial complex, with private prisons its most vibrant sector.[24] Many of these private prisons are located in economically depressed rural locations. Locating prisons in these areas helps to prop up the local tax base, generates local support, and not least allows for hyper-exploitation of cheap prison labor under repressive conditions (Young 2000).

The reserve army of prison labor is relatively plentiful in the USA since it is widely known that the USA has by far the world's highest rates of incarceration of any large country except for Russia, five to eight times higher than that of neighboring Canada (and the European Union).[25] The American prison population consists mainly of men, and disproportionately of black and, to a lesser extent, Hispanic males. At the end of 2000 American prisons and jails held 1,933,503 inmates, up from 330,000 inmates in 1972. The incarceration rate for young black males aged 25–29 years was an astonishing 13% of all young black men in that age group.[26] The racialized and gendered composition of US incarceration practices is illustrated in the following selected incarceration rates for both men and women combined, compiled on June 30, 2000: whites: 235 per 100,000; blacks: 1815 per 100,000; Latinos: 609 per 100,000; Asian: 99 per 100,000; Native Americans: 709 per 100,000. Of these, white males were incarcerated at the rate of 683 per 100,000; black males 4777 per 100,000; Hispanic males 1715 per 100,000; and as noted above, black males aged between 25–29: 13,118 per 100,000.[27] It is also well known that the USA, despite relatively universal condemnation from the rest of the world, continues to apply the death penalty, and indeed similar racial and gender-specific patterns apply to executions.

The prison industrial complex has grown rapidly ever since the Reagan Administration launched its "war on drugs," based on prohibition and the application of severe criminal sanctions for use and sale of illicit drugs, resulting in mass incarceration, whilst legal drugs such as antidepressants increasingly become part of everyday life in the USA and other OECD countries – in effect a legalized alteration of mind and mood in an increasingly somatic society.[28] As a University of Michigan Professor of Psychiatry and Psychology noted (in an article mainly concerned with the consequences for savings and investment of growing drug use among US executives and Wall Street traders):

Prescriptions for psychoactive drugs have increased from 131 million in 1988 to 233 million in 1998, with nearly 10 million prescriptions filled last year for Prozac alone. The market for antidepressants in the USA is now $6.3 billion per year. Additional huge numbers of people use herbs to influence their moods. [Roughly 20 million] people in the USA take antidepressants,... Wealthy stressed urbanites are especially likely to use them... Whether the overall mental health of the populace is improving remains an open question, however. Overall rates of depression seem stable or increasing in most technological countries, and the suicide rate is stubbornly unchanged despite all the new efforts to recognize and treat depression.[29]

Conclusion

In sum, it continues to be the case that many of the members of the culture of contentment are largely the beneficiaries of the increasingly privatized structures of the market and personal security, and when their anxieties take hold, they can palliate some of their fears with legalized narcosis. They are also beneficiaries of the structures of *de facto* unequal political representation and social reproduction: they have access to not only the politicians and bureaucracies but also the best schools, universities and medical care. They also enjoy freedom from the drudgery of everyday domestic work, partly because of transnational flows of (illegal) labor supply in the form of workers that tend to their children and look after their "properties."

By contrast, the frameworks of social reproduction and human security for most workers and the most vulnerable in the USA tend to be precarious, day to day (more immediate) in their time horizons, as well as subject to intense forms of surveillance by the state. Indeed whilst there has been a shift from welfare to workfare, and as social provisioning for many of the most vulnerable members of US society is being cut, there has been enormous expansion in outlays not only for policing, incarceration and private security, but also in general military expenditures since the end of the Cold War. And given what we have just described, it is perhaps not surprising that the well-funded, 1.4 million strong American military also provides not only an extended apparatus for policing US-led globalization, but also a surrogate form of social welfare in so far as it offers decent training and educational provision for its recruits. Not least it offers a disciplined institutional setting to foster a career path for its predominantly southern and western working-class recruits, especially for women, notably black women (15% of all officers and enlisted personnel are women, in contrast to virtually none 20 years ago).[30]

Indeed, not only women but also many of its Hispanic and black recruits view the military as an "equal opportunity" meritocratic institution, in stark contrast to many of their experiences in civilian life.[31] All of this helps to explain why minorities are over-represented in the US military ranks (and perhaps also why people drawn from the wealthy elites and Ivy League schools are notable by their absence, in contrast to the UK military).

Given the violent social landscape depicted above, and the racialized system of discipline and punishment (involving the incarceration of very large and disproportionate numbers of young black men), it is hardly surprising that the better educated black working-class men and especially black women are attracted to a military career. Indeed, whilst 60% of all enlisted men and women are white, blacks constitute 22% of all enlisted personnel (whereas blacks make up about 12.7% of the civilian population of the same age). Blacks are most heavily represented in administrative and support functions. The number of Hispanics in uniform also grew by about 30% over the last decade, and these mainly male recruits seem to be principally drawn to the ranks of the infantry and marines. Perhaps most striking, however, is that the number of enlisted black women. In the army, *half* of all enlisted women are black, outnumbering the whites that account for only 38%.[32]

Thus one of the paradoxes of globalization is that, as we shall see in Chapter 11, when US elites seek to "make globalization truly global" the military mobilization needed to realize this goal rests upon disproportionate numbers of the US working classes: particularly black women and working-class men.

Notes

1. I would like to thank Isabella Bakker and Tim Di Muzio for helpful comments on this chapter.
2. "What is Behind the Declines in Global Income Inequality and Poverty?" *IMF Survey*, March 17, 2003, 32 (5): 74–5.
3. According to the Princeton Population Clock world population totaled over 6.297 billion people on March 20, 2003. <opr.princeton.edu/popclock/>
4. "Such elites are... constituted by their positions in key strategic locations in transnational companies, banks, universities, think tanks, media companies, governments and international organizations such as the IMF, World Bank and OECD, and by the discourse of neo-liberal globalization. Their activities seek to make transnational capital a class 'for itself' by theorizing the world order and by synthesizing strategy. Key members are located in organizations at the apex of global knowledge, production and financial structures, as well as in key political parties and government agencies in the major capitalist states, notably in the members of the G7. This grouping has a public and a private face. Its members drawn from the private realm of civil society are intimately related to and form part of 'political society' at both 'national' and 'international' levels" (Gill 2003a: 169–70).
5. Joseph S. Nye, Jr. "Global Governance: Divided World, Shared Destiny and Improvised Accountability." The World Economic Forum's Annual Meetings were held in Davos on January 23–28, 2003. "Over 2,400 individuals from business, government, civil society, academia and media [who] participated in some 100 workshops." See <www.weforum.org/site/homepublic.nsf/Content/Global+Agenda+Atelier%5CGlobal+Agenda+Monitor>, accessed April 15, 2003.
6. The non-Americans in the top ten were Karl and Theo Albrecht of Germany (ranked third with $25.6 billion, source of wealth: "retail"), and Prince Alwaleed of Saudi

Arabia (ranked fifth with $17.7 billion, source of wealth: "investments," for example, he is the largest investor in Citicorp). See Kroll and Goldman (2003). As the UNDP pointed out in 1998, the combined wealth of the world's three richest people was greater than the total income of the 48 poorest nations. The 84 richest owned assets worth more than the total annual production (GDP) of China (1.2 billion people). The world's 225 billionaires were worth about $1 trillion, a sum roughly equal to annual incomes of just less than half of the global population (2.7 billion people). If $1 trillion (one thousand billion) had been redistributed to these 2.7 billion poor people, each of them would have received $370.37, more or less doubling their annual average incomes. See UNDP (1998). Some billionaires are philanthropists and voluntarily engage in redistribution, a good example being Bill Gates who has set up a foundation to provide, amongst other things, resources for public health in poorer countries.

7. Paul Krugman, "Plutocracy And Politics." *New York Times*, June 14, 2002.
8. In a typical factory for 7000 male employees, each earned an average of about $137 a month, for making Caterpillar and Wolverine boots. Each pair is sold in Western shops for the equivalent of a Chinese worker's monthly wages: "Almost every one of China's 150 million migrant workers has a similar story. Moving to a coastal city to work long hours on the factory floor represents for some an escape from the tyranny of life on the farm. For others it is a necessity; the rising cost of education, health care and living in rural areas has created a powerful force pushing workers to the coastal factories." Quoted in Dan Roberts and James Kynge, "A Better Life on the Production Line." *Financial Times Special Report: China*, February 6, 2003.
9. The worldwide campaign against sweatshop labor exploited by giant corporations has been gathering momentum. For example, "Nike has been targeted because of the treatment of the 500,000 workers, mostly women who make Nike footwear in countries like China, Indonesia, and Vietnam, using local contractors. The Nike campaign has become an international movement demanding that Nike accept independent monitoring of working conditions and its contractors' factories, and that workers be paid a living wage." See MacAdam (2003: 6).
10. "North America accounted for... 34%, of 1999 world military spending with the US alone accounting for 33%. Western Europe with 22% had the second largest share. [Between] 1989–1999... Eastern Europe's share fell from 34% to 7% with the collapse of the former Soviet Union and the Warsaw Pact. East Asia's share more than doubled, from 10% to 21%, primarily because China's estimated spending grew by 64%." Reported in US State Department *Factsheet* "Military Expenditures and Arms Transfers 1999–2000." Washington, D.C.: State Department, February 6, 2003. The USA's military build-up accelerated after 9/11.
11. Here we might recall the previous chapter on food security/hunger and note the rise of the "fast food" phenomenon, which is globalizing rapidly. Its spread has been coupled to a worldwide epidemic of obesity particularly amongst affluent populations. Diseases linked to obesity are now primary causes of ill health in North America. This is partly because of a process of deskilling (many no longer know how to cook fresh food) and partly because they do not have the time to prepare nutritious meals even if they have the skills (many work several part-time jobs with longer working hours). See Ritzer (1993), Schlosser (2001).
12. One in four vehicles sold in America is now an SUV. See Ed Crooks, "Highways to Harm." *Financial Times*, March 5, 2003.

13. Patricia Leigh Brown, "Among California's S.U.V. Owners, Only a Bit of Guilt in a New 'Anti' Effort." *New York Times*, February 8, 2003. This article prompted the following letter to the editor published on February 12, 2003:

    > It is disheartening to hear S.U.V. owners like the Marin County mother: "How else am I going to get four children from A to B?"... Our Toyota Corolla seated four kids easily, my own two plus their friends. How short sighted and arrogant for Americans to think that our super-consumption does not directly, immediately, jeopardize us and the rest of the world through global warming, oil dependency and the plundering of ever scantier resources! John Felstiner, Stanford, Calif., February 8, 2003.

14. An analysis of over 130,000 two-vehicle crashes, and others involving trucks, single-vehicle crashes and accidents involving pedestrians and cyclists showed that SUVs may make their drivers safer but they put other road users more at risk. See Michelle White, "The Arms Race on American Roads," Washington, D.C.: NBER Working Paper 9302, November 2002.
15. Danny Hakim, "Cloaked in Green, But Guzzling Gas: Japanese Carmakers Have Hybrids, But Their Attention is on Trucks." *New York Times*, April 19, 2003.
16. Mark Townsend, "Panic Room is a Must Have for Rich and Famous." *Observer*, June 22, 2002.
17. Julie Earle, "Personal Protection: Rich, Powerful and Afraid." *Financial Times*, April 2, 2003. All quotations in this paragraph were taken from this article. Rudy Giuliani, the Mayor of New York at the time of 9/11, has teamed up with Ernst and Young to begin a consulting firm that advises corporate clients on "security issues." See <www.giulianipartners.com/pr3.html>
18. Bob Herbert, "Casualties at Home." *New York Times*, March 27, 2003.
19. Bob Herbert, "Casualties at Home." *New York Times*, March 27, 2003. Growing numbers in the USA are also concerned at a new McCarthyism. The 15th anniversary celebration of a well-known baseball movie, *Bull Durham*, at the Baseball Hall of Fame in Cooperstown, N.Y., was abruptly canceled by the Hall's President, Dale Petroskey, a former press secretary under President (and former actor) Ronald Reagan, who feared that Tim Robbins and Susan Sarandon (two stars of the film) might express opposition to the event to the Iraq war. This caused a public outcry. See "Cooperstown Muffs One." Op-Ed, *New York Times*, April 12, 2003.
20. See David Cay Johnston, "Insurance Loophole Helps Rich." *New York Times*, April 1, 2003.
21. See David Cay Johnston, "Tax Inquiries Fall as Cheating Increases." *New York Times*, April 14, 2003.
22. Timothy Egan, "States, Facing Budget Shortfalls, Cut the Major and the Mundane." *New York Times*, April 21, 2003, emphasis added.
23. <www.fdic.gov/deposit/deposits/insured/index.html>, accessed March 19, 2003.
24. For extensive discussion on crime, social order and the prison industrial complex see the special edition of *Social Justice*, Fall 2000, 27 (3), and Parenti (1999).
25. The US incarceration rate in mid-2000 was 702 per 100,000 people (based on US Census Bureau estimate of national population of 275.1 million at mid-2000). The 2000 incarceration rate for Japan was 40, Sweden 60, Switzerland 85, Netherlands, France and Italy 90, Germany 95, Canada, Australia and Spain 110, UK 125, South Africa 400, Russia 699. See <www.sentencingproject.org/news/usno1.pdf>

26. Recent US prison population trends by year, prison population total, and prison population rate are 1992: 1,295,150 (505); 1995: 1,585,586 (600); 1998: 1,816,931 (669). See International Centre for Prison Studies, Kings College, London University, <www.prisonstudies.org/>
27. Statistics from US Bureau of Justice Statistics, June 30, 2000. Calculation for black adult men uses data from Tables 12 and 13 of the spreadsheet version of the Midyear 2000 BJS report. All references to Blacks and Whites are for what the Bureau of Justice Statistics and US Census refer to as "non-Hispanic blacks" and "non-Hispanic whites." Source: <www.prisonsucks.com/>, accessed October 9, 2001.
28. I use the adjective "somatic" in the ironic sense of Aldous Huxley's *Brave New World*, the imaginary dystopia where one of the key elements of social reproduction is "soma," a wonder drug developed over several years by thousands of scientists. Soma makes people high and happy, curing any form of melancholy, whilst having no side effects or leaving any hangover.
29. See Randolph M. Nesse, M.D. "Is the Market on Prozac?" <www.edge.org/3rd_culture/story/100.html>, accessed 7, April 2003. Nesse's personal website is <www-personal.umich.edu/~nesse/> According to the World Health Organization, which has recently focused attention on issues of "mental health," depression, often unrecognized, is now the second most common illness. "Women, at least in the industrialised West, are about twice as likely to suffer from depression as men, says the WHO, and depression sufferers are getting younger and younger all the time." <www.tribuneindia.com/1999/99mar31/health.htm#3>
30. Monica Davey, "Plans for Families, Degrees and Careers Come to Abrupt End in Iraq." *New York Times*, April 13, 2003.
31. See the extensive article by David M. Halbfinger and Steven A. Holmes, "Military Mirrors a Working-Class America." *New York Times*, March 30, 2003.
32. Data drawn from Halbfinger and Holmes, "Military Mirrors a Working-Class America." *New York Times*, March 30, 2003.

11
National In/Security on a Universal Scale[1]

Stephen Gill

Since the early 1980s, the US government launched a neo-liberal political offensive designed to restructure three main aspects of world order: (i) the internal social relations of capitalist states (for example, to strengthen capital relative to labor); (ii) the geopolitical and economic relations between the major capitalist states (the G7) and the rest of the world (North–South and East–West relations), and (iii) to create a more integrated world market.

In this regard I shall seek to show how, after the fall of the USSR, American global strategy has consisted of two main components:

1. efforts to mobilize and to lock in new constitutional governance frameworks; and
2. threatened/actual use of US military power to police, discipline and extend a globalizing world order.

The latter involves capacities for surveillance, rapid intervention and mass aerial warfare governed by new doctrines of "preventive" and "pre-emptive" war – against countries that potentially threaten not only the US homeland, but also its foreign assets.

Freed of the constraints of a significant traditional adversary that could countervail its military power, after the Soviet collapse the USA intensified the restructuring of its military to construct the capacity for unilateral military action as well as to extend its already significant surveillance technologies. There was a strategic shift away from containment of communism to a much more expansionist economic and military stance. It focused on combating terrorism, policing the so-called "rogue states" and perhaps more fundamentally, extending globalization.

Indeed, since 9/11 we have seen the extended use of this disciplinary apparatus, steered by a more conservative vision of American strategy than was manifest in the Clinton Administration, in ways that are connected to and build upon the ontology of fear and insecurity that seems to beset American society, and that was described in Chapter 10. This strategy has invoked the use of pre-emptive and preventive war, against actual or potential US adversaries, in contravention of international law in ways that suggest a radical restructuring of the normative structures of world order, with consequences for the international rules and statutes governing the use of organized violence that are only gradually being perceived (Falk 2003).

At the same time, building from the analysis of Chapter 10, we might suggest that because of the dominant American role in shaping particularly the military structures of world order, part of what is being globalized (universalized) in these processes is the redefinition of the nature and priorities associated with a much more assertive and conservative projection of US national in/security perspectives and interests.

With such issues in consideration, Chapter 11 highlights aspects of American economic and military strategy associated with the extension and policing of globalization. Indeed, Chapter 11 builds on and is inextricably linked to the arguments made in Chapter 10, which described how the social reproduction of affluence within the USA is linked to the extension of disciplinary neo-liberalism, and how this tends to generate corresponding patterns of human insecurity, not only in the USA but also worldwide. The result is that progressive forms of provisioning for social reproduction for the mass of the world's population have either been eroded, or are under attack.

Securing the world market

In what follows I focus on the two main dimensions of US strategy: the institutionalization of a new constitutionalist framework for the governance of the political economy ("securing the world market"), and the building of an extended coercive apparatus linked to new doctrines of national security premised on unchallenged American military predominance. At the end of the chapter I discuss the links between the new strategy and the 2003 war in Iraq. Here it might be noted initially, however, that the main aim of this new type of war is not the enlargement of territory, but the opening up of nations to freer flows of capital and enterprise and obtaining access to the oil that is central to the reproduction of the US "lifestyle."

In this section I focus on US efforts to create a more liberalized framework for globalization in trade and investment and a related world market in intellectual property, the latter being formalized in the WTO, and finally a brief discussion of efforts connected to creating a more integrated world capital market through the abolition of capital controls and other methods to lock in free international capital mobility. This dimension of US strategy helps American corporations to maintain access to foreign markets, supplies of foreign labor, raw materials and goods. Freer capital mobility also facilitates inflows of capital into the USA thus helping to fund its balance of payments deficits (the latter is of course a double-edged sword, since a crisis of confidence in the US economy could reverse these capital flows very rapidly indeed). Another flank of this strategy involves efforts to globalize US-style corporate governance structures/securities markets with freedom of corporate takeover/transfer of ownership titles. Thus American corporations can therefore find it easier to acquire overseas firms and assets previously shielded from "hostile" or foreign takeovers. Indeed, the vast majority of foreign direct investment in the 1990s was through mergers and acquisitions, not new investment. This type of investment does not expand productive potentials, indeed it is an effort to gain greater *control over* production structures.

If we recall the discussion in Chapter 10 of the wealthiest Americans we can indicate one way to start to understand how these governance initiatives are concerned with a particular pattern of the general reproduction of capital, and how this is linked to the social order within the USA. Indeed, as *Forbes* magazine's annual survey of billionaires illustrates, US plutocrats with the highest net worth have their money concentrated in software and computers (for example, Microsoft, Oracle, Dell), in media and entertainment (for example, Metromedia, Viacom) and in investment houses. The other main area of massive accumulation of wealth is retailing. For example, five members of the Walton family who own Wal-Mart stores (the world's biggest company in 2002) were tied as the seventh richest people on the planet, each with an estimated net worth of $16.5 billion (Kroll and Goldman 2003: 132). Not surprisingly each of these areas is reflected in the emphasis given in US foreign economic policy to creating new governance structures (new constitutional agreements): locking in guarantees for investment overseas, guaranteeing intellectual property rights for owners of software, as well as ensuring continued access to global sourcing for American brands to feed the endless US appetite for inexpensive consumer goods. As noted in Chapter 10, the shelves of Wal-Mart stores are packed with goods manufactured by cheap labor from China. This explains why the USA was keen to facilitate China's entry into the WTO and to lock in Chinese commitments to full repatriation of profits, and eventually to allow full foreign ownership of private enterprise, investment and sourcing for American corporations.

It is in this context we might note that governance regimes have been reshaped in the past 20 years in accordance with new constitutionalism and disciplinary neo-liberalism. The USA has tended to initiate many of these changes, and in turn, its corporations and consumers have tended to benefit most directly from the restructuring of trade, investment and financial and international business regulation during the past decade (Braithwaite and Drahos 2000).

In what follows I will simply indicate some of these trends and refer the reader to related work for a more in-depth and complete picture (Gill 2002a, 2002b, 2002c).

First, in *trade and investment* deeper and more extensive global economic integration has been associated with widening jurisdiction and competence of international organizations with new legal frameworks strongly influenced by the USA (for example, WTO, NAFTA). In addition, thousands of bilateral trade and investment agreements also form part of this deeper integration. This situation is also being ratified in the negotiations to institutionalize the General Agreement on Trade in Services in the WTO since in significant respects GATS can be seen as an investment agreement that includes rights of establishment and non-discrimination for foreign services firms. As noted in Chapter 2, GATS is intended to advance the liberalization process across not only communications services, but also in basic institutions of social reproduction such as education, as well as other social and cultural sectors; it may also serve to constrain certain types of social and health policies (Sinclair 2000).

US models have informed not only accounting standards but also legal concepts and dispute resolution procedures. Thus the US constitutional mechanism of judicial review has been reformulated internationally in the creation of dispute resolution mechanisms, with binding enforcement such as in the NAFTA and the World Trade Organization. Other US legal principles and concepts such as transparency are at the heart of trade and investment regulation. The institutionalization of American legal principles were central goals in US negotiating strategies for liberalization of trade and investment although, of course, the outcomes of such negotiations cannot be simply reduced to the effects of American power and strategy *per se* (Braithwaite and Drahos 2000).

Indeed, intellectual property rights are now treated increasingly as commodities, an issue that has become deeply controversial because of the ways that these affect rights to livelihood (see Chapter 9) as well as to health – for example, patent protection restricts access to medicines and vaccines to deal with epidemics and other diseases, in rich and especially poorer countries. This is an increasingly urgent concern since we have witnessed a re-emergence of serious global health problems involving growth in contagious diseases once thought conquered (for example, cholera), a proliferation of diseases associated with environmental degradation and pollution (for example, asthma among children, allergies), and new viruses (such as AIDS and SARS).[2] This has occurred amid a worldwide crisis in public health funding, that has been especially acute in Africa (Benatar 2001, 2002). Indeed, after World War II life expectancy increased throughout the world. This process has now apparently gone into reverse in a number of countries (notably in former communist-ruled nations of Eastern Europe and in much of Africa).

How such global health issues are treated is now partly shaped by the new trade and investment agreements. For example NAFTA's Chapter 11 provisions give private companies the right to sue governments for "takings" (expropriation of property) a concept again drawn from US jurisprudence (Schneiderman 2000). Takings can include actions that *might* lead to a decline in the expectation of future profits even when a government seems to be acting in the public interest to protect its industries for reasons of public health (the same would apply with respect to culture and information industries). Similar issues have arisen concerning the availability and cost of AIDS drugs, where the pharmaceutical firms have been drawn into litigation with South Africa. The drug corporations have resisted efforts to violate their legal rights related to Trade-Related Aspects of Intellectual Property (TRIPs). Also, TRIPs include detailed enforcement procedures which mirror step-by-step the administrative and judicial mechanisms in the USA (Correa 1999).

Among other things these institutional initiatives have allowed the USA to lock in access to foreign markets and to protect its firms' high technology and other intellectual property so as to strengthen American-owned capital relative to rivals (Barlow and Clarke 2000). In this context, the USA has established a commanding lead in core technologies associated with the information, communications and other industries of the so-called new economy (including defense). The period of accelerated globalization of intellectual property rights really began in earnest when the USA succeeded in linking trade to intellectual property rights in the Uruguay Round trade negotiations in 1994. American software, entertainment and pharmaceutical companies then successfully lobbied for an agreement with global coverage and enforcement mechanisms.[3]

Yet TRIPs has little to do with free trade since it involves locking-in rights of private monopolies over innovations, and so on; for example, through patents and other protections. This is why even some Neo-Classical economists have argued that TRIPs may undermine global welfare (and health) by preventing competition (for example, more open supply of medicines), an argument used very frequently by Third World governments. At the same time more left-leaning agencies such as UNCTAD and UNESCO were marginalized from any jurisdiction largely because they (like many Third World nations) favored principles to enhance technology transfer from North to South as well as binding codes of conduct for transnational corporations. The two UN organizations supported the principle that technology was part of the common heritage of humankind. Indeed, many developing countries and NGOs have strongly denounced particular aspects of TRIPs and call for its removal; for example, because of ethical objections to specific provisions such as Article 27.3(b), which deals with the patenting of life forms.

Prior to and in parallel with these initiatives, the USA, or more precisely its financial complex, has been at the vanguard of *restructuring and deregulation of the world financial system* (Cohen 1998; Helleiner 1994). Indeed, in significant respects the more liberalized system that emerged during the 1980s and 1990s has worked to recycle the trade surpluses of other nations (especially from Japan and South Korea, as well as from the European Union) to fund American expansion (and fund massive US payments deficits). The USA has also sought to press other governments not only for deregulation and privatization but also for changes in tax and bankruptcy policy, favoring higher indirect taxes, lower income and corporate taxes, as well as new legal protections for investors from expropriation – all measures that tend to reinforce the power of capital, including financial capital. Under pressure from the USA, the IMF and World Bank now use conditionality to give institution-building and policy advice on banking law, contract law, company law, and more generally on the role of the judiciary and specifically judicial review mechanisms modeled on American jurisprudence. It is worth noting that liberal reforms are more fully institutionalized when locked-in by law and backed by sanctions. Thus when liberalization and protection for private property rights are locked-in governments must accept not only privatization but also full *entry and exit rights* for investors, including rights of establishment and rights to repatriate capital or to move it offshore.

Pressing for many of the initiatives we have discussed in this section is what I call a supremacist historical bloc of public/private forces in the US state–civil society complex, along with its principal counterparts in the EU and to a lesser extent elsewhere in the G7 and other states (see Gill 2003a for discussion of the supremacist bloc). In the specific cases noted above, the most active elements of this historical bloc of forces involve a combination of the US government and a range of interests within American capitalism, for example, the financial complex (particularly huge institutional investors and Wall Street) and those associated with protection of intellectual property rights (for example, Silicon Valley, Hollywood and the image complex, the giant drug corporations, and so on).

Nevertheless, as capital has become more liberalized and globalized, the frequency and depth of economic crises has worsened and material dimensions of human insecurity may have increased, especially in much of the Third World. The 1997–98 global crisis was the worst since the Great Depression, with tens of millions of people impoverished and it illustrated the destabilizing effects of the free movement of transnational capital, such that even Neo-Classical economists have come to question the legitimacy and efficiency of free capital mobility (Bhagwati 1998). Many large institutional investors, corporations and super-wealthy individuals were bailed out when their investments went sour, ostensibly to prevent a more general financial collapse (that is, the risks of large investors or depositors were socialized). By contrast the costs of adjustment have been dumped on unprotected capital, unprotected workers and the most vulnerable members of society (that is, their risk has been privatized), and ultimately it will be ordinary taxpayers that meet the costs. Indeed, borrowers were generally forced to accept austerity frameworks as a condition of IMF and G7 loans. As Chapter 5 illustrates, this often meant reduced expenditures on programs of vital importance to most people and especially to the poor (social, health, education, and so on) in ways that have undermined human security and social welfare. Nevertheless, at the time of writing, the Bush Administration was pressing for free trade agreements to prohibit controls on capital movements (even in the event of an economic crisis) along the lines of two model bilateral agreements recently made with Chile and Singapore.[4]

Full spectrum dominance and globalization: US National Security Strategy

I now shift from a focus on issues of global economic governance to the use of military and surveillance power in emerging world order. So in this section, I initially discuss some of the ways in which this new apparatus of extended surveillance and military power have been developed by the USA, and then conclude with a reflection on how these are being used, and for what purposes, in the aftermath of 9/11.

Indeed, whilst there has been a great deal of continuity in both facets of US strategy (economic and military) since the end of the Cold War, the war in Iraq in 2003 seems to reflect an historical turning point. One can only speculate as to what this is ultimately likely to entail, although clearly, the war in Iraq has extended the Bush administration's open-ended war on terrorism to a strategy of pre-emption and regime change. This could mean not a new World War based upon mutually assured destruction and mass annihilation as some expected during the Cold War, but rather a combination of ongoing interventions and wars linked to the new US strategy of military dominance to not only police, but also to extend the frontiers of neo-liberal globalization.

One of the features of this type of warfare is the use of planners and software/weapons control so that the maximum amount of engagement is done from a distance, using bombing and other means to deny adversaries the chance of responding, inflicting casualties almost entirely to the "enemy" on the ground. This extended use of organized violence thus involves, as Bauman notes, a form of impunity. Its technical aspect relies on "electronic technology, which renders time instantaneous and annihilates the resistance of space" (Bauman 2001: 218).

It is in this context that we now explore some of the USA's plans for military globalization. In 1997 the Pentagon released a strategy document that promulgated the concept of "full spectrum dominance" maintained into the future through "full force integration." Its goal was to sustain superiority by synergizing US military technologies on land, sea, and air and in space. Indeed, the rapid militarization of space is seen as the most important strategic initiative for the USA in the twenty-first century to protect "US national interests and investments," not only from traditional rivals, but also from new challenges including those stemming from "a widening between 'haves' and 'have-nots'" (US Space Command 1997).[5] The new US conventional wisdom on strategy that emerged following the end of the Cold War was that challenges to its primacy were likely to be more diffuse, which implied that even its "friends" were potential targets of surveillance. Needless to say this created concerns in the European Union and elsewhere given the extensiveness of American intelligence networks.

When the airplane attacks destroyed the World Trade Center and hit the Pentagon, the rest of the world subsequently witnessed the use of American military power projection in Afghanistan and Iraq. In both cases the US leadership made it clear that this power would be used irrespective of whether it was sanctioned or legitimated by a UN mandate.

On June 6, 2002, the USA created the Department of Homeland Security, involving the most extensive reorganization of the US security apparatus since World War II, going well beyond an *ad hoc* system that combined 17 separate executive agencies. And, whereas one would have expected that the generality of the threat from mega-terrorism would have forged a bipartisan consensus on the enabling legislation of the new Department, "special interests" directly connected to the Republican Party benefited from various "riders" attached to the legislation. Thus giant pharmaceutical companies and US corporations that had registered in offshore jurisdictions such as the Bahamas had specific provisions inserted into the Homeland Security legislation so that they were, respectively, made exempt from class-action liability suits and from certain forms of taxation. In neither case did these provisions seem to have anything to do with the stated purposes of the legislation.[6]

However in this context, with very conservative figures such as Attorney General John Ashcroft at the vanguard, the federal government intensified domestic policing and surveillance, in ways that critics claimed threatened civil liberties and rights.[7] Indeed, although the US Constitution does not give sweeping emergency powers to the federal government, in practice these powers exist and are rarely subject to full judicial review. Such newly extended powers are now codified in a number of recent statutes, the most significant of which is the USA Patriot Act, which became law in October 2001.[8]

In addition, Admiral Poindexter, the former Reagan National Security Adviser who narrowly escaped imprisonment for his role in the Iran-Contra scandal, was made Director of the Office of Information Awareness at the Defense Advanced Research Projects Agency, charged with developing new surveillance technologies in light of 9/11.[9] Needless to say, Poindexter's appointment, and the wide remit attached to the new DARPA office has alarmed large numbers of civil libertarians in the USA. It is difficult to imagine this initiative – and related initiatives detailed below – will be confined to internal matters, since the USA has shaped the creation of universal international standards for data protocols. US strategists consider control over the basic infrastructure of networks an important power resource. The USA has both the largest corporations in these fields, as well as a massive intelligence apparatus associated with network capitalism. Indeed, US military theorists emphasize the need for US control over strategic nodes within global systems and networks, controlling rules of access and participation. This is viewed as part of a shift from old forms of war to "information age warfare," involving cyberwar and global communication systems (Fast 2001).

The above provides some of the background to the new *National Security Strategy of the United States*, which spells out changes stemming from conservative thinking since the late 1980s. At that time Secretary of State Powell, Vice President Cheney, and others attempted to formulate a new rationale for the military after the Cold War. The centerpiece of NSS is a reconfiguration of US strategy around two primary organizing principles: pre-emption and global dominance (US Government 2002).[10] The NSS document argues that the US is "menaced less by fleets and armies than by catastrophic technologies in the hands of the embittered few." Secretary of Defense Rumsfeld had earlier fleshed out the implications of this when he argued that the USA is moving away from "threat-based" strategy toward "a new capabilities-based approach to counter any potential threat through a variety of means" (Rumsfeld 2002). This includes the prerogative to strike first against actual or potential enemies.[11] On the other hand, Rumsfeld argued that twenty-first-century wars would entail the use of all elements of power, economic, diplomatic, financial, law enforcement, intelligence as well as overt and covert military operations. With respect to the latter the Pentagon is creating "an elite secret army with resources stretching across the full spectrum of covert capabilities."[12]

However, notwithstanding its commitment to the war on terrorism the present Bush Administration has been consistently clear that its military priorities lie in full spectrum dominance and this includes not only developing Star Wars (missile defense) but also increasing space-based and terrestrial surveillance structures. It has also stressed the need to build up US capacities to engage in information warfare, including a new secret agency located in the White House and in the Pentagon, called the Office of Strategic Influence (OSI), an initiative strongly criticized by many Americans after members of the Bush Administration made it clear that the OSI would use propaganda and disinformation campaigns to combat "anti-American" forces throughout the world. Also in July 2002, the Bush Administration announced the creation of the Office of Global Communications, a PR department to try to rehabilitate the US image abroad, especially in the Middle East and Europe. The department apparently grows out of the Coalition Information Center, partly established with British Prime Minister Blair's media guru, Alastair Campbell, to promote US–UK views during the Afghan war.[13]

A political counterpart to the military goals of the NSS has been dubbed the "Rice Doctrine" of "Realist multilateralism," the brainchild of Condoleezza

Rice that is consistent with the general goal of American strategy of establishing free markets, democracy and free trade, backed by US military force, if necessary to ensure "regime change."[14] Of course it is widely noted that the USA rejects multilateralism when it can, for example, rejecting the jurisdiction of the International Criminal Court for its citizens (reflecting an imperial conception of citizenship rights, with US citizens above international law), refusal to ratify the protocol to the Biological Weapons Convention, the rejection of the Kyoto Environmental Protocol and the scrapping of the ABM Treaty. On the other hand, the USA embraces multilateralism when it is needed, for example, in its war against terrorism and in the early stages of its preparation for the war against Iraq, planned long before 9/11 (Armstrong 2002).[15] It has also been widely noted that the USA tried to put together what it calls a "coalition of the willing," that is, a group of allies that would back its military action. Diplomats of the United Nations came to refer to this as the "coalition of the billing," since it was premised upon effectively buying votes at the UN to gain some legitimacy for its policy of war, a tactic that ultimately failed despite initial successes.[16] Indeed, such brittle commitment to multilateralism as is reflected in the Bush Administration is a position that prominent liberal internationalists firmly reject as counterproductive (Nye 2001).

With respect to issues of military surveillance, the Bush and Clinton Administrations reflect a considerable continuity. Thus in April 2001 it was announced that the secret National Reconnaissance Office of the USA had been authorized to undertake a massive expansion of its spy satellite systems (partly because other nations such as Russia, France, India and closer American allies such as Israel and Canada have satellite surveillance systems), in an initiative called Future Image Architecture. FIA is the most expensive venture ever undertaken by its intelligence agencies and will cost $25 billion over 20 years – by contrast the Manhattan Project to build the atomic bomb during World War II cost $20 billion in inflation-adjusted dollars. The new systems are intended to give a unilateral capacity for certain types of military action such as that recently witnessed in Iraq, allowing for more accurate targeting and bombing. This system fits well with the Bush Administration's priority of developing the military uses of space and the use of cyber warfare. It will be linked to powerful ground station computers that can analyze and distribute imagery (for example, battlefield pictures) rapidly to US government agencies.[17]

Prospects for World War III?

Many of the surveillance and other military technologies just discussed were used in the war in Iraq in 2003, which demonstrated the potency of the American military machine, as well as the American willingness to use its strategic power to extend its dominance over the resources and region of the Middle East.

Of course it is very well known that the current White House is both very sympathetic to the oil corporations and has concerns over long-term US energy security.[18] Much of the Bush Administration's immediate motivation for an attack on Iraq seems to be linked to this goal – to reassert and gain more fundamental long-term control over oil in the Middle East. (The US Department of Energy has estimated that Iraq may be able to provide the USA with up to half of its oil needs, and US energy and other corporations were lining up well before the war started – ready to take advantage of a post-war Iraqi oil boom.)

However, this war also might be the first of a new series of interventions designed to militarily lock-in and extend the US-led globalization project worldwide. In this regard, some may recall, that during one of the high points of the Cold War, the American sociologist C. Wright Mills published a book called *The Causes of World War Three* (1958). The argument of this book was built from his earlier thesis in *The Power Elite* (1956): that unaccountable elite power in the USA and in the Soviet Union, coupled to weapons of mass destruction, would inevitably lead to the outbreak of global war, unless rulers could be forced to turn scientific research into peaceful channels and break the drift towards war. With the benefit of hindsight, the eventual collapse of the Soviet Union showed that Mills was very wide of the mark: the leaders of the Soviet Union effectively surrendered of their own accord, although nuclear war was close on a number of occasions. However, now that the Cold War is over there are no significant military rivals on the horizon that might countervail American military power, in the way that the former Soviet Union was able to do.

It may well be, however, that future historians will argue in retrospect that 9/11 triggered the onset of a different kind of world war, one waged in the name of a new and perhaps more conservative and aggressive form of American imperialism, again with the very important caveat that no countervailing social and political forces prevent conservatives in the US government from pursuing their full-blown imperialist vision.

What seems to have occurred, with 9/11 as the catalyst, is that the USA has shifted its strategy well beyond President Clinton's concept of "democratic enlargement." Clinton's strategy tended to focus more on the institutionalization of disciplinary neo-liberalism using diplomatic and economic means to reshape the internal structures of governance of other states, of course, with the goal of making them more conducive to the expansion of American interests. By contrast, the Bush Administration's foreign policy team is a mixture of traditional Realism and different strands of Conservatism, with the latter greatly strengthened by the administration's responses to the mega-terrorist attacks. Thus whilst the administration contains not only traditional realists/assertive nationalists (such as Secretary of Defense Rumsfeld and National Security Adviser Condoleezza Rice) realist/pragmatists such as (Secretary of State Colin Powell), and traditional conservatives (such as Vice

President Cheney) of growing importance is a neo-conservative grouping that has been called the "democratic imperialists." Paul Wolfowitz (Deputy Secretary of Defense) is the leader of this faction in the administration, which has some of its intellectual roots in the Project for the New American Century.

Indeed, some believe that the democratic imperialists are becoming more influential within the Bush Administration. As Charles Kupchan of the Council on Foreign Relations has put it, these new imperialists have the (counter-) revolutionary aims of "transforming the world in America's image," or put differently they seek to extend the US-led globalization project on a worldwide basis.[19] Here it should be noted that Paul Wolfowitz was the principal author of a 1992 Pentagon strategy report for the first Bush Administration, one that had to be toned down before its publication since it was deemed to be too controversial at the time, although many of its ideas subsequently re-emerged in the new National Security Strategy document (US Government 2002). Wolfowitz is also the principal architect of the American strategy in Iraq, and many within American ruling circles are coming to the view that the decision to go to war there may galvanize a broader shift in American foreign policy – in a similar way to how the North Korean invasion of the South led to the adoption of the Truman Doctrine, and the Soviet invasion of Afghanistan set the stage for the Reagan Doctrine.[20]

The strategy of pre-emptive war and imperialism, if it continues, is bound to encounter massive resistance and seems likely to engender an increase in mega-terrorist threats. Resistance would, of course, assume many different forms. Some of it would involve traditional interstate realignments associated with a reformulated balance of power, and as such could be subject to institutionalization, diplomacy and negotiation. Some would take the form of popular resistance throughout the world, especially in the Middle East (for example, centering on the Palestinian question), and of course some of this would be peaceful, some more violent. In particular, significant conflicts could develop if the fall of Saddam's secular regime in Iraq were to be followed by a more fundamentalist Iraq, governed by forces akin to the Iran of the Ayatollahs. This would increase the forces hostile to the US presence in the region, and mishandling this challenge might portend greater use of suicide attacks on the USA and its allies, in so far as many of these more fundamentalist forces of resistance involve cults of martyrdom.

Thus it is worth concluding this volume by indicating some aspects of the viewpoint that lies behind this new American imperialist perspective. One rather stark example is the thinking of Thomas Barnett, an adviser to Secretary Rumsfeld and a Professor at the US Naval War College. Barnett outlined a theory behind a new US global strategy in an article for *Esquire* magazine in March 2003. Welcoming and anticipating the long-planned war in Iraq, he stated it "will mark the historical tipping point – the moment when Washington takes real ownership of strategic security in the age of globalization."[21]

Barnett believes the central strategic principle is that a country's potential to warrant a US military response is "inversely related to its globalization connectivity" (Barnett 2003: 4). Thus the new security paradigm for the USA is that *"disconnectedness defines danger"* (Barnett 2003: 1, emphasis in original).

Indeed, stripped bare of the moralistic rhetoric of President Bush, with its propensity to divide the world into a Manichean universe of good and evil, the new strategic map apparently circulating within Pentagon and intelligence services is avowedly materialistic. It is also equally simplified: it is premised upon a state's degree of integration into globalization (and thus its willingness to welcome and support capital and free enterprise).

This image of the global political economy is akin to that of World Systems theorists, however divided between countries integrated into the flows, transactions and networks of globalization and those who lie outside the globalization processes. Those most integrated, according to Barnett, have stable governments, rising living standards, and are aligned to the basic purposes of American power (these states comprise the "Core"). The Core would come to include states such as China who are increasingly integrated through trading capital flows, and although not democratic, at least have "stable government." Outside the Core are two categories of countries: (a) flanking or semi-peripheral states that are neither fully integrated into, nor fully outside globalization (the "Seam" states), and (b) those states that lie outside the globalization project and that constitute the main "strategic threat environment" to the US ("The Gap").

Thus Barnett proposes that US strategy should be to:

> 1) Increase the Core's immune system capabilities for responding to September 11-like system perturbations; 2) Work the Seam states to firewall the core from the Gap's worst exports, such as terror, drugs, and pandemics; and, most important, 3) shrink the Gap... the Middle East is the perfect place to start... (Barnett 2003: 4–5)

Barnett is fully aware that globalization creates winners and losers and that it can be a wrenching process, but stresses that the main resources for the new strategy will come from private investment, rather than from the public sector. However, its success requires expansion of the US military beyond its success in "deterring global war and obsolescing state-on-state war" to move into the "far more difficult sub-national conflicts and the dangerous transnational actors they spawn". He adds, in ways that refer us back to the earlier discussion of the lifestyles and paranoia of the affluent outlined in Chapter 10:

> I know most Americans do not want to hear this, but the real battlegrounds in the global war on terrorism are still over there. If gated communities and rent-a-cops were enough, September 11 never would have happened...

We ignore the Gap's existence at our own peril, because it will not go away until we as a nation respond to the challenge of making globalization truly global. (Barnett 2003: 7)

Notes

1. I thank Tyler Attwood and Tim Di Muzio for research for this chapter, and Isabella Bakker for comments.
2. Rates of asthma in America have doubled since 1980, and about 6% of all Americans have the disease. US asthma rates are much higher in poor urban areas, and a recent study has found that one in four children in central Harlem, a heavily polluted, poor and predominantly black area in New York City, has the disease. See Richard Perez-Pena, "Study Finds Asthma in 25% of Children in Central Harlem." *New York Times*, April 19, 2003.
3. United States corporations have influential business NGOs such as the Intellectual Property Committee (IPC) (members: Pfizer, IBM and DuPont, Bristol-Myers, FMC, General Electric, General Motors, Hewlett-Packard, Johnson & Johnson, Merck, Monsanto, Rockwell and Warner). IPC coordinated with Japan's Keidanren and with the Union of Industrial and Employers' Confederations of Europe (UNICE) to shape US positions. Others include the International Intellectual Property Alliance (IIPA), the most important copyright lobbyist in the world, an umbrella group of eight trade organizations including those in the music, movie, publishing, business equipment and information technology industries, and the Business Software Alliance (BSA).
4. Edward Alden, "US Backs Curbs on Capital Controls." *Financial Times*, April 2, 2003.
5. I am grateful to Tim Di Muzio for this example.
6. David Firestone, "Senate Votes, 90–9, to Set Up Homeland Security Department Geared to Fight Terrorism." *New York Times*, November 20, 2002; Jesse J. Holland, "Security Showdown Could Impact Future." *Washington Post*, November 18, 2002; Dan Morgan, "Homeland Bill Rider Aids Drugmakers." *Washington Post*, November 15, 2002.
7. For example, efforts by Attorney General Ashcroft to create (offshore) prison camps for US citizens declared as enemy combatants. See Jonathan Turley, "Camps for Citizens: Ashcroft's Hellish Vision." *Los Angeles Times*, August 14, 2002. The Bush Administration has also declared so-called First Amendment Zones (referring to the First Amendment right to freedom of speech). FAZs, now the norm at Bush public appearances, take the form of fenced-off areas for protesters that are usually several hundred yards away from the target of the protest. At a Florida rally for Jeb Bush in the 2002 gubernatorial election his brother, the President, appeared and seven protesters were arrested for refusing to move into such a Zone. The Secret Service claimed that such Zones are necessary for the President's safety, although they seem to have allowed Bush supporters much closer to the President. See "Zones Hinder Free Speech." *St Petersburg Times*, November 9, 2002.
8. The Uniting and Strengthening America by Providing Appropriate Tools Required to Intercept and Obstruct Terrorism (USA Patriot Act) is intended to better allow the US government "To deter and punish terrorist acts in the United States and around the world, to enhance law enforcement investigatory tools, and for other purposes." HR 3162 RDS: 107th Congress, October 24, 2001. The full text is posted

by the Electronic Privacy Information Center <www.epic.org/privacy/terrorism/hr3162.html>
9. The "Total Information Awareness System" aims to create an electronic dragnet of email, calling records, credit card and banking transactions and travel documents, without requiring a search warrant. It uses data mining techniques (used by scientists and marketers) to gather information from various databases, pursue links between people and groups and thus to respond to automatic alerts and share information more efficiently. See John Markoff, "Pentagon Plans a Computer System that Would Peek at Personal Data of Americans." *New York Times*, November 9, 2002. See <www.darpa.mil/iao/index.htm>
10. The document also devotes attention to management of regional conflicts, arms control and the promotion of global economic growth and alleviation of poverty through free markets, free enterprise and announcing a new Millennium Fund to aid the poor.
11. Max Boot, "Doctrine of the 'Big Enchilada.'" *Washington Post*, October 14, 2002; Max Boot, "Who Says We Never Strike First?" *New York Times*, October 4, 2002.
12. Rumsfeld's Defense Science Board 2002 Summer Study on Special Operations and Joint Forces in Support of Countering Terrorism, recommended combining "special ops, intelligence, cover and deception, information warfare, psyops, and covert forces" from the CIA and military agencies – the world of so-called "black operations" – into a single group called the Proactive, Pre-emptive Operations Groups (P2OG). This runs parallel with efforts to improve and link information databases and networks in the "war on terror." According to Rumsfeld, "Prevention and pre-emption are... the only defense against terrorism. Our task is to find and destroy the enemy before they strike us." Cited in William M. Arkin, "The Secret War." *Los Angeles Times*, October 27, 2002.
13. The office will apparently use Hollywood-style and Madison Avenue techniques to subtly spread its message, unlike the more upfront Voice of America radio network. It will work with foreign broadcasters and journalists to create positive images of the USA. Such an effort was called for by a Council on Foreign Relations taskforce, made of government officials, advertising and media executives who pointed out that the USA is seen by many abroad as arrogant, hypocritical, and self-absorbed. I thank Tyler Attwood for this point.
14. Walter Russell Mead, "Misunderstanding the Rice Doctrine." *Financial Times*, October 2, 2002.
15. It should also be emphasized that the NSS was not simply the result of 9/11 since it is built on the framework of conservative thinking that emerged in the late 1980s. More recently the conservative Project for the New American Century produced a strategy document in September 2000 called *Rebuilding America's Defenses: Strategies, Forces and Resources for a New Century*. In effect, this document is also a blueprint for US global domination, preserving primacy for unilateralism, with multilateral action only when it does not compromise US interests. William Kristol headed PNAC and its report was created by the key figures in the Bush administration foreign policy apparatus when they were out of office, for example, Cheney, Rumsfeld, Paul Wolfowitz, Jeb Bush and Lewis Libby (now Cheney's chief of staff).
16. Thalif Deen, "US Dollars Yielded Unanimous UN Vote against Iraq." Inter Press News Service, cited November 11, 2002, <www.commondreams.org/headlines02/1111-02.htm>

17. Joseph Fitchett, "Spying from Space: US to Sharpen the Focus." *International Herald Tribune*, April 10, 2001. Here it is worth adding that the US benefits from intelligence inputs from its major allies. Many of the electronic surveillance facilities of the English speaking countries are combined in the so-called ECHELON system that was enlarged between 1975 and 1995 to encompass virtually all electronic and telephone communications in Europe, analyzed through data mining software operating through Internet servers, with the information fed into huge computers known as "Dictionaries." Proof of this was found in 1998–99 by US intelligence specialist Jeffrey Richelson, via the Freedom of Information Act. He obtained documents that confirmed the existence, scale and expansion of the ECHELON system. See <www.zdnet.co.uk/news/2000/25/ns-16204.html>
18. Vice President Cheney chairs the White House Energy Policy Development Group, which in April 2001 commissioned the Council on Foreign Relations and the Baker Institute for Public Policy to produce a report on "energy security." The report concluded that the USA remained vulnerable to Iraq's destabilizing effect on the Middle East supply of oil and recommended that the USA build a new energy policy central to US domestic economic and foreign policy interests, revise strategy toward Iraq and rebuild a cohesive coalition of allies. Those advising on the report included Kenneth Lay (former Chief Executive of Enron), and executives of Shell, BP and Chevron-Texaco, as well as a former Kuwaiti oil minister.
19. Quoted by Stephen Fidler and Gerard Baker, "America's Democratic Imperialists." *Financial Times*, March 5, 2003.
20. Fidler and Baker, "America's Democratic Imperialists." *Financial Times*, March 5, 2003.
21. Barnett's website describes his work as follows: "At the Naval War College, Dr. Barnett serves as Director of the NewRuleSets.Project, an ambitious effort to draw new 'maps' of power and influence in the world economy so as to expand the US Military's – and specifically, the US Navy's – vision of where and how it can wield maximum influence across the international security environment of the Era of Globalization... The first phase of the project (January 2000–October 2001) was conducted in partnership with the Wall Street broker-dealer firm Cantor Fitzgerald, which hosted three full-day 'decision event' workshops atop World Trade Center 1 (Windows on the World). These workshops brought together elite leaders from the worlds of finance, national security, think tanks and industry to discuss the crucial 'flows' of globalization, with a special emphasis on Developing Asia." <www.nwc.navy.mil/newrulesets/thomas_barnett.htm>

Bibliography

Ahmad, A. 1995. The Politics of Literary Postcoloniality. *Race and Class*, 36 (3): 1–20.
Alexander, J., and C. T. Mohanty. 1994. Introduction: Geneologies, Legacies and Movements. In *Feminist Geneologies, Colonial Legacies, Democratic Futures*, edited by J. Alexander and C. T. Mohanty. New York: Routledge, xiii–xlii.
Altvater, E. 1993. *The Future of the Market: An Essay on the Regulation of Money and Nature after the Collapse of "Actually Existing Socialism"*. London: Verso.
Altvater, E., and B. Mahnkopf. 2002. *Globalisierung der Unsicherheit: Arbeit im Schatten, Schmutziges Geld und informelle Politik*. Muenster: Westfaelisches Damfboot.
Amano, K. 2001. Sokoku to Tenno-Sei (Homeland and Emperor System). *Impaction*, 126: 74–81.
Amin, S. 2000. Economic Globalization and Political Universalism: Conflicting Issues. *Journal of World Systems Research*, VI (3, Fall/Winter): 581–622.
Anderson, P. 1974. *Passages from Antiquity to Feudalism*. London: NLB.
Araghi, F. 1995. Global Depeasantization. *The Sociological Quarterly*, 36 (2): 337–68.
Araghi, F. 2000. The Great Global Enclosure of Our Times. In *Hungry for Profit: The Agribusiness Threat to Farmers, Food and the Environment*, edited by F. Magdoff et al. New York: Monthly Review Press, 145–60.
Arat-Koc, S. 2003. Whose Social Reproduction? Transnational Motherhood and Challenges to Feminist Political Economy. Paper to *Rethinking Social Reproduction*, March 14, at York University, Toronto.
Armstrong, D. 2002. Dick Cheney's Song of America: Drafting a Plan for Global Dominance. *Harper's Magazine*, October, 76–83.
Armstrong, P. et al. 1985. *Feminist Marxism or Marxist Feminism: A Debate*. Toronto: Garamond Press.
Arrighi, G. 1994. *The Long Twentieth Century – Money, Power and the Origins of Our Times*. London: Verso.
Aslanbeigui, N., and G. Summerfield. 2001. Risk, Gender, and Development in the 21st Century. *International Journal of Politics, Culture and Society*, 15 (1): 7–26.
Atinc, T. M., and M. Walton. 1998 *Social Consequences of the East Asian Financial Crisis* World Bank, <www.worldbank.org/eapsocial/library/socconsq/>
ATTAC. 2003. *Die Hoffnung Hat Die Angst Besiegt*. Berlin: Scientific Board of ATTAC.
Bailey, M. 2000 *Agricultural Trade and the Livelihoods of Small Farmers* Oxfam GB Policy Department, March, <www.oxfam.org.uk/policy/papers/agricultural_trade/agric.htm>
Bakker, I. 1989. The Political Economy of Gender. In *The New Canadian Political Economy*, edited by W. Clement and G. Williams. Montreal: McGill-Queens Press, 99–115.
Bakker, I. 1991. Pay Equity and Economic Restructuring: The Polarization of Policy? In *Pay Equity: A Feminist Assessment*, edited by J. Fudge and P. McDermott. Toronto: University of Toronto Press, 254–80.
Bakker, I., ed. 1994. *The Strategic Silence: Gender and Economic Policy*. London: Zed Books.
Bakker, I., ed. 1996a. *Rethinking Restructuring: Gender and Change in Canada*. Toronto: University of Toronto Press.
Bakker, I. 1996b. Deconstructing Macro-Economics through a Feminist Lens. In *Women and Canadian Public Policy*, edited by J. Brodie. Toronto: Harcourt Brace, 31–56.

Bakker, I. 1997. Identity, Interests and Ideology: The Gendered Terrain of Global Restructuring. In *Globalization, Democratization and Multilateralism*, edited by S. Gill. London, Tokyo: Macmillan, UN University Press, 127–39.
Bakker, I. 1998. *Unpaid Work and Macroeconomics: New Discussions, New Tools for Action.* Ottawa: Status of Women Canada.
Bakker, I. 1999. Neoliberal Governance and the New Gender Order. *Working Papers*, 1 (1): 49–59.
Bakker, I. 2000. (Contributing Author) Accountability for the Progress of Women. In *Progress of the World's Women*, edited by D. Elson. New York: UNIFEM, 108–28.
Bakker, I. 2001. Neoliberal Governance and the Reprivatization of Social Reproduction. Paper to *International Studies Association*, March 23–27, at New Orleans.
Bannon, J. F. 1966. *Indian Labor in the Spanish Indies*. Boston: Heath.
Banting, K., and C. Beach, eds. 1994. *Labor Market Polarization and Social Policy Reform*. Kingston: Queen's University, School of Policy Studies.
Barlow, M., and T. Clarke. 2000 *A WTO Primer: An Activists' Guide to the World Trade Organization* Council of Canadians, <www.canadians.org/>
Barndt, D. 1997. Bio/Cultural Diversity and Equity in Post-NAFTA Mexico (Or: Tomasita Comes North While Big Mac Goes South). In *Global Justice, Global Democracy*, edited by J. Drydyk and P. Penz. Winnipeg: Fernwood Publishing, 55–69.
Barndt, D. 2002. *Tangled Routes: Women, Work and Globalization on the Tomato Trail*. Lanham: Rowman & Littlefield.
Barnett, T. 2003. The Pentagon's New Map: It Explains Why We're Going to War, and Why We'll Keep Going to War. *Esquire* 1–11, <www.nwc.navy.mil/newrulesets/ThePentagonsNewMap.htm>
Barrett, M., and M. McIntosh. 1982. *The Anti-Social Family*. London: Verso.
Bauman, Z. 2001. *The Individualized Society*. Cambridge, UK; Malden, MA: Polity Press.
Becerra, L. et al. 2002. Argentina: An Alternative Proposal to Overcome the Crisis. *Monthly Review*, 53 (11): 24–34.
Beck, U. 2000. *What is Globalization?* Translated by P. Camiller. Malden, MA: Polity Press.
Beck, U. 2002. *Redefining Power in a Global Era*, <globaldimensions.net/articles/Beck.html>
Beck, U., and E. Beck-Gernsheim. 2002. *Individualization: Institutionalized Individualism and Its Social and Political Consequences*. London: Sage.
Bello, W. 1999. Asian Financial Crisis: The Movie. *The Ecologist*, 29 (1): 28–32.
Benatar, S. R. 2001. South Africa's Transition in a Globalizing World: H.I.V./A.I.D.S. As a Window and a Mirror. *International Affairs*, 77 (2): 347–60.
Benatar, S. R. 2002. The HIV/AIDS Pandemic: A Sign of Instability in a Complex Global System. *Journal of Medicine and Philosophy*, 27 (2): 163–77.
Benería, L. 1999. Globalization, Gender and the Davos Man. *Feminist Economics*, 5 (3): 61–83.
Benería, L., and G. Sen. 1997. Accumulation, Reproduction and Women's Role in Economic Development: Boserup Revisited. In *The Women, Gender and Development Reader*, edited by N. Vasvanathan, et al. London: Zed Books, 42–50.
Bentham, J. 1995. *The Panopticon Writings*. London; New York: Verso.
Bergeron, S. 2001. Political Economy Discourses of Globalization and Feminist Politics. *Signs*, 26 (4): 983–1006.
Bhagwati, J. 1998. The Capital Myth: The Difference between Trade in Widgets and Dollars. *Foreign Affairs*, 77 (3): 7–12.
Boris, E., and E. Pruegel. 1996. *Homeworkers in Global Perspective: Invisible No More*. New York: Routledge.

Bové, J., and F. Dufour. 2001. *The World Is Not for Sale: Farmers against Junk Food*. London: Verso.
Braithwaite, J., and P. Drahos. 2000. *Global Business Regulation*. Cambridge: Cambridge University Press.
Braudel, F. 1980. *On History*. Chicago: University of Chicago Press.
Braudel, F. 1982. *Civilization and Capitalism, 15th–18th Century*. New York: Harper & Row.
Brodie, J. 1994. Shifting the Boundaries: Gender and the Politics of Restructuring. In *The Strategic Silence: Gender and Economic Policy*, edited by I. Bakker. London: Zed Press, 46–60.
Brodie, J., ed. 1996. *Women and Canadian Public Policy*. Toronto: Harcourt Brace & Company.
Brodie, J. 1997. Meso Discourses: State Forms and the Gendering of Liberal-Democratic Citizenship. *Citizenship Studies*, 1 (2): 223–42.
Brodie, J. 2002a. Citizenship and Solidarity: Reflections on the Canadian Way. *Citizenship Studies*, 6 (4): 377–94.
Brodie, J. 2002b. The Great Undoing: State Formation, Gender Politics, and Social Policy in Canada. In *Western Welfare in Decline: Globalization and Women's Poverty*, edited by C. Kingfisher. Philadelphia: University of Pennsylvania Press, 90–110.
Brodie, J. 2003 (in press). Globalization and the Social Question. In *States Under Seige: Global Governance in the Semiperiphery*, edited by S. Clarkson and M. Cohen. London: Zed Books.
Butler, J. E. 1898. *Personal Reminiscences of a Great Crusade*. London: H. Marshall.
Cagatay, N., and S. Ozler. 1995. Feminization of the Labor Force: The Effects of Long-Term Development and Structural Adjustment. *World Development*, 23 (11): 1883–94.
Campaign 2000. 2001. *Family Security in Insecure Times: Tackling Canada's Social Deficit*, November bulletin. Available at <www.campaign2000.ca/rc/01bulletin/Nov01Bulletin4p.pdf>
Carvalho, F. et al. 2000. *Brazil Report: Economic Adjustment and Social Disadjustment*, <www.chasque.net/frontpage/socwatch/2000/eng/pdf2000countries/brazileng.pdf>
Castels, S., and M. J. Miller. 1993. *The Age of Migration: International Population Movements in the Modern World*. New York: Guilford Press.
Cerny, P. G. 1993. *Finance and World Politics: Markets, Regimes, and States in the Post-Hegemonic Era*. Aldershot: Edward Elgar.
Chatterjee, P. 1986. *Nationalist Thought and the Colonial World*. London: Zed Books.
Chossudovsky, M. 1997. *The Globalization of Poverty: The Impacts of IMF and World Bank Reforms*. Penang: Third World Network.
Cleaver, H. 1977. Food, Famine and the International Crisis. *Zerowork*, (2): 7–77.
Cohen, B. J. 1998. *The Geography of Money*. Ithaca: Cornell University Press.
Cohen, M. 1997. From the Welfare State to Vampire Capitalism. In *Women and the Canadian Welfare State*, edited by P. Evans and G. Wekerle. Toronto: University of Toronto Press, 28–67.
Connell, R. W. 1987. *Gender and Power: Society, the Person and Sexual Politics*. Cambridge: Polity Press.
Connell, R. W. 2000. *The Men and the Boys*. Cambridge: Polity Press.
Cook, J. et al., eds. 2000. *Towards a Gendered Political Economy*. London: Macmillan.
Correa, C. M. 1999. *Intellectual Property Rights, the WTO, and Developing Countries: The TRIPS Agreement and Policy Options*. New York: Zed Books.
Cox, R. 1981. Social Forces, States and World Orders: Beyond International Relations Theory. *Millennium*, 12 (2): 116–55.

Cox, R. W. 1987. *Production, Power, and World Order: Social Forces in the Making of History*. New York: Columbia University Press.

Culpeper, R. 2002. Approaches to Globalization and Inequality within the International System. Paper to *Social Development in International Organizations*, March 15, at Geneva.

Cutler, A. C. 1997. Artifice, Ideology and Paradox: The Public/Private Distinction in International Law. *Review of International Political Economy*, 4 (2): 261–85.

Daly, M., and G. Standing. 2001. Introduction. In *Care Work: The Quest for Security*, edited by M. Daly. Geneva: International Labor Organization, 1–12.

Davis, M. 1990. *City of Quartz: Excavating the Future in Los Angeles*. London; New York: Verso.

Davis, M. 1998. *Ecology of Fear: Los Angeles and the Imagination of Disaster*. New York: Metropolitan Books.

Davis, M. 2001. *Late Victorian Holocausts: El Niño Famines and the Making of the Third World*. London: Verso.

Dawkins, K. 1999. *Agricultural Prices and Trade Policy: Evaluating and Correcting the Uruguay Round Agreement on Agriculture*. Paper to UNCTAD, December 12–14, at Geneva.

Deacon, B. 1997. *Global Social Policy: International Organizations and the Future of Welfare*. London: Sage.

Dean, M. 2000. *Governmentality: Power and Rule in Modern Society*. London: Sage.

Dias Martins, M. 2000. The MST Challenge to Neoliberalism. *Latin American Perspectives*, 27 (5): 33–45.

Dixon, J. 2002. *The Changing Chicken: Chooks, Cooks and Culinary Culture*. Sydney: University of New South Wales Press.

Dower, J. W. 1999. *Embracing Defeat: Japan in the Wake of World War II*. New York: W.W. Norton & Company.

Eichengreen, B. 1998. *Globalizing Capital: A History of the International Monetary System*. Princeton, NJ: Princeton University Press.

Einarsson, P. 2001. *The Disagreement on Agriculture*. <www.grain.org/publications/mar012-en.cfm>

Elson, D. 1995. Male Bias in Macro Economics: The Case of Structural Adjustment. In *Male Bias in the Development Process*, edited by D. Elson. Manchester: Manchester University Press, 164–90.

Elson, D. 1997. Economic Paradigms Old and New: The Case of Human Development. In *Global Development Fifty Years after Bretton Woods: Essays in Honour of Gerald K Helleiner*, edited by R. Culpeper *et al*. Basingstoke; New York: Macmillan; St. Martin's Press; in association with the North–South Institute, 50–71.

Elson, D. 1998. The Economic, the Political and the Domestic: Businesses, States and Households in the Organisation of Production. *New Political Economy*, 3 (2): 189–209.

Elson, D. 1999. Labor Markets as Gendered Institutions: Equality, Efficiency and Empowerment Issues. *World Development*, 23 (3): 611–27.

Escobar, A. 1996. *Encountering Development: The Making and the Unmaking of the Third World*. Princeton, NJ: Princeton University Press.

Falk, R. 2003. *The Great Terror War*. New York: Olive Branch.

Fanon, F., and J.-P. Sartre. 1963. *The Wretched of the Earth*. Translated by C. Farrington. New York: Grove.

Fast, W. R. 2001. *Knowledge Strategies: Balancing Ends, Ways, and Means in the Information Age* [Report by Lieutenant Colonel, United States Army]. Institute for National Strategic Studies, July 3, 2001, <www.ndu.edu/inss/siws/cont.html>

Ferguson, S. 1998. Building on the Strengths of the Socialist Feminist Tradition. *New Politics*, 7 (2): 89–100.
Fitzpatrick, T. 2001. *Welfare Theory: An Introduction*. Basingstoke: Palgrave Macmillan.
Flassbeck, H. 2002. Lehrstück am Rio de la Plata. *Blätter für deutsche und Internationale Politik*, 2: 135–37.
Flavio de Almeida, L., and F. R. Sánchez. 2000. The Landless Workers' Movement and Social Struggles against Neoliberalism. *Latin American Perspectives*, 22 (5): 11–32.
Floro, M., and G. Dymski. 2000. Financial Crisis, Gender, and Power: An Analytical Framework. *World Development*, 28 (7): 1269–83.
Folbre, N. 2001. *The Invisible Heart: Economics and Family Values*. New York: New Press.
Folbre, N., and J. A. Nelson. 2000. For Love or Money-or Both? *Journal of Economic Perspectives*, 14 (4): 123–40.
Food First. 2000. *Fact Sheet: Food Aid in the New Millennium – Genetically Engineered Food and Foreign Assistance*, <www.foodfirst.org/pubs/factsheet/2000/biotechfs.1.html>
Fraser, N. 1997. From Redistribution to Recognition? Dilemmas of Justice in a "Poststructuralist" Age. *New Left Review*, (212): 68–93.
Friedman, M. 1962. *Capitalism and Freedom*. Chicago: University of Chicago Press.
Friedmann, H. 1982. The Political Economy of Food: The Rise and Fall of the Postwar International Food Order. *American Journal of Sociology*, 88: 248–86.
Friedmann, H. 1990. The Origins of Third World Food Dependence. In *The Food Question: Profits Versus People?*, edited by H. Bernstein et al. New York: Monthly Review Press, 13–31.
Friedmann, H. 1993. The Political Economy of Food: A Global Crisis. *New Left Review*, (197): 27–59.
Friedmann, H., and P. McMichael. 1989. Agriculture and the State System: The Rise and Decline of National Agricultures, 1870 to the Present. *Sociologia Ruralis*, XIX (2): 89–121.
Fujime, Y. 1998. *Sei No Rekishigaku (A History of Sexuality)*. Tokyo: Fuji Press.
Fukuda, T. 1993. *Yoshihara Ha Konna Tokoro De Gozaimashita: Kuruwa No Onna-Tachi No Showa-Shi (Yoshiwara Was Like This: A History of the Showa Era Kuruwa Women)*. Tokyo: Shakai Shiso-Sha.
Furtado, X. 2000. Human Security and Asia's Financial Crisis. *International Journal*, LV (3): 355–73.
Gabriel, C., and L. Macdonald. 1996. NAFTA and Economic Restructuring: Some Gender and Race Implications. In *Rethinking Restructuring: Gender and Change in Canada*, edited by I. Bakker. Toronto: University of Toronto Press, 165–86.
Gago, V., and D. Stzulwar. 2002. *Colectivo Situaciones*. Buenos Aires: Interview by Bettina Köhler and Ulrich Brand.
Galbraith, J. K. 1992. *The Culture of Contentment*. Boston: Houghton Mifflin.
Gandy, O. J. 1993. *The Panoptic Sort: A Political Economy of Personal Information*. Boulder: Westview.
Gill, S. 1995a. Globalisation, Market Civilisation, and Disciplinary Neoliberalism. *Millennium*, 23 (3): 399–423.
Gill, S. 1995b. The Global Panopticon?: The Neo-Liberal State, Economic Life and Democratic Surveillance. *Alternatives*, 20 (1): 1–49.
Gill, S. 1997. Transformation and Innovation in the Study of World Order. In *Innovation and Transformation in International Studies*, edited by S. Gill and J. H. Mittelman. Cambridge: Cambridge University Press, 5–24.
Gill, S. 1998a. New Constitutionalism, Democratisation and Global Political Economy. *Pacifica Review*, 10 (1): 23–38.

Gill, S. 1998b. European Governance & New Constitutionalism: EMU & Alternatives to Disciplinary Neo-Liberalism in Europe. *New Political Economy*, 3 (1): 5–26.
Gill, S. 1999. The Geopolitics of the Asian Crisis. *Monthly Review*, 50 (10): 1–10.
Gill, S. 2000a. Toward a Postmodern Prince? The Battle in Seattle as a Moment in the New Politics of Globalisation. *Millennium*, 29 (1): 131–41.
Gill, S. 2000b. The Constitution of Global Capitalism. Paper to *International Studies Association*, March 15, 2000, at Los Angeles.
Gill, S. 2001a. Constitutionalizing Inequality & the Clash of Globalizations. Paper to *International Studies Association*, February 21–24, at Chicago.
Gill, S. 2001b. Transparency Capitalism & Security in the Post-Cold War Order. Paper to *Gender, Political Economy and Human Security*, October 5, at York University, Toronto.
Gill, S. 2002a. Constitutionalizing Inequality and the Clash of Globalizations. *International Studies Review*, 4 (3): 47–65.
Gill, S. 2002b. Supremacy and Surveillance Power in Global Capitalism. *Das Argument 248*, 44 (5/6): 21–33.
Gill, S. 2002c. Privatization of the State and Social Reproduction? GATS and New Constitutionalism. Paper to *GATS: Trading Development?*, September 20–21, at the Centre for the Study of Globalisation and Regionalisation, University of Warwick.
Gill, S. 2003a. *Power and Resistance in the New World Order*. Basingstoke: Palgrave Macmillan.
Gill, S. 2003b. American Transparency Capitalism and Human Security: A Contradiction in Terms? *Global Change, Peace and Security*, 15 (1): 9–25.
Gill, S., and D. Law. 1988. *The Global Political Economy: Perspectives, Problems, and Policies*. Baltimore: Johns Hopkins University Press.
Goodman, D. *et al.* 1987. *From Farming to Biotechnology*. Oxford: Basil Blackwell.
Gorelick, S. 2000. Facing the Farm Crisis. *The Ecologist*, 30 (4): 28–32.
GPI Atlantic. 1998 *The Economic Value of Civic and Voluntary Work in Nova Scotia*. GPI Atlantic Publications, <www.gpiatlantic.org/ab_volunteer.shtml>
Gramsci, A. 1971. *Selections from the Prison Notebooks of Antonio Gramsci*, translated by Q. Hoare and G. Nowell-Smith. New York: International Publishers.
Gray, J. 1999. *False Dawn: The Delusions of Global Capitalism*. London: Granta Books.
Gregory, J. *et al.*, eds. 1999. *Women, Work and Inequality: The Challenge of Equal Pay in a Deregulated Labor Market*. London: Macmillan.
Grewal, I., and C. Kaplan. 1994. Introduction: Transnational Feminist Practices and Questions of Postmodernity. In *Scattered Hegemonies: Postmodernity and Transnational Feminist Practices*. Minneapolis: University of Minnesota Press, 1–33.
Grown, C. *et al.* 2000. Introduction. *World Development*, 28 (7): 1145–56.
Guest, D. 1985. *The Emergence of Social Security in Canada*. Vancouver: University of British Columbia Press.
Haddad, L., *et al.* 1995. The Gender Dimensions of Economic Adjustment Policies: Potential Interactions and Evidence to Date. *World Development*, 23 (6): 881–96.
Hampson, F. O. 2002. *Madness in the Multitude: Human Security and World Disorder*. Toronto: Oxford University Press.
Hanochi, S. 1996. *1949 Nen Kousho- Seido Haishi Regime No Keisei to Henyo (Formation and Transformation of the 1949 Abolitionist Regime)*. Yokohama: Meiji Gakuin University unpublished manuscript.
Hanochi, S. 1998a. A Historical Perspective on the Japanese Sex Trade. *REFUGE*, 17 (5): 19–23.

Hanochi, S. 1998b. Are Post-Colonial Feminists for or against the Hegemonic Alliance?: The Case of Anti-Global Sex Trade Movements. Paper to *SGIR-ISA Joint Conference*, September 16–19, at Vienna, Austria.

Hanochi, S. 1999. The Globalization of the Sex Trade into Japan. Paper to *Asian Dialogue on Trafficking in Women and Children*, March 21–23, at Tokyo.

Hanochi, S. 2001. Gender No Global Human Security Theory Ni Mukete (Towards a Gender-Based Global Human Security Theory). *Associe*, (5): 244–58.

Haraway, D. J. 1991. *Simians, Cyborgs, and Women: The Reinvention of Nature*. New York: Routledge.

Harder, L. 1999. Depoliticizing Insurgency: The Politics of Family in Alberta. In *Feminism, Political Economy and the State: Contested Terrain*, edited by P. Armstrong and P. Connelly. Toronto: Canadian Scholars' Press, 177–204.

Hardt, M., and A. Negri. 2000. *Empire*. Cambridge, MA: Harvard University Press.

Harrod, J. 1987. *Power, Production, and the Unprotected Worker*. New York: Columbia University Press.

Harrod, J. 2001. Power, Production and the Unprotected Worker: Rationalities, World Views and Global Change. Paper to *International Studies Association*, February 20–24, at Chicago.

Hartsock, N. 2001. Domination, Globalization: Toward a Feminist Analytic. Paper to *Domination and Ideology in High-Tech Capitalism*, May 24–27, at Berlin.

Harvey, D. 1989. *The Condition of Postmodernity*. Oxford: Blackwell.

Harvey, D. 1990. Between Space and Time: Reflections on the Geographical Imagination. *Annals of the Association of American Geographers*, 80 (3): 418–34.

Harvey, D. 1996. *Justice, Nature & the Geography of Difference*. Oxford: Blackwell.

Hay, C. 1998. Globalization, Welfare Retrenchment and the Logic of No Alternative: Why Second-Best Won't Do. *Journal of Social Policy*, 24 (4): 525–32.

Hayek, F. A. v. 1944. *The Road to Serfdom*. Chicago: University of Chicago Press.

Helleiner, E. 1994. *States and the Reemergence of Global Finance – from Bretton Woods to the 1990's*. Ithaca: Cornell University Press.

Himmelfarb, G. 1984. *The Idea of Poverty: England in an Industrial Age*. New York: Alfred A. Knopf.

Himmelweit, S. 1999. Domestic Labor. In *The Elgar Companion to Feminist Economics*, edited by J. Peterson and M. Lewis. Cheltenham: Elgar, 126–35.

Hirsch, J. 1995. *Der Nationale Wettbewerbsstaat. Staat, Demokratie und Politik im globalen Kapitalismus*. Berlin: Edition ID-Archiv.

Hobsbawm, E. J. 1968. *Industry and Empire*. Harmondsworth: Penguin.

Hobsbawm, E. 1994. *Age of Extremes – the Short Twentieth Century – 1914–1991*. London: Michael Joseph.

Hollifield, J. F. 1994. Immigration and Republicanism in France: The Hidden Consensus. In *Controlling Immigration: A Global Perspective*, edited by W. A. Cornelius et al. Stanford: Stanford University Press, 143–75.

Hosoya, C., and H. Nagayo, eds. 2001. *Nichi Bei Kankei Shi (History of Japan–U.S. Relations)*. Tokyo: Yuhikaku.

Huffschmid, J. 2002. *Politische Ökonomie der Finanzmärkte*. Hamburg: VSA.

Humphries, J., and J. Rubery. 1984. The Reconstitution of the Supply Side of the Labor Market: The Relative Autonomy of Social Reproduction. *Cambridge Journal of Economics*, 8 (1): 331–46.

Ignatieff, M. 1995. The Myth of Citizenship. In *Theories of Citizenship*, edited by R. Beiner. Albany: SUNY Press, 53–78.

Ignatiev, N. 1995. *How the Irish Became White*. New York: Routledge.

ILO 2003. *World Commission on the Social Dimensions of Globalization.* <http://www.ilo.org/public/english/wcsdg/globali/index.htm>
IMF. 1998. *Capital Account Liberalisation: Theoretical and Practical Aspects.* Washington, D.C.: IMF.
IMF. 2001. *World Economic Outlook.* Washington, D.C.: IMF.
Immigration Office: Japan Ministry of Justice. 1996. *Gaikokujin Geinoujin Ni Kansuru Nyukoku-Shinsa-Kijun No Kaisei Tou Ni Tsuite (Concerning Reforms of Immigration Standards for Foreign Entertainers).* Kokusai Jinken: International Human Rights.
Ismi, A. 1998. World Bank: Plunder with a Human Face. *Z Magazine* (February) 9–12.
Jacobson, M. F. 1998. *Whiteness of a Different Color.* London: Harvard University Press.
Jenson, J. 1986. Gender and Reproduction or Babies and the State. *Studies in Political Economy,* (20): 9–46.
Josephson, M. 1934. *The Robber Barons: The Great American Capitalists, 1861–1901.* New York: Harcourt Brace.
Kabeer, N. 1991. Cultural Dopes or Rational Fools? Women and Labor Supply in the Bangladesh Garment Industry. *European Journal of Development Research,* 3 (1): 133–60.
Kang, S.-J., and S. Yoshimi. 2001. *Global Ka No Enkinhou (Perspective of Globalization).* Tokyo: Iwanami.
Kim, W. B. 1998. Sub-Regional Economic Integration and Labor Migration in East Asia. In *Migration and Regional Economic Integration in Asia.* Paris: Organization for Economic Cooperation and Development, 33–42.
Kimbrell, A. 1998. Why Biotechnology and High-Tech Agriculture Cannot Feed the World. *The Ecologist,* 28 (5): 294–8.
Krasner, S. 2000. Compromising Westphalia. In *The Global Transformation Reader: An Introduction to the Globalization Debate,* edited by D. Held and A. McGrew. London: Polity Press, 124–35.
Kroll, L., and L. Goldman. 2003. Billionaires – the World's Richest People. *Forbes,* 171 (6): 87–142.
Kuyek, D. 2000. *ISAAA in Asia: Promoting Corporate Profits in the Name of the Poor.* <www.grain.org/publications/reports/isaaa.htm>
Lacher, H. 1999. Embedded Liberalism, Disembedded Markets: Reconceptualising the Pax Americana. *New Political Economy,* 4 (3): 343–60.
Lappé, F. M., and A. Lappé. 2002. *Hope's Edge.* New York: Tarcher/Putnam.
Leach, B. 1996. Behind Closed Doors: Homework Policy and Lost Possibilities for Change. In *Rethinking Restructuring: Gender and Change in Canada,* edited by I. Bakker. Toronto: University of Toronto Press, 203–16.
Lee, M. A. 2000. *The Beast Reawakens: Fascism's Resurgence from Hitler's Spymasters to Today's Neo-Nazi Groups and Right-Wing Extremists.* London: Routledge.
Lehman, K., and A. Krebs. 1996. Control of the World's Food Supply. In *The Case against the Global Economy and for a Turn toward the Local,* edited by J. Mander and E. Goldsmith. San Francisco: Sierra Club Books, 122–30.
LeQuesne, C. 1997. The World Trade Organisation and Food Security. Paper to *Talk to UK Food Group,* July 15.
Lim, J. 2000. The Effects of the East Asian Crisis on the Employment of Women and Men: The Philippine Case. *World Development,* 28 (7): 1285–306.
Lim, L. L., ed. 1998. *The Sex Sector: The Economics and Social Bases of Prostitution in South East Asia.* Geneva: ILO.
Lister, R. 1997. Citizenship: Towards a Feminist Synthesis. *Feminist Review,* 57 (1): 28–48.
MacAdam, M. 2003. Campaign against Exploitation of Foreign Workers Unites Activists. *Canadian Centre for Policy Alternatives Monitor,* 9 (9): 1, 6–7.

McMichael, P. 1994. GATT, Global Regulation and the Construction of a New Hegemonic Order. In *Critical Perspectives on Rural Change, Vol 5: Agricultural Regulation*, edited by P. Lowe, *et al*. London: David Fulton Publishers, 163–90.

McMichael, P. 1999. The Global Crisis of Wage Labour. *Studies in Political Economy*, 58: 11–40.

McMichael, P. 2000. *Development and Social Change. A Global Perspective*. Thousand Oaks, CA: Pine Forge Press.

McNally, D. 1998. Globalization on Trial: Crisis and Class Struggle in Asia. *Monthly Review*, 50 (4): 1–14.

Madeley, J. 2000a. *Hungry for Trade*. London and New York: Zed Books.

Madeley, J. 2000b. *Crops and Robbers: Biopiracy and the Patenting of Staple Food Crops*. Action Aid, <www.actionaid.org/resources/pdfs/crops_robbers.pdf>

Malhotra, K. 1996. The Uruguay Round of GATT: The World Trade Organization and Small Farmers. Paper to *Regional Conference on Monocultural Cropping in Southeast Asia Social/Environmental Impacts and Sustainable Alternatives*, June 3–6, at Songkhla, Thailand.

Mark, J. 2001. Brazil's MST: Taking Back the Land. *Multinational Monitor*, (January): 10–12.

Maroney, H. J., and M. Luxton. 1987. *Feminism and Political Economy*. Toronto: Methuen.

Martin, P. L. 1994. Germany: Reluctant Land of Immigration. In *Controlling Immigration: A Global Perspective*, edited by W. A. Cornelius *et al*. Stanford: Stanford University Press, 189–225.

Marx, K. 1964. *Economic and Philosophic Manuscripts of 1844*. Translated by M. Mulligan. New York: International Publishers.

Marx, K. 1971. *The Grundrisse*. New York: Harper & Row.

Marx, K. 1973. *Surveys from Exile: Political Writings Volume 2*. Translated by D. Fernbach. London: Allen Lane, New Left Review.

Marx, K. 1976. *Capital: A Critique of Political Economy*. Translated by B. Fowkes. New York: Penguin.

Massey, D. S. 1996. The Age of Extremes: Concentrated Affluence and Poverty in the Twenty-First Century. *Demography*, 33 (4): 395–412.

Molyneux, M. 1979. Beyond the Domestic Labor Debate. *New Left Review*, 116 (July–August): 3–27.

Molyneux, M. 1985. Mobilization without Emancipation? Women's Interests and the State in Nicaragua. *Feminist Studies*, 11 (2): 227–54.

Mori, K. 1999. *Lanfu to Senjo-No-Sei (Comfort Women and Sexuality of War)*. Tokyo: Shincho Press.

Morisaki, K. 1976. *Karayuki-San (Girls Going to Work in Asia)*. Tokyo: Asahi Press.

Murphy, C. N., and M. K. Pasha, eds. 2002. *International Relations and the New Inequality*. Oxford: Blackwell.

Murphy, S. 1999. WTO, Agricultural Deregulation and Food Security. *Globalization Challenge Initiative*, 4 (34): 1–4.

Mushakoji, K. 1996. Multilateralism in a Multi-Cultural World: Notes for a Theory of Occultation. In *The New Realism: Perspectives on Multilateralism and World Order*, edited by R. W. Cox. London: Macmillan, 83–108.

Mushakoji, K. 2001. Suppression of Trafficking and Promotion of Sex Industry: Criminality in/of Neoliberal Hegemony. *Journal of Global and Inter-Cultural Studies*, 3 (March): 1–23.

Mushakoji, K., ed. 2002. *Atarashii Nihon No Katachi (New Face of Japan)*. Tokyo: Fujiwara Press.

Nayar, J. 2000. Doing Law Differently. *New Internationalist*, 330: 20–1.
Nesiah, V. 1993. Toward a Feminist Internationality: A Critique of US Feminist Legal Scholarship. *Harvard Women's Law Journal*, 16: 189–210.
Norberg-Hodge, H., et al. 2001. *From the Ground Up: Rethinking Industrial Agriculture*. London: Zed Books.
Nussbaum, M. 2000. *Women and Human Development: The Capabilities Approach*. Cambridge: Cambridge University Press.
Nye, J. S. 2001. *The Paradox of American Power: Why the World's Only Superpower Can't Go It Alone*. New York: Oxford University Press.
OECD. 2001. *Financial Market Trends No. 79*. Organization for Economic Cooperation and Development, <www.oecd.org/pdf/M00007000/M00007473.pdf>
OECD. 2002. *Migration and Labor Market in Asia. Recent Trends and Policies*. Paris: OECD.
Ohmae, K. 1995. *The End of the Nation State*. London: Collins.
Oishi, M. 1995. *Nihon Kenpo Shi (History of the Japanese Constitution)*. Tokyo: Yuhikaku.
Okuda, M., and J. Tajima, eds. 1998. *Shinjuku No Ajia-Kei Gikokujin (Asian Foreigners in Shinjuku)*. Tokyo: Mekon Press.
Orlanda Pinnasi, M. F. Cabral and M. C. Lourencao. 2001. An Interview with Joao Pedro Stedile. *Latin American Perspectives*, 27 (5): 46–62.
Ostry, S. 1998. Looking Back to Look Forward: The Multilateral Trade System after 50 Years. Paper to *Symposium on the World Trading System*, April 30, at Geneva.
Palan, R. 1998. Trying to Have Your Cake and Eating It: How and Why the State System Has Created Offshore. *International Studies Quarterly*, 42 (3): 625–44.
Papademetriou, D. G., and K. A. Hamilton. 2000. *Reinventing Japan: Immigration's Role in Shaping Japan's Future*. Washington, D.C.: Carnegie Endowment.
Parenti, C. 1999. *Lockdown America: Police and Prisons in the Age of Crisis*. London: Verso.
Paringaux, R. P. 2001. The Deliberate Destruction of Agriculture. India: Free Markets, Empty Bellies. *Le Monde Diplomatique*, (September): 1–9.
Pasha, M. K., and A. I. Samatar. 1996. The Resurgence of Islam. In *Globalization: Critical Reflections*, edited by J. H. Mittelman. Boulder: Lynne Rienner, 187–201.
Patel, R., and A. Delwiche. 2002. The Profits of Famine: Southern Africa's Long Decade of Hunger. *Food First*, 8 (4): 1–8.
Perez Baltodano, A. 1999. Social Policy and Social Order in Transnational Societies. In *Transnational Social Policies: The New Development Challenges of Globalization*, edited by D. Morales-Gomez. Ottawa: International Development Research Centre, 19–41.
Persaud, R. B. 1997. Franz Fanon, Race and World Order. In *Innovation and Transformation in International Studies*, edited by S. Gill and J. H. Mittelman. Cambridge; New York: Cambridge University Press, 170–84.
Persaud, R. B., and C. Lusane. 2000. The New Economy, Globalisation, and the Impact on African Americans. *Race and Class*, 42 (1): 21–34.
Peterson, V. S. 2003. *A Critical Rewriting of Global Political Economy: Integrating Reproductive, Productive and Virtual Economies*. London: Routledge.
Philipps, L. 1996. Tax Policy and the Gendered Distribution of Wealth. In *Rethinking Restructuring: Gender and Change in Canada*, edited by I. Bakker. Toronto: University of Toronto Press, 141–62.
Philipps, L. 2002. Tax Law and Social Reproduction: The Gender of Fiscal Policy in an Age of Privatization. In *Privatization, Law and the Challenge to Feminism*, edited by B. Cossman and J. Fudge. Toronto: University of Toronto Press, 41–85.
Phillips, K. P. 2002. *Wealth and Democracy: A Political History of the American Rich*. New York: Broadway Books.

Phongpaichit, P., S. Piriyarangsan, and N. Treerat. 1998. *Guns, Girls, Gambling, Ganja: Thailand's Illegal Economy and Public Policy*. Chieng Mai: Silkworm Books.

Picchio, A. 1992. *Social Reproduction, the Political Economy of the Labor Market*. Cambridge: Cambridge University Press.

Pierson, C. 1998. *Beyond the Welfare State? The New Political Economy of Welfare*. University Park: Pennsylvania State University Press.

Pistorius, R., and J. v. Wijk. 1999. *The Exploitation of Plant Genetic Information: Political Strategies in Crop Development*. London: CAB International.

Polanyi, K. 1957. *The Great Transformation: The Political and Economic Origins of Our Time*. Boston: Beacon.

Polanyi, K. 2000. Our Obsolete Market Mentality. In *Transformations of Capitalism: Economy, Society, and the State in Modern Times*, edited by H. F. Dahms. New York: New York University Press, pp. 137–50.

Public Citizen 2001. *Down on the Farm: Nafta's Seven-Year War on Farmers and Ranchers in the U.S., Canada and Mexico*, February, 2003, <www.citizen.org/documents/ACFF2.pdf>

Rai, S. M. 2002. *Gender and the Political Economy of Development*. Cambridge: Polity Press.

Ramond, J. 2001. *Guide to the New UN Trafficking Protocol*. North Amherst: Coalition Against Trafficking in Women.

Repak, T. 1995. *Waiting on Washington: Central American Workers in the Nation's Capital*. Philadelphia: Temple University Press.

Riley, M. 2002. *Education Matters: General Agreement on Trade in Services* International Gender and Trade Network, <www.genderandtrade.net/EconoLit/GATSeduc.pdf>

Ritchie, M. 1993. *Breaking the Deadlock: The United States and Agricultural Policy in the Uruguay Round*. Minneapolis: Institute for Agriculture and Trade Policy.

Ritchie, M. 1999 *The World Trade Organization and the Human Right to Food Security* [General Assembly]. International Cooperative Agriculture Organization, August 29, <www.agricoop.org/activities/mark_ritchie.pdf>

Ritzer, G. 1993. *The McDonaldization of Society: An Investigation into the Changing Character of Contemporary Social Life*. Thousand Oaks, CA: Pine Forge Press.

Rodrik, D. 1997. *Has Globalization Gone Too Far?* Washington D.C.: Institute of International Economics.

Rose, N. 1999. *Powers of Freedom: Reframing Political Thought*. Cambridge: Cambridge University Press.

Ruggie, J. G. 1982. International Regimes, Transactions and Change: Embedded Liberalism in the Post-War Order. *International Organisation*, 36 (3): 379–415.

Ruggie, J. G. 1997. *Globalization and the Embedded Liberal Compromise: The End of an Era?* Max Planck Institute for the Study of Societies, <www.mpi-fg-koeln.mpg.de/pu/workpap/wp-97-1.html>

Rumsfeld, D. 2002. Transforming the Military. *Foreign Affairs*, 81 (3): 20–32.

Rupert, M. 1995. *Producing Hegemony: The Politics of Mass Production and American Global Power*. Cambridge [England]; New York: Cambridge University Press.

Said, E. W. 1993. *Culture and Imperialism*. New York: Knopf; Distributed by Random House.

Salzinger, L. 2001. Making Fantasies Real: Producing Women and Men on the Maquila Shop Floor. *NACLA: Report on the Americas*, XXXIV (5): 13–19.

Sassen, S. 1988. *The Mobility of Labor and Capital: A Study in International Investment and Labor Flow*. Cambridge: Cambridge University Press.

Sassen, S. 1996. *Losing Control? Sovereignty in an Age of Globalization*. New York: Columbia University Press.
Sassen, S. 1998a. *Globalization and Its Discontents*. New York: New Press.
Sassen, S. 1998b. Towards a Feminist Analytics of the Global Economy. In *Globalization and Its Discontents*. New York: New Press, 81–110.
Sassen, S. 2000. Women's Burden: Counter-Geographies of Globalization and the Feminization of Survival. *Journal of International Affairs*, 53 (2): 503–24.
Sassen, S. 2002. Countergeographies of Globalization: The Feminization of Survival. Paper to *Gender Budgets, Financial Markets, Financing for Development*, February 19–20, Berlin.
Sbragia, A. 2000. Governance, the State, and the Market: What Is Going On? *Governance: An International Journal of Policy and Administration*, 13 (2): 243–51.
Schaeffer, R. 1995. Free Trade Agreements: Their Impact on Agriculture and the Environment. In *Food and Agrarian Orders in the World-Economy*, edited by P. McMichael. Westport: Praeger, 255–75.
Schlosser, E. 2001. *Fast Food Nation: What the All-American Meal Is Doing to the World*. London: Allen Lane, Penguin Press.
Schneiderman, D. 2000. Investment Rules and the New Constitutionalism. *Law and Social Inquiry*, 25 (3): 757–87.
Schneiderman, D. 2003. The Old and the New Constitutionalism. In *Reinventing Canada: Politics in the 21st Century*, edited by J. Brodie and L. Trimble. Toronto: Prentice Hall, 243–58.
Scobie, J. 1840. *Hill Coolies: A Brief Exposure of the Deplorable Condition of the Hill Coolies in British Guiana and Mauritius*. London: Harvey and Darton.
Seguino, S. 2000. Accounting for Gender in Asian Economic Growth. *Feminist Economics*, 6 (3): 27–58.
Sen, G. 1997. Globalization, Justice and Equity: A Gender Perspective. *Development*, 40 (2): 21–6.
Sen, G. and S. O. Correa. 2000. *Gender Justice and Economic Justice: Reflections on the Five Year Reviews of the UN Conferences of the 1990s*. <www.dawn.org.fj/global/health/gender_justice.html>
Shiva, V. 2000. *Stolen Harvest. The Hijacking of the Global Food Supply*. Boston: South End Press.
Simmons, H. 1996. *The French National Front: The Extremist Challenge to Democracy*. Boulder: Westview.
Simpson, L. B. 1929. *The Encomienda in New Spain: Forced Native Labor in the Spanish Colonies, 1492–1550*. Berkeley: University of California Press.
Sinclair, S. 2000. *GATS: How the WTO's New "Services" Negotiations Threaten Democracy*. Ottawa: Canadian Centre for Policy Alternatives.
Singh, A., and A. Zammit. 2000. International Capital Flows: Identifying the Gender Dimensions. *World Development*, 28 (7): 1249–68.
Slok, J. 2001. The Different Impacts of Social and Economic Developments on Men's and Women's Labor Force Participation in Korea. *East Asia Environment and Social Development Unit, World Bank: Newsletter*, April, (3) 1–4.
Smith, A. M. 1994. *New Right Discourse on Race & Sexuality: Britain 1968–1990*. Cambridge: Cambridge University Press.
Soederberg, S. 2003. Unravelling Washington's Judgement Calls: The Cases of Chile and Malaysian Capital Controls. *Antipode* (forthcoming).
Soros, G. 1998. *The Crisis of Global Capitalism: Open Society Endangered*. New York: PublicAffairs.

Soysal, Y. N. 2001. Changing Citizenship in Europe: Remarks on Postnational Membership and the National State. In *Rethinking European Welfare*, edited by J. Fink et al. London: Sage, 65–75.
Spieldoch, A. 2002. *When a Terrible Situation Gets Worse: Reflections on Argentina from a Gender Perspective*, <www.genderandtrade.net/PaperSeries/occasionalSeries.htm>
Spivak, G. C. et al., eds. 1996. *The Spivak Reader*. New York: Routledge.
Standing, G. 1989. Global Feminization through Flexible Labor. *World Development*, 17 (7): 1077–95.
Steinmo, S. 1993. *Taxation and Democracy: Swedish, British, and American Approaches to Financing the Modern State*. New Haven; London: Yale University Press.
Stiglitz, J. 1998. More Instruments and Broader Goals: Toward the Post-Washington Consensus. *WIDER Annual Lecture*, January 7, at Helsinki.
Stiglitz, J. 2002. *Globalization and Its Discontents*. New York: W.W. Norton and Company.
Strange, S. 1994. *States and Markets*. London; New York: Pinter.
Suzuki, Y. 2002. *Tenno-Sei, Ianfu, Feminism (Emperor System, Comfort Women, Feminism)*. Tokyo: Impact-Shuppan kai.
Swank, D. 2002. *Global Capital, Political Institutions and Policy Change in Developed Welfare Societies*. Cambridge: Cambridge University Press.
Takaki, R. 1993. *A Different Mirror: A History of Multicultural America*. New York: Little, Brown.
Toennies, F. 2001. *Community and Civil Society*. Cambridge: Cambridge University Press.
Truong, T.-D. 2000. A Feminist Perspective on the Asian Miracle and Crisis: Enlarging the Conceptual Map of Human Development. *Journal of Human Development*, 1 (1): 159–64.
Truong, T.-D. 2001. Human Trafficking and Organized Crime. *Institute of Social Studies Working Papers*, (339): 1–27.
UNDP. 1994. *Human Development Report 1994*. New York: Oxford University Press.
UNDP. 1997. *Human Development Report 1997*. New York: Oxford University Press.
UNDP. 1998. *Human Development Report 1998*. New York: Oxford University Press.
UNDP. 1999. *Human Development Report 1999*. New York: Oxford University Press.
UNDP. 2000. *Human Development Report 2000*. New York: Oxford University Press.
UNDP. 2002. *Human Development Report 2002*. New York: Oxford University Press.
UNICEF. 2001. *Profiting from Abuse: An Investigation into the Sexual Exploitation of Our Children*. New York: United Nations.
UNIFEM. 2002. *Progress of the World's Women: A Biennial Report*. New York: UNIFEM.
UNRISD. 1995. *States of Disarray. The Social Effects of Globalization*. Geneva: United Nations.
US Government. 2002. *The National Security Strategy of the United States of America*. The White House, <www.whitehouse.gov/nsc/nss.html>
U.S. President's Commission on Migratory Labor. 1951. *Migratory Labor in American Agriculture*. Washington, D.C.: Government Printing Office.
US Space Command 1997. *Vision for 2020*. US Department of Defense, <www.gsinstitute.org/resources/extras/vision_2020.pdf>
van der Pijl, K. 1998. *Transnational Classes and International Relations*. London: Routledge.
van Staveren, I. 2002. Global Finance and Gender. In *Civil Society and Global Finance*, edited by J. A. Scholte and A. Schnabel. London, Tokyo: Routledge, United Nations University Press, 228–46.
Vanders, L. et al., eds. 2000. *Poverty in World Politics: Whose Global Era?* New York: St. Martin's Press; London: Macmillan; in association with Millennium: Journal of International Studies.

Waring, M. 1999. *Counting for Nothing: What Men Value and What Women Are Worth.* Toronto: University of Toronto Press.
Watkins, K. 1996. Free Trade and Farm Fallacies: From the Uruguay Round to the World Food Summit. *The Ecologist,* 26 (6): 244–55.
WEF. 2003. *Global Agenda Monitor: Building Trust.* World Economic Forum, January 23–28.
Woolley, F. 1995. *Women and the Canada Assistance Plan.* Ottawa: Status of Women Canada.
World Bank. 1997. *World Development Report.* Washington, D.C.: Oxford University Press.
World Bank. 2002. *Building Institutions for Markets: World Development Report 2002.* Washington, D.C.: Oxford University Press.
Yeates, N. 1999. Social Politics and Policy in an Era of Globalization: Critical Reflections. *Social Policy and Administration,* 33 (4): 372–93.
Yoon, B.-S. 1998. Koreanische Frauen in der globalen Ökonomie. Industrialisierung und Geschlechterpolitik in Südkorea. *PROKLA,* 111 (June): 217–34.
Young, B. 1998. Genderregime und Staat in der globalen Netzwerkökonomie. *Prokla 111,* 28 (2): 175–98.
Young, B. 1999. Global Capitalism without a Global Citizenry. *Working Papers,* 1 (1): 39–48.
Young, B. 2001a. The "Mistress" and the "Maid" in the Globalized Economy. In *Working Classes: Global Realities Socialist Register 2001,* edited by L. Panitch and C. Leys. London: Merlin Press, 264–76.
Young, B. 2001b. Globalization and Gender: A European Perspective. In *Gender, Globalization and Democratization,* edited by R. M. Kelly *et al.* Lanham: Rowman and Littlefield Publishers, 27–47.
Young, C. 2000. Punishing Labor: Why Labor Should Oppose the Prison Industrial Complex. *New Labor Forum,* 7 (Fall–Winter): 41–52.
Zhiqin, S. 2000. Women and Social Security: Impact of Financial Crisis. Shandong: Academy of Social Sciences, China (unpublished paper).

Index

accumulation, 5, 21, 24, 27, 35, 46, 50–6, 61, 77, 79, 90, 95, 106, 124, 126, 128, 130, 134, 163, 165, 172, 191, 193, 196. *See also* capital, power
 flexible, 7, 13, 99–100
 global, 4, 27
 primitive, 4, 19, 34, 165, 195. *See also* enclosures, expropriation
 social structure of, 137
 transnational, 45, 69
affluence, 149, 166, 179, 190, 209. *See also* plutocracy, social reproduction
Afghanistan, 51, 215, 219
Africa, 172, 211
agency, 18–19, 21–2, 24, 132, 216. *See also* hegemony, power, state
agribusiness, 166, 169, 172, 175–6, 180ff, 195. *See also* food security, intellectual property rights
agriculture, 26, 37, 170, 178, 182–3, 188. *See also* farming, food
 agro-exporting, 170, 175, 178–9
 cash crops, 178
 farm subsidies, 172–5
 peasant farmers, 177, 183
  Indian, 179
  Mexican, 181.
Albrecht, Karl, 205 fn 6
Albrecht, Theo, 205 fn 6
Algeria, 140
alienation, 4, 48. *See also* labour, estranged
Al-Queda, 13
Altvater, Elmar, 75, 155
America, United States of, 7–8, 12, 36–8, 44, 51, 63, 73, 100, 108, 117–18, 130ff, 143, 168, 170, 175ff
 agriculture, 172–4. *See also* agribusiness, food
 asthma in, 221 fn 2. *See also* health
 Defense Advanced Research Projects Agency, 215
 Department of Energy, 218
 Department of Homeland Security, 215
 Federal Deposit Insurance Corporation, 201
 Federal Reserve, 105
 financial complex, 213. *See also* Wall Street
 First Amendment Zones, 221 fn 7
 foreign policy, 167, 196, 210, 218–19
 Freedom to Farm Act, 180
 Future Image Architecture, 217. *See also* military, panopticism, surveillance
 global dominance, 216–17
 grand strategy, 208–9
 imperialism, 218–19
 incarceration, 202, 206 fn 25, 26 & 27. *See also* panopticism, prison industrial complex
 intelligence agencies, 215
 Internal Revenue Service, 199
 jurisprudence, 141, 212–13. *See also* new constitutionalism
 labour supply, 143. *See also* labor
 leadership, 32
 Middle East, 217
 military, 87, 203, 214ff
 multilateralism, 217
 national security, 92, 209, 214, 216, 218. *See also* security
 National Reconnaissance Office, 217
 Naval War College, 219
 obesity in, 205 fn 11
 Office of Global Communications, 216
 Office of Information Awareness, 215, 222 fn 9
 Office of Strategic Influence, 216
 Patriot Act, 215, 221 fn 8. *See also* panopticism, surveillance, terrorism
 Pentagon, 168, 192, 214ff
 Personal Responsibility and Work Opportunity Reconciliation Act, 63
 Proactive, Pre-emptive Operations Groups (P2OG) 222 fn 12
 Project for the New American Century, 217, 219, 222 fn 15
 protectionism, 173
 Star Wars, 216
 Total Information Awareness System, 222 fn 9. *See also* panopticism, surveillance, terrorism
 Union of Concerned Scientists, 197
Anderson, Perry, 125
apartheid, 138

Archer Daniel Midlands Inc, 181
Argentina, 31, 100, 103ff, 181
  currency board, 109
  deflation, 108
  deindustrialization, 105
  financial crises, 99, 103–4, 120–1
  monetary policy, 108
  popular protest, 122
  privatization, 105
  social collapse, 104, 119
arms trade, 13
Ashcroft, John, 215
Asia, 7–8, 88, 91, 93, 95, 104, 110, 113, 121, 131, 139, 143, 158, 172
  economic miracle, 103, 111–12
  financial crises, 100, 103, 107, 111ff
  gender order, 112
  trafficking in, 84
AstraZeneca, 183
atomization, 7, 13, 82
Australia, 131, 135, 139
Aventis Inc, 183

Baghdad, 168
Bahamas, 13, 215
balance of power, 219
balanced-budget laws, 70, 200. *See also* fiscal crisis, new constitutionalism
Barndt, Deborah, 180
Barnett, Thomas, 219–20, 223 fn 21
Bauman, Zygmunt, 214
Beck, Ulrich, 55, 57, 59, 61, 63
Belgium, 140
Bengal, Hill Coolies 135. *See also* labor
Bentham, Jeremy, 200–1
billionaires, 192–3, 210. *See also* affluence, plutocracy
biodiversity, 166, 170, 183, 185
bioengineering, 181
biological reproduction, 4, 77, 110, 152. *See also* social reproduction
biopiracy, 183
bioserfdom, 185
biotechnology, 182–4
Blair, Anthony (Tony) 216
Block, John, 174–5
bond rating, 56
bondage, 88, 134, 155. *See also* sex industry, trafficking
Bosnia, 59
Bové, Jose, 181
Braudel, Fernand, 192
Brazil, 104–8, 118, 121–2, 139, 171, 181, 186
  financial crisis, 103, 105–7, 118–22
  IMF rescue, 120

Bretton Woods, 170
Britain, 8, 86, 136, 140, 192, 201
British Petroleum, 218
Bull Durham (baseball movie, USA) 206 fn 19
Bush, George H., 196, 219
Bush, George W., 199, 214, 217–18, 220
  doctrine of war, 32
Bush, Jeb, 217
Butler, Josephine, 97 fn 2

Cairns Group, 172
California, 165, 181
Cambodia, 127
Campbell, Alastair, 216
campesinos, 179
Canada, 43–5, 56, 66ff, 118, 135, 177, 179, 181, 195, 202, 217
capital, 4, 8, 11–12, 19, 20–1, 25–9, 35–6, 54, 56, 68–9, 75, 79, 163–5, 169, 172, 186–7, 191, 193, 198, 200, 212, 220. *See also* accumulation, class, power
  controls, 56, 105, 209, 214
  Argentina. *See corralito*
  devaluation, 105
  ecological, 179
  finance, 11, 213
  flight, 56, 105, 121
  foreign, 25, 81, 105, 111
  global, 56–7, 70, 116
  market, 12, 35, 55–6, 69, 104, 116, 209
  mobility, 13, 26, 28, 31, 48, 69, 104, 116, 209, 213,
  power, 4, 8, 9, 12, 26, 56, 107, 108, 109, 163, 166, 213
  public bailouts, 100
  regulation, 35
  reproduction of, 21, 193–4, 210
  restructuring of, 15
  security of, 4, 19, 31, 33, 44, 158, 166, 188
capital punishment, 167. *See also* America, United States of, incarceration
capitalism, 23, 27, 52, 54–5, 60, 73, 77, 124–5, 129, 134, 146
  American, 135, 213
  corporate, 192, 193
  crony, 44, 111
  global, 10, 12, 14, 19, 34, 60, 106, 119, 195
  network, 216
  state, 111
Cardoso, Fernando Henrique, 106, 118,186

care economy, 22, 28, 45, 64ff, 108, 110–15, 120. *See also* social reproduction
caregivers, 74, 79, 107, 114
Cargill Inc, 172, 181
Caribbean
  migrant workers from 81
  slavery in 134–5
Carter, James (Jimmy) 192
Cartesian dualism, 22
Cayman Islands, 13
central banks, 31, 106. *See also* capital controls, currency board, finance, new constitutionalism
charity. *See* voluntary sector
Cheney, Richard (Dick) 216–19
Chevron Inc, 218
Chief Executive Officers (CEOs) 198
child care, 74, 81, 117
childbearing, 21, 63, 77, 110
Chile, 176, 214
China, 35, 88–9, 127, 171, 191, 194, 210, 220
  workers, 194–5, 210
Chirac, Jacques, 141
citizenship, 11, 29, 44–5, 52ff, 125–7, 138, 141, 184, 188, 201, 217
civil society, 5, 24–5, 27, 31, 33, 50, 59, 61, 70, 74–5, 87, 90, 92, 101, 140, 147, 151–3, 195. *See also* hegemony, legitimacy, power, state
  counter-movements, 52, 123, 170
  Japanese, 149
class, 6–7, 18–19, 23, 29, 33, 38, 62, 66, 76, 81, 86, 107, 109, 192, 201, 203. *See also* capital, plutocracy, labour, power
  conflict, 53, 199
  formation, 21
  professional, 104
  struggle, 60
Clinton, William Jefferson (Bill) 209, 217–18
Cold War, 10–11, 50, 83, 141, 170–1, 203, 214ff
collateral damage, 159
collective bargaining, 54, 74
colonialism, 7, 27, 96
commercialization, 62
commodification, 7, 13–14, 18, 20–1, 26, 34, 61, 76, 81–2, 87, 99, 109, 125, 129, 169, 173, 183
commodity form, 21, 24
common sense, 24, 35
communism, 10, 23, 35, 141
  containment of, 170, 208

comparative advantage, 170, 172, 176
conditionality. *See* structural adjustment
consciousness, 17, 22
  cosmopolitan, 192
  revolutionary, 195
constitution. *See* new constitutionalism
consumerism, 10, 167
consumption, 8, 14, 20, 56, 76, 114, 169, 173, 181, 184, 187, 193, 196–7
Continental Inc, 172
corporations, 44, 192
  American, 210ff
  consolidation, 175
  Iraq, 218
  pharmaceutical, 183, 212ff
  rights, 173
  transnational, 55ff, 180–1, 193, 212
  welfare, 167, 201
corralito, 121. *See also* capital, controls
Council on Foreign Relations (New York) 216, 218–19
Cox, Robert, 3, 6, 25, 130
credit. *See* debt, debt crisis, finance
crime, 10, 58. *See also* trafficking, sex industries
  Chinese Mafia (Triads) 94 151, 158
  Japanese Mafia (*yakuzas*) 95, 151ff
  organized, 7, 13, 38, 67, 94, 146, 149, 152, 155, 160
  trafficking, 92
  transnational, 93ff, 101, 147, 150, 156ff
culture, 18, 20ff, 34, 37, 53, 61, 87ff, 126–7, 129, 137, 159, 166–7, 184–6, 192–6, 203, 212. *See also* hegemony, consumption, marketisation, market civilization
currency boards, 106, 109, 119. *See also* Argentina, central banks, financial crises, new constitutionalism

da Silva, Luiz Inacio Lula, 106, 119
Darwinism, social 167
Davos, Switzerland, 26. *See also* World Economic Forum
debt, 11–12, 39, 56–7, 94, 109, 115, 117, 151, 177, 179
debt crisis, 26, 34, 35, 103, 105, 118, 177, 194
Dell Inc, 210
democracy, 4, 10, 12, 22, 31–2, 44–5, 47, 57, 60ff, 73ff, 82, 90, 96, 108, 122–3, 127, 134, 166, 169, 182ff, 217ff
democratic imperialism, 168, 219
deregulation, 47, 57, 58, 60, 81, 86, 111, 118–19, 165, 173, 174, 180, 212. *See also* accumulation, market, restructuring, disciplinary neo-liberalism

determinism, 57–8
developing countries. *See* South
development, 5, 9, 10–11, 169
   human, 29
   neo-liberal, 27
disciplinary neo-liberalism, 5, 8–9, 12–13, 18, 29, 31ff, 46, 68–9, 74, 84, 92ff, 104–5, 108–11, 121, 160, 164, 166, 190–1, 196, 209–10, 218
discrimination, 87, 112, 167
dislocation, social, 48, 59, 191
dohan (Japanese escorts) 148ff, 156
double movement, 63, 79. *See also* Polanyi, Karl
Douglas, Fredrick, 136
Dunning, T.J., 164
DuPont Inc, 183

ECHELON, 217, 222–3 fn 17. *See also* surveillance, panopticism
ecology, 8, 26. *See also* agriculture, environment
economic crises. *See* financial crises
economic growth, 47, 61, 69, 78, 90, 110, 112, 120, 142, 191, 216
education, 4–5, 11–12, 18, 20, 22, 28, 32–4, 39, 54, 63, 67, 72, 76, 109, 110, 135, 166–7, 187, 194, 211, 214
ejidos (community owned lands, Mexico) 35
Elson, Diane 41ff, 78, 107, 109–10
elites, 10, 13, 43–4, 47, 50, 104, 192–3, 195–6, 204. *See also* class, globalization, power
emancipation, 18, 23–4
enclosure movement, 4, 195. *See also* accumulation, primitive; expropriation, privitization
Enron Corp, 218
entertainment, 38, 94, 110, 112, 115, 152, 198, 210, 212. *See also* sex industry
environment, 8, 10, 13. *See also* ecology, agriculture
   crises, 11
   degradation, 50, 62, 106, 211
epistemology, 17, 24
ethnic cleansing, 106
ethnicity, 76, 129, 159
Europe, 86, 93, 136–7, 142, 170–1, 177, 211, 216. *See also* European Union
   Eastern, 136–7, 205 fn 10, 211
   labour supply, 139
   medieval, 14
   protectionism, 173
European Union, 25, 142, 175, 184, 202, 213, 215. *See also* Europe
   currency crisis, 103

Common Agricultural Policy, 173
exploitation, 6–8, 14, 18, 19, 21, 24, 26, 31, 34–5, 38, 87, 89, 93ff, 126, 136–8, 143, 146, 148, 150ff, 163–5, 194, 202. *See also* labor, serfdom, slavery
   economic, 127, 146
   intensification, 34
   racial, 96, 133
   sexual, 46, 101. *See also* labor, migration, trafficking
export subsidies, 175
expropriation, 4, 23, 33, 75, 184, 212–13. *See also* accumulation, primitive; enclosure movement; privatization

family, 21, 24–5, 29, 100, 108ff, 122, 128, 185
   autonomization, 62–4
   nuclear, 34, 53–4, 63
   wage, 18–19, 34ff, 45, 54, 64, 69, 74–5, 78, 109, 194, 201
famine, 178–9, 184. *See also* food
farming, 122, 166, 170ff. *See also* agriculture, food
fascism, 81
Feminism, 4, 6, 23, 26, 32–3, 54, 62, 75, 77, 81, 86–7, 113. *See also* gender
Feminist Political Economy, 14, 17, 68, 77
feminization of survival, 11, 18, 19, 34, 35, 37, 107, 115. *See also* Sassen, Saskia
Feuerbach, Ludwig, 18
fictitious commodities, 40 fn 4, 76. *See also* Polanyi, Karl
Filipinas, in Japanese sex industries 148–51, 155–8
finance, 5, 11, 55, 67, 107, 170, 186, 210. *See also* capital, Wall Street
   globalization, 56
financial crises, 7, 10, 62, 82, 99, 100ff, 116, 118, 191
   Argentina, 103–4, 118–21
   Asia, 49, 111ff
   Brazil, 105–7, 118–21
   contagion, 103
   social consequences, 103ff
   and social reproduction, 104–7
First World. *See* North
fiscal
   crises, 11–12, 28, 32, 39, 45
   discipline, 76, 104, 108–9, 112, 118ff. *See also* balanced-budget laws, new constitutionalism
   policy, 30, 61, 68, 70, 75, 82, 108
Fitzpatrick, Tony, 61

fixed exchange rate, 106. *See also* new constitutionalism, currency board
Folbre, Nancy, 54
food, 37, 39, 169ff, 182. *See also* agriculture, farming
  aid, 171, 184–5
  commons, 166
  consumer product, 173
  dependency, 171
  'from nowhere', 170ff, 177, 180
  'from somewhere', 170, 185
  genetically modified. *See* biotechnology
  scarcity, 183
  security, 8, 37, 120, 166, 169, 170ff, 196
  self-sufficiency, 166, 170ff
  sovereignty, 166, 170, 185, 188
  supply, 178
  surplus, 171, 173
Ford Foundation, 164
foreign aid, 169, 171
France, 86, 140, 217
free enterprise, 31, 43, 216, 220. *See also* capitalism; market, free
free trade. *See* trade agreements, WTO
Free Trade Area of the Americas (FTAAA) 181
freedom, 11, 18, 21, 23, 27, 31, 34, 49, 50, 59, 68–9, 85–6, 127, 134, 147, 156, 164, 185, 198, 203, 210, 215
full spectrum dominance, 168, 214, 216. *See also* America, United States of; military
fundamentalism, 168
fuzoku-gyo (leisure/sex industry, Japan) 151

gated communities, 168, 196, 201, 220. *See also* affluence, social enclavization
Gates, William (Bill) 193
Gemeinschaft (community) 156, 159, 161 fn14
Gesellschaft (society) 159, 161 fn14
gender, 6–7, 18ff, 33, 62ff, 79, 81, 96, 100, 107–8, 112, 128–9, 133, 138. *See also* Feminism
  commodity form, 21
  erosion, 62, 66, 81
  intensification, 62, 66
  norms, 112–13, 118, 122
  orders, 7, 18, 29, 33–4, 44–5, 53–4, 62, 66–8, 74ff, 108, 118, 122.
    Fordist, 109
    regime, 66, 68, 76, 80–1, 108, 114
    stability, 82
    transformation, 108
  roles, 113, 122
  structural adjustment, 26
gene patenting, 183
General Agreement on Tariffs and Trade (GATT) 6, 28, 30, 36, 38, 39, 170ff, 211. *See also* trade, WTO
General Agreement on Trade in Services (GATS) 28, 36. *See also* trade, WTO
genetic diversity, 183
Germany, 86, 118, 141–2, 193
Ghandi, Mahatma, 99
Gillanders, Arbuthnot & Company, Calcutta 134
globalism, 47ff
globality, 44, 47, 49, 58–9
globalization, 3ff, 34, 38, 44, 46, 55, 58, 73, 78, 81, 92–3, 101ff, 122, 133, 143, 153, 156ff, 167–8, 190, 192, 204, 208, 212, 219–20
  above, from, 8, 14, 104, 111, 122, 192
  anti-, 50
  below, from, 8, 14, 123, 166, 194
  Canada and, 66
  clash of, 14, 123
  corporate, 168–9, 171, 185, 187
  economic, 30, 57
  military, 214
  neo-liberal, 32, 43, 83, 86, 94, 101, 104, 117, 119, 146–7, 158, 166, 209, 214. *See also* disciplinary neo-liberalism and new constitutionalism
  policing, 209
  US-led, 166, 196, 203, 219
governance, 4ff, 18, 24ff, 38, 47, 58ff, 74, 96, 99, 107, 164, 166, 208, 210
  corporate, 44, 210
  defined, 5
  economic, 106, 214
  global, 5, 7, 33, 64, 164, 193. *See also* disciplinary neo-liberalism, new constitutionalism
  neo-liberal, 5, 30, 43–4, 48, 51–3, 58, 64–9, 100, 111, 163, 200
Gramsci, Antonio, 17, 20ff
  hegemony, 22, 27
  and historical economism, 22
  primary education, 20
Gray, John, 51
Great Depression (1930s) 52, 78, 201, 213
green revolution, 171, 178, 182. *See also* agriculture, farming, food
Group of Eight (G8) 30
Group of Seven (G7) 27, 30, 95, 104, 150, 157, 192, 204 fn 4, 208, 213–14
guest workers, 141–2. *See also* labor, migration, exploitation

Haraway, Donna, 62, 66
Hardt, Michael, 58
Harrod, Jeffrey, 7, 15 fn1, 130
Harvey, David, 192
health, 4–5, 10–12, 18, 26, 28, 32–6, 39, 50, 54, 67, 72, 76, 87, 107, 109, 110, 114, 118, 120, 130–1, 144, 187, 193–6, 199–200, 203, 211–12, 214
hegemony, 22–7, 160. *See also* civil society, dominance, Gramsci, Antonio, power, state, supremacy
Herbert, Bob, 199
Himmelfarb, Gertrude, 53
Hispanics, 167, 204
historical bloc, 24–5. *See also* hegemony, power, state
supremacist, 213
historical materialism, 23–4, 27
Hitler, Adolf, 141
HIV/AIDS, 59, 64, 110, 211–12
Hollywood, 213
Honda Inc, 197
Honduras, 177
Hong Kong, 95, 116, 138, 158, 194
Hudson's Bay Company, 195
human development, 47–51, 67, 107, 164
Human Development Index, 44, 68
human in/security, 4, 8ff, 26, 32, 39, 44, 47–8, 50ff, 80ff, 93, 99, 101, 103ff, 112, 122, 147, 153–4, 163ff, 179, 190–1, 196, 203, 209, 213–14. *See also* security
human rights, 10–11, 29, 32, 59, 115, 123, 147, 152, 157
hunger, 10, 106, 119, 182ff, 196. *See also* agriculture, food security, starvation
Huxley, Aldous, 207 fn 28
hyperinflation, 105

identity, 18, 23–6, 34, 92, 96, 101, 126, 136, 138, 165
Ignatieff, Michael, 51
Ignatiev, Noel, 136
immigration, 7, 100, 118, 130ff, 141–2, 144. *See also* migration
imperialism, 7, 87
  American, 218–19
India, 36, 127, 167, 170, 176, 178, 191, 217
individualism, 67, 71, 86, 167
  methodological, 22
  possessive, 10, 13, 33, 68, 75
individualization, 44, 63, 71, 81, 108, 118

Indonesia, 111, 114, 116, 127, 131, 139, 195
industrialization, 52–3, 76, 143, 171, 173
inequality, 7ff, 22, 34, 44, 48, 50ff, 62ff, 81, 101, 106, 109, 113, 121, 125, 165ff, 191, 201
inflation targets, 31, 106. *See also* central banks, new constitutionalism.
informal economy, 21, 29, 33, 64, 67, 68, 75, 79, 101, 109, 114, 146, 150, 152, 155ff,
insecurity. *See* human in/security
institutional investors, 213
integration, 9, 170, 220. *See also* market, world
  deep, 30, 166, 211
  economic, 211
  shallow, 30
intellectual property rights, 183–4, 209, 211–12. *See also* TRIPS
Intellectual Property Committee (USA) 221 fn 3
intellectuals, 88, 192
interdependence, 59
International Criminal Court, 217
international financial institutions, 27, 105. *See also* World Bank, International Monetary Fund
International Labour Organization, 101, 147
international law, 73, 95, 157, 209, 217
International Monetary Fund, 31, 34ff, 45, 49, 103ff, 170, 177, 191–2, 213–14. *See also* central banks, international financial institutions, structural adjustment, World Bank
intervention. *See also* war
  humanitarian, 59
  preventive, 51
investment, 5, 29, 34, 56, 61, 166–7, 209–10
  agreements, 30, 38
  bilateral, 211
  foreign, 105–6, 116, 118, 138, 210
  private, 27
investors, 5, 12, 28, 31, 45, 69, 100, 165, 213. *See also* capital, finance
  confidence, 45, 105
  foreign, 105, 121
Iran, 219
Iran-Contra Scandal (1983–88) 215
Iraq, 8, 32, 167, 168, 196, 199, 203, 209, 214–19
Ireland, 136
Ishihara, Shintaro, 93, 151
Israel, 217

Italy, 118, 136, 140

Japan, 38, 46, 83ff, 90, 116–17, 126–7, 131, 138, 140ff, 184, 197, 213
  Anti-Prostitution Law, 95
  brothel system, 86ff, 96
  colonization, 85, 87
  Commission for the Study of the Constitution, 84
  constitutional politics, 45, 83ff
  deflation, 103
  economic crisis, 94
  Emperor Meiji, 84–5
  Fuzoku-Eigyou Ho (Law Concerning Sex Industries) 91, 150
  internationalization, 89
  Meiji Constitution, 84ff, 96
  modernization, 88
  post-colonial, 85
  Showa State form, 96
  Tokugawa Shogunate, 87
Japanese Filipino Children (JFCs) 152–3
japa-yuki-san (women trafficked into Japan) Robert 91
Jihad (holy striving) 159
Josephson, Matthew, 163
judicial review, 31, 211, 213, 215. See also new constitutionalism

Kabuki-cho (Tokyo sex district) 92, 94–5, 150, 156, 158
kara-yuki-san (Japanese women trafficked into Asia) 89
Keynesianism, 34, 37, 75, 91
Korea, 88, 27, 131, 213
  labor force, 112–13
  unemployment, 114
Kristol, William, 217
Kroll Inc, 198
Krugman, Paul, 199
Kupchan, Charles, 219
kuruwa (bonded slave trafficking) 87ff
Kuwait, 131, 218

labor, 6, 14, 18–21, 54, 64, 74, 90, 101, 107, 113, 138, 147, 158, 164, 180, 193, 208. *See also* alienation, exploitation, migration, trafficking
  aristocracy, 193
  -capital relation, 19
  colonial division of, 170
  Chinese
    migrant 94
    indentured, 127, 135–7
    factory workers 194–5, 210
  disposable, 7–8, 130ff, 139
  division of, 54, 68, 74, 76, 100, 107, 121, 128–9, 172
  domestic, 30–1, 37, 38, 51, 54, 57, 62, 64, 67, 74, 76ff, 91, 100, 105ff, 173ff, 181, 199ff, 215, 218
  estranged, 21, 23. *See also* alienation
  female, 34, 79
  feminization of, 7, 33, 66, 80–1, 118, 126
  flexibility, 33, 108, 126, 130–2, 143, 193, 198
  foreign, 125, 137, 139, 141, 144, 151, 210
  global supply, 126, 144
  hierarchies, 39, 129
  immigrant, 37, 92, 126ff, 136, 144, 147, 158, 182. *See also* trafficking, migration
  indentured, 8, 135ff, 148
  Indian, 134
  intermediaries, 101, 131
  Irish, 136
  Italian, 137
  Mexican, 139, 143
  mobility, 138
  organized, 132
  power, 26, 33, 53, 77, 110, 125, 131
  primary market, 100, 130
  primitive market, 130, 132
  prison, 202
  professional, 28, 38, 61
  racialization, 6, 100, 130, 138, 144
  reproduction of, 32, 35, 44, 62, 67–8, 77, 154
  scarcity, 129
  secondary market, 100, 117, 130
  segmentation, 130
  sexual division of, 54, 109
  skilled, 36
  slave, 110
  spot market, 131
  subcontracting, 79
  subordination, 194
  subsumption, 36, 124, 126
  supply, 6, 124–5, 131–5, 139, 143, 195, 203
  temporary. *See* labour intermediaries
  undocumented, 38, 45, 100
  unpaid, 62ff, 71ff, 107, 112
  unprotected, 6, 13, 148
  wage-, 21, 182, 195
laissez-faire, 48, 51ff
land reform, 121, 187
Latin America, 7, 35, 95, 103–4, 106, 110, 118, 172
Lay, Kenneth, 223 fn 18

Le Pen, Jean-Marie, 141
League of Nations, 87, 90
legitimacy, 10, 13, 25, 28, 50ff, 116, 163, 182ff, 213, 217. *See also* hegemony, civil society, power, state, supremacy
Lesotho, 178
Libby, Lewis, 221 fn 15
liberalism, 10, 179. *See also* disciplinary neo-liberalism
  abstract, 130
  classical, 79
  economic, 48, 50ff
liberalization, 28, 30, 33, 111, 116, 119, 185, 211, 213
  agriculture, 172, 174
  economic, 49
  finance, 191
  reform, 29
  services, 6. *See also* GATS
  trade, 47, 109, 177, 182, 191
lifestyle, 34, 196. *See also* affluence
  in United States, 8, 167ff
Locke, John, 33, 75
London, 13, 170
Los Albornoz (Argentinian tragi-comedy) 100
Los Angeles, 197

macroeconomic policy, 31. *See also* central banks, fiscal, disciplinary neo-liberalism, new constitutionalism
Madres de la Plaza de Mayo (Mothers of the disappeared, Argentina) 123
Mahathir, Mohamad, 51
Malawi, 178
Malaysia, 51, 111, 114, 127, 131, 139
mama-san (Japanese madams) 149, 151, 153–6
Manhattan Project, 217
marginalization, 48, 54, 61, 100, 133, 137, 159–60, 176, 177, 188, 194–5, 212
Maria Luz Incident (1873) 88
Marin County, California, 196–7
market
  civilization, 5, 10, 21, 193, 195
  economy, 53, 65
  forces, 20, 30–1, 48, 66, 69, 73, 76, 81, 83–4, 109, 166, 180, 194. *See also* disciplinary neo-liberalism
  free, 33, 95, 99, 111, 169, 178, 216
  fundamentalism, 48
  world, 6, 25–6, 3738, 146–7, 153, 157, 166, 171ff, 181, 208–9
marketization, 172

Marshall Plan, 171
Massey, Douglas 202
Marx, Karl, 6, 9, 17, 36, 127, 163–4, 194
  human property, 23, 29
  private property, 24
  species-being, 18ff
  value, 124
Marxism, 22–3, 129, 164
materialism, 22
Mauritius, 135
McNally, David, 103
Menem, Carlos, 105, 119
mergers and acquisitions, 210
methodology, 17, 24
Metromedia Inc, 210
Mexico, 67, 132, 179
  Constitution, 35
  financial crises, 103
Microsoft Inc, 210
Middle East, 117, 196, 216–19
migration, 8, 12, 15, 19, 68, 87, 90–2, 95, 125, 127, 141ff, 155–8, 180, 194, *See also* immigration, labor, trafficking
  Central America, unprotected labour from 118, 132
  Caribbean workers, 81
  exploitative, 147, 151–8
  feminization, 7
  global, 38
  illegal, 151, 155
  theory, 127–9
militarization, 197
  of space, 214
military, 32, 46, 51, 85ff, 109, 123, 151, 160, 166–8, 171, 196, 203–4, 208–9, 214–16, 220
  technology, 217
  United States, 8, 32
millenarianism, 7
Mills, C. Wright, 218
missile defence. *See* Star Wars
modernity, 14, 55, 125
monetary policy, 60–1, 119, 126, 141. *See also* central banks, new constitutionalism
money-laundering, 13
monoculture, 166, 171
Monsanto Inc, 182–3
Morocco, 140
Movimento dos Trabalhadores Rurais Sem Terra (Landless Workers Movement, Brazil) 186–7
Mozambique, 178
Mujahiddin, 159
multilateralism, 216
Myanmar, 127, 139

Nagasaki, 87
Nanking Massacre (1937) 89
Napoleonic Wars (1799–1815) 136
National Front (France) 141
nationalism, 81
Nazism, 141
Negri, Antonio, 58
neo-liberalism, 27, 47, 63, 80, 129, 158, 160, 165, 169, 173, 178, 208. *See also* disciplinary neo-liberalism, new constitutionalism
   Argentina, 100ff
   consensus, 70. *See also* Washington Consensus
   discourse, 50, 69
   economists, 212
   experiment, 49, 62, 64
   food security, 174
   globalization, 83, 86, 94, 101, 104, 146–7, 158, 166
   governance, 67–9
   ideology, 171, 174
   political economy, 37, 44, 57, 60ff, 73, 79 82, 169, 173, 182, 198
   reform, 27, 29, 81
   restructuring, 67, 77, 108, 111, 118
new constitutionalism, 5, 10, 12, 18, 27, 28–31, 38, 45–6, 48, 57, 61, 68–9, 74, 84, 90, 92, 95, 104, 121, 164, 166, 208ff. *See also* governance, disciplinary neo-liberalism
New International Economic Order, 29
New York, 198
New Zealand, 135
Nike Inc, 194, 205 fn 9
Non-Governmental Organizations, 153ff, 212
North, 9, 25–6, 34–5, 47–8, 51, 58, 62, 64, 73–4, 78, 87, 89, 96, 130, 138, 140, 146, 151, 173–4, 176, 180–1, 195ff, 208, 212. *See also* Group of Seven (G7)
North American Free Trade Agreement (NAFTA) 30, 35, 45, 57, 61, 73, 179ff, 211–12. *See also* trade agreements
   Chapter 11 provisions, 212
Novartis, 183
nuclear weapons, 85
Nye, Joseph, 192

occultation, 147, 151ff
offshore, 13, 28, 158, 192, 196, 213, 215. *See also* finance, taxation
Ohio, 200
oil, 117, 181, 196–7, 209, 218

oiran (bonded slavery of young poor women, Japan) 87
okiya (creditors in the bondage contract, Japan) 88
ontology, 17–23
Operation Get Out (Malaysia) 139
Oracle Inc, 210
Organization for Economic Cooperation and Development (OECD) 5, 33, 36–7, 69, 71, 80–1, 95–6, 104, 116, 127, 158, 160, 172, 175–6, 186, 192ff, 200, 202
Organization for Petroleum Exporting Countries (OPEC) 117
Owaki, Masako, 152
Oxfam, 176

Pakistan, 127
Palestine, 219
Palocci, Antonio, 119
panic rooms, 167, 198, 206 fn 17
panopticism, 196, *See* surveillance; America, United States of, incarceration
Panopticon Plan (Jeremy Bentham) 200
panpan (prostitutes to the US military occupation forces in Japan) 91
paradox of necessity, 44, 58, 60
paradox of scale, 44, 58, 60
paradox of sustainability, 44, 58, 61
patents. *See* intellectual property rights
   on life forms, 212
paternalism, 60
patriarchy, 6, 87
   state, 83
peace movement, 81
Peru, 139, 177
philanthropy. *See* voluntary sector, charity
Philippines, 38, 67, 81, 113, 116, 127, 139, 146ff, 155, 183
   colonization, 87
Philipps, Lisa 70–2, 74
Pillsbury Inc, 181
plutocracy, 167, 192–3, 210. *See also* affluence, billionaires
Poindexter, John, 215
Polanyi, Karl, 21, 27, 43, 52–3, 59, 60, 62, 76–7, 81
Political Economy, 24, 27
   Feminist and Radical, 3, 14
   global, 3ff, 23ff, 39, 46, 55, 73, 106, 109, 138, 160, 163, 191, 220
political order, 14, 24, 34, 61
pollution, 59, 211
pornography, 101

Porto Alegre. *See* World Social Forum
potato famine (Ireland, 1845–50) 136
poverty, 37–8, 44, 48, 53, 57, 63ff, 70–1, 79, 93, 100ff, 111, 119ff, 164, 177–8, 182, 198, 216. *See also* human development, human in/security
Powell, Colin, 216, 218
Powell, J. Enoch, 140
power, 3, 6, 9, 13–14, 17, 19, 2324, 39, 67, 83–4, 93, 147, 160, 168, 191, 200. *See also* capital, hegemony, legitimacy
  military, 196
  network, 10, 13
  political, 5
Prince Alwaleed of Saudi Arabia, 193
prison industrial complex, 202
private property, 18, 23–4, 29, 31, 70, 72, 75, 86, 122, 137, 172, 183, 185–6, 213. *See also* property rights
private sector, 61, 70, 72–3, 78, 110, 138
privatization, 28, 32, 35–6, 47, 58, 60, 72, 79, 111, 178, 213. *See also* accumulation, primitive; enclosure movement, expropriation
  Argentina, 105, 119
  and food security, 169, 172
  Mexico, 35
  of risk, 34, 77, 167, 213
  state assets, 19
production, 3ff, 15, 19, 21, 26, 28, 33, 39, 52, 67, 74, 76, 82, 84, 100, 126, 147, 160, 164, 175, 194–6
  globalization of, 56
  relations, 26
  transnational, 108
profit, 18, 36, 38, 45, 56, 67, 72, 94, 115, 122, 132, 135, 146, 158, 165–6, 173, 178, 187. *See also* accumulation, capital
property rights, 31, 33, 75, 86, 106, 131, 210, 212–13. *See also* private property rights
prostitution, 39, 83, 86ff, 94, 100–1, 110ff, 148ff. *See also* brothel system, sex industry, trafficking
provisioning, 4, 7. *See also* care economy, social reproduction
Prozac, 203
Public Citizen, 179ff
public goods, 47, 68ff, 79, 110, 112, 122
public policy, 4, 12, 15, 31, 47–8, 52–3, 56, 61, 65, 68. *See also* Keynesianism, disciplinary neo-liberalism, structural adjustment
public sector, 47, 61, 72, 73, 78–9, 104, 110, 119, 220

quotidian, concept of the, 153, 157

race, 7, 18–19, 21, 23, 26, 29, 33, 38, 56, 62, 66, 81, 109, 117, 121, 125, 129, 133ff, 159, 201. *See also* discrimination, inequality
racial domination, 141
racial ideology, 135
racialization, 125–6, 132, 136, 138, 144, 191, 204
racism, 46, 81, 86–7, 96, 125, 137, 140, 153, 167
racist hierarchy in world order , 93, 96
rationality, 75, 125, 193
Reagan Doctrine, 219
Reagan, Ronald, 202, 215
Realism, 218
Reardon, Betty, 153
redistribution, 11, 37, 56, 63, 65, 76, 78, 164, 184, 193
refugees, 68
regime change, 32, 76, 168, 214, 217
regulation, 5, 15, 67, 69, 73
  labour market, 73
  national, 47, 48
  neo-liberal, 84
religious fundamentalism, 7
remittances, 36ff, 62, 67, 94, 116, 150, 152. *See also* migration
reprivatization, 18, 63, 68, 76ff
  and social reproduction, 66, 79
resistance, 6, 9, 14, 18, 21, 23–4, 27, 35, 44, 50, 99, 140, 154, 163, 195, 214, 219
restructuring, 3, 11, 15, 29, 69, 70, 72, 109, 191, 194, 212
  corporate, 78
  economic, 80, 109, 116
  global, 29, 38
  labor market, 75
  neo-liberal, 67, 76–7, 82, 108, 111, 118
  post-Fordist, 7
  state, 66, 106
revolution, 29, 31, 35, 143
Rhodesia, 138
Rice, Condoleeza, 217–18
Richelson, Jeffrey 223 fn 17
risk, 81, 167
  individualization of, 44
  privatization of, 34, 77, 167
  socialization of, 167
robber barons, 163, 165
Ruggie, John G., 74

ruling class, 10, 12–13, 83, 88, 192
  Japanese, 151
Rumsfeld, Donald, 216ff
Russia, 95, 202, 217
  financial crises, 103

sabotage, economic, 163
San Francisco, 196
Sassen, Saskia, 11, 12, 38, 115, 129. *See also* feminization of survival
Saudi Arabia, 193
Savings and Loans bailout, USA (1989–90) 201
Seattle, 177
security, 9
  of capital, 12, 121, 157, 190
  human in/security, 4, 8ff, 26, 32, 39, 44, 47–8, 50ff, 80ff, 93, 99, 101, 103ff, 112, 122, 147, 153–4, 163ff, 179, 190–1, 196, 203, 209, 213–14
  national, 4, 10–12, 50
  private, 198
  three concepts of, 9
Seed Satyagraha Movement (India) 185
September 11th (9/11) 51, 167–8, 198, 209, 214ff
serfdom, 94. *See also* labor, slavery
Severe Acute Respiratory Syndrome (SARS) 211
sex
  industry, 6, 13, 46, 83ff, 90, 95, 101, 110, 146ff, 195. *See also* trafficking
  slavery, 92, 96
  tourism, 91, 96, 148
  workers, 91–2, 101, 147ff
sexuality, 21, 26, 34, 62
Shell, 218
Shinjuku, Tokyo, 94–5
Shiva, Vandana, 184
shock therapy 38, *See also* financial crises, IMF, structural adjustment programs
Silicon Valley, 213
Singapore, 111, 127, 131, 138–9, 214
slavery, 7, 8, 93, 125, 134ff, 148, 194. *See also* serfdom, sex industries
social enclavisation, 167, 201. *See also* gated community
social exclusion, 62, 101, 146–7
social forces, 4, 12, 23ff, 53, 60, 76, 81, 133, 168, 172, 196
social formation, 4, 8, 19, 22–3, 34, 46, 83, 133, 167, 191
social justice, 29, 59
social programs, 39, 58, 61, 64–6, 199, 201

social protection, 4, 25, 36, 52, 59, 76, 101
social relations, 6, 7, 13, 18, 20ff, 49, 55, 104, 124ff, 138, 164, 169, 183, 188, 208
social reproduction, 3ff, 31–5, 39, 52, 54, 60–7, 76–8, 83, 88, 99, 103, 106, 109, 128, 152, 160, 163ff, 172, 182, 190–1, 196, 203
  of affluence, 8, 196ff
  crisis of, 37, 39, 51, 107, 113, 117, 169
  definition of, 17–18, 32, 67, 107
  governance of, 33–4
  informalization and, 68
  key components of, 77, 110
  migration and, 147
  privatization and, 34–5, 67–8, 82
  progressive, 166
  racialized, 124
  sustainability of, 47
  transnational, 36
social security, 54, 61, 67, 75, 90, 147, 200. *See also* welfare, workfare
social services, 28, 71, 72, 109, 122
social wage, 36, 67, 74, 77, 164, 188
socialization, 4, 21, 156, 191–2
  of risk, 4, 18, 33, 37, 67, 77, 191, 200–1
software industry, 131, 143–4, 210ff
Somalia, 59
Soros, George, 44
South, the, 25–6, 34, 48, 51, 57–8, 62, 64, 74, 89, 91, 95–6, 101, 111–13, 122, 146, 151, 173–6, 180ff, 195, 202, 208, 212. *See also* Third World
South Africa, 123, 138
  AIDS crisis, 212
Southeast Asia, 7
sovereignty, 12–13, 55ff, 109, 130, 133, 138, 184
Soviet Union, 8, 30, 32, 208, 218
  and Afghanistan, 219
Spain, 120, 140
species-being, 18, 21ff, 190
Sports Utility Vehicles (SUVs) 196–7, 206 fn 13 & 14. *See also* affluence, lifestyle
Sri Lanka, 127
starvation, 37, 169, 178. *See also* agriculture, food, poverty, subsistence
state, 4–5, 8, 11ff, 24–5, 29, 54, 56, 60, 62, 74, 77, 126, 147–8, 152, 170ff. *See also* hegemony, legitimacy, power
  authority, 10
  capitalism, 23–4, 35
  fiscal crisis of, 28

liberal, 55
nationalization, 86
privatization, 28, 35
restructuring, 5, 30, 33, 66, 69, 70ff
sovereignty, 12
welfare, 35
Stedile, Joao Pedro, 187
Stiglitz, Joseph, 44, 49
stock market bubble of the 1990s, 44
stock options, 130
structural adjustment programs, 34, 38, 48, 57, 109–10, 177. *See also* international financial institutions, International Monetary Fund, shock therapy, World Bank
Sub-Saharan Africa, 140
subsistence, 4, 6ff, 20–1, 32, 39, 51, 75, 107, 110, 178, 180, 195. *See also* agriculture, food, starvation
surveillance, 12, 51, 54, 56, 93, 96, 149, 151, 157, 159, 166–7, 196ff, 208, 214ff. *See also* America, United States of; ECHELON, panopticism
Japan, 86, 95
military, 217
technology, 215
Swank, Duane, 57
Swaziland, 178
Switzerland, 13, 196

Taipei, 138
Taiwan, 95
taxation, 28, 56, 60, 63, 70, 72, 78, 192, 213
avoidance, 199. *See also* offshore
capital friendly, 58
progressive, 54, 74
regressive, 28
tayus (master entertainers, Japan) 88
technocratic neutrality, 70
technology, 10, 47, 59, 78, 129, 160, 182–3, 203, 208, 212ff
transfer, 171, 212
terrorism, 7, 10, 13, 51, 92, 146, 158–9, 167, 198, 208, 214ff. *See also* September 11[th,] surveillance
war against, 14
Texaco Inc, 218
Thailand, 111, 113ff, 116, 139, 153
Third World, 6, 26, 29, 37, 56, 100, 130, 171, 182, 212, 213. *See also* South
Tokyo, 87, 92, 94, 149, 151, 156, 158
trade, 5, 61, 170–1, 181, 209–10
agreements, 45, 73. *See also* investment, GATT, GATS, NAFTA, TRIPS, WTO
bilateral, 30, 211

blocs, 69
protectionism, 174
Trade Related Aspects of Intellectual Property Rights (TRIPS) 184, 212. *See also* intellectual property rights
trafficking, 13, 38, 83, 87, 89–91, 95, 101, 106, 115–17, 146–8, 150ff
children, 101
criminalization of, 96
definition of, 101
in human organs, 115
sex, 21, 67, 84, 99. *See also* sex industry
women, 87, 91ff
transgenic technology, 182ff. *See also* biotechnology
transparency. *See* surveillance, panopticism
Trilateral Commission, 192
Truman Doctrine, 219
Truman, Harry S., 171
Tunisia, 140
Turkey, 171
financial crises, 103
Tyson Foods Inc, 181

underdevelopment, 51, 88
unemployment, 10, 38–9, 48, 54, 60, 67, 78, 100, 106, 113ff, 143, 177, 186
insurance, 75
union-busting, 132
unionization, 33, 194. *See also* labor
United Arab Emirates, 131
United Nations, 10, 28–9, 32, 44, 90, 117, 157–8, 170, 191, 212, 215, 217
Biological Weapons Convention, 217
Biosafety Protocol, 184
Commission on Human Rights, 152
Conference on the Environment, Rio, 196
Conference on Trade and Development, 185, 212
Convention Against Trafficking, 90
Convention Against Transnational Organized Crime, 157
Convention on Biological Diversity, 184
Economic, Social and Cultural Organization, 187, 212
Food and Agricultural Organization (FAO) 171, 176–7
Human Development Program, 4, 9, 10–11, 28ff, 48, 5051, 67–8, 78, 190, 193
Kyoto Environmental Protocol, 87, 217
Relief and Rehabilitation Administration, 171
UNICEF, 101
UNIFEM, 63

United Nations *continued*
  Universal Declaration of Human Rights, 59
  World Food Programme, 184
Uruguay Round, 173ff, 212. *See also* GATT, GATS, TRIPS, WTO

Veblen, Thorstein, 163
Venezuela, 181
Via Campesina, 182, 185–6
Viacom Inc, 210
Vietnam, 127, 195
Virginia, 135
voluntary sector, 71–2

Wall Street, 165, 202, 213. *See also* finance
  security in, 198
Wal-Mart Inc, 181, 195, 210
war, 9, 209. *See also* intervention, Iraq, terrorism, September 11th, world order
  Afghanistan, 216
  cyber-, 216–7
  economic, 13
  information, 216
  in Iraq, 8, 214, 217–18
  on drugs, 202
  on terrorism, 51, 160
  nuclear, 218
  pre-emptive, 32, 168, 208–9, 214, 216
  preventive, 32, 51, 168, 208ff
Washington consensus, 48–9, 103, 118–9. *See also* international financial institutions, IMF, structural adjustment, World Bank
Washington DC, 31, 48–9, 100, 103, 105, 118ff, 143, 168, 179, 196–7, 215, 219
weapons of mass destruction, 218
welfare, 4–5, 29, 32, 37, 56, 61ff, 79, 200–1, 212. *See also* social security, workfare
welfare state, 47, 53ff, 73–4, 173. *See also* social security, workfare
  reform, 116–17

Wolfowitz, Paul, 217, 222 fn 15
women, 18–19, 24, 29, 33–4, 45, 62, 73, 106, 117. *See also* gender
  comfort, 89
  migration. *See* trafficking, sex industry
  polarization of, 80
  unpaid labour, 64
workfare, 63, 70, 167, 200–1, 203. *See also* social security, welfare
World Bank, 5, 26ff, 35, 38, 44, 49, 109, 111–12, 114, 122, 177, 191–2, 213. *See also* international financial institutions, IMF, structural adjustment, Washington consensus
World Economic Forum (WEF) 50–1, 61, 192, 195. *See also* globalization, plutocracy, capital
world order, 4ff, 23–5, 28, 32–3, 46, 68, 74, 82, 99, 125, 146, 166, 190–1, 196, 209
  new, 168, 208, 214
  ontology, 23
World Social Forum (WSF) 50, 195. *See also* resistance, globalization
World Systems Theory, 220
World Trade Center, 215
World Trade Organization (WTO) 28ff, 38, 45, 49, 57, 70, 106, 172, 174–5, 177, 179ff, 209ff
  Agreement on Agriculture, 172–6
World War I, 86, 140
World War II, 29–30, 86, 108, 140, 166, 170, 200, 211, 215, 217
World War III, prospects for 217

xenophobia, 140, 142, 151, 156

Yokohama, 88

Zambia, 178, 184
Zapatistas, 35
zashiki (brothel saloons, Japan) 88
Zimbabwe, 174